THE EUROSCEPTIC CHALLENGE

In recent years, Eurosceptic and nationalist forces have been gaining ground in the European Union. Their rhetoric has changed the political discourse, shaking the ideal of an ever closer union to its core. However, the specific legal changes brought about by this political turn have often remained obscure. How does Euroscepticism manifest itself in the law and policies of the EU Member States?

This book seeks to understand to what extent Eurosceptic attitudes translate into legislative, administrative and judicial practices that challenge EU law and governance in the Member States. It reveals the many facets of national resistance that the EU is currently facing, ranging from open defiance to ignorance of EU law. It includes perspectives from the entire Union: from old and new, western and eastern, troublesome and (ostensibly) compliant Member States.

Bringing together experts from law and political science, this timely book offers unique insights into the reception – and sometimes rejection – of EU law in the Member States. It is essential reading for anyone interested in the current challenges and the future of the European Union.

Volume 4 in the series EU Law in the Member States

EU Law in the Member States

Located at the cross-section between EU law, comparative law and socio-legal studies, *EU Law in the Member States* explores the interaction of EU law and national legal systems by analysing comparative evidence of the impact landmark EU measures – from CJEU decisions and secondary legislation to soft-law – have had across different Member States. The nature and operation of EU law has traditionally been analysed in a highly 'centralised' way, through the lenses of Brussels and Luxembourg, and in terms of the Treaty and its interpretation by the Court of Justice. Beneath this orthodoxy, however, lies the complex world of the genuine life of EU law in the Member States. Judicial and administrative practices across the Union's 28 Member States considerably qualify and sometimes even challenge the long-standing assumption that doctrines such as the direct effect and supremacy of EU law ensure a uniform and effective application of its provisions.

Each volume brings together leading academics, national experts and practitioners in order to draw conclusions both for EU law generally and the specific area in question on the basis of Member State reports and broader horizontal papers, and will be of interest to generalist EU lawyers and specialists in each field across the Member States. Academic audiences will benefit from the tight integration of national case studies and doctrinal analysis, whilst practitioners and policy makers will find systematically presented comparative evidence and commentary.

Series Editors
Jeremias Prassl
Michal Bobek

Volume 1: *Viking, Laval* and Beyond
Edited by Mark Freedland and Jeremias Prassl

Volume 2: Central European Judges under the European Influence: The Transformative Power of the EU Revisited
Edited by Michal Bobek

Volume 3: Air Passenger Rights, Ten Years On
Edited by Jeremias Prassl and Michal Bobek

Volume 4: The Eurosceptic Challenge
Edited by Clara Rauchegger and Anna Wallerman

The Eurosceptic Challenge

National Implementation and Interpretation of EU Law

Edited by
Clara Rauchegger
and
Anna Wallerman

· H A R T ·
OXFORD · LONDON · NEW YORK · NEW DELHI · SYDNEY

HART PUBLISHING

Bloomsbury Publishing Plc

Kemp House, Chawley Park, Cumnor Hill, Oxford, OX2 9PH, UK

HART PUBLISHING, the Hart/Stag logo, BLOOMSBURY and the Diana logo are trademarks of Bloomsbury Publishing Plc

First published in Great Britain 2019

Copyright © The editors and contributors severally 2019

The editors and contributors have asserted their right under the Copyright, Designs and Patents Act 1988 to be identified as Authors of this work.

All rights reserved. No part of this publication may be reproduced or transmitted in any form or by any means, electronic or mechanical, including photocopying, recording, or any information storage or retrieval system, without prior permission in writing from the publishers.

While every care has been taken to ensure the accuracy of this work, no responsibility for loss or damage occasioned to any person acting or refraining from action as a result of any statement in it can be accepted by the authors, editors or publishers.

All UK Government legislation and other public sector information used in the work is Crown Copyright ©. All House of Lords and House of Commons information used in the work is Parliamentary Copyright ©. This information is reused under the terms of the Open Government Licence v3.0 (http://www.nationalarchives.gov.uk/doc/open-government-licence/version/3) except where otherwise stated.

All Eur-lex material used in the work is © European Union, http://eur-lex.europa.eu/, 1998–2019.

A catalogue record for this book is available from the British Library.

Library of Congress Cataloging-in-Publication data

Names: Rauchegger, Clara, editor. | Wallerman, Anna, editor.

Title: The Eurosceptic challenge : national implementation and interpretation of EU law / edited by Clara Rauchegger and Anna Wallerman.

Description: Oxford [UK] ; Chicago, Illinois : Hart Publishing, 2019. | Series: EU law in the member states ; volume 4 | Includes bibliographical references and index.

Identifiers: LCCN 2019021096 (print) | LCCN 2019021908 (ebook) | ISBN 9781509927661 (EPub) | ISBN 9781509927654 (hardback : alk. paper)

Subjects: LCSH: Law—European Union countries—Interpretation and construction. | Freedom of movement—European Union countries. | Antitrust law—European Union countries.

Classification: LCC KJE947 (ebook) | LCC KJE947 .E97 2019 (print) | DDC 341.242/2—dc23

LC record available at https://lccn.loc.gov/2019021096

ISBN: HB: 978-1-50992-765-4
ePDF: 978-1-50992-767-8
ePub: 978-1-50992-766-1

Typeset by Compuscript Ltd, Shannon
Printed and bound in Great Britain by CPI Group (UK) Ltd, Croydon CR0 4YY

To find out more about our authors and books visit www.hartpublishing.co.uk. Here you will find extracts, author information, details of forthcoming events and the option to sign up for our newsletters.

Table of Contents

List of Contributors vii

Prologue: (EU Law) Scholarship in (Times of) Crisis? xi
Michal Bobek

Introduction 1
Clara Rauchegger and Anna Wallerman

PART I
NATIONAL EUROSCEPTICISM AND THE EU INSTITUTIONS

1. *EU Policies in Times of Populist Radical Right Euroscepticism: Which Future?* 7
   Gerda Falkner and Georg Plattner

2. *Does Euroscepticism Influence Compliance and Enforcement of EU Law in the Member States?* 27
   Dimiter Toshkov

PART II
EUROSCEPTIC GOVERNMENTS AND THEIR POLICIES

3. *The New Italian Government between Break and Continuity: Political Discourse and Constitutional Practices* 47
   Luigi Gianniti and Barbara Guastaferro

4. *Poland's Defiance Against the CJEU in the* Puszcza Białowieska *Case (C-441/17)* 67
   Przemysław Tacik

5. *Hungarian Economic Patriotism and Internal Market Law: Questioning Fundamental Freedoms and Disregarding Fundamental Rights* 87
   Mónika Papp and Marton Varju

PART III
CASE STUDIES ON MIGRATION AND FREE MOVEMENT OF PEOPLE

6. *Schengen, Migration – and the Resurrection of the Westphalian Nation-State?* 109
   Peter Thalmann

7. *'Euroreluctance' at the Heart of Europe? Challenges to the Free Movement of People in Luxembourg* 135
   Catherine Warin

PART IV
RESISTANCE WITHIN AND AGAINST THE PRELIMINARY REFERENCE PROCEDURE

8. *Who is the National Judge? A Typology of Judicial Attitudes and Behaviours Regarding Preliminary References* 155
   Anna Wallerman

9. *Attitude or Aptitude? Explaining the Lack of Preliminary References in Dutch Competition Law Cases* 175
   Jesse Claassen

10. *Reluctance to Participate in the Preliminary Ruling Procedure as a Challenge to EU Law: A Case Study on Slovenia and Croatia* 191
    Monika Glavina

11. *Game of Courts: The Effects of Constitutional Judicial Conflicts on Polish Judges' Co-operation with the CJEU* 213
    Juan A Mayoral

PART V
CONCLUSIONS

12. *National Resistance Against EU Law and Governance: Degrees and Manifestations* 229
    Clara Rauchegger and Anna Wallerman

Index 249

List of Contributors

Michal Bobek has been Advocate General at the Court of Justice of the EU since October 2015. He obtained master's degrees in law and in international relations from the Charles University (Prague); a Diploma in English law and the law of the EU at the University of Cambridge; a Magister Juris at the University of Oxford, St Edmund Hall; and a doctorate at the European University Institute, Florence. He was a Legal Secretary to the President of the Supreme Administrative Court of the Czech Republic and Head of the Research and Documentation Department of that court; a Fellow at the Institute of European and Comparative Law of the University of Oxford; Professor at the College of Europe in Bruges, with further visiting appointments in Europe and overseas. He (co)authored over a dozen books and numerous articles on European law, comparative (public) law, and legal theory.

Jesse Claassen, LLM (Nijmegen), is a PhD candidate in EU Law at the Radboud University Nijmegen, the Netherlands. In his PhD research, he examines the motives of national courts when deciding whether to refer preliminary questions to the CJEU. The project runs parallel to the project of Dr Jasper Krommendijk, funded with a grant of the Netherlands Organisation for Scientific Research, titled 'It Takes Two to Tango. The Preliminary Reference Dance between the Court of Justice of the European Union and National Courts'.

Gerda Falkner, ao Univ-Prof Mag Dr, is the Director of the Centre for European Integration Research, and a professor of political science, at the University of Vienna in Austria. Her publications cover a range of topics within European Integration Studies, with publishers such as Oxford University Press, Cambridge University Press, Routledge, and the leading international journals in the field.

Luigi Gianniti, PhD (University of Bologna), is Counsellor of the Italian Senate, where he directs the Research Service. He has been Head of Cabinet of the Minister of European Affairs, Enzo Moavero Milanesi. In addition to his professional activity, he has held courses and conducted research activities in constitutional law at various Italian universities, including at "Sapienza" University and the University of Firenze. He has been Professor of Parliamentary Law at the Department of Political Science, "Roma Tre" University and at the LUISS School of Government. He is the author of several publications in renowned Italian journals. His recent publications include Corso di diritto parlamentare (co-authored with N Lupo).

List of Contributors

Monika Glavina is a PhD candidate at the Centre for Legal Theory and Empirical Research at the Faculty of Law, KU Leuven, where she also works as a researcher under the ERC-granted EUTHORITY Project. Monika has obtained a master's degree from the Faculty of Law at the University of Zagreb and a master's degree from the Legal Department at the Central European University. Her research interests include empirical legal research, judicial behaviour, and the Europeanisation of national judiciary. In her PhD dissertation, Monika focuses on the incentives and constraints for the application of EU law among EU Member State judges.

Barbara Guastaferro, PhD (University of Padua) is Tenured Assistant Professor of Constitutional Law at the University of Naples "Federico II". She was previously Research Fellow in Law at Durham Law School, within the framework of the "Neo-Federalism" Project (funded by the European Research Council). In 2011 she was awarded the prestigious Hauser Global Law Scholarship to financially support her post-doctoral studies at New York University School of Law, where she was an Emile Noël Fellow in 2011/2012. She is author of several publications in the field of EU Law, Comparative and Constitutional Law, and Constitutional and Democratic Theory.

Juan A Mayoral, LLM PhD (European University Institute and Centre for Advanced Study in the Social Sciences – Juan March Institute) is Assistant Professor in Law and Politics in the Centre of Excellence for International Courts (iCourts) at the University of Copenhagen. His research interests include judicial comparative politics, EU law and politics, and empirical methods.

Mónika Papp, PhD (Eötvös Loránd) is a research fellow at the Centre for Social Sciences, Hungarian Academy of Sciences and a Senior Lecturer at Eötvös Loránd University, Faculty of Law, Budapest. Her key research interests lie in EU internal market law and EU competition law. She has published in English especially on economic patriotism, economic particularism, on the application of EU state aid rules in Hungary and on the application of EU competition rules by the Hungarian judiciary.

Georg Plattner, MA (Vienna) is a PhD candidate and research assistant at the Centre for European Integration Research (EIF) at the University of Vienna in Austria. Before his current position, he was a visiting researcher on a scholarship granted by the Israeli Ministry of Foreign Affairs at Tel Aviv University. His research interests include populist radical right parties in Europe, European Integration, and EU Security, Defence and Foreign Policies.

Clara Rauchegger, MMag (Innsbruck) LLM PhD (Cambridge), is Assistant Professor of European law at the University of Innsbruck and Erwin Schrödinger Fellow of the Austrian Science Fund (FWF). She has previously been a Max Weber Postdoctoral Fellow at the European University Institute in Florence. She holds a PhD from the University of Cambridge, where she was a scholar of the Arts and Humanities Research Council and the Austrian Academy of Sciences.

Her research interests lie at the intersections of EU and domestic constitutional law, with a particular focus on fundamental rights protection.

Przemysław Tacik, LLD (Kraków) PhD (Kraków), is Assistant Professor at the Institute of European Studies at the Jagiellonian University in Kraków. He holds PhDs in philosophy (2014) and law (2016). He has been a visiting scholar at the SUNY at Buffalo, Université de Nice, Universität Heidelberg, Max-Planck-Institut für ausländisches öffentliches Recht und Völkerrecht, Universidade de Lisboa, Paris-Lodron Universität Salzburg and Université Paris 1 – Panthéon Sorbonne. He has authored three books in Polish, as well as over 30 articles in English and Polish. His interest include international law, human rights, animal studies, critical theory and contemporary philosophy.

Peter Thalmann, MMag (Vienna) MJur (Oxford) Dr (Vienna), is Assistant Professor at the Institute for European and International Law at the Vienna University of Economics and Business. He has previously been a visiting research affiliate at the University of Oxford, an associate with a Vienna-based law firm, and a guest professor at the China-EU School of Law in Beijing. His research interests include EU and domestic constitutional law, as well as internal market and competition law.

Dimiter Toshkov, PhD (Leiden) is an Associate Professor at the Institute of Public Administration at Leiden University in the Netherlands and a Jean Monnet Fellow at the Robert Schuman Centre for Advanced Studies at the European University Institute. His research interests include European governance and politics, comparative public policy, immigration, and research methodology.

Marton Varju, PhD (Hull) is a senior research fellow at the Hungarian Academy of Sciences, Centre for Social Sciences, Institute of Legal Studies and a senior legal advisor at the Hungarian Supreme Court, Administrative and Labour Division. He is also a fellow at the Centre for Ethics and Law in Biomedicine, Central European University, Budapest. His research interests lie in EU public and economic law, the intersection of the law and the political economy of European economic integration, and the ethics and law of the regulation of human biotechnologies.

Anna Wallerman, LLD (Gothenburg) is an Associate Senior Lecturer and a Ragnar Söderberg Postdoctoral Fellow in Law at the University of Gothenburg. She has previously been a Max Weber Postdoctoral Fellow at the European University Institute and held visiting fellowships at the Universities of Zurich and Oxford. Her research interests include national and European procedural law, judicial reasoning and decision making, and legal empirical studies.

Catherine Warin, a graduate of the Institut d'Etudes Politiques de Paris (Sciences Po), holds a PhD from the University of Luxembourg. Her research focuses on the rights and functions of individuals in the EU's multilevel legal order. She is registered with the Luxembourgish bar and her main practice areas are immigration law, labour law and data protection law.

Prologue: (EU Law) Scholarship in (Times of) Crisis?

MICHAL BOBEK*

I. THE VALUE OF COMPARATIVE EU LAW

IS THERE SUCH a thing as 'comparative EU law'? The more traditional answer would be that there is only one system of EU law, with its unity or uniformity, in the judicial realm ultimately ensured by the Court of Justice through the preliminary rulings procedure, being one of the key defining elements of that legal order.[1] Without necessarily harbouring any normative agenda as to whether it is a good thing, or a bad thing, or a truly pluralist thing, comparative studies of EU law on the national level simply acknowledge that 'EU law on the ground' might be somewhat different from the central orthodoxy. To the bare bones of what are indeed uniform or directly applicable rules, national layers implementing substantive rules are added, then a national institutional and procedural set-up, but also the overall national judicial practice and approaches. The result is of course rather different. Much like an image projected from an overhead projector, one transparency sheet is indeed the same everywhere. But where two or more additional sheets are different at the local level, so too is the ensuing picture.

Why should (the study of) EU law pay any attention to those national layers? First, on the basic level, as with any other normative system, there is an issue of social responsiveness and social relevance. Any efficient system of norms should be interested in the effects on the ground of what has already been enacted or decided, but also in current and likely problems. Both of those dimensions, the pre-decision and the post-decision ones, should then ideally be taken into account in ongoing legislative or judicial endeavours.

Second, there is perhaps an additional reason why the study of national processes matters for EU law in particular. Any legal order is normative in nature. There is, however, a considerable difference between the national legal orders and EU law in terms of what lies beneath this normativity. In national

---

* All opinions expressed are strictly personal to the author.
[1] See, eg, *Opinion 2/13* (Accession of the EU to the ECHR) EU:C:2014:2454, paras 174–76 and the case law cited therein.

legal orders, the normativity is supported by recognisable constitutional authority on the one hand and hierarchy and coercion on the other. Thus, in pragmatic terms, a positivist national legal order does not need to be that concerned with non-compliance and the divergence between normativity and reality. With respect to positivist and state-centred normative systems, these two levels may even be fairly disconnected. Again, any sensible legal system naturally ought to ensure that there are no large gaps between the normative and the real.[2] But sociological challenges to the law based on non-compliance and lack of responsiveness of the law are less severe, as there is the ultimate instrument of coercion.

The problem of EU law, but at the same time its nobility and uniqueness, lies in the absence of clear constitutional authority and its own coercive mechanisms. In EU law, it is compliance that fuels normativity. The assumed acceptance of EU law in the Member States became part of the normative narrative of what EU law is and why it exists. EU law has incorporated Member States' acceptance of and compliance into its normative narrative and legitimacy. In other words, at the root of EU laws does not lie 'should' but rather 'is'. Thus, where a positivist national legal order relying on a normative underpinning in terms of constitutional authority and ultimate coercion is allowed not to bother much about compliance, EU law faces a dual void: constitutional and coercive. It is for that reason that acceptance and compliance 'on the ground' is perhaps far more important for EU law than for national legal systems. That is also why the comparative study of the practice on the ground matters much more, not just for fans of legal sociology.

Finally, it ought to be underlined that within such a structure, the proposition that the Court of Justice and the national courts are joint vessels is not a disguised claim of EU law primacy and the command for national courts to follow the Court's guidance. It is a simple acknowledgment of the fact that the exchange between the courts in Europe is now much more multifaceted and multidirectional.[3] It entails more than the traditionally conceived top-down dimension of the Court of Justice in exchange with the national court(s) through the preliminary rulings procedure. There is also the lively bottom-up dimension of the conversation, occurring not just by the comparative study of national systems in and by the Court.[4] An often overlooked fact is that the national courts

---

[2] While of course acknowledging that in every legal system there will be certain leeway in between what the supreme jurisdiction says the law is and what the law genuinely is on the ground, in lower courts and the courts of first instance. As metaphorically put, supreme jurisdictions will frequently be but lighthouses in symbolic fields, mostly relying on the persuasive power of their judgments. F Bruinsma, 'A Socio-Legal Analysis of the Legitimacy of Highest Courts' in N Huls, M Adams and J Bomhoff (eds), *The Legitimacy of Highest Court's Rulings: Judicial Deliberations and Beyond* (The Hague, TMC Asser Press, 2009) 73.

[3] For a detailed description see, eg, M Bobek, 'Europeanization of Public Law' in S Cassese, A von Bogdandy and P Huber (eds), *The Max Planck Handbook in European Public Law: Volume I: The Administrative State* (Oxford, Oxford University Press, 2017).

[4] See, eg, K Lenaerts, 'Interlocking Legal Orders in the European Union and Comparative Law' (2003) 52 *International & Comparative Law Quarterly* 873.

set the agenda for the Court of Justice, by the choice of question they make to the Court and how those questions are phrased. Furthermore, the same national courts may also engage by taking other kinds of decisions, whereby they might wish to signal certain matters to the Court without necessarily making a request for a preliminary ruling in that individual case. Finally, over the last two decades or so, there has been an increased 'horizontality' of exchanges between the Member States and their courts, within but also beyond the scope of EU law, in the form of various networks and associations, sometimes with but sometimes also without the participation of the European institutions and courts.[5]

All these avenues of exchange, further fuelled and enhanced by technologies allowing for instantaneous communication and data sharing, allow for ample feedback and opportunity for reflection. Feedback and reflection are perhaps even more welcome within an already highly evolved legal order, such as that of the EU today, which might run the risk of gradually being trapped in its own highly specialised debates. It is often the case that the more evolved and detailed a system is, the more self-referential it becomes. Therefore, also in this regard the study of comparative EU law, mapping the realities on the ground, as well as personal exchanges with national judges and practitioners, helps the EU to remain responsive and engaged with issues that are indeed of concern to national practice. It is only by reading such studies and the expression of concerns that one realises, for example, that the national judges are likely to be more interested in a helpful answer on the (often rather technical) merits of a case than they would be, for example, in hair splitting taxonomies of types of direct effect.[6]

II. A PERMANENT CRISIS?

This volume provides much valued feedback and reflection in terms of national practice in a number of Member States. It does so by focusing on three different strands of challenges to EU law in the Member States: (i) general or systemic challenges by Eurosceptic parties and governments; (ii) sectoral case studies in the areas of migration and free movement of people; and (iii) by revisiting some elements of the truly Hamletian question of EU comparative law studies focusing on the national judiciaries: to refer or not to refer (to the Court with a request for a preliminary ruling).

---

[5] Further see, eg, M Claes and M de Visser, 'Are You Networked Yet? On Dialogues in European Judicial Networks' (2012) 8 *Utrecht Law Review* 100 or the same in 'Courts United? On European Judicial Networks' in B de Witte and A Vauchez (eds), *Lawyering Europe: European Law as a Transnational Social Field* (Oxford, Hart Publishing, 2013).

[6] This is of course not to say that such topics are not important. But, in a way, the discussion on them, as passionate as it might be, tends to be a highly advanced discussion between specialised EU law scholarship and the Court, not necessarily finding much traction or interest at the national (judicial) level.

The common denominator, sometimes expressed, sometimes implied, is called *crisis*. It appears to be an overall crisis of (integrationist) faith, captured at various levels, or stages of progression, ranging from (open) disobedience and defiance, to Euroscepticism and challenge to EU law (or EU governance), and eventually arriving in some cases at a 'mere' resistance, 'Euro-reluctance', or a 'lack of' something.

Buzzwords in EU scholarly discourse change with the times. It is sufficient to look at the titles of academic articles or books of the past decades: after the initial wave of communitarian and supranational enchantment, the word of the day changed to 'Europeanisation', then of course 'enlargement', 'reform', and/or 'deepening', coupled with quite a degree of institutional optimism, then gradually pluralist (ideally constitutional or whatever other adjective preceding pluralist). The last ten years or so are the age of crises: monetary and fiscal, Eurozone, then that of refugees, the rule of law, and then Brexit. Prefixes change, but the crisis stays. Either or all of these are then said to translate, eventually, into a crisis of faith into the European integration project.

Without wishing to downplay or disparage the gravity of any of the above, one may wonder whether a 'permanent crisis' is still a crisis, or a new normality. The Oxford Online Dictionary defines crisis as 'a time of intense difficulty or danger' or as 'the turning point of a disease when an important change takes place, indicating either recovery or death'.[7]

Thus, of course, a crisis might last for some time. However, as not only people versed in Marxist and Trotsky's theories might guess, similar to a 'permanent revolution',[8] a 'permanent crisis' is also unlikely to be a realistic recipe for any society. Indeed, after a while, the crises, or rather the issues and the controversies that have been raised thereby, become the new normality. Provided that the patient is at that stage still alive, it is thus fair to assume that there has been some sort of recovery.

III. SCHOLARSHIP AND CRISIS

Finally, at the cross-section of both of the issues outlined above lurks the question: what ought to be the role of scholarship in times of crisis? Perhaps first and foremost, it ought to be critical and detached already at the evaluative and terminological level. Instead of automatically taking over and running with the fashionable terms of the day, it ought to critically examine them in the first place. Is there really a crisis worth that name? Is the edifice really crumbling?

---

[7] https://en.oxforddictionaries.com/definition/crisis (last accessed on 30 December 2018).
[8] First articulated at the level of political programme in K Marx and F Engels, *Address of the Central Committee to the Communist League* (London, March 1850), and later notably developed by L Trotsky, *The Permanent Revolution* (1929).

Or is there perhaps just (often cyclical) readjustment to new facts and realities? Are Member States indeed becoming increasingly Eurosceptic, with that mood being translated into national application and enforcement of EU law? Does that also translate into the decrease in the number of references from national courts to the Court, and/or into an overall disengagement? This volume already promises valuable insights into those issues.

Second, the more complex deontological issues arise once one finds that there indeed is a crisis, however it is labelled. What is the role of (not just EU law) scholarship then, in particular in the face of structural challenges that could undermine the very foundations of the entire edifice? To remain critical, detached, and seemingly value-neutral? Or to become engaged at the level of promoting certain policies and in the defence of standards and norms?

Posing that question is certainly no call for 'value-free-scientific-nihilism' in law. It is rather the acknowledgment of the fact that in the (modern) European tradition, including the European Continent and the English common law tradition, the key source of legitimacy for (legal) scholarship has been of a *seemingly* apolitical, detached rational nature. Whether it had been, from the beginning of the nineteenth century onwards, the 'mere' exegesis and dogmatic interpretation of the new codes, or later in particular in the Germanic tradition the more constructive, unifying nature of the legal scholarship, that tradition has been dogmatic, positivist, and analytical, but rarely *openly* political.[9]

Both those expressions are important: 'seemingly' and 'openly'. There is of course no disguising that much more has been going on beneath the surface, with certain policies, values and ideas, in particular in given areas, or as far as certain legal issues were concerned, frequently implanted within the legal discourse as a seemingly objective necessity of the law, with considerable value-orientated or political preferences hidden in such arguments. However, yet again, the overall rules of the game on the surface are different: the scholar is the expert who is listened to, or at least used to be in that tradition, not because of his origin or beliefs, but because of his objective, detached rational authority.[10]

---

[9] Generally see, eg, S Vogenauer, 'An Empire of Light? II: Learning and Lawmaking in Germany Today' (2006) 26 *OJLS* 627 (on Germany); A Braun, 'Professors and Judges in Italy: It Takes Two to Tango' (2006) 26 *OJLS* 665 (on Italy); N Duxbury, *Jurists and Judges: An Essay on Influence* (Oxford, Hart Publishing, 2001) (on England and France); and, by contrast, A Arnull, 'The Americanization of EU Law Scholarship' in A Arnull and others (eds), *Continuity and Change in EU Law: Essays in Honour of Sir Francis Jacobs* (Oxford, Oxford University Press, 2008) (on EU law scholarship), concluding in fact, in spite of the title, that those two traditions are still very much separate.

[10] In the sense of Weberian formal rationality as the foundation of modern society and its system of law – see M Weber, *Wirtschaft und Gesellschaft: Grundriss der verstehenden Soziologie*, 5th edn (Tübingen, Mohr Siebeck, 1972) 496 ff. Interestingly (or rather sadly) enough, the explicit rejection of 'experts' and their opinions and replacement by shared beliefs and/or personality, that one encounters in some parts of Europe today, is something that would be normally associated with pre-modern, in particular medieval personal or religious authority. See, eg, P Becker and R Von Krosigk, 'New Perspectives on the History of Bureaucratic and Scientific Subjects' in P Becker and R von Krosigk (eds), *Figures of Authority* (Bern, Peter Lang, 2008) 16.

There is nonetheless another side to the same coin: the further scholarly work strays away from that source of legitimacy, the more easily its calls might be discarded as being 'just another opinion'. Thus, becoming engaged in the way of openly promoting certain policy could come with a price tag attached in terms of legitimacy and acceptance.

This does not mean that it ought not to be done – quite the contrary. Sometimes it is useful and in some situations, it becomes an imperative. It is very difficult to generalise in this regard, since not all crises are the same. Their context differs vastly. From the (not so remote) European past, in particular in the eastern and south-eastern parts of the EU, we know the clearly negative examples, such as when legal scholarship and its individual representatives, in order to preserve the remnants of self-respect, but sometimes also simply in order to be left alone, chooses internal exile instead of engagement and challenge. The key idea then becomes to move, for the time being or even permanently, into areas that are considered to be 'ideology-free', or at least 'ideology-light', such as certain technical areas of law, or empirical legal methods.[11] Quite interestingly, the same 'self-defence' mechanism, applied not only to social sciences but also to judicial work, then produced certain self-justification myths of 'ideology-free' judging in certain areas, such as some areas of private law.[12] One matter is clear: neither of them really work.

Next to the Scylla of 'hiding one's head in the sand' is the Charybdis of political or even politicised engagement, in which knowledge and science is made a servant to a cause. A key element of the formal rationality on which modern scientific legitimacy is based is that, with regard to facts, cognition precedes demonstration. The cognition method is believed to be neutral and objective.[13] Reversing that order, or rather engaging in demonstration in the sense of defending a policy or an idea, no matter what (or rather irrespective of any cognition), indeed crosses the borderline between a normative argument and

---

[11] Suggesting then that apart from the compulsory citation of the latest Communist Party resolution in the introduction and then perhaps paying lip service to it in the conclusion, but the rest of the work was 'objective' and 'scientific', untainted by the prevailing social context.

[12] With that myth having been thoroughly debunked, certainly with regard to totalitarian regimes, in which the new law and its interpretative tenets claimed indeed to be permeating the entire old legal order, also including (seemingly 'neutral') areas such as family law, law of contract etc. Further see, eg, B Rüthers, *Die unbegrenzte Auslegung: Zum Wandel der Privatrechtsordnung im Nationalsozialismus* (Tübingen, Mohr Siebeck, 1968) (on Nazi Germany); I Markovits, *Justice in Lüritz: Experiencing Socialist Law in East Germany* (Princeton, Princeton University Press, 2010) (on the former GDR) or O Ulč, *Malá doznání okresního soudce* [*Small Confessions of a District Court Judge*] (68 Publishers 1974) (on Communist Czechoslovakia).

[13] Captured in the pure Cartesian tradition as 'Et il est bien meilleur de ne jamais penser à chercher la vérité d'aucune chose que de le faire sans méthode ... par méthode, j'entends des règles certaines et aisées, grâce auxquelles tous ceux qui les auront exactement observées, n'admettront jamais rien de faux pour vrai et ... parviendront à la connaissance vraie de toutes les choses dont leur esprit sera capable.' In R Descartes, *Discours de la méthode* (Paris, Flammarion, 2000) 124–25.

a political pamphlet.[14] The umbilical cord of any scientific legitimacy becomes completely severed.

Thus, from the past crises, there is only so much that one can learn. Each one tends to be different. Naturally, the past gives us some indications as to when there might no longer be scholarship in times of crisis, but rather a scholarship in crisis. However, apart from such extreme cases, legal scholarship, also or even especially in times of crisis, will always be appreciated in the same way it has always been: as the key guide in our understanding, interpretation, and further development of the law.

---

[14] Yet again, from the experience in the former Communist bloc, there was a certain rule of 'ideologically reversed proportions' – the closer a certain topic was to an official political dogma, the less space there was for any independent cognition. All that was needed was 'scientific demonstration' as to why that dogma is correct. A fascinating example of such intellectual inventiveness can raise the issue of comparability of laws of socialist and capitalist countries and ways in which that comparability was 'scientifically' denied ('proving' a previous political pronouncement on the inherent incomparability of those systems). See, eg, V Knapp, Verträge im tschechoslowakischen Recht (1962/1963) 27 *Rabels Zeitschrift für ausländisches und internationales Privatrecht* 495, firmly denying the possibility of any comparison, and, on the other hand, U Drobnig, 'Comparability of Socialist and Non-Socialist Systems of Law' (1977) 3 *Tel Aviv University Studies in Law* 45, or H-J Bartels, *Methode und Gegenstand intersystemarer Rechtsvergleichung* (Tübingen, Mohr Siebeck, 1982) analysing those statements from the 'capitalist' side. The latter author also notes that it was common that the authors from the Eastern bloc used to articulate certain views in official publication and then speak differently in person in the semi-privacy of international conferences (Bartels, *Methode*, 55).

Introduction

CLARA RAUCHEGGER AND ANNA WALLERMAN

IN RECENT YEARS, Eurosceptic and nationalist forces have been gaining ground in many Member States. The ideal of an ever closer union, built on fundamental freedoms and the rule of law, has been shaken by the United Kingdom's decision to leave the European Union (EU) and by illiberal developments in Hungary and Poland. Anti-immigration sentiments are at the core of the Eurosceptic agenda. The free movement of persons and the influx of third-country refugees have tended to be particularly controversial in the Member States.

However, while political scientists have examined public opinion towards the EU and legal scholars have focused on mechanisms aimed at ensuring compliance with EU law, we still do not know what the Eurosceptic challenge precisely consists of. Do governments and/or political parties criticise particular pieces of EU law and policy, and do they propose, or take, initiatives that are incompatible with those of the Union? Does Euroscepticism manifest itself in domestic legislation or case law?

This collection seeks to provide an overview of the many facets of national resistance that the EU is currently facing. Our aim was to look beyond the rhetoric of political leaders to the legal and administrative measures that are actually taken within the Member States. We wish to divert the attention away from claims and pledges to concrete actions. All the national developments brought together in this collection represent challenges to the implementation, effect and authority of EU law in the Member States. We made a deliberate choice to not only focus on the most extreme expressions of Euroscepticism and on the Member States that are known to be highly critical of the EU. Rather, the challenges examined here take many forms and manifestations, ranging from the gauntlet thrown in open defiance to perfectly innocent – and yet equally troublesome – ignorance. The combined effect of the latter kind of obstacles can be as problematic as outright opposition to EU law and governance.

While it is impossible to give a comprehensive account of all kinds of national resistance against the EU in a single volume, we have included perspectives from the entire Union, from old and new, western and eastern, troublesome and (ostensibly) compliant Member States. Naturally and for good reasons, a lot of attention has been directed towards Hungary and Poland, in recent scholarship in general but also in this volume. However, the chapters that follow demonstrate that Euroscepticism or challenges to EU law and governance do not only occur in the newer Member States. Only one prominent example has consciously been left out. The United Kingdom's withdrawal from the EU is, of course, in some ways the ultimate act of Euroscepticism. However, Brexit is not a good fit for this collection because it is not really an internal challenge to the effect and authority of EU law and governance. Moreover, the specific regulatory and administrative consequences of Brexit remain to be revealed.

The collection is divided into five parts. Part I contains two chapters that examine Member States' Euroscepticism from a comprehensive perspective, using qualitative and quantitative political science methodology. These two contributions provide an overview of the effects of rising Euroscepticism in national political parties and governments. In chapter one, **Gerda Falkner** and **Georg Plattner** analyse the policies of national far-right populist parties represented in the European Parliament. They argue that while these parties are generally hostile to the deepening of European integration, their policy preferences are not coherent enough to form a united front. However, the rise of these parties could lead to a proliferation of anti-EU attitudes and to non-co-operative antagonism in EU institutions and Member States. In chapter two, **Dimiter Toshkov** discusses the consequences of Euroscepticism in government and among the general public for compliance with EU law. Surprisingly, his study shows that Eurosceptic Member States are no more likely than other Member States to be subject to infringement proceedings, and no less likely, when such procedures occur, to receive a judgment in their favour. This could indicate that Euroscepticism has more bark than bite, for instance because Eurosceptic governments are balanced by their civil servants or because of anticipated higher degrees of surveillance that deters non-compliance.

This idea carries over to Part II of this volume, which consists of detailed sectoral and national case studies of the most evidently Eurosceptic governments: those of Italy, Hungary and Poland. **Luigi Gianniti** and **Barbara Guastaferro**, in chapter three, examine the actions taken by the Italian populist coalition government of the Five Stars Movement and the League during its first time in office. In parallel to Toshkov's findings, Gianniti and Guastaferro find that the Eurosceptic policies of the League, in particular, were attenuated by the separation of powers between government, Prime Minister, President, and Parliament. They therefore conclude that the new government's impact on Italy's stance towards the EU has so far been less than one might have expected.

However, this optimism is shaken when **Przemysław Tacik** turns to Poland in chapter four and analyses the Polish Government's responses to rulings of the Court of Justice of the EU (CJEU) on the illegality of logging activities in the Białowieża primeval forest. Tacik observes that government representatives deliberately and consistently sought to undermine the Court's authority by spreading disinformation and whipping up nationalism. Rational legal discourse was thereby made all but impossible. This threatens not only the effectiveness of EU law but the very fundamental democratic values of the Union.

Chapter five focuses on the Union's other *enfant terrible*: Hungary. Looking beyond the constitutional and judicial reforms that have given rise to much discussion and analysis, **Mónika Papp** and **Marton Varju** turn their attention to the economic policy of the Orbán government. They show that Hungarian economic policy since 2010 has taken a patriotic turn by moving away from the liberal values underpinning the internal market and often coming into conflict with EU free movement law. While the concrete reforms have at least on some occasions been successfully challenged in court, Papp and Varju argue that the national policies examined in the chapter are symptomatic of a fundamental ideological conflict between the EU and the current Hungarian administration.

Part III is dedicated to different aspects of free movement within the EU, which, as stated above, seems to be particularly controversial. This part includes two case studies on the free movement of persons and the Schengen system. In chapter six, **Peter Thalmann** examines whether the widespread departure from open EU internal borders in the wake of the 2015 migration crisis has been a suitable and necessary response to 'a serious threat to public policy or internal security' pursuant to EU law. Thalmann does not rule out that the reinstitution of border controls may have been compatible with the exceptions provided for in the Schengen regime. However, he notes that the very existence of far-reaching exceptions puts into question the ideal of a Europe without internal state borders. Chapter seven takes on the classical question of intra-EU free movement of persons. **Catherine Warin** shows that even Luxembourg – a deeply European, founding Member State, which thrives on free movement – is reluctant to give full effect to its EU law obligations towards frontier and migrant workers. While suggesting that misunderstandings and limited legislative capacity may partly explain this reluctance, Warin observes that implementation of EU law is often minimalistic and corrected only following judicial intervention. This suggests at least a certain 'Euroreluctance', if not Euroscepticism.

In Part IV, attention shifts towards the judiciary and in particular the relationship between national courts and the CJEU. Chapter eight, by **Anna Wallerman**, offers a framework to capture the attitudes of national judges. Drawing on the Dworkinian superjudge Hercules, Wallerman introduces three heroines of her own: three judges who personify institutionalist, legalist and activist explanations for judicial behaviour. Her characterisation of three types of judge help us to achieve a more nuanced understanding of the nature of the relationship between national courts and the CJEU, and the effects of each attitude on ensuring Member State compliance with EU law.

Chapter nine offers a positive account of the national judge. **Jesse Claassen** focuses on an area where harmonisation is substantial, competition law, and the Netherlands – a jurisdiction which, although not untouched by nationalist and Eurosceptic sentiments, has a reputation of being generally pro-integration. Claassen argues that in this case a scarcity of preliminary references should be interpreted not as a sign of rebellion and challenge, but as one of successful integration. Dutch competition law judges, he argues, do not refer to the CJEU because they do not need to; they have fully embraced EU law and are quite capable of applying it on their own accord.

Shifting the focus from one of the founding to two of the newer Member States, **Monika Glavina** in chapter ten examines obstacles to referrals to the CJEU through interviews with judges in Slovenia and Croatia. She argues that while previous studies have searched for one dominant explanation for national judges' propensity to refer, in reality judges are influenced by a number of different considerations ranging from personal preferences to institutional incentives. Crucially, Glavina finds little support for the idea that judges refrain from referring in order to lessen or challenge the influence of EU law in their national legal order. In chapter eleven, **Juan Mayoral** discusses the effects of a conflict between the CJEU and national constitutional courts. Based on a survey of Polish judges that was conducted before the populist PiS government came to power, Mayoral shows that the guidance of national constitutional courts may outweigh that provided by the CJEU where case law at the national and Union levels conflicts. Mayoral argues that this severely limits the national judiciary's potential to function as a counter-weight to a Eurosceptic government. Indeed, the judiciary may itself turn Eurosceptic under the influence of a politically predisposed peak court.

The volume is brought to a close by Part V (chapter twelve), in which the editors compare and contrast the findings of the preceding 11 chapters and confront them with the broader literature on Euroscepticism and compliance.

The contributions to this volume were discussed at a workshop organised by the editors at the European University Institute in June 2018. We are grateful to the Max Weber Programme, the Law Department and the Robert Schuman Centre for Advanced Studies for financial support, and to the Max Weber Team for helping us with the practical arrangements of the event. We would also like to express our gratitude to the anonymous reviewers who generously volunteered their time and whose comments greatly contributed to the quality of the volume. The professionalism and dedication of the fantastic team at Hart Publishing made our job as editors as easy and painless as possible. Lastly, we would like to thank Anna Khalfaoui for her superb editorial assistance.

Part I

National Euroscepticism
and the EU Institutions

1
EU Policies in Times of Populist Radical Right Euroscepticism: Which Future?

GERDA FALKNER AND GEORG PLATTNER*

I. INTRODUCTION: THE EUROSCEPTIC CHALLENGE AND EU POLICIES

THIS BOOK REACHES beyond the usual top-down perspective of EU law, and it does so in many different ways. The following chapter adds to these multiple perspectives by turning the readers' attention to populist radical right parties in the Member States and in the European Parliament (EP). What are their ideas for potentially reforming existing EU policies, such as the Economic and Monetary Union, EU environmental policy, and EU social policy? Where do these parties agree across countries and where not? Who disagrees with whom?

Given mounting right-wing electoral successes, we need in-depth knowledge about what these comparatively novel actors could bring about for policies that nowadays stretch far beyond the national level and, most importantly for our purposes, include the EU. One of the fundamental challenges these parties pose is their profound defiance of several policies developed over decades by the EU. This speaks to one of the major issues of our times: how will today's major challengers to traditional democracy and of established European collaboration among states affect the EU?

The most likely scenario would involve the active reform of EU policies. Populist radical right parties (PRRPs) could form a bloc in day-to-day policy making (most importantly, in the EP, but also in all other institutions) to reform relevant EU policies according to one common template. If and where they are not strong enough in numbers, they may look out for additional ad hoc coalition

---

*We are grateful for the research assistance provided by Olof Karlsson and Florian Sowa. Support during Gerda Falkner's Schuman Fellowship in the Robert Schuman Centre at the European University Institute in spring 2018 is gratefully acknowledged.

partners from other parties. European governments are already led more often by representatives of the political right than left, and of the 11 populist parties in power in the EU, either alone or as coalition partners, seven could be described as PRRPs.

Table 1.1 Populist parties in government (EU28, by 8 November 2018)

	Left-wing populist parties	Centrist populist parties	Populist radical right parties
Governing alone			Poland (PiS)
Leading a coalition	Greece (Syriza)	Czech Republic (ANO) Italy (M5S) Slovenia (LMS)	Hungary (Fidesz)
In a coalition			Austria (FPÖ) (CON led) Latvia (NA) (CON led) Slovakia (SNS) (SD led) Bulgaria (ATAKA) (CON led) Italy (Lega) (POP led)
Total Number	1	3	7

Source: Own compilation.

Table 1.1 indicates that PRRPs are no longer fringe parties, which suggests that their impact on policies, including at the EU level, is likely to grow. However, the policy clout of the PRRPs would be expected to be larger if they were coherent in their objectives and motivations. By contrast, if PRRPs pull in opposite directions, their claims could more easily cancel each other out, so that their effect would be limited.[1]

So far, PRRPs have usually been considered as a bloc by political scientists because of their relative coherence on national policies and their general (but unspecific) Euroscepticism. Our study examines this assumption by comparing the parties' programmes on specific EU policies. This chapter presents selected data from a wider research project and compares the programmatic claims of 16 national PRRPs with seats in the EP – according to the book's ambition to study the intersection of national and EU levels. It seems to us that the combined challenge arising from many individual policy changes may, at least in the long run, challenge existing EU law, and attract as much attention as the – to date much more debated – issue of Brexit.

Our research question asks if the PRRPs' programmatic documents expose a coherent vision regarding the reform of EU policies. It was necessary to build on established knowledge to determine the political parties to be included in our

---

[1] At least on the policy level; this may be different at the level of political styles and campaigning.

analysis. Thus, this project based itself on the rich political science literature analysing political parties. In other words, this study does not aim to establish which political party in the EU could or should be labelled 'populist radical right' or has elements of a RRRP, be it the 'populist', 'radical' or 'right'. Instead, we use the political parties identified as 'PRRPs' by the literature. The seminal work by Cas Mudde from 2007 is used for the definition of key characteristics of the parties in question.[2]

The relevant literature specifies that 'populist radical right' parties are 'populist' in that they present themselves as the sole legitimate representatives of 'the pure people' whilst the other parties are regarded as part of 'the corrupt elite';[3] are 'radical' in their 'opposition to some key features of liberal democracy, most notably pluralism and the constitutional protection of minorities';[4] and are 'right' in that they believe 'the main inequalities between people to be natural and outside the purview of the state'.[5]

Following the mainstream consensus regarding a cluster of parties that are labelled PRRPs,[6] we identify 16 national parties that are represented in the 8th European Parliament (2014–2019) as the objects of our study. Laid down in Table 1.2, this study covers 16 PRRPs: to the six parties identified in 2007 by Mudde, the Austrian FPÖ, the Belgian VB, the Danish DF, the Italian LN, the Swedish SD and the French FN;[7] this chapter adds the Hungarian Jobbik, the German AfD, and the Dutch PVV, discussed by Mudde in later research;[8] the Latvian NA;[9] the Polish PiS, which significantly changed after 2007;[10] the Finnish PS;[11] the British UKIP after its recent transformation;[12] and finally, the Lithuanian PTT.[13]

---

[2] C Mudde, *Populist Radical Right Parties in Europe* (Cambridge, Cambridge University Press, 2007).
[3] ibid 23.
[4] ibid 25.
[5] ibid 26.
[6] The literature does not use the same definitions uniformly nor does it come to the same conclusions as to which specific party is populist, radical or right. For the purpose of our project, we adopted a compromise definition seemingly accepted by a majority of researchers.
[7] Mudde, *Populist Radical Right Parties in Europe* (2007). Not all parties were covered by Mudde in 2007 and some transformed into PRRPs only after his reference 2007 study on PRRPs in Europe.
[8] See C Mudde, *On Extremism and Democracy in Europe* (Abingdon, Routledge, 2016) 43 ff; C Mudde (ed), *The Populist Radical Right: A Reader* (Routledge Studies in Extremism and Democracy) (Abingdon, Routledge, 2017) 15 f.
[9] D Auers and A Kasekamp, 'Comparing Radical-Right Populism in Estonia and Latvia' in R Wodak, B Mral and M Khosravinik (eds), *Right-Wing Populism in Europe: Politics and Discourse* (London, A&C Black, 2013).
[10] R Pankowski, *The Populist Radical Right in Poland: The Patriots* (Abingdon, Taylor & Francis, 2010).
[11] D Arter, 'The Breakthrough of Another West European Populist Radical Right Party? The Case of the True Finns' (2010) 45 *Government and Opposition* 484.
[12] M Goodwin and J Dennison, 'The Radical Right in the United Kingdom' in J Rydgren (ed), *The Oxford Handbook of the Radical Right* (New York, Oxford University Press, 2018).
[13] W Van der Brug et al, 'Radical right parties: Their voters and their electoral competitors' in J Rydgren (ed), *Class Politics and the Radical Right* (Abingdon, Routledge, 2012).

Table 1.2 Populist radical right Members of the European Parliament (MEPs) (overall: 172 of 751 MEPs, or 22.9 per cent) included in our study[14]

PRRPs	English name	Abbreviation	Country	EP seats
Prawo i Sprawiedliwość	Law and Justice	PiS	Poland	14
Dansk Folkeparti	Danish People's Party	DF	Denmark	3
Perussuomalaiset	The Finns	PS	Finland	2
Nacionālā apvienība 'Visu Latvijai!' – 'Tēvzemei un Brīvībai/LNNK'	National Alliance	NA	Latvia	1
United Kingdom Independence Party	United Kingdom Independence Party	UKIP	United Kingdom	20
Sverigedemokraterna	Sweden Democrats	SD	Sweden	2
Partija Tvarka ir teisingumas	Order and Justice	PTT	Lithuania	1
Front National	National Front	FN	France	19
Lega Nord	Northern League	LN	Italy	5
Freiheitliche Partei Österreichs	Austrian Freedom Party	FPÖ	Austria	4
Partij voor de Vrijheid	Party for Freedom	PVV	Netherlands	4
Kongres Nowej Prawicy	Congress of the New Right	KNP	Poland	2
Alternative für Deutschland	Alternative for Germany	AfD	Germany	2
Vlaams Belang	Flemish Interest	VB	Belgium	1
Jobbik Magyarországért Mozgalom	Jobbik	Jobbik	Hungary	3
KORWiN	KORWiN	KORWiN	Poland	1

Source: Adapted from European Parliament (2018).[15]

[14] The project does not include the Hungarian Fidesz party of PM Viktor Órban, even though the party can be described as PRRP, or at least as making PRR politics; see Mudde, *On Extremism and Democracy in Europe*, above n 8, 44 ff. This is because the party is not part of a political group in the EP that hosts more than one PRRP. Note that our wider project also compares the EU-level party groups with each other and the parties in them, hence we chose only groups with more than one PRRP. In any case, Fidesz has not published any party programme (since 2007) or EP election manifesto (since 2009) in recent years. Excluded from our study are, moreover, three (former) members of the ENF whose 'parties' published no programme (at least, not before this project's cut-off date by the end of 2016).

[15] European Parliament, 'List of Current Members (MEPs)' (2018), available at www.europarl.europa.eu/meps/en/full-list.html.

II. METHODOLOGY

Our study covers all available programmatic documents of these parties in their most recent versions (i.e. 31 individual documents).[16] This includes all 16 PRRPs' election manifestos for the EP election of 2014; the official party programmes of all relevant national parties by the end of 2016 or, in the absence of such a document, the latest election programmes for pre-2016 national elections; and a few relevant policy documents that present the specific claims of any such party with regard to a specific EU policy.[17] Election manifestos in particular, but also party programmes, are an outstanding source for extracting a party's policy position because they embody a common denominator, regardless of the party's internal structure. Our study closes a prominent gap in research since existing studies have looked at other, more indirect, sources for the assessment of policy positions. This includes votes on specific issues in the EP, but these votes are much more eclectic and not representative of a party's own priorities regarding a specific EU policy.[18] Furthermore, expert interviews and surveys, the second source for policy positions that is often relied on, offer valuable, but secondary assessments.[19] Campaign statements as reported in the media may include more recent policy demands but are often ad hoc.[20] By contrast, the party documents can be expected to be more impartial and as close as we can get to these parties' common guidelines of will and intent.[21]

We use the method of qualitative content analysis to establish how coherent or incoherent the PRRPs' policy ideas are.[22] Our coding units are all specific statements, over 450 claims, pertaining to any EU policy or any item falling within a specific EU policy.[23] The statements are then compared to the EU's policy goals and instruments, as extracted from the EU's primary law (Treaty on European Union/TEU, Treaty on the Functioning of the European Union/TFEU, Charter of Fundamental Rights, etc.), as well as the relevant secondary

---

[16] All documents in other languages were translated into English by experts supervised by Georg Plattner at the Centre for European Integration Research, University of Vienna.

[17] The manifestos for the European elections in 2014 have by courtesy been shared with the researchers by the Euromanifestos Project 2014 conducted at the University of Mannheim. The party programmes were collected on the parties' websites. Further documents were retrieved from the parties' websites and through a search of the sources mentioned in secondary literature.

[18] M Cavallaro, D Flacher and MA Zanetti, 'Radical Right Parties and European Economic Integration: Evidence from the Seventh European Parliament' (2018) 19 *European Union Politics* 321.

[19] L Hooghe and G Marks, 'Cleavage Theory Meets Europe's Crises: Lipset, Rokkan, and the Transnational Cleavage' (2007) 25 *Journal of European Public Policy* 109.

[20] S Hutter, H Kriesi and G Vidal, Old Versus New Politics: The Political Spaces in Southern Europe in Times of Crises' (2018) 24 *Party Politics* 10.

[21] M Laver, K Benoit and J Garry, 'Extracting Policy Positions from Political Texts Using Words as Data' (2003) 97 *American Political Science Review* 311.

[22] K Krippendorff, *Content Analysis: An Introduction to its Methodology* (Thousand Oaks, CA, SAGE Publications, 2004).

[23] Excluding double claims with essentially identical content, the dataset consists of 352 claims.

law documents (Directives, Regulations, etc.). Each specific goal, instrument or setting of a relevant policy is one specific code. 'Double claims' are not counted where they are coherent with each other but are covered individually where they are contradictory. Our findings are aggregated on the level of policy items and later of entire EU policies.

Our coding includes both the direction and the depth of any specific policy claim contained in the PRRPs' documents studied. Regarding direction, we follow Bauer and Knill's quest for increased or decreased governmental commitment in specific sectors.[24] 'Policy dismantling' (Bauer and Knill's primary research interest) occurs when the number of policy instruments or the intensity of their settings are lowered; the status quo scenario results in no change; or a number of changes lead to the same status if balanced out. Policy expansion is an increase in the number of policy instruments or the intensity of their settings. Regarding the intensity of suggested policy change, we follow Hall's concept: first order change refers to new settings of existing instruments; second order change to new instruments or fewer instruments than before; and third order change to new (ordering of) goals of the policy or cancellation of previous goals.[25]

As to the policy change's coherence, we distinguish between 'absolute coherence' and 'goal coherence'. 'Absolute coherence' is achieved if there are no inconsistencies on any level of claimed policy change.[26] 'Goal coherence' means coherence regarding the proposed change on the level of goals.[27]

On the level of EU policies, we distinguish three clusters that are concerned with different overarching policy topics: core state powers (section III); a new politics cluster (section IV); and a socio-economic cluster (section V).[28] This chapter only discusses policy areas that received more than ten statements from parties and, hence, excludes areas that are of interest to only a few of the relevant parties.

---

[24] MW Bauer and C Knill, 'Understanding Policy Dismantling: An Analytical Framework' in MW Bauer et al (eds), *Dismantling Public Policy: Preferences, Strategies, and Effects* (Oxford, Oxford University Press, 2012); MW Bauer and C Knill, 'A Conceptual Framework for the Comparative Analysis of Policy Change: Measurement, Explanation and Strategies of Policy Dismantling' (2014) 16 *Journal of Comparative Policy Analysis: Research and Practice* 28.

[25] PA Hall, 'Policy Paradigms, Social Learning, and the State: The Case of Economic Policymaking in Britain' (1993) 25 *Comparative Politics* 275.

[26] This means that all parties want the same direction of change (status quo, extension or dismantling) regarding goals, instruments and settings in the policy.

[27] In our research design, we agreed that the picture on the level of instruments or settings could be comparatively more varied and still warrant a qualification of coherence. If there is goal coherence, the overall picture can be considered 'rather coherent' if at least 75+ per cent of the issues show coherence, and 'rather incoherent' if 25+ per cent do not. As the concluding section outlines, this was irrelevant as to lack of goal coherence.

[28] The policy claims that do not correlate with the three broad expectation-based clusters (eg claims regarding institutional issues) were pooled in a fourth cluster ('Other') and are not analysed here.

III. (IN-)COHERENCE IN CLUSTER 1: CORE STATE POWERS

The first cluster deals with policies that are concerned with core state powers. Core state powers are the powers of a state that ensure its monopoly of legitimate coercion and its monetary autonomy.[29] The cluster in our study comprises three different policy areas, set out in Table 1.3: the EU's Foreign Policy, Defence and Security, intra-EU border control, and the EU's economic and monetary policies. Table 1.4 represents the policy claims in this cluster.

Table 1.3 National PRRPs' policy claims in EU policy areas: depth of change for core state powers

	Policy area	Total number of claims	Goals	Instruments	Settings
Core state powers cluster	Foreign policy, defence and security	41	18	23	0
	+ Special case: geopolitical orientation	13	0	0	0
	EU internal border control	22	19	3	0
	Economic and monetary policies	33	18	15	0
	TOTAL	109	55	41	

Source: Own compilation.

Table 1.4 PRRPs' policy claims in EU policy areas: direction of change for core state powers

	Policy area	Total number of claims	Dismantling	Status quo	Extension
Core state powers cluster	Foreign policy, defence and security	41	32	3	6
	+ Special case: geopolitical orientation	13	0	0	0
	EU internal border control	22	17	3	2
	Economic and monetary policies	33	29	2	2
	TOTAL:	109	78	8	10

Source: Own compilation.

[29] P Genschel and M Jachtenfuchs, 'More Integration, Less Federation: The European Integration of Core State Powers' (2016) 23 *Journal of European Public Policy* 42.

A. Common Foreign, Defence and Security Policies

Let us first focus on the EU's common foreign, defence and security policies, which have by far the most statements of all policy areas in the cluster. At first glance, the parties do indeed oppose attempts to integrate this policy area at the EU level: when it comes to the RRPs' predominant direction of change, dismantling is much more prominent (78 per cent) than extending the policy.

On a closer look, however, the picture becomes more nuanced. On the EU's Common Foreign and Security Policy (CFSP), there would be absolute coherence towards dismantling goals and instruments if the Lithuanian PTT did not support the CFSP as a policy goal in rather general terms and if the Latvian NA did not support one of the CFSP's instruments, the Eastern Partnership. Dismantling is claimed seven times regarding the goal of developing a common foreign policy (German AfD, French FN, Polish KNP, Italian LN, Dutch PVV, Polish PiS, Latvian NA) and four times regarding instruments ('EEAS': German AfD, Italian LN, Belgian VB; 'Embassies': Dutch PVV).

Another topic, usually connected to the foreign and security policy realm, deserves our attention. 'Geopolitical orientation' is neither a goal nor an instrument and cannot, hence, be coded like the claims discussed above. Nevertheless, geopolitical orientation is a crucial factor to understand the general directions of a state's external policies. It seems that, considering the global constellation of alliances, there is a default line cutting through the PRRPs. One camp is rather pro-NATO/pro-USA or anti-Russia, with four national parties: Lithuanian PTT, German AfD,[30] Polish PiS and Dutch PVV. Another group's leaning is rather anti-NATO/anti-US or pro-Russia, with four national parties as well: the Austrian FPÖ, Hungarian Jobbik, French FN and Italian LN. In other words: out of the eight national PRRPs that lay out their preferred geopolitical orientation, an equal number falls in two opposing camps.

Considering the main goal of the EU's defence policy of a Common Security and Defence Policy (CSDP), goal coherence would be achieved among the PRRPs, if one party did not instead opt for more common defence policy. The Austrian FPÖ argued at the party conference in 2013 that it would welcome it 'if the EU strives for a self-reliant defence architecture that is independent of NATO and the USA'.[31] This stands in stark contrast to the other PRRPs on the issue, as can be seen in the following quote from the Danish DF:

> The Danish People's Party is a supporter of Denmark upholding its freedom and sovereignty through membership in NATO and the UN ... The Danish People's Party is an opponent of the EU creating an independent defence. Attempts at creating

---

[30] The German AfD may be misrepresented by its own programmatic claim, since the party consistently positions itself pro-Russia in the domestic public discourse; see M Amann and P Lokshin, 'Moscow's Fifth Column. German Populists Forge Ties with Russia', *Der Spiegel* (27 April 2016).

[31] Freiheitliche Partei Österreichs, *Für ein freies Europa – Zuerst Österreicher, dann Europäer!* (Vienna, 2013) 2.

a European defence with its own command structure will unavoidably lead to the strengthening of isolationist forces in the USA, which can prove fatal for Europe.[32]

The Danish DF is one of nine PRRPs calling for the dismantling of a CSDP (Finnish PS, Swedish SD, Belgian VB, Dutch PVV, French FN, Italian LN, German AfD, and Polish KNP).

The picture is mixed on the CSDP's policy instruments. All six claims regarding an 'EU Army' (a prospective instrument) are made with the intent to abolish the option. Regarding 'Missions', three parties opt for extending the counter-terrorism activities of the EU (Italian LN, Lithuanian PTT, German AfD); one calls for regional co-operation to enable participation in missions (Latvian NA); and four call for the dismantling of all missions (Austrian FPÖ, the Finnish PS, the Dutch PVV and British UKIP). On the issue of 'Joint Procurement', there is also strong incoherence: two parties are against any harmonisation (Finnish PS, Belgian VB), while the Italian LN strives to extend this instrument.

B. Intra-EU Border Control

The second EU policy of interest here is border control regarding intra-EU borders. Here, we look at the controversial issue of the Member States' control over their own borders and who enters their territory coming from other Member States. This includes the free movement of people.[33]

This policy area also shows significant incoherence on the issue level, with a nevertheless significant 77 per cent of the overall statements favouring dismantling. All three EU policy goals (on the absence of internal border controls, the free movement of persons, and the free movement of workers) are incoherent in their relevant statements; the same goes for the one instrument debated – the AfD in 2014 preferred keeping the status quo regarding the 'Right of Residence' whereas the Swedish SD favoured the dismantling of this instrument.

Looking at the three goals more closely, there is a stark contrast between the Eastern PRRPs on the one hand, and the Western and Northern PRRPs on the other.

The main goal in this area is the 'Absence of Internal Border Controls', where eight parties strive for the dismantling of this goal and the reinstatement of national border controls. The Swedish SD, for example, argues that 'in order to protect our citizens and others from trafficking, burglary, drugs and migrating crime, we want to see the reinstatement of border protection'.[34] The only party that is in favour of extending this goal is the Polish KNP.

---

[32] Dansk Folkeparti, *Arbejdsprogram* (Copenhagen, 2014) 110.
[33] Note that this policy area does not include external migration which is part of the 'New Politics Cluster' in our analysis.
[34] Sverigedemokraterna, *EU-Valplattform* (Stockholm, 2014) 7.

Regarding the second goal, 'Free Movement of Persons', the Polish KNP again argues for what we code as an extension: 'We will strive to maintain and extend the principle of free travel of people ("Schengen") ... We do not need any institutional superstructure and bureaucratic absurdities for this.'[35] Three parties oppose this position (Dutch PVV, Austrian FPÖ and Italian LN).

Regarding the third goal, 'Free Movement of Workers', four parties want to dismantle the policy goal altogether. Concerning this policy goal, we also find an internal contradiction within the German AfD. In its 2014 document, the party argues in favour of the status quo (as does the Latvian NA). But in the AfD's 2016 party programme, the party explicitly opposes the free movement of workers.

C. Economic and Monetary Policies

The final policy area in this cluster is concerned with economic and monetary policies. These policies concern the core state power of controlling one's own currency and economy. This policy area shows less division than the first two, but is still incoherent regarding both main goals. Two statements that confirm the status quo regarding the goal of a 'Monetary Union' (by the Latvian NA) and an 'Economic Union' (by the Finnish PS) prevent goal coherence in this area. Three parties favour the dismantling of the Economic Union (French FN, Dutch PVV and Italian LN). Overall, the area shows a strong majority of 88 per cent in favour of dismantling.

Regarding the Monetary Union, 13 parties out of 16 favour its dismantling. The statement by the Italian LN illustrates the opposition of many PRRPs to the common currency:

> Out of the Euro – Immediately! Exiting the euro is possible and necessary (...). Going back to our currency is the first step to return having employment and to value our skills, show our qualities to the world and look to a future of prosperity with hope.[36]

On the level of instruments, the parties agree on the dismantling of the 'European Semester' (the French FN, the Belgian VB and the Hungarian Jobbik); the parties are incoherent regarding the 'Banking Union' (the Latvian NA wants to extend it, the Swedish SD and the German AfD to dismantle it), and the 'European Stability Mechanism' (ESM) (seven parties want to dismantle the ESM, the only exception being the Hungarian Jobbik, which claims it should be extended).

This section illustrates, first, that the cluster of EU policies which we can subsume under 'core state powers' shows significant incoherence between PRRPs. Second, principled nationalism at best is applied by many, but not all, PRRPs. Drawing on the typical characteristics highlighted for PRRPs in the literature on

---

[35] Kongres Nowej Prawicy, *Program* (Warsaw, 2015) Section III, 8.
[36] Lega Nord, *Programma Elettorale* (Rome, 2014) 15 f.

national parties, one could have reasonably expected PRRPs to opt against any additional shift of competences to the EU level, particularly regarding policies associated with core state powers. However, those who assume that PRRPs never ask for increased supranational co-operation are proven wrong.

IV. (IN-)COHERENCE IN CLUSTER 2: 'NEW POLITICS'

Next, we look at the 'New Politics' cluster, which is concerned with the cultural dimension, liberal policies and new issues such as the environment and migration. This cluster also includes three policy areas that have been coded in our content analysis, as Table 1.5 illustrates: anti-discrimination policies; environmental policies; and migration policies. Table 1.6 represents the policy claims in the new politics cluster.

Table 1.5 National PRRPs' policy claims in EU policy areas: depth of change for 'New Politics' cluster

	Policy area	Total number of claims	Goals	Instruments	Settings
'New Politics' cluster	Anti-discrimination policies	28	28	0	0
	Environmental policies	43	22	21	0
	Migration policies	30	18	12	0
	TOTAL	101	68	33	

Source: Own compilation.

Table 1.6 PRRPs' policy claims in EU policy areas: direction of change for 'New Politics' cluster

	Policy area	Total number of claims	Dismantling	Status quo	Extension
'New Politics' cluster	Anti-discrimination policies	28	25	2	1
	Environmental policies	43	26	8	9
	Migration policies	30	21	5	4
	TOTAL:	101	72	15	14

Source: Own compilation.

A. Anti-Discrimination Policies

In this cluster, we first discuss the policy area of anti-discrimination policies. This is the policy area with the fewest overall statements in the area. It concerns all matters of discrimination against people because of their ethnicity, sex, gender, sexuality, religion or belief. The statements in the policy area are overwhelmingly made in favour of dismantling (89 per cent).

That we find comparatively less incoherence in the policy area of anti-discrimination policies does not bode well for principles such as freedom of religion, in particular when it comes to persons (perceived to be) of Muslim faith. Most parties pay lip service to freedom of religion but then undermine it by either directly excluding one religion from the remit of this principle or by referencing one religion as more important than others. The Dutch PVV is one of the most outspoken parties regarding the freedom of religion: 'Islam is not a religion but a totalitarian ideology. No headscarves in the health care sector, education, town hall or any other government buildings; also not with subsidized organizations. Forbid the burqa and the quran, tax headscarves.'[37] All nine parties that voice claims on this policy goal are calling for dismantling (Danish DF, Lithuanian PTT, Swedish SD, British UKIP, French FN, German AfD, Austrian FPÖ, and Belgian VB).

The parties are also in coherence with regard to two more goals where they also call for dismantling: four parties put forward statements that oppose (implicitly or explicitly) the 'Right to Found a Family' for non-heterosexual couples (Lithuanian PTT, German AfD, Austrian FPÖ and Italian LN). Furthermore, four parties also oppose the policy goal of 'Equality between Men and Women' (Polish PiS, German AfD, Austrian FPÖ and Polish KORWiN).

Three statements by parties are standing in the way of absolute coherence of the populist radical right on anti-discrimination policies. One is the Austrian FPÖ, which is the only party positioning itself against the reintroduction of the death penalty, whereas three parties are in favour of it (French FN, Polish KNP and Polish KORWiN). The second is the Dutch PVV's 'support' for LGBTQ non-discrimination. Although this claim has been voiced in the context of anti-Muslim agitation,[38] the well-known Dutch culture of liberalism regarding sexual orientation suggests that there may indeed be intra-group divergence. The third incoherence is the Hungarian Jobbik, which calls on the EU to protect ethnic minorities. While Jobbik only calls for improved protection for its own ethnos, the statement nevertheless has to be coded as a call for extension.[39]

---

[37] Partij voor de Vrijheid, *Hún Brussel, óns Nederland* (Amsterdam, 2012) 37.

[38] 'Gay emancipation: We defend our homosexuals against the advancing Islam', ibid 45.

[39] 'The cause of Hungarian minorities has become a subject debated on EU political forums on a daily basis, since Hungarians are the biggest disenfranchised minority of the EU. We have to achieve that Hungarian communities living on the territories lost after World War I gain autonomy and we have to stop the legal, political and also physical atrocities directed against them. We have to achieve that the Slovakian Language Act and the Beneš decrees that defy all kinds of fundamental rights are repealed'; Jobbik Magyarországért Mozgalom, *Nemzetek Európája. A Jobbik programja a magyar önrendelkezésért és a társadalmi felemelkedésért* (Budapest, 2014) 48.

B. Environmental Policies

The next policy area studied in this cluster is the environment, which is concerned with all topics related to energy, agriculture or climate change. Overall, there seems to be greater incoherence than in the first policy area, and all goals but one are incoherent. It is also the policy area with the smallest majority for dismantling of all, with only 60 per cent. Here, we find once more that only Eastern European parties seem to favour these EU policies, while the Western and Northern PRRPs consistently oppose EU environmental policies.

One of the main goals in this area is that of achieving a 'Low-Carbon Economy by 2050'. This policy is opposed by seven parties. Nevertheless, the positions are incoherent overall, since the Latvian NA calls for extending the policy:

> The energy policy should be geared to the economic growth of the state … and the more effective use of resources. We do not think that the figures achieved by the EU are suitable targets; only concrete numbers allow us to achieve even greater goals.[40]

The party follows up this statement by proposing several national laws that go beyond the EU's stated requirements for achieving a low-carbon economy.

The German AfD, among others, goes in the opposite direction with its statements regarding carbon monoxide:

> Climate changes have occurred as long as the earth exists. The climate protection policy is based on hypothetical climate models, which in turn are based on computer-generated simulations of the IPCC (International Panel on Climate Change). Carbon dioxide (CO_2), however, is not a harmful substance, but part and parcel of life.[41]

The party, in this statement, denies the very necessity of the EU's policy goal, since it does not recognise CO_2 as a danger and denies anthropogenic climate change altogether. While the EU's policy is geared towards combatting climate change and accepts it as man-made, the German party clearly positions itself amongst those who deny humanity's responsibility in it.

Regarding the other goals in the area, four parties want to dismantle the 'Common Agriculture Policy' (CAP) (Danish DF, Dutch PVV, Belgian VB, Hungarian Jobbik), while the Latvian NA confirms the status quo of the policy.

The 'Promotion of Energy Efficiency and Energy Saving and the Development of New and Renewable Forms of Energy', another policy goal in the area of the environment that is concerned with the development of renewable energies, is opposed by the British UKIP and the German AfD, but supported with a call for extension by the Lithuanian PTT.

---

[40] Nacionālā apvienība 'Visu Latvijai!' – 'Tēvzemei un Brīvībai/LNNK' (2012) *Programma* (Riga, 2012) 17.
[41] Alternative für Deutschland, *Programm für Deutschland* (Stuttgart, 2016) 79.

The final goal in the area is concerned with the 'Free Movement of Safe and Wholesome Food'. It is opposed by the Danish DF, the Swedish SD and the French FN, which demand a national authority over the raising of standards and imposition of restrictions on foodstuffs from outside their respective countries. The two Scandinavian political parties do so in the name of animal welfare and opposing cruelty against animals. The Hungarian Jobbik supports the status quo of the policy goal.

The policy instruments in the area are equally contested between the parties. The PRRPs are coherent in extending two policy instruments: the extension of the EU's 'Energy Security Strategy' is supported by the Finnish PS and the Lithuanian PTT; and the extension of the instrument of 'Food Information to Consumers' by the Finnish PS, the German AfD and the Hungarian Jobbik.

The parties are coherently calling for dismantling two instruments: the 'Emissions Trading System' is opposed by the Finnish PS and the British UKIP, and the 'Renewable Energy Directive' is met with resistance by the British UKIP and the Hungarian Jobbik.

The statements are incoherent regarding two policy instruments: CAP's instrument of 'Direct Support' is supported with a statement favouring the status quo by the Lithuanian PTT and opposed by the German AfD, the Danish DF and the Swedish SD. Finally, 'Safe Nuclear Energy' is opposed by the Austrian FPÖ and supported by the Finnish PS, the Dutch PVV and the Hungarian Jobbik.

C. Migration Policies

The final policy area in this cluster is migration policies, which concerns external migration into the EU. In this policy area, there is a majority of 70 per cent of the statements in favour of dismantling.

The area is coherent regarding the main goal of the policy which is a 'Common Policy on Immigration'. All seven parties which put forward claims opt for dismantling. They argue that immigration should be the domain of the nation state and oppose a supranational approach to the issue.

The second major goal in the area is a 'Common Policy on Asylum'. This goal would also be coherent if it were not for the German AfD's internal contradiction between its 2014 and 2016 documents, which can be explained by the evolution of the AfD into a full-fledged PRRP between 2014 and 2016. In 2014, the party argued in favour of a common approach to asylum:

> The resulting social and financial consequences [of asylum seekers] have to be distributed fairly between the Member States. The peripheral states should not bear the brunt of the asylum policy. In the EU, common minimal standards for housing and support should be established.[42]

---

[42] Alternative für Deutschland, *Mut zu Deutschland – Für ein Europa der Vielfalt* (Erfurt, 2014) 16.

In their 2016 document, the AfD argued that asylum seekers should be only allowed to do so in 'protection and asylum centres' in safe states. All asylum seekers that are already in Europe would have to return to those centres.[43] This is coded as a call for dismantling the common EU approach to asylum, since the EU now sees the right to apply for asylum in Europe as an integral part of the process. Six other parties favour dismantling this policy goal, with five of them (Finnish PS, Swedish SD, British UKIP, Belgian VB, Italian LN) arguing in favour of the nation state as the sole decision maker. The Austrian FPÖ, like the AfD, calls for asylum centres outside the EU. Disregarding the statement by the AfD from 2014, a time where the party was still not a fully developed PRRP, we see goal coherence regarding a common EU asylum policy.

The parties which put forward statements, even if they are only three, are also goal coherent regarding the third goal in the area: a 'Common Policy on Monitoring and Management of EU External Borders' (Finnish PS, Belgian VB, and German AfD). All of them call for a policy extension. This is also the reason for the high number of claims for extension in the policy area. This may at first come as a surprise given the general assumption that these parties oppose progressive migration policies and supranational authority on the matter. However, the three parties seem to simply transfer their ideological goal of closed borders to the European level, and this is coded as a call for extension.

The level of instruments is more diverse. The parties are incoherent regarding the 'Dublin Regulation' with the Finnish PS and the Austrian FPÖ supporting the status quo, while the Danish DF and the Italian LN call for its dismantling. They are also incoherent regarding the 'Schengen Visa System' (the Latvian NA supports the status quo, and the Danish DF favours dismantling). They are, however, coherent regarding the third policy instrument which is the 'Family Reunification Directive'. All three parties that put forward claims on this issue call for its dismantling (Swedish SD, French FN and Belgian VB).

This section's main finding is that this cluster shows more coherence than the first cluster of core state powers, at least on the level of goals. Nevertheless, there are policy goals and instruments that are incoherent in this cluster as well, and even in all three policy areas. From the perspective of the new 'transnational cleavage' literature, one could have expected the PRRPs to be generally coherent in their opposition against liberal policies and the extension of policies at the EU level.[44] The results in this cluster corroborate this assumption only to a certain extent since the PRRPs also disagree on numerous policy reforms in the cluster.

V. (IN-)COHERENCE IN CLUSTER 3: SOCIO-ECONOMIC POLICIES

Let us turn, finally, to the third cluster that is used to analyse the policy coherence of PRRPs, namely, the Socio-economic cluster. Only two policy areas are

[43] Alternative für Deutschland, *Programm für Deutschland* (Stuttgart, 2016) 59.
[44] Hooghe and Marks, 'Cleavage Theory Meets Europe's Crises' (2007).

included in this cluster: the Single Market and social policy. It is the cluster with by far the fewest statements by PRRPs (see Table 1.7 below). Table 1.8 lays down the policy claims in the Socio-economic cluster.

Table 1.7 National PRRPs' policy claims in EU policy areas: depth of change for socio-economic cluster

	Policy area	Total number of claims	Goals	Instruments	Settings
Socio-economic cluster	Single market	24	12	12	0
	Social policy	20	13	7	0
	TOTAL	44	25	19	

Source: Own compilation.

Table 1.8 PRRPs' policy claims in EU policy areas: direction of change for socio-economic cluster

	Policy area	Total number of claims	Dismantling	Status quo	Extension
Socio-economic cluster	Single market	24	17	2	5
	Social policy	20	16	2	2
	TOTAL:	44	33	4	7

Source: Own compilation.

A. Single Market

First, let us take a look at the policy area that is concerned with the EU's main policy initiative of all, the Single Market. The EU's major instruments to realise this are the 'four freedoms', i.e. the free movement of goods, persons, services and capital (see Article 26 TFEU). Again, there is a majority of statements by the PRRPs that favour dismantling, although significantly smaller than in most of the other policy areas (71 per cent).

With the exception of the Latvian NA and the Polish KNP, all parties that put forward claims (eight parties) are opposed to the main EU goal of the area: the establishment of a 'Common Market without Internal Frontiers'. The Latvian NA shows its support for the single market, with a focus on services: 'NA works towards the goal of absolute openness of the market for services.'[45]

---

[45] Nacionālā apvienība 'Visu Latvijai!' – 'Tēvzemei un Brīvībai/LNNK', *40000 Letter Manifesto for the European Elections 2014* (Riga, 2014) 2.

The majority of PRRPs oppose the single market, and the French FN can serve as an example of the position of most of the parties in our study:

> It is suitable to put tariff rights in place so that a fair competition with countries whose competitive advantage has come from social dumping and currency manipulation is again possible. We advocate an intelligent protectionism that allows to undo the deindustrialization of France (500,000 jobs lost in 5 years) but also to contain the transfers of technology that we see today.[46]

Most of the parties do argue for (at least sectoral) closing of their national markets, similarly but not as openly as the French FN in the above quote.

Regarding the second goal in the policy area that appears in the documents, the establishment of a 'Functioning Energy Market', the Latvian NA and the Italian LN favour the EU energy market. Two parties want to dismantle the EU-wide Energy Market (Hungarian Jobbik and Belgian VB).

On the level of instruments, the German AfD and the French FN oppose liberalisation in the area of 'Services of General Interest'. The AfD, at the same time, is in favour of extending the 'Supranational EU Competition Policy', which puts the party in conflict with the French FN, Italian LN and the Danish DF and Hungarian Jobbik. The Polish PiS, Italian LN and Hungarian Jobbik are against the 'Right of Establishment' when it comes to the purchase of agricultural land, but the Latvian NA is in favour of the status quo.

B. Social Policy

In the final policy area of our analysis, Social Policy, incoherence prevails again (with 'just' 67 per cent of the statements in favour of dismantling). Three Eastern PRRPs (Lithuanian PTT, Polish PiS, and Latvian NA) prefer extending EU policy commitment or status quo in this policy area. The Lithuanian PTT argues in favour of 'Proper Social Protection': 'We will strive to ensure that the criteria for a person to be eligible for a minimum benefit system are aligned throughout the European Union'.[47] Eight parties oppose EU-wide social services, with the Belgian VB offering a short sentence that serves as an example: 'No "social union" with synchronization of social security'.[48]

The Polish PiS wants a new 'EU-Wide Child Support System' to encourage EU citizens to reproduce, which is coded as a call for extension of a (as of yet not-existing) policy goal. The Danish DF, Dutch PVV and Hungarian Jobbik want to scrap the 'Economic, Social and Territorial Cohesion' policy goal, whereas the Latvian NA is content with the status quo.

---

[46] Front National, *Notre Projet: Programme Politique du Front National* (Paris, 2011) 72.
[47] Partija Tvarka ir Teisingumas, *Laisvai tautai* (Vilnius, 2014) 5.
[48] Vlaams Belang, *Verkiezingsprogramma – Uw Stock Achter de Deur* (Brussels, 2014) 9.

On the level of instruments, the Polish KNP supports the status quo of the Posting of Workers Directive, whereas the Swedish SD, the French FN, the Italian LN, the Dutch PVV and the Belgian VB all call for dismantling it (albeit for not always the same, or very clear, reasons).

To conclude this section, socio-economic policies are the cluster which, by far, has the fewest statements by PRR parties and a significant amount of incoherence. This confirms what would be expected by the relevant literature, i.e. a comparatively low interest in and no common approach to socio-economic policies.[49]

VI. CONCLUSIONS: AN EVER-CLOSER POPULIST RADICAL RIGHT?

This chapter presented Europe's Populist Radical Right Parties' programmatic claims for the reform of the EU in three policy clusters and eight policies: foreign and defence policies; internal border control; monetary and economic policies, anti-discrimination; external migration; the environment; social policies; and Single Market policies. All parties for which programmatic texts were studied in our project had been classified as PRRPs by earlier authors and it was therefore important to assess whether these parties formed a harmonious chorus when it comes to their claims regarding these important fields of EU activity.

We find the comparatively highest amount of coherence in the 'New Politics' cluster, where the parties agree on most issues regarding non-discrimination and migration. The few calls for extension in the area of migration are not necessarily contradictory either as they are mainly concerned with hard EU external borders and the idea of a 'fortress Europe'. An interesting finding in this cluster is the clear division between Western and Eastern European PRRPs in environmental policies, with the latter favouring policy extension and the former strictly opposing it (some of them even rejecting the dangers of climate change and carbon dioxide emissions).

Coherence is lower than expected in the 'Core State Powers' cluster, with the PRRPs explicitly disagreeing on almost all of the policy goals regarding foreign, defence and security policies; the Economic and Monetary Union; and the EU's internal borders. The division regarding internal borders runs, again, between East European PRRPs and their Western counterparts, with the former sometimes advocating open borders inside the EU and the latter consistently wanting to restore national borders.

Finally, incoherence again prevails in the socio-economic cluster in both social and internal market policies.

Overall, we find rather significant incoherence in all three clusters and in all policies. In short, this suggests that the scenario of 'joint reform pressure by

---

[49] Mudde, *Populist Radical Right Parties in Europe* 25; J Rydgren, 'The Sociology of the Radical Right' (2007) 33 *Annual Review of Sociology* 241, 245.

a bloc of PRRPs' does not seem very likely – at least, if these parties stay true to their programmatic claims.

Therefore, for those who promote joint EU-level problem solving, it would seem that the main upcoming danger may be less of an agreed line of reforms for these novel actors. The main change may then rather be a form of 'hollowing out' of EU-level policy making due to a proliferation of anti-EU attitudes, on a more general plain and/or non-co-operative antagonism. A blockage of further development of policies may still result, considering that the traditional pro-European camps have been losing out in terms of votes and seats recently and that they may do so even more in the upcoming 2019 EP elections. Overall, there are many more claims calling for the dismantlement of EU policy in our three overarching clusters (75 per cent) than for policy extension (12 per cent) or preserving the status quo (13 per cent). This confirms the general assumption that these parties' attitudes are primarily EU-hostile. In any case, however, the hollowing out of European integration would procedurally differ significantly from joint reform of specific EU policies by the PRRPs.

A final note of caution: having highlighted the main finding of our empirical study, i.e. considerable incoherence of the PRRPs' programmatic ideas for EU policy reforms, it bears mentioning again that programmatic statements of political parties are clearly *only one among many important factors* shaping the behaviour of parties. Such statements cannot be expected to mechanically determine the outcome of policy-making processes. Further crucial influences will come, for example, from:

- individual political leaders, whose opinions in the specific group of parties studied could be more changeable than usually;
- the PRRPs' interactions with the party apparatus, with the party membership, with each other, and with the media; and
- the resulting dynamics between many countries and levels of governance in Europe.

Moreover, how stable the PRRPs' claims will be in the long run remains to be seen, regarding not only general EU scepticism but, more specifically, concrete EU policies.

Even assuming a fair amount of volatility, attention should still be paid to these parties' programmes. In fact, they are the major reference point against which both researchers and electorates are and will be able to measure the PRRPs' actions if they make gains in the EP, the European Council, and the European Commission. Party programmes appear to be the comparatively least volatile claims parties make. Compared to expert surveys on similar issues, which are also a tremendously useful tool for research, programmatic documents present the authors' direct voice without interpretation by anyone else than, by necessity, our research team classifying all claims in an identical manner. Claims voiced by party representatives in election campaigns, in turn, may be more up to date than party programmes or expert surveys – but they are also more ad hoc. Contrasting programme-based findings with those of other approaches is a promising area of further research.

For all these reasons, the study of programmatic documents represents one crucial step to better understand what the coming into power of ever more populist radical right parties may actually mean in terms of challenges to EU law and governance, as discussed in this book at large, and in terms of the EU's various policies and their potential future reform, more specifically.

2

Does Euroscepticism Influence Compliance and Enforcement of EU Law in the Member States?

DIMITER TOSHKOV*

I. INTRODUCTION

CONTESTING EUROPEAN INTEGRATION is not a new phenomenon. Historically, the establishment and progressive institutionalisation of the European Union (EU) has had to overcome significant scepticism and outright resistance from powerful social groups and political actors across the continent. Yet, the challenge of Euroscepticism has become especially acute in the second decade of the twenty-first century with shifting levels of public support for the EU; the imminent exit of the United Kingdom from the Union (as of late 2018); a rising number of openly Eurosceptic parties in governments across Europe; and high-profile conflicts between the European Commission on the one hand, and Italy, Hungary and Poland on the other.

The conflicts with Hungary and Poland are especially alarming, even if not the most politically salient, because they pose a challenge to the rule of law within the EU. The EU is a community of law, and its impact is mostly exercised through rules and regulations, rather than money or raw power. Therefore, conflicts centred on the rule of law and the application of EU rules can undermine the very basis of the EU. Moreover, the effects of such conflicts can quickly spill over to block the decision-making machinery of the EU as, in many areas, supermajorities are still needed for the EU to act. And they can drive further alienation from and public dissatisfaction with 'Brussels'.

---

* A previous version of this chapter was presented at the conference 'Challenges to EU Law and Governance in the Member States', European University Institute, Florence, 8 June 2018. I am grateful to Clara Rauchegger, Anna Wallerman, and an anonymous reviewer for useful comments on the draft. The data used in this chapter has been collected with the support of the Netherlands Organization for Scientific Research, VENI Grant number 451-11-023.

Against this background, it is important to consider the possible influence of Euroscepticism on compliance and enforcement of EU law. Compliance, broadly conceived, includes the transposition of EU directives into national legislation, as well as the practical implementation (application) of EU legal acts, and the process of enforcement of these acts by national authorities. EU-level enforcement relates to the monitoring and enforcement of national implementation and the sanctioning of non-compliant behaviour of the Member States by the EU institutions.

Daily compliance with individual EU regulations lacks the salience of broad political conflicts over European integration. The enforcement of individual EU directives rarely reaches the high media profile of conflicts over the budget or migration policy. Yet, individual compliance shortcomings can quickly accumulate to a failure of the EU legal system, and by extension, of the EU as a whole. Therefore, if Euroscepticism significantly influences levels and forms of non-compliance, it will have another, more indirect and subtle, mechanism to derail the process of European integration.

One can easily imagine reasons why Eurosceptic countries and governments should exhibit routinely worse compliance behaviour than their counterparts with more pro-European governments and societies. After all, not only would they be expected to oppose the advance of Europeanisation in general, but also they would be more likely to oppose particular EU policies and pieces of legislation. At the same time, one can also muster good arguments why Euroscepticism should *not* be able to affect compliance significantly: legal implementation remains largely outside the interest of politicians, and enforcement is negotiated and adjudicated in an institutional environment where expert opinions and legal arguments are supposed to dominate over partisan claims and political concerns. Hence, the question whether Euroscepticism affects compliance with EU law needs to be settled empirically.

This chapter reviews existing studies and analyses original data to answer this empirical question, after unpacking the theoretical arguments sketched above at greater length in the next section. The review covers studies of transposition and implementation of EU law. The analysis of original data is focused on the infringement procedures – the main tools at the EU's disposal to enforce compliance with its rules. In addition to the oft-studied infringement cases that are opened against different Member States, I focus on two additional aspects relating to the conduct of the infringement procedures: the share of opened cases that are settled (before they reach adjudication) and the share of adjudicated cases that Member States win in court (at the expense of the Commission). I relate each of these three aspects to the Euroscepticism of the government in power in the Member State and national public opinion for the period 2004–2015. I seek evidence of the influence of these two forms of Euroscepticism on the patterns of infringement procedures using statistical methods of analysis.

To clarify, this chapter presents a *positive* empirical analysis of the relationship between Euroscepticism and compliance with EU law, rather than a *normative* treatment of the connection between the two, or a *legal* analysis of compliance with particular legislations. The advantage of this positive empirical approach is that it can reveal the effect of Euroscepticism in the patterns of aggregate data; an effect that would not be visible, or would be impossible to prove, when one looks at individual cases or the direct evidence presented by the parties involved in the enforcement process.

The results from the analysis suggest that there is no empirical evidence that Euroscepticism, both in its public and party-political manifestations, affects the patterns of enforcement of EU law. If anything, it appears from the data that higher public and government support for the EU is associated with *more* infringement cases at the Court of Justice of the European Union (CJEU), with more judgments on infringement cases delivered, and with a higher share of wins for the Member State in the judgments. But these associations are likely driven by general and unrelated trends in the development of infringement procedures and Euroscepticism. Nevertheless, even if we discount the positive association between Euroscepticism and compliance that we find in the data, there is no evidence of a negative one.

II. EUROSCEPTICISM AND COMPLIANCE: THEORETICAL CONSIDERATIONS

This section unpacks the theoretical considerations related to the possible influence of Euroscepticism on compliance with EU law. To start with, it is useful to rehearse the reasons why individual Member States may be unwilling to comply with the rules and regulations agreed upon collectively by the EU.

A. Capabilities and Willingness for (Non)Compliance with EU Law

The existing social-scientific literature typically distinguishes between two broad sets of reasons for (non)compliance with EU law: one related to capacities and another related to willingness and incentives.[1] Administrative and other capacities, including available human and financial resources, are important factors influencing the transposition and implementation of EU rules, and we need not review the details of their influence in this chapter.[2]

However, we should note that capacity is not completely exogenous from general willingness to comply. Countries and governments that consider

---

[1] TA Börzel, 'Non-Compliance in the European Union: Pathology or Statistical Artefact?' (2001) 8 *Journal of European Public Policy* 803.

[2] See O Treib, 'Implementing and Complying with EU Governance Outputs' (2014) 9 *Living Reviews in European Governance* 1; D Toshkov, 'Taking Stock: A Review of Quantitative Studies of Transposition and Implementation of EU Law' (2010), available at https://ideas.repec.org/p/erp/eifxxx/p0009.html.

compliance with the EU laws important as a goal in its own right will invest in building the necessary institutions and capacities. Countries that do not consider compliance important will fail to do so. Hence, the effect of capacity on compliance is only partly independent from the effect of willingness. As a result, one cannot make a clear distinction between voluntary (based on willingness) and non-voluntary (based on limited capacities) non-compliance.

B. Why Would Member States not be Willing to Comply with EU Law?

What are the sources of Member States' willingness to avoid compliance? Before we zero in on the possible influence of Euroscepticism, we have to consider the broader context of incentives relating to compliance in a multi-level system of governance. Not all incentives for Member States' non-compliance need to be derived from systemic distrust of the EU.

First, in many policy areas Member States can be outvoted during the decision-making stage, therefore facing a situation where they have to apply legal acts with which they have (openly) disagreed with for substantive reasons.

Second, as the period between proposal, adoption, transposition and ultimately implementation of EU law can be long, the government that supported the adoption of a directive may not be the same government having to implement it.

Third, and relatedly, the department that led the negotiation of the adoption of an EU legal act might not be the same department charged with application of that same act, even within the same government.

Fourth, even if a government is in principle in favour of the provisions of a new common policy, it may still face incentives to comply less then fully once the policy is adopted. Individual governments may have incentives to free-ride on the efforts of the others in order to spare the costs but bear the benefits of the common policy. As we know from the classic analyses of collective action problems,[3] such incentives can quickly unravel co-operation, because the dominant strategy of each government is not to comply, even if collectively all governments can agree about the desirability of the policy. Of course, collective action problems arise only in certain types of situation and from a particular combination of incentives. Nevertheless, it can be argued that in many areas of EU involvement, such as environmental protection, fisheries, competition policy, etc. the threat of collective action problems and free-riding is endemic. Indeed, the whole process of European integration can be interpreted as one massive collective action problem. All in all, there are good reasons to expect that in many cases national governments may not want to comply fully and on time

---

[3] G Hardin, 'The Tragedy of the Commons' (1968) 162 *Science* 1243; E Ostrom, *Governing the Commons* (Cambridge, Cambridge University Press, 1990).

with EU laws and policies, even if in principle they support the EU and the process of European integration.

How does Euroscepticism enter the calculus of willingness to comply? By Euroscepticism we mean systemic, generalised distrust of the EU and its institutions and opposition to the principle and practice of European integration. Euroscepticism can take different forms and can be expressed both at the societal level, as manifested in public opinion and attitudes, and at the level of political parties, as manifested in parties' positions and actions.[4] Both societal and party-level Euroscepticism may be related to the willingness to comply.

First, Eurosceptic parties are more likely to oppose particular pieces of EU legislation, because of concerns about the increasing reach of EU laws and policies.

Second, they are less likely to value timely and correct compliance as goals in their own right.

Third, Eurosceptic politicians, civil servants, and other public officials may obstruct the daily practical implementation of EU rules through actions and inaction that are hard to monitor, detect, and correct.

Fourth, Eurosceptic parties may actually benefit by engaging in open conflicts with the EU institutions over compliance, as this gives them the chance to portray themselves as defenders of their nations and to signal their opposition to the EU.

Fifth, a Eurosceptic public may be less likely no notify national compliance's failures to the EU institutions, obstructing a crucial mechanism for compliance and enforcement.

Before we jump to the conclusion that, as theoretical reasons exist for Euroscepticism to increase non-compliance, this must necessarily be the case, we have to consider the EU institutional framework for enforcing laws and policies.

C. Institutions for Enforcing EU Law and Opportunities for Non-Compliance

When it comes to the *opportunities* of national governments to shirk on commitments made in Brussels, there are several important ones to consider.

First, EU legal acts, and directives in particular, typically allow for considerable amounts of discretion, which Member States can use to accommodate national interests, legal traditions and political concerns.[5] Some discretionary

---

[4] A Szczerbiak and P Taggart (eds), *Opposing Europe? The Comparative Party Politics of Euroscepticism: Volume 1 Case Studies and Country Surveys* (Oxford, Oxford University Press, 2008); S Vasilopoulou, 'Varieties of Euroscepticism: The Case of the European Extreme Right' (2009) 5 *Journal of Contemporary European Research* 3; B Leruth, N Startin and S Usherwood (eds), *The Routledge Handbook of Euroscepticism* (New York, Routledge, 2017).

[5] B Steunenberg and D Toshkov, 'Comparing Transposition in the 27 Member States of the EU: The Impact of Discretion and Legal Fit' (2009) 16 *Journal of European Public Policy* 951.

allowances result from formal exceptions, derogations, or transitionary periods. Others arise from ambiguous language or lack of detail. Moreover, the boundaries of discretion might be unclear, so that it is not obvious whether a national interpretation is compatible with the provisions of the EU legal act or not.

Second, there are often considerable delays between the adoption of an EU legal act and the date at which the act itself or the national transposition measure must enter into force. These delays provide opportunities for Member States to 'drag their feet' when implementing EU rules and to delay their effects.

In addition to discretion and delays, the most important opportunity for (temporary) non-compliance is offered by the EU's relatively weak system of institutions to monitor and enforce the implementation of its rules. The EU enforcement system might be considered strong when compared with other international organisations, but it is much weaker than enforcement systems in unitary and federal states. It is intrinsically hard to police the implementation of tens of thousands of legal acts in 28 different countries, each with its own legal system, administrative structures, and language(s). It is even more so given the very limited capacity of the European Commission, which is designated as the 'guardian of the Treaties'.[6] In the light of the huge information asymmetry between the Commission, as the principal, and the national governments, as the agents of EU legal implementation, transgressions at the national level may very well go unnoticed or a considerable amount of time may pass before the Commission detects non-compliance, during which the Member State will be spared the cost of implementation.[7]

Even if and when the Commission detects a possible infringement, this is only the start of the enforcement process. It can take a long time before a Member State faces any tangible sanctions for its non-compliant behaviour. The first infringement procedure, under Article 258 TFEU, follows several stages. At the end of it, even if an infringement is declared by the Court of Justice of the European Union (CJEU), the Member State will not face immediate financial or other material sanctions. Only after a second ruling on a separate procedure under Article 260 TFEU can financial sanctions (as a lump sum and periodic payments) be imposed on the Member State.

In addition to the lengthy period and many hurdles that the enforcement process must pass through before the threat of financial sanctions becomes imminent, the infringement procedures offer plenty of opportunities to negotiate compliance. Before a case gets decided by the CJEU, the Commission has considerable discretion in deciding whether to open a formal procedure, whether and when to escalate the process to the next stage, and whether to refer the case

---

[6] M Smith, *Centralised Enforcement, Legitimacy and Good Governance in the EU* (London, Routledge Cavendish, 2009), 138.

[7] For an overview of the Commission's enforcement tools, see European Court of Auditors, 'Landscape Review: Putting EU Law into Practice: The European Commission's Oversight Responsibilities under Article 17(1) of the Treaty on European Union' (2018), available at www.eca.europa.eu/Lists/ECADocuments/LR_EU_LAW/LR_EU_LAW_EN.pdf.

to the CJEU. In this phase of the process, sometimes called 'management' or 'negotiation',[8] the Commission tries to ascertain not only the state of national implementation, but also the reasons for non-compliance and the constraints that the Member State faces.

In the Commission's understanding, going to court and imposing financial penalties is only a weapon of last resort. The EU has also created additional institutional mechanisms, like SOLVIT and EU Pilot, that aim to support the voluntary resolution of conflicts over the implementation of EU law before the triggering of the infringement procedure.[9] To sum up, the lengthy enforcement procedure in which the enforcer has far-reaching discretion (and faces little accountability) in how to handle a suspected infringement provides ample opportunities for Member States which are unwilling to comply to try to negotiate their way out of sanctions or simply drag their feet until faced with a judgment under Article 260 TFEU.

It is interesting to consider what would happen if a Member State failed to comply with a judgment under Article 260 TFEU, i.e. refused to pay the financial penalties. Such a possibility has not materialised so far, despite Member States having been ordered to pay fines until compliance has been achieved in many cases. The options available to the EU to enforce compliance with the CJEU's judgments are, however, unclear. The political consequences of employing such options (for example, withholding payments from the EU budget) are even less clear.

A failure to comply, even after a judgment under Article 260 TFEU, might result not only from the obstinacy of a Member State (unwillingness), but from a physical inability (lack of capacity) to do so. The national government would be in the unfortunate situation of having to pay a periodic fine, without being able, in spite of its own goodwill, to comply with the EU rule (for example, about bringing air quality above a certain standard in the short run.) This situation certainly would be bad for the Member State, but also for the EU, which would be seen as irrational and vindictive for punishing a country for something that is outside of its control. This puts the Commission in a precarious position where it needs to decide whether a Member State has the capacity but not the willingness to comply or whether the Member State faces real obstacles in complying. In the first case, referral to the CJEU may help and even be necessary, but in the second case, 'negotiation' and support might be better strategies. Of course, this strategic calculus is clear to the Member States as well, which can try to exploit the uncertainty to their advantage by exaggerating the difficulties they face in complying.

---

[8] J Tallberg, 'Paths to Compliance: Enforcement, Management and the European Union' (2002) 56 *International Organization* 609.

[9] See European Commission, 'EU Single Market: Single Market Scoreboard', available at http://ec.europa.eu/internal_market/scoreboard/.

Other relevant aspects of the enforcement system relate to the audience costs of pursuing infringement cases (i.e. the bad publicity for the EU resulting from having open conflicts with its Member States); the fact that infringement procedures are not single-shot but repeated interactions (i.e. the Commission needs to concern itself with its long-term reputation as an agent of enforcement); and issue linkages between enforcement and decision making (i.e. the Commission 'negotiating' compliance with existing legal acts while simultaneously trying to win the support of the Member States for new legislation). All these aspects provide leeway for national governments that lack the willingness to comply with EU laws and policies to delay or avoid compliance, to engage in lengthy negotiations and legal battles over infringements, and to link up compliance issues to more general conflicts over decision making and the overall course of European integration.

Evidently, delays and incorrect transposition and implementation need not result from an outright refusal to comply, but only from an incentive to push the boundaries of discretion to their limits. But even if a particularly Eurosceptic government is more likely to want to interpret the text of the EU legal act, this may still result in non-compliance, as adapting the text of a directive takes time and can run into deadlock created by national actors.[10]

Overall, if we can expect Eurosceptic governments and societies are less willing to comply with EU laws and policies, the EU system of multi-level governance offers ample opportunities for such effects to play out.

We face complications when considering how such effects will manifest themselves in empirical data. Since the processes of compliance and enforcement are strategic, meaning that the relevant actors do not decide independently but in anticipation of the other actors' moves, detecting different conflict patterns in data is not straightforward.[11] As an example, consider a government required to implement a directive that it has openly opposed during the decision-making stage, because of general Euroscepticism and substantive policy concerns. This government will be expected to attempt to delay or avoid compliance. But precisely because these incentives are obvious, the Commission will be expected to monitor closely the government's actions and promptly pursue enforcement actions against the Member State, if transposition and legal implementation are delayed. If the government, which anticipates the Commission's diligence, would be deterred by eventual enforcement actions, this may lead to timely compliance. As a result, even if there were high incentives for the government

---

[10] M Haverland, 'National Adaptation to European Integration: The Importance of Institutional Veto Points' (2000) 20 *Journal of Public Policy* 83.

[11] JC Fjelstul and CJ Carrubba, 'The Politics of International Oversight: Strategic Monitoring and Legal Compliance in the European Union' (2018) 112 *American Political Science Review* 1; T König and L Mäder, 'The Strategic Nature of Compliance: An Empirical Evaluation of Law Implementation in the Central Monitoring System of the European Union' (2014) 58 *American Journal of Political Science* 246.

to avoid compliance, this would not necessarily feature in the data as an additional, or a lengthier, infringement procedure. On the contrary, it could lead to a quicker than average referral to the CJEU as the Commission would be less likely to suspect limited capability as the reason for non-compliance.

The strategic nature of compliance can lead to another selection effect that can mask the influence of Euroscepticism on compliance.[12] If the Commission anticipates that a Eurosceptic government will fight harder and be less likely to budge when faced with an infringement procedure, the Commission may refrain from starting enforcement actions in the first place and be more likely to settle the case before the CJEU reaches a judgment. This would lead to fewer infringement cases opened and fewer judgments delivered against Eurosceptic countries, but not because these states are more compliant. Note, however, that according to this logic, when infringement cases against Eurosceptic government *do* reach the judgment stage, the Commission is likely to win a higher percentage of the judgments.

D. Are There Constraints on Political Influence on Compliance?

In addition to the strategic aspects of enforcement, there are other reasons why the political preferences of national governments, and Euroscepticism in particular, may have no discernible impact of implementation and compliance. Typically, legal implementation is of no interest to politicians. In most cases, the issues are too technical and there are no political points to be scored. While decision making often attracts media attention, legal implementation rarely does. The legal implementation stage, including the drafting of national transposition measures, is the realm of bureaucrats and legal experts, where politicians rarely venture and in which they quickly lose interest.

Moreover, the implementation of EU law is often in the hands of civil servants and experts that are part of dense cross-national networks of public officials who have institutionalised forums for exchange of information and 'best practices'.[13] Such forums are used by the European Commission to support compliance with EU laws, for example by issuing technical guidelines or sharing data on national performance. National officials participating in such networks are deeply socialised in the shared ethos of the profession and relatively insulated from direct political pressures at home. As a result, any push for

---

[12] JC Fjelstul and CJ Carrubba, 'The Politics of International Oversight: Strategic Monitoring and Legal Compliance in the European Union' (2018) 112 *American Political Science Review* 1.

[13] L Andonova and I Tuta, 'Transnational Networks and Paths to EU Environmental Compliance: Evidence from New Member States' (2014) 52 *Journal of Common Market Studies* 775; M Scholten, 'Mind the trend! Enforcement of EU law has been moving to "Brussels"' (2017) 24 *Journal of European Public Policy* 1348.

non-compliance by politicians in the Member States' capitals would be filtered through the actions of civil servants who care about the perception of their peers from other countries. Relatedly, legal implementation nowadays often involves a host of European and national agencies as well,[14] and such organisations are even further isolated from the influence of politicians and public pressure.

As to the conduct of the infringement procedures, in principle ministers and the cabinet determine how the country should react (i.e. amend legislation, initiate more costly implementation action, or go to the next stage of the infringement procedures); the details of the national strategy are, once again, in the hands of civil servants and legal experts. The exchange of information between the Commission and the Member States can involve highly technical matters and/or complicated legal issues out of the remit of politicians. The discourse during the infringement procedures is based on legal arguments and expert opinions, not on political claims, which reduces the scope of influence of the government and public.

Combining these theoretical considerations, it is clear that (a) governments may have many incentives to delay and avoid compliance and (b) the EU enforcement system allows ample opportunities for doing so. Yet (c) other considerations lead us to expect that even when national governments espouse Eurosceptic preferences, these may not easily translate into non-compliance, as legal implementation and enforcement are strategic and relatively insulated from political interest and control. Therefore, which of these considerations prevails in practice and whether one can detect the influence of Euroscepticism on compliance in empirical data remain empirical questions. The next sections of this chapter engage with these crucial questions by reviewing the existing empirical literature on compliance and by providing an original analysis of infringement data.

III. EUROSCEPTICISM AND COMPLIANCE: THE EMPIRICAL EVIDENCE

A. Literature Review: Transposition and Implementation

The empirical analysis of the influence of Euroscepticism on compliance with EU law already has a long history. Early on, Lampinen and Uusikyla found a negative but not statistically significant effect of public attitudes towards the EU on transposition rates in a study covering all policy sectors and 12 Member States for the period 1990–1995.[15] Bergman examined the influence of public support for EU membership on the implementation performance of the (then 15)

---

[14] E Versluis and E Tarr, 'Improving Compliance with European Union Law via Agencies: The Case of the European Railway Agency' (2013) 51 *Journal of Common Market Studies* 316.

[15] R Lampinen and P Uusikyla, 'Implementation Deficit: Why Member States do not Comply with EU Directives?' (1998) 21 *Scandinavian Political Studies* 231.

EU Member States for the period 1996–1998.[16] Bergman found evidence for a negative and significant effect which ran contrary to expectations, namely that less public support leads to fewer infringements. Mbaye also found evidence of a negative and significant effect by examining data on the initiation of infringement procedures.[17]

These results have not been confirmed in subsequent studies. Börzel et al, as well as Siegel, found no effect of public support for EU membership on the occurrence of infringement procedures.[18] Similarly, Kaeding found no effect on transposition timelines in a study covering all directives in one policy sector – transport – in five countries over a period of almost 50 years.[19] The same conclusion was reached by Steunenberg and Rhinard, who examined an even larger sample of transposition cases in four policy areas.[20] In a recent article, Williams argued that 'member state governments do slow transposition in response to higher aggregate public Euroskepticism'.[21] Zhelyazkova et al concluded that societal EU support does not affect the '[national] implementers' outperformance of national legislation'.[22] Thus, the implementing agents did not go further in compliance than the national transposition texts.

While these studies examine the influence of public support for the EU, another set of empirical analyses focuses on the impact of the European integration preferences of the political parties in government. Jensen found a positive but not significant effect of pro-EU government positions on compliance, looking at infringement procedures in the field of social policy for the EU-15 during the period 1978–2000.[23] The same conclusion was reached by Linos looking at a similar sample but with a focus on transposition timeliness

---

[16] T Bergman, 'The European Union as the Next Step of Delegation and Accountability' (2000) 37 *European Journal of Political Research* 415.

[17] H Mbaye, 'Why National States Comply with Supranational Law: Explaining Implementation Infringements in the European Union, 1972–1993' (2001) 2 *European Union Politics* 259.

[18] TA Börzel, M Dudziak, T Hofmann, D Panke and C Sprungk, 'Recalcitrance, Inefficiency and Support for European Integration: Why Member States Do (Not) Comply with European Law' (2007) Center for European Studies Harvard, available at ces.fas.harvard.edu/uploads/files/Working-Papers-Archives/CES_WP151.pdf; TA Börzel, T Hofmann, D Panke and C Sprungk, 'Obstinate and Inefficient: Why Member States Do Not Comply with European Law' (2010) 43 *Comparative Political Studies* 1363; S Siegel, 'Law and Order in the European Union: Explaining Variations in Compliance with European Union Law' (2006) available at https://www.ssoar.info/ssoar/bitstream/handle/document/11351/ssoar-2006-siegel-law_and_order_in_the.pdf?sequence=1.

[19] M Kaeding, 'Determinants of Transposition Delay in the European Union' (2006) 26 *Journal of Public Policy* 229.

[20] B Steunenberg and M Rhinard, 'The Transposition of European Law in EU Member States: Between Process and Politics' (2010) 2 *European Political Science Review* 495.

[21] CJ Williams, 'Responding Through Transposition: Public Euroskepticism and European Policy Implementation' (2016) 10 *European Political Science Review* 51, 51.

[22] A Zhelyazkova, C Kaya and R Schrama, 'When Practice Goes beyond Legislators' Expectations: Analysis of Practical Implementation Exceeding Legal Compliance with EU Directives' (2018) 56 *Journal of Common Market Studies* 520, 532.

[23] CB Jensen, 'Implementing Europe: A Question of Oversight' 8 *European Union Politics* 451.

rather than infringements.[24] Zhelyazkova et al found that 'high EU support by the party of the prime minister is not sufficient to ensure compliance [in low-capacity countries] and low support cannot disrupt day-to-day administrative practices in the implementation process [in high-capacity Member States]'.[25] Kaya found a positive but not robustly significant effect of the EU support of the party of the prime minister on compliance.[26]

Interestingly, there is strong evidence that pro-European governments better transposed EU legislation during the period of preparation before the EU's Eastern enlargement. While all former communist states from Central and Eastern Europe achieved remarkable success in transposing the huge body of EU legislation prior to their accession to the EU in 2004 and 2007, within this group, governments with more EU-supportive positions transposed better and faster.[27]

To summarise, with the exception of the period of Eastern enlargement for the acceding countries, there is no evidence that more Eurosceptic governments are associated with worse compliance outcomes. On balance, the existing literature does not lend credence to the hypothesis that public support in favour of the EU is related to the compliance performance of the Member States, either across countries or over time.

It is also relevant that there is no consistent evidence that express disagreement with a directive (e.g. a vote against the adoption of the directive in the Council of Ministers) leads to worse compliance.[28]

B. Analysis of Infringement Patterns

To complement existing studies, this chapter offers an original empirical analysis of the impact of Euroscepticism on data generated by infringement

---

[24] K Linos, 'How Can International Organizations Shape National Welfare States? Evidence From Compliance With European Union Directives' (2007) 40 *Comparative Political Studies* 547.

[25] A Zhelyazkova, C Kaya and R Schrama, 'Notified and Substantive Compliance with EU Law in Enlarged Europe: Evidence from Four Policy Areas' (2017) 24 *Journal of European Public Policy* 216.

[26] C Kaya, 'The Impact of Interest Group Diversity on Legal Implementation in the European Union' (2018) 25 *Journal of European Public Policy* 567.

[27] P Hille and C Knill, 'It's the Bureaucracy, Stupid: The Implementation of the Acquis Communautaire in EU Candidate Countries 1999–2003' (2006) 7 *European Union Politics* 531; D Toshkov, 'Transposition of EU Social Policy in the New Member-States' (2007) 17 *Journal of European Social Policy* 335; D Toshkov, 'Embracing European Law: Transposition of EU directives in Central and Eastern Europe' (2008) 9 *European Union Politics* 379; R Zubek and K Staronova, 'Ministerial Transposition of EU Directives: Can Oversight Improve Performance?' (2010) available at https://eif.univie.ac.at/downloads/workingpapers/wp2010-09.pdf.

[28] R Thomson, 'Opposition through the Back Door in the Transposition of EU Directives' (2010) 11 *European Union Politics* 577; R Thomson, R Torenvield and J Arregui, 'The Paradox of Compliance: Infringements and Delays in Transposing European Union Directives' (2007) 37 *British Journal of Political Science* 685; A Zhelyazkova and R Torenvlied, 'The Time-Dependent Effect of Conflict in the Council on Delays in the Transposition of EU Directives' (2009) 10 *European Union Politics* 35; T König and L Mäder, 'The Strategic Nature of Compliance: An Empirical Evaluation of Law Implementation in the Central Monitoring System of the European Union' (2014) 58 *American Journal of Political Science* 246.

procedures. The focus of the analysis is on the period 2004–2015 and it covers all EU Member States except for Croatia, Cyprus and Malta due to data availability.

Three aspects of the infringement procedures are analysed: the total number of cases per country per year that reach the CJEU; the total number of judgments on infringement procedures delivered; and the share of Member States' wins, ie judgments in which the case is decided partly or fully in favour of a Member State. Data on these variables is extracted from the CURIA database.[29]

Two aspects of Euroscepticism are considered. The first one is public attitudes. This is measured as the percentage of people who tend to trust the European Commission from all respondents in a country. The variable is measured yearly and derives from the Standard Eurobarometer surveys of public opinion in the EU.[30] The choice to focus on trust in the European Commission is based on the fact that the Commission is the central body in the system of enforcement. In practice, however, attitudes towards the different EU institutions and the EU in general are very highly correlated;[31] therefore the precise choice does not matter that much.

The second aspect of Euroscepticism that is considered is the ideological position of the Member States' governments on the pro/anti-EU spectrum. These positions are measured as the weighted average of the pro/anti EU positions of the parties in government in a country in each year. The parties' positions themselves are derived using text analysis of the party manifestos, as made available from the Manifesto project.[32]

The method of analysis used is multiple linear regression of each aspect of infringements on both public and government support towards to the EU (the two are not highly correlated). Multiple linear regression summarises the relationship between a dependent (response) variable and a set of independent (predictor, covariate) variables by fitting a linear equation to the observed data.[33] Some of the reported statistical models also include state- and year-level control variables. Such control variables can remove bias and clarify the relationships between the variables of interest when working with time-series cross-sectional data. In principle, the dependent variables are bounded and not normally distributed, so that a negative binomial rather than a linear specification of the regression models may have been more appropriate. In practice,

---

[29] Available at https://curia.europa.eu; for details see D Toshkov, 'Compliance and Enforcement of EU law: Who Wins, Who Loses, and Who Settles' (2016), available at wp.peio.me/wp-content/uploads/PEIO9/102_80_1443441937982_Toshkov28092015.pdf.

[30] The surveys are available at http://ec.europa.eu/commfrontoffice/publicopinion/index.cfm.

[31] See, eg, A Schlenker, 'Supranational, Intergovernmental or Demoicratic Legitimacy? Citizens' Evaluations of the EU' (2015) 16 *European Politics and Society* 581.

[32] P Lehmann, J Lewandowski, T Matthieß, N Merz, S Regel and A Werner, 'Manifesto Corpus' (2018) available at https://visuals.manifesto-project.wzb.eu/mpdb-shiny/cmp_dashboard_dataset/.

[33] For a modern introduction to statistical methods for data analysis, see A Gelman and J Hill, *Data Analysis Using Regression and Multilevel Hierarchical Models* (New York, Cambridge University Press, 2014).

however, the results are similar to the ones based on linear regressions, therefore the latter are preferred due to easier interpretation.

Table 2.1 reports the results from the estimation of linear regression models of the total number of infringement cases registered at the CJEU. In Model 1a only public and government EU support are entered as covariates. The estimated effects of these variables are positive. This implies that higher public and government support for the EU are associated with a higher number of infringement cases. This runs contrary to the anticipated finding that more Eurosceptic governments and countries will be associated with more infringement procedures. The positive coefficients are robust to the inclusion of country dummies, and actually more than double in size (*cf* Model 1b). This implies that once the average cross-country differences in their number of infringement cases are considered, the effects of public and government support are even stronger and more precisely estimated.

Table 2.1 Linear regression models of total number of infringement cases registered against a Member State for the period 2004–2015 per country per year. Raw coefficients with standard errors in parentheses. Significance codes: *** 0.001 ** 0.01 * 0.05 ` 0.10

Variable	Model 1a	Model 1b	Model 1c	Model 1d
(Intercept)	0.29 (2.03)	–12.60 (2.60)***	17.00 (2.74)***	1.61 (3.74)
Public EU support	0.14 (0.04)***	0.38 (0.04)***	–0.01 (0.04)	0.21 (0.05)***
Government EU support	0.52 (0.32)	1.08 (0.33)**	0.11 (0.28)	0.67 (0.32)*
State controls	/	yes	/	yes
Year controls	/	/	yes	yes
Adj. R-squared	0.06	0.54	0.32	0.62

However, when we include year dummies that take into account common trends across the countries in a year, the effects of support for the EU disappear (*cf* Model 1c). This suggests that the effects of these variables are driven by contemporaneous changes across the countries. The general decline in trust in the European Commission and the general decrease of governmental support for the EU over the period of study coincide with a general decline in the number of infringement procedures registered at the Court (see Figure 2.1). But the forces that lead to these parallel time trends can have very different causes.

For example, the decline in infringement procedure at the CJEU is driven to a large extent by the lower number of new legislative acts adopted and the institutionalisation of mechanisms such as SOLVIT and EU Pilot. Hence, despite the regression results, we should not conclude that high support for the EU causes countries to receive more infringement cases.

Figure 2.1 Trends in infringement procedures and EU support (2004–2015)

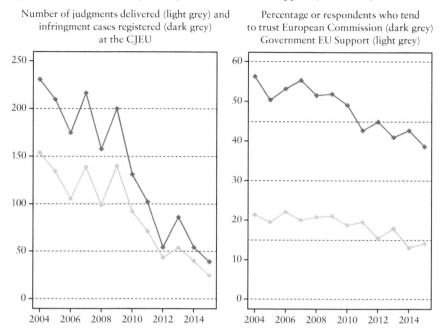

Table 2.2 looks at the number of judgments on infringement cases delivered. It is necessary to examine this variable separately since a large share of cases which are filed are withdrawn before the Court makes a decision, either because the Member State eventually complied with the legal act or some other settlement has been reached. The result of the regressions again suggests positive effects of support for the EU on the number of judgments on infringement cases against a Member State. These positive effects are estimated as large and more significant once state dummies are included in the model.

Table 2.2 Linear regression models of total number of judgments on infringement cases received by a Member State for the period 2004–2015 per country per year. Raw coefficients with standard errors in parentheses. Significance codes: *** 0.001 ** 0.01 * 0.05 ` 0.10

Variable	Model 2a	Model 2b	Model 2c	Model 2d
(Intercept)	1.85 (1.04)	−5.81 (1.86)**	13.50 (1.89)***	5.06 (2.69)
Public EU support	0.05 (0.03)*	0.21 (0.03)***	−0.05 (0.03)`	0.07 (0.04)`
Government EU support	0.37 (0.22)	0.68 (0.24)**	0.10 (0.19)	0.39 (0.23)`
State controls	/	yes	/	yes
Year controls	/	/	yes	yes
Adj. R-squared	0.02	0.49	0.29	0.57

But in a similar fashion to the models of the total number of cases in Table 2.1, once time controls are introduced, the positive effects disappear, and, in fact, there is a significant (at the 0.10 level) negative effect for public support of the EU.

This pattern of results suggests that the time dimension of the data drives a strong positive correlation between EU support and the number of judgments received. But as explained above, this can be explained by time trends which push the time series in the same direction but have completely unrelated causes. At the same time, the cross-country variation that is brought to light once we control for the time trends suggests a negative correlation between public support for the EU and the number of infringement judgments. In other words, once the general trends of declining number of judgments and increasing Euroscepticism are filtered out, Member States with more Eurosceptic populations are likely to be the subject of a higher number of judgments on infringement cases in a given year.

Table 2.3 Linear regression models of the share of wins on infringement cases by a Member State for the period 2004–2015 per country per year. Raw coefficients with standard errors in parentheses. Significance codes: *** 0.001 ** 0.01 * 0.05 ` 0.10.

Variable	Model 3a	Model 3b	Model 3c	Model 3d
(Intercept)	0.49 (0.09)***	0.56 (0.17)**	0.23 (0.13)`	5.06 (2.69)
Public EU support	–0.005 (0.002)**	–0.006 (0.002)**	–0.001 (0.002)	0.003 (0.003)
Government EU support	0.005 (0.014)	–0.006 (0.022)	0.008 (0.012)	0.005 (0.020)
State controls	/	yes	/	yes
Year controls	/	/	yes	yes
Adj. R-squared	0.03	0.06	0.19	0.25

The final set of models looks at the share of Court's judgments on infringement cases that are fully or partially in favour of the Member State (Table 2.3). Without controlling for time, public EU support has a significant negative association with the share of cases that the Member State wins. This would seem to suggest that countries with higher Euroscepticism would be more successful before the CJEU. But, again, this association disappears once year dummies are included, therefore, it is likely driven by common time trends rather than cross-sectional variation between the countries.

IV. CONCLUSION

This chapter set out to evaluate the evidence for a possible effect of Euroscepticism on patterns of compliance with EU law in the European Union. It argued that this question must be settled empirically, since reasonable theoretical considerations suggest that Eurosceptic governments and countries may want to avoid and delay compliance, but also that they can be constrained in systematically doing so.

The review of the empirical literature identified a large number of studies that have looked at the problem since the late 1990s. The literature's findings are inconclusive and, overall, do not provide evidence for a connection between either public or government support for the EU, on the one hand, and various indicators of compliance, such as transposition timeliness and correctness, implementation failures, or infringement procedures, on the other.

The results from the original empirical analysis of infringement data supports this view. It finds no systematic empirical evidence that public and government Euroscepticism affect the patterns of enforcement of EU law. In fact, when unadjusted for time trends, the data shows that higher public and government support for the EU is associated with more infringement cases at the CJEU; more judgments on infringement cases delivered; and a higher share of wins for the Member States in the judgments. These associations, however, are likely to be driven by general trends in the development of infringement numbers and Euroscepticism that are largely independent. Regardless of our interpretation of this positive association between Euroscepticism and compliance in the data, it does not support the hypothesis that there is a negative effect in reality.

At the moment, we can only speculate as to why there is no discernible systematic negative effect of Euroscepticism on compliance and enforcement at the aggregate level. One could note that while Eurosceptic governments often fail to comply with EU law and become subject to infringement procedures, this is also the case for Europhile governments. Non-compliance is not a phenomenon reserved for Eurosceptic Member States.

A second relevant reason is that some of the most Eurosceptic governments in Northern Europe have professional, efficient administrations and strong cultures of compliance,[34] which insulate the transposition and daily application of EU law from political pressures. This relates to the idea, discussed in the theoretical section, that compliance with EU law is typically the province of bureaucrats, embedded in dense transnational networks in which experts play a big role and politicians rarely venture.

A third possible partial explanation of the null results of the analysis relates to the measures of Euroscepticism used. Popular support for the EU in some of the Member States portrayed as Eurosceptic, such as Hungary and Poland, is actually quite high, as evidenced in the Eurobarometer surveys of public opinion. Political parties' Euroscepticism is not always captured in their manifestos – the texts on which the measure used in this empirical study were based.

---

[34] G Falkner, O Treib, M Hartlapp and S Leiber, *Complying with Europe: EU Harmonisation and Soft Law in the Member States* (Cambridge, Cambridge University Press, 2005).

The selection effect discussed in the theoretical section could also account to some extent for the empirical patterns found in the analysis. If the Commission carefully picks its battles with more Eurosceptic Member States, this would explain why such governments face fewer infringements and judgments. But the selection effect is not consistent with the finding that more Eurosceptic governments win a higher share of the infringement cases in which the CJEU delivers a judgment – or, at least, exhibit similar success rates to more EU supportive governments. If the Commission was especially careful in selecting cases to bring to the Court when facing a Eurosceptic government, it should win a higher, not a lower, share of these cases.

Future research should examine the question of whether there are differences in the types of infringement that Eurosceptic and Europhile Member States are subject to. It may be that Eurosceptic Member States face more infringement cases about incorrect application rather than delayed transposition, as the latter is easier to monitor. In addition, infringements by Eurosceptic Member States could be concentrated in areas where the EU is expanding its reach, such as justice and home affairs, rather than in areas where it has a long-established presence, such as the internal market. More generally, social scientists and legal scholars should closely examine the actual mechanisms through which Eurosceptic governments and national populations can influence (or not) compliance with and enforcement of EU law.

Part II

Eurosceptic Governments and Their Policies

3

The New Italian Government between Break and Continuity: Political Discourse and Constitutional Practices

LUIGI GIANNITI AND BARBARA GUASTAFERRO*

I. ITALY AND THE EUROPEAN UNION

ITALY, AS ONE of the founding Member States of the European project, has always been a substantially Euro-friendly country. Although this attitude did not necessarily lead to a speedy and correct implementation of EU law into domestic law, the quite high – although decreasing – rate of infringement procedures against Italy may be explained in bureaucratic terms (relating to a burdensome and highly centralised administrative system) rather than political terms (relating to a legislative branch overtly acting against EU policies).[1] In this respect, it is worth emphasising four (related) institutional aspects characterising Italy's relationship with the European Union (EU).

First, as with other European constitutions born after World War II and founded upon a rejection of totalitarianism and its overwhelming centralisation of sovereignty, Italy's Constitution is characterised by a significant openness towards international law.[2] Article 11 of the Constitution, which is one of the

---

* Within the framework of a joint reflection, Luigi Gianniti is the author of sections IV–VIII and Barbara Guastaferro of sections I–III. Luigi Gianniti's views and opinions expressed in this chapter are those of the author and do not reflect the official position of the Italian Senate. All the translations of Italian primary sources – such as political manifestos, institutional speeches of the Prime Ministers and political declarations – are the authors'.

[1] For a general overview on the topic, see M Cartabia and JHH Weiler, *L'Italia in Europa: Profili istituzionali e costituzionali* (Bologna, Il Mulino, 2000).

[2] The roots of this phenomenon can be traced to even earlier, to what, in the 1930s, Mirkine-Guetzévitch called the 'internationalization of modern constitutions'; see B Mirkine Guetzévitch, *Les nouvelles tendances du droit constitutionnel* (Paris, Marcel Giard, 1931) 48, quoted in G Martinico, 'Constitutionalism, Resistance and Openness: Comparative Law Reflections on Constitutionalism in Postnational Governance' (2016) 35 *Yearbook of European Law* 318.

foundational principles of the Republic, provides for limitations of sovereignty in favour of international organisations protecting peace and justice among nations.[3] Although this Article was conceived with the United Nations in mind (since the European Communities did not exist during the drafting of the Italian Constitution), it was always considered to be – also by the Italian Constitutional Court – a sound basis for Italy's membership of, first, the European Communities, and then of the EU. Besides Article 11, which has belonged to the Constitution since its inception, a new Article dedicated to the European Union was introduced in 2001. As per Article 117, paragraph 1, '*Legislative powers* shall be vested in the State and the Regions *in compliance with* the Constitution and with *the constraints deriving from EU legislation* and international obligations' (emphasis added).

The second aspect worth emphasising is that, unlike several EU Member States which experienced harsh parliamentary and political debates or required a referendum often blocking the European project (as happened with the Treaty establishing a Constitution for Europe), Italy did not challenge any of the significant steps of the European integration process. All the Treaties of the European Communities and of the EU, increasing supranational competences, were ratified with large majorities by the Italian Parliament.[4] As an example, the Italian Parliament was the first to ratify the Treaty establishing a Constitution for Europe (which never entered into force because of the failure of the referenda in France and the Netherlands).[5] Moreover, Italy approved the Lisbon Treaty in 2008 with a unanimous vote within both the House of Deputies and the Senate. Although our Constitution does not require any referendum, there was no adverse public opinion or rhetorical revolt against the political deepening of the European project.

The third, related, aspect is that Italy never revised the Constitution to accommodate the significant changes triggered by EU Treaties. The 'limitation of sovereignty' clause provided by Article 11 was considered broad enough to provide a constitutional foundation for the transfer of powers contemplated by all EC and EU Treaty amendments. In contrast to other countries, for example, no specific constitutional amendment was required to endorse the extension of electoral rights to non-Italian citizens.[6] The great adaptability and openness of

---

[3] Article 11: 'Italy agrees on conditions of equality with other States, to the limitation of sovereignty that may be necessary to a world order ensuring peace and justice among the Nations'. On the constitutional foundations of EU membership, see G Martinico, B Guastaferro, and O Pollicino, 'The Constitution of Italy: Axiological Continuity between the Domestic and International Levels of Governance?' in A Albi and S Bardutzky (eds), *The Role of National Constitutions in the European and Global Governance* (The Hague, TMC Asser Press, 2019).

[4] According to Arts 80 and 87 of the Constitution, ratification is by the President of the Republic, but in some enumerated cases – which cover a wide spectrum of treaties – a previous act of Parliament is required.

[5] The House of Deputies approved the draft Constitutional Treaty on 25 January 2005, with only 28 votes against, and the Senate voted on 6 April 2005, with only 16 votes against.

[6] This was, for example, the case in other Member States, as noted in the European Parliament's comparative study by L Besselink, M Claes, Š Imamovic and JH Reestman, *National Constitutional*

the Italian Constitution towards EU law was then backed and strengthened by a gradual acknowledgment of the principle of supremacy in the case law of the Italian Constitutional Court. EU legislation enjoys a higher rank and supersedes domestic ordinary law in cases of conflict, as long as it respects the core principles and the constitutional identity of the Italian Republic.[7]

The fourth aspect concerns the instruments that have been used to ensure a smooth implementation of EU law. Italy, indeed, was the first country to contemplate a legal instrument to ensure a timely implementation of EU law by the national Parliament. The necessity of a sound legislative instrument providing for a general framework to regulate Italian participation in the EU was particularly felt in the light of the Constitution's laconic provisions on the topic and significant implementation delays. The very first instrument was Law No 86 of 9 March 1989 (the *Legge La Pergola*), and the following Law No 11 of 4 February 2005 (the *Legge Buttiglione*). Currently, the procedures through which the Italian Parliament interacts with the EU are provided by Law No 234 of 2012.[8] The latter is very important because, first, it introduces appropriate procedures to implement the new forms of participation of the Italian Parliament in the EU decision-making process set out by the Treaty of Lisbon (including the subsidiarity check in the context of the early warning mechanism),[9] and, second, it strengthens the possibility for the Italian Parliament to control and influence the activity of the Executive within the EU context.[10]

Against this backdrop, outlining a sound and co-operative relationship between Italy and the EU, it may be easy to see the Conte government, which has ruled Italy since the complex 2018 elections, as an outspoken Eurosceptic government. According to this narrative, the current government first and foremost challenges the EU financial rules which constrain all those policies necessary to face the economic crisis and to avoid the collapse of the welfare state. However, this chapter argues that there is a strong mismatch between the political discourse of some of the Italian political parties' leaders, who have sometimes put the very core of the European project under pressure particularly

---

Avenues for further European Integration (2014), available at www.europarl.europa.eu/RegData/etudes/etudes/join/2014/493046/IPOL-JURI_ET%282014%29493046_EN.pdf 147.

[7] A general account of the Italian Constitutional Court's case law concerning EU law can be found in M Cartabia and B Guastaferro, 'Italy' in M Claes, S Griller et al (eds), *Member States' Constitutions and EU Integration* (Oxford, Hart Publishing, 2019, forthcoming). More generally on the Italian Constitutional Court, see V Barsotti, P Carozza, M Cartabia and A Simoncini (eds), *Italian Constitutional Justice in Global Context* (Oxford, Oxford University Press, 2016).

[8] Entitled 'General rules on Italy's participation in the formation and implementation of legislation and policies of the European Union', in force since 19 January 2013.

[9] For a general overview on the Lisbon innovation related to subsidiarity and parliamentary democracy, see M Cartabia, N Lupo and A Simoncini (eds), *Democracy and Subsidiarity in the EU* (Bologna, Il Mulino, 2012); A Manzella, 'The Role of Parliaments in the Democratic Life of the Union' in S Micossi and GL Tosato (eds), *The European Union in the 21st Century: Perspectives from the Lisbon Treaty* (Brussels, Centre for European Policy Studies, 2009) 257 et seq.

[10] For a recent and general account of the power of the Italian Parliament in EU affairs, see N Lupo and G Piccirilli (eds), *The Italian Parliament in the European Union* (Oxford, Hart Publishing, 2017).

during the electoral campaign (see sections II–III), and Italy's concrete constitutional and institutional practices which usually comply with EU law and governance (see sections IV–VII). Most importantly, the constitutional role played by the Italian President Mattarella and the position held by the Italian Prime Minister Conte within the EU's intergovernmental arena have substantially tempered the Eurosceptic attitude of Italian political leaders.

II. THE CHANGING LANDSCAPE OF ITALIAN POLITICS AND THE 2018 ELECTION

The wave of Euroscepticism which characterised the 2018 Italian election dates back to the great economic and financial crisis. The approval of the Treaty on Stability, Coordination and Governance in the European and Monetary Union in 2012, sponsored by the Monti government, was accompanied by the first revision of the Constitution to comply with 'external' guidelines. The 2012 constitutional amendment changed Article 81 of the Constitution to comply with the 'Fiscal Compact' guidelines on balanced budget.[11] The constitutional amendment, besides being quite a novelty for our constitutional praxis, generated a generalised scapegoating strategy against the EU, which was accused of being responsible for the several budgetary cuts made to the welfare state stemming from the scarcity of financial resources. Although the Fiscal Compact was a Treaty outside the institutional framework of the EU, the political discourse's narrative ran as follows: we *need* to introduce the balanced budget provision into the Constitution, since Europe *asks for* it. Moreover, explicit references to EU law were introduced in the contextual revision of Articles 97 and 119 of the Constitution, which, respectively, required public administrations and lower levels of government (such as regions, municipalities etc.) to ensure compliance with the EU's economic and financial constraints.[12] The parliamentary debate, although very poor,[13] was more tormented than usual and raised several criticisms.[14]

---

[11] Constitutional Law No 1 of 20 April 2012; Art 81 states that: 'The State shall balance revenue and expenditure in its budget, taking account of the adverse and favourable phases of the economic cycle.'

[12] Art 97: 'General government entities, in accordance with EU law, shall ensure balanced budgets and the sustainability of public debt.' Art 119 subjects the budgetary autonomy of municipalities, provinces and metropolitan cities to the 'obligation to balance their budget' and requires them to 'contribute to securing compliance with the economic and financial constraints imposed under European Union law'.

[13] See L Pierdominici, 'Constitutional Change through Emergency Decrees: The Abolition of Provinces in Italy' in T Beukers, B de Witte and C Kilpatrick (eds), *Constitutional Change through Euro-Crisis Law* (Cambridge, Cambridge University Press, 2017) who points out that in both Chambers and in the relevant parliamentary committees, the procedure for authorisation of the Fiscal Compact was combined with other procedures related to the Treaty amendment in Art 136(3) TFEU and the ESM Treaty.

[14] The Fiscal Compact obtained 368 votes in favour and 68 votes against in the House of Deputies (The League and the Five Stars Movement, which currently back the Conte government, voted against).

Consistently with the Eurosceptic and populist nature of many recent electoral campaigns in Europe, the 2018 Italian electoral campaign was characterised by this kind of argument. Interestingly enough, while domestic elections are usually relatively blind and agnostic towards Europe, the EU promptly entered the political debate as the 'enemy' of the populist and anti-integration parties. Some commentators emphasised that in light of the thinner distinguishing line between left-wing and right-wing political parties, the "classic" bipolar competition was replaced by a new bipolarism opposing EU and anti-EU parties or pro-national sovereignty and pro-Europe parties.[15]

This chapter focuses on the Eurosceptic turn of the new Italian Government, led by Prime Minister Giuseppe Conte and supported in Parliament by a political majority mainly composed of parliamentarians of two political parties: 'The League' (Lega), led by Matteo Salvini, and the 'Five Stars Movement' (Movimento 5 stelle), led by Luigi Di Maio – both of them Vice-Presidents of the Council. This chapter details the approaches to the EU enshrined in the political platforms of these two parties. It leaves aside the pro-Europe or anti-Europe approach of the political parties currently opposing rather than supporting the government.

III. THE EUROSCEPTIC PLATFORMS OF THE LEAGUE AND THE FIVE STARS MOVEMENT AND THE CONSTITUTIONAL SAFEGUARDS TEMPERING THEM

The Five Stars Movement's political manifesto for the 2018 elections did not mention the EU. While the Five Stars Movement did not take any position on foreign and EU policy, at least in the past the party had openly challenged the European project. Indeed, the idea of a referendum against the euro was one of the main goals of the political party since its inception and only recently disappeared from the political agenda. Nonetheless, the founding father of the party, Beppe Grillo, even after the elections of March 2018, discussed a proposal concerning such a referendum in an interview released to the international press.[16] The position on the topic was very ambiguous, with the referendum considered sometimes as a necessary goal to allow 'the people' to have a say on European affairs; sometimes as the last possible course of action; and sometimes as something which does not deserve to enter the political manifesto. Many commentators noted that the avowed Euroscepticism of the Five Stars Movement, which was born as an anti-system party and which sat in opposition following the previous general election, was significantly dampened ahead of

---

[15] N Verola, 'La nuova geografia della politica europea' (2018) 2 *Astrid Rassegna* 1.
[16] N Vidal, 'Beppe Grillo: "Je parle de la réalité à travers le filtre de cet esprit diabolique"', *PUTSCH* (4 May 2018) available at putsch.media/20180504/interviews/interviews-culture/beppe-grillo-je-parle-de-la-realite-a-travers-le-filtre-de-cet-esprit-diabolique/.

the 2018 general election. The Movement, which was predicted to win in the poll by several surveys, started to develop a more 'institutional' side. Consistently, Europe, which had often been depicted as the enemy in the past, was expressly referred to as 'our home' by Luigi Di Maio.[17] The challenge to the EU's budgetary limit of 3 per cent deficit to GDP, enshrined in the Stability and Growth Pact, had the same fate as the demands for a referendum on the euro. Luigi Di Maio, just a few months before the elections, had called the limit an 'absolute contradiction' triggering the reaction of the European Economic Affairs Commissioner Pierre Moscovici.[18] Yet, ahead of the 2018 election, no proposal for revising the Treaties on this issue was included in the Five Stars Movement's official manifesto.

The League's political manifesto, in contrast, contained an entire section dedicated to Europe. The section opened on the following slogan: 'Yes to the Europe of peoples, peace and freedom. No to the Europe of bureaucrats and speculators.'[19] This section was divided into several sub-sections outlining objectives for the EU's future. The first sub-section's heading was 'Back to the pre-Maastricht era'. After emphasising the geostrategic crucial role of Italy for Europe and the Mediterranean area, the section defined the EU as a

> gigantic supranational body, devoid of any democratic legitimacy, and structured through a sprawling bureaucratic structure that dictates the agenda to our Governments, also to the detriment of the physical and economic protection of the citizens of the individual Member States.

It also blamed the euro as 'the main cause of our economic decline, a currency tailored for Germany and multinationals and contrary to the need of Italy and small business'. The same sub-section mentioned the outspoken goal to 'stay within the European Union only on condition that we re-discuss all the Treaties that place constraints on the exercise of our full and legitimate sovereignty, returning to the European Economic Community before the Maastricht Treaty'.

Another sub-section featured under the label of 'the Constitution as a guarantee of sovereignty'. It stated that, while Article 11 of our Constitution clearly states that Italy can limit its sovereignty in favour of international organisations whose goal is to achieve the peace and justice among the nations,

> [t]he EU is not among these organisations. For this reason also the German Constitutional Court, which also has a Constitution circumscribing the possible transfer of sovereignty, clarified that any European Treaty provision which is in conflict with the Constitution must be rejected.

---

[17] C Sarra, 'La svolta di Di Maio: "L'Unione europea è la nostra casa"', *il Giornale* (6 February 2018), available at www.ilgiornale.it/news/politica/svolta-maio-lunione-europea-nostra-casa-1491143.html.

[18] '"Italia a rischio geopolitico", l'Ue affonda le politiche di Di Maio e 5 Stelle', *Today* (16 January 2018) available at www.today.it/politica/elezioni/politiche-2018/m5s-europa-scontro.html.

[19] The political manifesto can be found at the following website: www.leganord.org/il-movimento/politiche-2018.

Another subsection was dedicated to 'the revision of the European Treaties' to go back to the pre-Maastricht era, namely to

> a form of free and peaceful cooperation between States of purely economic nature; a profound correction of the functioning of the internal market aimed at: eradicating the internal dumping of the Union; abolishing the rules not familiar with the common traditions of the Member States; stopping the excess of homologation, which kills biodiversity and favours only productions on a multinational scale.

Most importantly, this same sub-section listed a series of 'sovereignties' to be recovered through the revision of the Treaties: 'the economic and monetary sovereignty' to only give the EU competence on commercial policy; the 'territorial sovereignty' allowing each State to have full control of its own borders through the abolition of the Schengen agreement and the Dublin Regulation; the 'legislative sovereignty', expressly professing the supremacy of national law over EU law; and the 'restoring of subsidiarity' to bring back almost all shared and supporting competences to the Member States and by strengthening the monitoring function of the Parliament and the Regions in scrutinising EU acts.

Finally, in another subsection entitled 'less money, less waste, more subsidiarity and more autonomy', The League first proposed to re-discuss Italy's contribution to the EU in the light of Brexit, asking the Commission for a significant reduction in the financial endowment of the next Multiannual Financial Framework. Second, The League demanded an end to any further transfer of responsibilities to Brussels, reducing EU competences to what is necessary and feasible. Finally, The League called for the suppression of all seats left vacant by the British Members of the European Parliament to prevent the establishment of any pan-European college. Such a college, it argued, would be contrary to the citizens' needs for democracy and accountability and would increase the distance between the electorate and the elected representatives.

As the electoral campaign illustrates, The League and the Five Stars Movement were the foremost populist and Eurosceptic political parties running for the 2018 Italian general election. The complex outcome of the 2018 elections, where none of the political parties and coalitions gained the necessary majority to constitute a government, brought an alliance between the Five Stars Movement and The League.[20] Until then, The League was a smaller political party of a broader right-wing coalition. The League, however, separated itself from the coalition to merge with the Five Stars Movement so as to reach the necessary majority to present a government. Tellingly, the two parties' political leaders, Luigi Di Maio and Matteo Salvini, have since behaved as Vice-Presidents of the

---

[20] On the difficulties in creating the government and on the several pressures of the 2018 electoral scenario on consolidated and longstanding constitutional practices, see S Staiano, 'La forma di governo italiana: permanenza e transizione' (2018) 2 *Osservatorio costituzionale*, available at www.osservatorioaic.it/images/rivista/pdf/Staiano%20(pronto).pdf.

Council of Ministers. They chose a third person, not belonging to politics but the academic word, Giuseppe Conte, as the Prime Minister. As they had not been allies during the campaign, The League and the Five Stars Movement signed a 'Contract of Government' outlining the goals of the new coalition supporting the government.[21] The positions on Europe enshrined in the contract were substantially more nuanced than those professed during the electoral campaign. The alliance between the most populist and Eurosceptic Italian parties, together with their call in favour of deficit spending and the partial revision of the Treaties, alarmed both the markets and international observers. The President of the Republic, Sergio Mattarella, in exercising his power under Article 92 of the Constitution to appoint the President of the Council of Ministers (and, upon his/her suggestions, the Ministers) paid significant attention to the composition of the government in order to escape expressly Eurosceptic positions. Indeed, he warned of investors' concerns on the future of Italy which threatened the country's financial stability, and he asserted that Italy's membership of the EU is a fundamental choice enshrined in the core principles of the Italian Constitution.[22]

These events show, on the one hand, that the Eurosceptic turn of the new political majority should not be underestimated. This Euroscepticism could negatively impact on the implementation of EU law in specific areas. As an example, the leader of The League, Matteo Salvini, in his capacity as Minister of the Interior, challenged during the recent migration crisis the Dublin Regulation and put pressure on the EU to alter Italy's reception of migrants and refugees.[23] On the other hand, the role of the Italian President and the approach of the Conte government to the EU – analysed in the following paragraphs – suggest that Italy's membership of the EU and compliance with EU obligations are so embedded in the constitutional culture as to constitute significant constitutional safeguards against a Eurosceptic drift in the Italian Republic. Thus, it is interesting to highlight the mismatch between the Eurosceptic tone of the political discourse surrounding the 2018 elections and the institutional attitude and

---

[21] An English summary of the government contract is available at www.ilblogdellestelle.it/2018/05/summary_of_the_contract_for_the_government_of_change_in_italy.html.

[22] The declaration of the President of the Republic (27 May 2018) can be found at www.quirinale.it/elementi/1345. President Sergio Mattarella's declaration, triggering a reshuffling in the initial composition of the government proposed by President Conte, generated an in-depth scholarly debate on the constitutional prerogatives of the President of the Republic relating to the formation of the government envisaged by Art 92. See, among others, A D'Aloia, 'Nomina dei ministri, interessi costituzionali fondamentali e poteri del Presidente della Repubblica. Appunti a margine del caso Savona' (2018) 2 *Osservatorio costituzionale*; and D Tega and M Massa, 'Why the Italian President's Decision was Legitimate', *VerfBlog* (28 May 2018), available at verfassungsblog.de/why-the-italian-presidents-decision-was-legitimate/.

[23] On the possible inconsistency of the so-called 'Security Decree' with both Italian constitutional law and EU law, see AM Cecere, 'Le iscrizioni anagrafiche per gli stranieri richiedenti protezione internazionale dopo il d.l. n.113 del 2018, il cd. Decreto Salvini. Quando il legislatore demagogicamente orientato disorienta l'amministrazione pubblica' (2019) 3 *federalismi.it*.

practices of Prime Minister Conte almost in line with the European guidelines, to which we now turn.

IV. THE APPROACH OF THE CONTE GOVERNMENT TO THE EU

Part of the first drafts of the so-called 'government contract' had alarmed observers, fostering a widespread perception that the attitude of the new Italian Government towards the EU would radically change. Fears revolved around Italy's membership of the Eurozone, the role of the Central Bank, and the impact of the Italian Government's Euroscepticism towards the Economic and Monetary Union on the price of the Italian Government's bonds on the markets. Nevertheless, the section on Europe in the final version of the government contract, specifically point 29, was substantially in line with Italy's traditional role in the European integration process. The government contract proposes, for example, that the EU's first objective should be 'promoting the balanced economic and social progress of the continent'. It further envisages a strengthening of the role and powers of the European Parliament. The proposal to revise the structure of the Eurozone's economic governance, while entailing a critical attitude towards current European policies, is at the same time proactive: aimed at strengthening the institutions and common policies as essential tools to overcome asymmetries and promote a more balanced economic and social progress.

The first point to emphasise, then, is the discrepancy between, on the one hand, public statements made by leaders and many representatives of government parties and, on the other, the new government's public documents and institutional statements. The main debates held in the Italian Parliament on EU policies – from the birth of the new government in June 2018 until the end of that year – show that the tone significantly differs from the blunt attacks against Europe that characterised the electoral campaign that we previously analysed.

The European Council – institutionalised by the Treaty of Lisbon and given the crucial role of politically guiding the Union – provides us with ample empirical evidence as it began to meet almost monthly. During the economic crisis, it was also supported by the Euro Summit – i.e. the (informal) institution that only includes the heads of state of the Eurozone. The Euro Summit is an institution envisaged by Article 12 of the European Fiscal Compact, outside the EU's institutional framework. This undoubtedly intergovernmental development has progressively changed the EU's institutional balance, but it has been accompanied by the strengthening of mechanisms and procedures for monitoring state representatives' actions in the European Council within the various Member States. In Italy, for example, the political decision, taken at a European Council meeting, to join the fiscal compact prompted former Prime Minister Mario Monti to request a prior discussion with the two Chambers of the Italian Parliament which ended with a vote. The Prime Minister has since systematically reported to the Chambers before each European Council. These debates have generally ended with the approval of acts of guidance. Most importantly, the Law No 234 of 2012 now regulates this informal practice. Article 4 provides that, before each European Council meeting, the government must illustrate its position to the Chambers and commit itself to take into consideration any act of guidance that they may pass. At the Chambers' request, the government must report to the relevant parliamentary body before EU Council meetings. Article 4 also states that the government must inform the relevant parliamentary bodies on results in the European Council and EU Council within 15 days.

Against this backdrop, the following section reviews the speeches made by Prime Minister Conte during the debates held in the two Chambers before the meetings of the European Council in June, October and December 2018.

V. THE 'GOVERNMENT IN PARLIAMENT': EUROPE AND THE CONFIDENCE MOTION

The first confrontation between Prime Minister Conte and the Parliament took place on 5 June 2018. The Prime Minister presented the government's programme and asked for the confidence of the two Chambers. The new Prime Minister began by noting that 'the political forces composing the majority supporting the government have been accused of being populist, anti-system'.[24] He argued that populism can be considered as 'the attitude of the ruling class to listen to the needs of the people' and that being 'anti-system' means 'aiming at introducing a new system that removes old privileges and incrustations of power'. Conte asked for the confidence of the Parliament 'in favour not only of a government team, but also of a project: a project to change Italy'. The Prime Minister noted that this project 'was formalised in a contract between the two political forces that make up the parliamentary majority'.

Illustrating the contents of the government contract on the EU, Conte spoke of the need to eliminate 'the growth gap between Italy and the European Union ... in a framework of financial stability and market confidence'. Conte specifically observed that

> we are facing a situation in which the interests of Italy at this stage of European construction coincide with the general interests of Europe and with the aim of preventing its possible decline. Europe is our home – it is the home of all of us. As a founding country, we are fully entitled to claim a stronger and fairer Europe, in which the economic and monetary union is oriented to protect the needs of citizens, to more effectively balance the principles of responsibility and solidarity.[25]

Any polemical statements made by members of the governmental majority, during the debates held in the Chamber of Deputies and in the Senate and

---

[24] Senato della Repubblica, 5 June 2018 (authors' translation).
[25] Senato della Repubblica, 5 June 2018 (authors' translation).

especially before the media, the two Chambers endorsed the Conte government with a large majority. The motion of confidence passed by the two Chambers expressly noted 'the full alignment of the political and administrative policy expressed by the Prime Minister with the contents of the Government contract of change signed by the 5 Stars Movement and The League'.[26]

The Prime Minister's statements before Parliament, the government contract and the documents approved by the Chambers are all in substantial continuity with Italy's traditional European policy: for a stronger Union able to overcome the imbalances between countries, combining the principles of responsibility and solidarity, in a framework of financial stability and market confidence.

If we want to find a partially critical element, where the Italian position seems to be different from the EU one, we can point to a passage in the government contract and in the programmatic declarations of the Prime Minister concerning relations with Russia. Here, the Prime Minister promotes 'a review of the system of sanctions'. It may be recalled that during the last confrontation between the centre-left government led by Gentiloni and the Parliament on 12 December 2017, before the elections of March 2018, the representatives of The League had expressly requested that the government go 'to Europe to ask for the lifting of sanctions against Russia'.[27] This theme is also present in The League's 2018 political manifesto.

VI. THE 'GOVERNMENT IN PARLIAMENT' BEFORE THE MEETINGS OF THE EUROPEAN COUNCIL

Less than a month after he took office, Prime Minister Conte returned to the Parliament ahead of a meeting of the European Council in June, the first European Council of the new government.

In this debate, entirely dedicated to Europe, the Prime Minister began by stating the need for an attitude, a 'determination', before the European Council that marks 'that change, in the method and in the substance that I announced before these Chambers, and that since the first day of this government I committed myself to propose in all international and European contexts, with the strength and awareness of a government that speaks in Europe with one voice, firm and resolute'.[28]

That European Council meeting was focused on migration policies. Here, Prime Minister Conte emphasised before Parliament that it was a negotiating success 'to avoid a draft proposal for conclusions which was clearly inadequate to offer an effective solution to the problem of immigration: a draft that runs

---

[26] Senato della Repubblica, 5 June 2018, Annex A (authors' translation).
[27] Senato della Repubblica, 12 December 2017, Intervention of senator Centinaio (authors' translation).
[28] Camera dei deputati, 27 June 2018 (authors' translation).

counter to the policies of our country'. Conte then presented to the Italian Parliament a detailed proposal based on the following objectives: strengthening relations between EU and third countries of transit; create international protection centres in transit countries; strengthen the external borders of the Union; go beyond the Dublin Regulation and the criterion of the country of first entry; and ask the EU and its Member States to assume a common European responsibility for persons rescued at sea, since 'the obligation to rescue imposed by international conventions cannot become an obligation to implement and apply those conventions on behalf of all'. According to Conte, 'we cannot take everyone to Italy or Spain, we need reception centres in more than one European country to safeguard the rights of those who arrive and to avoid problems of public order and overcrowding'. These statements indicate an attitude more assertive – but not radically different – than in the past, especially if compared to an Italian migration management system which Conte described as 'ha[ving] saved the honour of Europe in the Mediterranean' for years.[29]

On economic issues, in view of the Euro Summit scheduled on 29 June 2018, Conte reiterated the objective of 'eliminating the growth gap between Italy and the European Union in a framework of financial stability and market confidence'. Rather, he posited, 'It is time to advance the sharing of risk which so far has remained too far behind'. Such sharing should not include conditionality. In this perspective, Conte opposed a reform of the European Stability Mechanism (ESM), which 'far from operating with equalising purposes, ends up forcing some countries towards predefined restructuring paths with substantial exhaustion of the power to elaborate effective economic policies in autonomy'. On the recurring question of European sanctions against Russia, Conte only reaffirmed 'the principle that the renewal of sanctions should not be automatic'. He further committed the government, through the resolution approved at the end of the debate, 'to act within the European framework in order to re-open spaces for collaboration and dialogue with the Russian Federation, for example by proposing a reshaping of the sanctions' to exclude certain sectors. Unanimity is required for the renewal of sanctions. Therefore, the opposition of a single country would be enough to lift them. On this issue, which is politically sensitive for the government forces and on which the unilateral decision of the Italian Government could have determined a precise outcome, the guidelines approved in Parliament do not indicate any breakdown of European solidarity.

Thus, issues which are bitterly and heatedly debated in the media – nourished particularly by the declarations of the Vice-Presidents of the Council – are not as divisive in parliamentary records. In this respect, Senator Casini hinted to a 'double-track strategy', during a debate in which he shared the Prime Minister's position in the field of migration inspired by 'a communitarian or even federalist vision of Europe', while criticising the public positions taken by the Minister

---

[29] Camera dei deputati, 27 June 2018 (authors' translation).

of the Interior and leader of The League Salvini, inspired by 'a sovereign and intergovernmental vision of Europe'.[30]

On 16 October, President Conte returned to report to both Chambers of Parliament on the European Council of 17 and 18 October and on the related meeting of the Euro Summit – although there is no legislative obligation as far as the latter is concerned. This choice confirms the growing role of the Euro Summit which, although defined as an 'informal' institution in the Fiscal Compact, is becoming increasingly important in the institutional life of the Union: the real forum where the regulatory evolution of the EU's economic governance is also discussed.

The topics covered by Prime Minister Conte to Parliament were: migration policies; the issue of Brexit; the negotiation of the multiannual European budget (the so-called multiannual financial framework); and, finally, the governance of the Eurozone and, in particular, the completion of the banking union.

Most importantly, Prime Minister Conte illustrated the objectives of the new government's first budget plan, submitted a few days earlier to the European Commission following a parliamentary vote of the two chambers by qualified majority.[31] This plan authorised the government to borrow significantly more than what had previously been agreed with the European Commission.

Prime Minister Conte used the opportunity of the debate on the European Council to 'underline the urgency of a change of agenda for the European Union, which must increasingly focus on the needs of civil society, be closer to peoples and citizens'. In this context, the Italian Government, according to Conte, could be proud of its economic manoeuvre presented in Brussels. Prime Minister Conte did not detail the process and essentially concentrated on the objectives. He avoided mentioning the details and most controversial issues bound to arise in the confrontation with the European Commission in the following days and months. The resolution, approved by the majority at the end of the debate, only makes a general reference to the opportunity to

> take all the initiatives necessary to create a high-level working group that examines the current European institutional architecture and the current economic policy, in order to propose solutions in line with the objectives of growing stability and full employment explicitly provided for by the treaties.[32]

This recommendation, which is certainly uncontroversial, featured in the document presented by the Minister for European Affairs Paolo Savona to Parliament and the European Commission entitled 'A Politeia for a different, stronger and fairer Europe'.[33] Other and more controversial proposals contained in this

---

[30] Senato della Repubblica, 27 June 2018, Intervention of senator Casini (authors' translation).
[31] Senate, Session No 046 (11 October 2018) available at www.senato.it/japp/bgt/showdoc/18/Resaula/0/1077147/index.html?part=doc_dc-ressten_rs-gentit_ddddln1bnad2018).
[32] Senato della Repubblica, 16 October 2018 (authors' translation).
[33] P Savona, 'A Politeia for a different, stronger and fairer Europe' (2018) available at www.politicheeuropee.gov.it/en/minister/speeches/a-politeia-for-a-different-stronger-and-fairer-europe/.

document were echoed in Members of Parliament's speeches – including by Claudio Borghi, President of the Budget Committee of the Chamber, and by the new leader of the Five Stars Movement, Francesco D'Uva[34] – but were not included in the resolutions which concluded the debates in the Chamber and the Senate.[35]

Prime Minister Conte, once again, took non-divisive positions on the priorities of the European Council meeting. On the question of sanctions against Russia, he used even less critical language than in the past, stating that the discussion on the topic should 'maintain ... the unity of the position of the European Union in relation to Moscow'. This quote indicates that the unity of the EU's position is the main asset to be preserved.

On 11 December 2018, Prime Minister Conte gave both Chambers a statement on the last 2018 meetings of the European Council and the Euro Summit.

The priorities were the question of Brexit (over which no disagreements arose among Italian political parties during the debate); the progress of the Common Security and Defence Policy; and again sanctions against Russia. Here, Prime Minister Conte again stressed Italy's reservations about sanctions but, again, did not openly dissent. Conte said that 'Italy intends to be consistent with its own respectful approach to the European choices'.[36] Conte did not engage on another issue which the media, on the basis of statements released by ministers and members of the two governing parties, had hypothesised could form a breaking point with EU policy: the updating of the mandate of Operation Sofia requested by Italy itself. Veto procedures were not activated, as in the case of sanctions against Russia, although the Treaties also require the unanimous consent of Member States on this matter. The most relevant issues in Conte's speech were those related to the agenda of the Euro Summit.

Conte reported the disagreements of the 4 December 2018 Eurogroup meeting. The Prime Minister placed Italy among the Member States favouring new solutions for a Eurozone common budget aimed at pursuing convergence and increasing competitiveness, in support of an effective function of stabilisation. The Prime Minister declared he was disappointed by the incomplete implementation of the banking union. He pointed out, in particular, that 'the further postponement of decisions on the deposit insurance scheme is for us the signal of a Europe that continues to be conditioned by the markets rather than conditioning and guiding them'. Conte then reiterated Italy's reservations about an intergovernmental approach to the reform of the ESM's governance. Conte argued that the ESM should not irreversibly undermine the prerogatives of the European Commission, particularly in terms of fiscal surveillance.

Prime Minister Conte, therefore, once again espoused the traditional Italian position favouring the reform of the Eurozone's governance, based on

---

[34] Camera dei deputati, 16 October 2018, interventions of hon. Borghi and D'Uva.
[35] Senato della Repubblica, 16 October 2018, Annex A.
[36] Camera dei deputati, 11 December 2018 (authors' translation).

the Community method and characterised by tools aimed at the mutualisation of risks.

VII. THE TORMENTED APPROVAL OF THE 2019 BUDGET

The 11 December 2018 debate is of particular interest because it provided an opportunity for the Prime Minister to report to Parliament on the outcome of the dialogue with the European Commission on the Italian budget package for 2019–2021.[37]

On 27 September, the Italian Government approved a draft budget bill which was clearly inconsistent with the recommendations adopted by the Council of the EU on 11 July 2018. In the following days, representatives of the government and the supporting coalition parties released statements critical of the EU as a whole; the President of the European Commission; and the competent Commissioners. The spreads between Italian bonds and German bonds exceeded 300 points. On 11 October, the Italian Parliament approved an Updated Note to the Economic and Financial Document which authorised considerable borrowing to carry out the measures provided for by the budget package. Criticism from, among others, the Fiscal Council (the Parliamentary Budget Office) and the Bank of Italy were not taken into consideration.[38] Instead, these institutions were themselves subjected to criticism by representatives of the majority.

Based on this prior parliamentary authorisation, the Council of Ministers approved on 15 October the draft budget law and sent the draft budget planning document summarising its content to the European Commission, in accordance with the European Semester's rules. In authorising the presentation of this budget plan to the Chambers, the President of the Republic formally urged 'the Government to develop – also during parliamentary scrutiny – a debate and a constructive dialogue with the European institutions'. This discussion began immediately with a letter from the European Commission requesting clarification on the proposed budget.[39] The Minister of Economic Affairs replied on 22 October by defending the plan's approach and proposals.[40] The following day, the European Commission sent a formal critical opinion on the draft budget document, asking Italian authorities to present a revised text.[41] In the meantime,

---

[37] Camera dei deputati, 11 December 2018.
[38] Chamber of Deputies, 'La Nota di aggiornamento del DEF 2018' (8 October 2018) available at temi.camera.it/leg18/temi/nota-di-aggiornamento-del-def-2018.html.
[39] Letter from Valdis Dombrovskis and Pierre Moscovisi (18 October 2018), available at ec.europa.eu/info/sites/info/files/economy-finance/18_10_18_commission_letter_to_italy_en_0_1.pdf.
[40] Letter from Giovanni Tria (22 October 2018), available at www.mef.gov.it/inevidenza/documenti/Letter_to_VD_and_PM_-_22-10-2018.pdf.
[41] European Commission Opinion on the Draft Budgetary Plan of Italy and requesting Italy to submit a revised Draft Budgetary Plan (23 October 2018) C(2018) 7510 final, available at ec.europa.eu/info/sites/info/files/economy-finance/2019_dbp_opinion_it_en.pdf.

the parliamentary procedure was ongoing in the Chamber of Deputies, and the government considered the European Commission's comments on the content of the budget plan as largely irrelevant.

This discussion phase ended on 21 November when the European Commission, in its decision on the 2019 draft budget document, adopted a report pursuant to Article 126(3) TFEU.[42] The report stated that Italy's public debt in relation to GDP did not comply with the debt rule. In the Commission's view, this justified the opening of an excessive deficit procedure. This procedure, although provided in the Treaties, had never been used before. Following the November meeting of the Economic and Financial Committee, the Eurogroup, at its meeting on 4 December, also endorsed the European Commission's assessment and invited Italy to take the necessary measures to comply with the Stability and Growth Pact.[43]

On 8 December, the Chamber of Deputies approved the budgetary plan in the terms contested by European authorities. In parallel, however, the dialogue between the Italian Government and the European Commission was becoming more intense to avoid the opening of an excessive deficit procedure. These were days of frantic confrontation, which directly involved Prime Minister Conte, as well as the Ministers for Economic Affairs, Tria, and Foreign Affairs, Moavero Milanesi. On 28 November, Tria talked of prospects for a shared solution in the Senate. This did not result in any changes to the text of the draft bill still examined by the Chamber, which, as mentioned above, was approved a few days later. The scrutiny of the Senate was essentially blocked, pending the outcome of the negotiations.

While reporting on the 11 December European Council, as mentioned above, the Prime Minister informed Parliament as to the state of negotiations. He took the lead in negotiations himself, with the aim of reaching solutions 'within the perimeter traced by the rules and constraints of public finance stemming from Italian membership of the EU and to the eurozone'.[44]

The opportunity to conclude negotiations with the European Commission came at the European Council meeting.

On 19 December, immediately after a press release issued by the competent European Commissioners, Pierre Moscovici and Valdis Dombrovskis,[45] Prime Minister Conte again released a statement before the Senate to describe adjustments to the draft budget bill. These measures were later translated into

---

[42] European Commission, Report on Italy prepared in accordance with Art 126(3) of the Treaty on the Functioning of the European Union (21 November 2018) COM(2018) 809 final.

[43] European Council, 'Eurogroup Statement on the Draft Budgetary Plans for 2019' (4 December 2019) available at www.consilium.europa.eu/en/press/press-releases/2018/12/04/eurogroup-statement-on-the-draft-budgetary-plans-for-2019/.

[44] Camera dei deputati, 11 December 2018 (authors' translation).

[45] European Commission, 'Vice-President Valdis Dombrovskis: College read-out and remarks on the Italian budget' (19 December 2018) available at europa.eu/rapid/press-release_SPEECH-18-6886_en.htm.

radical changes to the structure of the draft bill (in the form of governmental amendments. Those amendments were discussed and approved by the Senate in a text in which the government asked for a vote of confidence on 22 December. That text was then approved, without changes, by the Chamber, at the end of December, just in time to avoid the country operating on a provisional budget in 2019. This procedure was in many ways anomalous and without real precedent. It was, hence, loudly challenged by political forces of the opposition.

It is important to stress that, although the draft budget bill first occasioned a sharp confrontation with the European Commission, the agreement reached in the end is consistent with European rules and their interpretations by the European Commission. In striking this agreement, the Italian Parliament intervened on the substance of the draft budget in an unprecedented way.

VIII. CONCLUDING REMARKS

The aforementioned events show the close interrelationship between the institutional dynamics of the EU and the political and institutional balances within the Member States. This is also confirmed by the evolution of the role of Prime Minister Conte. As a personality not involved in politics during the electoral campaign, he was initially seen as rather weak; a simple guarantor of the government contract; obscured in the Italian public debate by the initiatives and statements of the two Vice-Presidents of the Council, Luigi Di Maio and Matteo Salvini, respectively leaders of the two political formations that gave rise to the government itself – the Five Stars Movement and The League.

That the Prime Minister is the only person entitled to represent Italy in the European Council and in the Eurogroup meetings progressively strengthened Prime Minister Conte as the leader of the government. The most complex political challenge – the negotiation with the European Commission and the Council on the draft budget bill – was conducted personally by the Prime Minister, assisted by the Minister of Economy and the Minister of Foreign Affairs. Incidentally, the Minister of Foreign Affairs' role in this negotiation was quite unusual, but it was justified by the personality of Minister Moavero and the need to find an agreement with the EU authorities, in which the dynamics of intergovernmental negotiations and of international negotiations played an essential role.

The result of the negotiations allowed to reach a point of equilibrium 'within the perimeter traced by the rules and constraints of public finance stemming from Italian membership [of] the European Union and to the Euro-zone' as acknowledged by Conte himself.[46] If, on the one hand, this negotiation was successful and increased the autonomy and political role of the Prime Minister,

---

[46] Camera dei deputati, 11 December 2018 (authors' translation).

then on the other hand, it significantly reduced the possibilities of parliamentary scrutiny as the discussions on the bill were blocked till an agreement was reached with the European institutions. The Italian Constitutional Court itself recently denounced the 'anomalous acceleration' of parliamentary processes in the approval of the 2019 budget.[47]

The anomalous acceleration of parliamentary scrutiny is explained by the fact that the debates on the budget law revolved around one of the unsolved elements of the government contract. This document, being a shared programme between two very different political formations, did not define the sensitive and controversial issue of fiscal policy. Nor did it provide clues on how to ensure consistency and coherence with EU law, particularly in light of the strong Euroscepticism of the two parties emphasised in the first sections of this chapter. By contrast, in many EU countries ruled by coalition governments (the Dutch experience comes to mind, for instance), the coalition agreement defined in great details the coalition's understanding of fiscal policy and its compatibility with EU policies.

The new Italian Government's uncertainty on fiscal policy unduly delayed any assessment of this policy in light of EU goals; even though Italian law mandates that the law governing the budget cycle should involve the Parliament in the complex and timely cycle of the European semester from the very first phase of setting national priorities.[48] The events of December 2018, and the consequent infringement upon parliamentary prerogatives, stemmed from the government's choice to only start negotiating with the EU institutions in the final steps of the budget approval process. This negotiation was conducted exclusively by the government and, more specifically, by the Prime Minister, all the more so because of the tight timescale. By informing and updating the Parliament on the state of the negotiations and on their progress, especially in their final stages, the Prime Minister provided the Parliament with the opportunity to develop its function of control and monitoring over the activity of the Government: to the detriment, however, of the exercise of its legislative function.

The so-called 'executive-dominance' issue, through which the EU contributes to the strengthening of national executives over their Parliaments,[49] was further

---

[47] Ruling of Italian Constitutional Court (www.cortecostituzionale.it/documenti/comunicatistampa/CC_CS_20190110182534.pdf).

[48] On this point, see L Gianniti and N Lupo (eds), *Corso di diritto parlamentare*, 3rd edn (Bologna, Il Mulino, 2018) 290. In a comparative perspective, to evaluate the adaptation strategies of national parliaments with respect to the cycle of the European semester, see V Kreilinger, 'National Parliaments, Surveillance Mechanisms ad Ownership in the Euro Area' (2016) available at www.delorsinstitut.de/2015/wpcontent/uploads/2016/03/Nat.Parl_.SurveillanceOwnership-Kreilinger-JDIB-Mar16.pdf.

[49] On the notion of executive government, see F Fabbrini-Somsen, 'Introduction: A New Look at the Form of Government of the European Union and the Eurozone' in F Fabbrini, E Hirsch Ballin and H Somsen (eds), *What Form of Government for the European Union and the Eurozone?* (Oxford, Oxford University Press, 2015) 2.

bolstered by the economic and financial crisis and is widespread throughout EU Member States.[50] In the Italian case, however, these dynamics took place in a particularly accentuated and blatant way which impacted on both the legislative process and the domestic institutional balance. Nevertheless, in this peculiar historical moment, the strengthening of the executive might benefit the European project. It might, indeed, secure the long-standing friendly relationship between Italy and the EU, at least tempering the great Eurosceptic impetus of the 2018 electoral campaign.

[50] B Guastaferro, 'Procedures vis-à-vis the "Masters of the Treaties": the Parliamentary Role in the Revision of the Treaties' in N Lupo and G Piccirilli (eds), *The Italian Parliament in the European Union* (Oxford, Hart Publishing, 2017).

4

Poland's Defiance Against the CJEU in the Puszcza Białowieska Case (C-441/17)

PRZEMYSŁAW TACIK

I. INTRODUCTION

POLAND OCCUPIES A special place on the map of anti-European populism today. The paralysis and subsequent take-over of the Polish Constitutional Court, the direct attack on the independence of the judiciary and the long-lasting undermining of the rule of law have become symbols of how a country which still officially belongs to the family of liberal democracies can transform into a hybrid regime which defies EU law and democratic standards. The far-right majority which has been holding power since 2015 has strengthened the position of the executive and weakened independent institutions, in particular the judiciary.[1]

The emerging hybrid regime has been described by some commentators as a 'populist state' or 'illiberal democracy'.[2] In this sliding towards authoritarianism, the ruling majority has branded as its enemies both domestic defenders of liberal standards, such as the separation of power and the independence of the judiciary, and the EU. Domestic defenders of liberal standards are portrayed not only as allegedly compromised by previous liberal governments' politics, but as historically bankrupt in their focus on individual and liberal rights instead of giving priority to the national community.[3] The EU is usually referred to as an instrument of foreign, predominantly German, influence on the sovereign

---

[1] A good overview of the key developments in Poland's undermining of the rule of law can be found in: S Jankovic, 'Polish Democracy Under Threat? An Issue of Mere Politics or a Real Danger?' (2016) 9 *Baltic Journal of Law & Politics* 49.

[2] L Pech and KL Scheppele, 'Illiberalism Within: Rule of Law Backsliding in the EU' (2017) 19 *Cambridge Yearbook of European Legal Studies* 4.

[3] A Modrzejewski, 'Catholic and Nationalist Populism in the Current Poland' (2017) 10 *Perspective Politice* 23.

Polish state.[4] Consequently, the EU and Polish defendants of the rule of law are identified (in a sense rightly) as members of the same camp. Against the liberal consensus, the rule of law is presented as a biased ideology which is not worth autotelic respect.

This approach of the ruling majority has led to tensions with the domestic judiciary, in particular the Constitutional Court, until the nominations of new judges by the Polish Government in December 2016, and the Supreme Court. Tensions have also risen with the European Union.[5] The European Commission (EC) engaged in dialogue with Poland under the Rule of Law Framework for close to two years.[6] On 20 December 2017, the EC famously invited the Council to find that there is a clear risk of a serious breach of the rule of law in Poland under Article 7(1) TEU.[7] One of the most recent and important areas of tension between Poland and the EC has been the December 2017 law on the Supreme Court.[8] This prompted the Commission to apply for a declaration of failure to fulfil obligations.[9] Through an interim measures order in October 2018,[10] Poland revoked some of the measures which undermined the independence of the Supreme Court.[11] Nonetheless, there remain other areas of conflict in which Poland's defiance of the EU, the rule of law and the authority of the Court of Justice of the European Union (CJEU) authority is noticeable.

One of these was the conflict over Poland's intrusive operations in the Białowieża Forest, the last well-preserved primeval forest in Europe. Many organisations, environmentalists and scientists joined forces to defend the forest as its wood was sold for the profit of the state company Lasy Państwowe, which administers Polish public forests. The activities in Białowieża were brought forward before the CJEU. While the forest's devastation was the case's focus, the case also illustrated the destructive potential of populists' methods of undermining the rule of law and the judiciary's independence. As will be argued, the Polish Government's stance in this case not only displayed anti-European rhetoric making ostensible use of nationalist clichés, but also challenged the

---

[4] ibid 25.
[5] See RD Kelemen, 'Europe's Other Democratic Deficit: National Authoritarianism in Europe's Democratic Union' (2017) 522 *Government and Opposition* 211.
[6] European Commission (EC), 'Rule of Law in Poland: Commission starts dialogue' (13 January 2016) WM/16/2030, available at europa.eu/rapid/press-release_WM-16-2030_en.htm.
[7] EC, 'Reasoned Proposal in Accordance with Article 7(1) of The Treaty on European Union Regarding the Rule of Law in Poland' (20 December 2018) COM(2017) 835 final; see also EC, 'Rule of Law: European Commission takes next step in infringement procedure to protect the independence of the Polish Supreme Court' (14 August 2016) IP/18/4987, available at europa.eu/rapid/press-release_IP-18-4987_en.htm.
[8] Law on the Supreme Court (8 December 2017), Legislative Journal of the Republic of Poland from 2 January 2018, 5.
[9] Action brought on 2 October 2018 – Case C-619/18 *European Commission v Republic of Poland* (2018/C 427/39).
[10] Ordonnance du Vice-Président de la Cour, Case C-619/18 *European Commission v Republic of Poland*, 19 October 2018, C-619/18 R, EU:C:2018:852.
[11] Law on the amendment of the Law on the Supreme Court (26 November 2018).

foundations of rational discourse which enables meaningful communication between the judiciary and the parties to the proceedings. Consequently, the CJEU adopted unprecedented legal measures to exert its authority over Poland.

This chapter analyses the *Białowieża* case to analyse one of the paths that contemporary far-right populism in Europe may take in challenging cornerstones of the rule of law, namely judicial neutrality, objectivity and rational assessment. The growing league of anti-European nationalists – on the rise not only in Eastern Europe, where it flourished a few years ago, but at the heart of old Western democracies, such as Italy, Austria and Germany – poses a complex threat to the EU's functioning. Beyond rhetorical attacks on European institutions and EU law, the rise of populism threatens the very existence of rational, value-based discourse on which the EU is based.

The chapter first analyses the *Białowieża* case, focusing chiefly on the clash between the language and reasoning used, on one side, by the CJEU and the EC and, on the other, the rhetoric of the Polish Government.[12] This section outlines discursive strategies of a staunchly anti-European and anti-liberal government. The chapter then places the Polish Government's discursive position in this case in the broader context of contemporary populist upsurge. Finally, it draws conclusions about the challenge posed to the EU by the authoritarian turn in Eastern countries and populism's expansion in Western countries.

II. THE *BIAŁOWIEŻA* CASE AND THE BOUNDARIES OF LEGAL DISCOURSE

In 2016 Poland, then ruled for nearly half a year by a new far-right coalition, began massive intrusive operations in one of the best preserved primeval European forests. This led to infringement proceedings before the CJEU, which ended on 17 April 2018 when the Grand Chamber delivered its judgment.[13] This case's true significance is to be found not in the judgment itself, but in the

---

[12] It might seem dubious to perceive the CJEU and the EC as belonging to one group opposed to the Polish Government. Nonetheless, as I will demonstrate, between these two 'camps' there was a significant division in terms of the type of arguments, ways of communication and values. Even if such an analysis runs the risk of misrepresenting the proper relation between the EC as one of the parties and the CJEU as the court, I believe it to be legitimate insofar as it points to the divergence between the legal discourse of the two EU institutions and the populist rhetoric of the Polish Government. In terms of discourse analysis, the CJEU and the EC were much closer to each other than to the Polish Government, despite the obvious difference in the role they played in the proceedings. Incidentally, even within the legal discourse there were demands that the EC and the CJEU engage in a concerted action to defend the rule of law and the Białowieża Forest – see TT Koncewicz, 'The Białowieża case. A Tragedy in Six Acts' (23 May 2018), available at https://reconnect-europe.eu/blog/the-bialowieza-case/. Perhaps then it might be legitimate to ask whether the unprecedented assault on the rule of law demands actions that blur the sacrosanct distinction between the Court and the parties.

[13] Judgment of 17 April 2018, *Commission v Poland (Forêt de Białowieża)*, C-441/17, EU:C:2018:255.

proceedings before the Court and the accompanying statements of the Polish Government. In order to determine the case's impact on the effectiveness and authority of EU law, it is necessary to begin with its origins.

A. The Destruction of the Białowieża Forest and the Infringement Procedure

The Białowieża Forest (*Puszcza Białowieska*) is a unique environmental treasure. As one of the last and the largest remnant of primeval forests that once covered large parts of Europe, it is an exceptional habitat of flora and fauna. It straddles the border between Eastern Poland and Western Belarus and enjoys protection in both countries. Classified as national parks in Poland[14] and Belarus,[15] the Białowieża Forest, since 2014, has been listed on the UNESCO World Heritage List.[16]

This unique area demands special methods of conservation.[17] As pointed out by the UNESCO World Heritage Centre, 'only some of the ecosystems represented in the property (wet meadows, wetlands, river corridors) require maintenance through active management, due to the decrease of water flow and absence of agriculture (hay cutting)'.[18] Apart from these areas, the primeval forest should be left to its own self-regulation. As a result, the forest abounds in dead trees which decay naturally.

A large part of the Białowieża Forest in Poland is located outside the Białowieża National Park and, hence, benefits from much weaker levels of protection. It is administered not by the National Park authorities, but by the Forestry Office.[19] Logging is practised in these areas, up to limits established by the Polish Minister for the Environment. On 25 March 2016, Minister Jan Szyszko, who took office after the victory of the right-wing coalition led by the 'Law and Justice' party in October 2015,[20] significantly raised the upper limit of wood to be harvested from the forest in the years 2013–2021 – from

---

[14] The forest is protected by the Polish legal order on three levels. The Law on the Nature Protection of 2004 defines the duties of the public authorities concerning the protection of nature and gives a legal basis for creating and maintaining national parks, (2004) *Legislative Journal* No 92, Art 8 at 882. A part of the forest has constituted the Białowieża National Park since 1932 (reconstituted after World War II in 1947). The Ordinance of the Minister for the Environment from 7 November 2014 establishes the general plan for protection of the national park, (2014) *Legislative Journal* at 1735. Finally, there are acts at the lowest level, issued by the Director of the national park. Nonetheless, this protection applies only to the part of the forest which is covered by the Białowieża National Park.

[15] www.belarus.by/en/travel/belarus-life/belovezhskaya-pushcha.

[16] Decision No 38 COM 8B.12 adopted by the World Heritage Committee at its 38th session (Doha, 2014), WHC-14/38.COM/16 172–74.

[17] ibid 172–73.

[18] ibid 172.

[19] These areas are protected only by the Law on Forests of 1991, which applies to all forests in the country in a generally uniform way. As a result, from the point of view of the general law, parts of the Białowieża Forest are treated identically to any other forest.

[20] https://parlament2015.pkw.gov.pl/347.

63,000 to 188,000 cubic metres.[21] This decision (the so-called '2016 Annex') was justified by the purported need to remove dead trees from the forest to prevent the spread of parasitic saproxylic beetles that feed on wood.[22] 'Sanitary pruning', reforestation and restoration were planned. In 2007, the Białowieża Forest was designated by the 'Habitats Directive' as a site of Community importance,[23] as well as a Special Protection Area of Birds under the so-called 'Birds Directive'.[24] The EC quickly expressed concerns, sending a letter of formal notice to the Polish authorities in June 2016 urging them to 'make sure that the conservation and protection requirements of the EU's rules are complied with'.[25] Poland did not respond to the letter and continued logging.[26]

The 2016 Annex was met with widespread criticism from pro-environment movements and activists. This opposition only gained momentum after logging increased in 2017 following Decision No. 51 of the General Director of the Forestry Office of 17 February 2017 on the removal of trees in the Białowieża Forest.[27] Sharing the views of numerous scientists and environmental organisations, the EC lodged an action against Poland on 20 July 2017 for failure to fulfil obligations under Article 258 TFEU (the specified provisions of the Habitats and Birds Directives) in approving the decisions on logging without taking into account the risk to natural habitats and species of birds.[28] The Commission

---

[21] Decision of the Minister for the Environment No DLP-I.6.11.16.2016 on the approval of the annex to the Forest Management Plan of 25 March 2016. See also Reuters, 'Polish minister approves tripling of logging in ancient forest' (25 March 2016) available at https://in.reuters.com/article/us-poland-environment-forest-idINKCN0WR15H.

[22] 'Saproxylic beetles' is a general term for insects which feed on dead wood. Among them, a specific species of spruce bark beetles was labelled as the main threat to the forest.

[23] Council Directive (EC) 92/43/EEC on the conservation of natural habitats and of wild fauna and flora [1992] OJ 1992 L 206, p 7, as amended by Council Directive (EC) 2013/17/EU adapting certain directives in the field of environment, by reason of the accession of the Republic of Croatia [2013] OJ L158/193 ('the Habitats Directive'). Art 3 of the Directive establishes 'Natura 2000', a coherent European ecological network of special areas of conservation. It is meant to 'enable the natural habitat types and the species' habitats concerned to be maintained or, where appropriate, restored at a favourable conservation status in their natural range.' (Art 3(1)).

[24] Directive 2009/147/EC of the European Parliament and of the Council of 30 November 2009 on the conservation of wild birds [2010] OJ L20/7), as amended by Council Directive (EC) 2013/17 adapting certain directives in the field of environment, by reason of the accession of the Republic of Croatia [2013] OJ L158/193 ('the Birds Directive').

[25] EC, 'April infringements package: key decisions' (27 April 2017) available at europa.eu/rapid/press-release_MEMO-17-1045_EN.htm.

[26] ibid.

[27] Decision of the General Director of the Forestry Office No 51 (17 February 2017) ZU.6004.1.2017, available at bip.lasy.gov.pl/pl/bip/uregulowania_wewnetrzne.

[28] The Commission lodged four allegations, claiming that Poland had failed (1) to fulfil its obligations under Art 6(3) of the Habitats Directive by approving an appendix to a forest management plan for the Białowieża Forest District without satisfying itself that it would not adversely affect the integrity of the Białowieża Forest Site of Community Importance, (2) to fulfil its obligations under Art 6(1) of the Habitats Directive and under Art 4(1) and (2) of the Birds Directive by not taking the necessary conservation measures corresponding to the ecological requirements of natural habitat types and birds, (3) to fulfil its obligations under Art 12(1)(a) and (d) of the Habitats Directive by not guaranteeing the strict protection of some species of saproxylic beetles, and (4) to fulfil its obligations under Art 5(b) and (d) of the Birds Directive by not guaranteeing the protection of some species of birds.

also requested, pursuant to Article 160(7) of the CJEU's Rules of Procedure, that interim measures be granted before the defendant submitted its observations, because of the risk of serious and irreparable damage to the habitats and the integrity of the Białowieża Forest. The EC argued that the Forest is unique as it contains very old trees, including centenary ones, and, due to natural self-regulation, is a habitat for many species which cannot be found in human-regulated forests.

B. Infringement Proceedings and the Undermining of Judicial Authority

By the order of 27 July 2017, the Vice-President of the Court granted the request for interim measures.[29] Poland was ordered to immediately stop all logging activities and removal of dead trees except in cases of threats to public security. The order was issued before the Polish Government presented any statements. Acting on the basis of Article 160(7), the Vice-President established that the EC's claims were not unsubstantiated prima facie and that the logging could cause grave and irreparable damage to the forest.[30] The change from a non-regulated forest to a cultivated one would irrevocably alter the nature of the Natura 2000 site protected by EU law. The Vice-President noted that granting the order did not significantly undermine the national measures against the European spruce bark beetle taken by the Polish authorities. In particular, he found plausible the EC's argument that such measures did not constitute appropriate protection measures. Thus, the Vice-President clearly shared the Commission's views that in a non-regulated forest, propagation of saproxylic beetles is a natural process.

It is worth noting that the ruling in the interim measures proceedings was not solely based on scientifically established facts. The facts could not be a full ground of the ruling without their value-based interpretation as to how to preserve the forest. Undoubtedly, the behaviour, propagation and effects of the bark beetle can be verified by science and the EU courts have only general capacity to assess coherence and persuasiveness of scientific arguments.[31] Nonetheless, such knowledge does not determine per se whether the propagation of the beetle should be prevented. A value-informed use of expertise must decide whether a given measure should be adopted. The Vice-President's order may be interpreted as applying a particular version of the precautionary principle, whereby this principle is generally used by international courts to defer to national decision making.[32] In application of this principle, '[t]he emphasis falls instead on

---

[29] Ordonnance du Vice-Président de la Cour, *Commission v Poland (Forêt de Białowieża)*, 27 July 2017, C-441/17 R, EU:C:2017:622.

[30] ibid, para 17 and paras 18–20.

[31] See I Van Damme, 'The Assessment of Expert Evidence in International Adjudication' (2018) 9 *Journal of International Dispute Settlement* 407.

[32] CE Foster, *Science and the Precautionary Principle in International Courts and Tribunals. Expert Evidence, Burden of Proof and Finality* (Cambridge, Cambridge University Press, 2011) 18–21.

the limitations of scientific prediction, and the need for decision making that errs on the side of allowing for worst-case scenarios.'[33] In the *Białowieża* case, however, the precautionary principle was used to put in doubt the efficiency and proportionality of a purportedly environmental measure adopted by the Polish authorities. Whereas the Polish Government presented logging as a protective method meant to combat an alleged environmental catastrophe, the Vice-President's order appears to take the national measure itself as a threat.

The Polish authorities deliberately ignored the Vice-President's order. Not only did logging openly continue, but dead old spruces were transported away from the Forest. Activists and NGOs documented the activities undertaken against the order and found that the pace of logging did not relent after 27 July 2017.[34] To justify its actions, the Polish Ministry of Environment began to invoke the public safety clause referred to by the Vice-President in the interim order. The Ministry claimed that deforestation was necessary to protect public roads from falling branches. The Polish authorities seemingly did not take this excuse seriously and were merely providing another pretext for logging. Indeed, promptly after the order was issued, the Regional Director of the Forestry Office called for a thorough re-assessment of the public safety needs. This led to the adoption of a new definition of safety need so broad as to allow the Forestry Office to undertake pruning and logging in almost all parts of the Białowieża Forest.[35] Such operations were deemed admissible to protect roads, tourist facilities, areas of understorey collection or sites full of dry and dead wood. Moreover, excessive safety margins were adopted which effectively expanded the scope of the allowed activities.

In parallel, the Polish Ministry for the Environment undertook a campaign denouncing the forest's defenders as 'ecoterrorists'.[36] Environmental movements and organisations were officially criticised, whereas associations of hunters were promoted on the basis of allegedly representing an adequate approach to nature and ecology. The Ministry went as far as to notify the Ministry of Social Education of the need to modify the teaching content of biology classes in schools.[37] Hunting was to be presented as a method of protecting nature in the name of nature itself. Hunters were to be invited to schools to teach students about their activities and their views on the environment.

---

[33] ibid, 18.
[34] See Report on the Damaging of the Białowieża Forest (*Puszcza Białowieska – raport z dewastacji. Wyniki społecznej kontroli działalności Lasów Państwowych w Puszczy Białowieskiej w 2017 roku*), available at dzikapolska.org/puszcza-bialowieska-raport-dewastacji/, 24.
[35] ibid, 29–31.
[36] M Chołodowski, A Gurgul and J Suchecka, *Szyszko tnie ekoterrorystów*, Gazeta Wyborcza (31 July 2017), available at wyborcza.pl/7,75398,22174459,szyszko-tnie-ekoterrorystow.html; M Chołodowski, *Szyszko: Ekoterroryści atakują księdza Duszkiewicza. Ekolodzy: nie doszło do ataku* (17 August 2017), available at bialystok.wyborcza.pl/bialystok/7,35241,22242813,szyszko-ekoterrorysci-atakuja-ksiedza-ekolodzy-nie-doszlo.html.
[37] M Chołodowski, A Gurgul and J Suchecka, *Szyszko tnie ekoterrorystów* (2017).

Alongside abusing the public safety clause – allegedly in compliance with the Vice-President's order – the Polish Ministry for the Environment began to openly contest the authority of the Court. In July 2017 the Environmental Minister Szyszko organised a press conference to which he brought a jar full of bark beetles, claiming that 48 million of such beetles were 'at large' and that these should be totally eradicated by the end of 2017.[38] His statements were manifestly incoherent: on the one hand, he maintained that Poland acted according to EU law, but on the other hand he claimed that the problem stemmed from misunderstandings 'in basic issues'. He also promised to defend his stance against 'those who do not know the laws of nature and the specificity of the Poles'.[39] He also dismissed the ecologist activists' attempts to block logging in the forest. In a press interview, he claimed that 'EU specialists are not capable of distinguishing a bark beetle from a frog', while delays in logging would cause irreversible damage.[40]

The actions of the Polish authorities were an unprecedented case of open and daring disregard of a CJEU interim measures order.[41] This was denounced by CJEU judge Marek Safjan, although to no reaction from the government.[42] The disconcertingly defiant stance of the Polish Government, displayed also in proceedings before the CJEU, prompted the European Commission to supplement its application for interim measures by requesting that the Court additionally order Poland to pay a periodic penalty payment if it failed to comply with the orders made by the Court. Owing to Poland's requests and the importance of the case, the matter was referred to the Court and, later, to the Grand Chamber.

Finally, on 20 November 2017 the Grand Chamber delivered its ruling on interim measures under the expedited procedure, re-asserting the order to stop the active forest management operations.[43] In order to prevent the abuse of the

---

[38] ibid.

[39] ibid.

[40] M Orłowski, *Szyszko: Unijni specjaliści nie potrafią odróżnić kornika od żaby*, Gazeta Wyborcza (3 August 2018), available at wyborcza.pl/7,75398,22184794,szyszko-unijni-specjalisci-nie-potrafia-odroznic-kornika-od.html.

[41] For this reason, it was the most important case that the EC referred to the CJEU against Poland in 2017. See EC, 'Monitoring of Application of Union Law. 2017 Annual Report', Part III 142; see also TA Borzel, T Hofmann and D Panke, 'Caving in or Sitting it out? Longitudinal Patterns of Non-Compliance in the European Union' (2012) 19 *Journal of European Public Policy* 454; R Grzeszczak, IP Karolewski, *Białowieza Forest, the Spruce Bark Beetle and the EU Law Controversy in Poland* (27 November 2017), available at verfassungsblog.de/bialowieza-forest-the-spruce-bark-beetle-and-the-eu-law-controversy-in-poland/.

[42] P Kośmiński, *Puszcza Białowieska. Trybunał Sprawiedliwości UE swoje, PiS swoje. "To sytuacja bez precedensu"*, Gazeta Wyborcza (1 August 2018), available at wyborcza.pl/7,75398,22177187,puszcza-bialowieska-trybunal-sprawiedliwosci-ue-swoje-pis.html.

[43] Order of 20 November 2017, *Commission v Poland (Forêt de Białowieża)*, C-441/17 R, EU:C:2017:877.

public safety clause, the CJEU resorted to very strict language as to the order's exceptions:

> Exceptionally, the Republic of Poland may continue to take the measures referred to in paragraph 1 of the operative part of the present order where they are strictly necessary, and in so far as they are proportionate, in order to ensure, directly and immediately, the public safety of persons, on condition that other, less radical measures are impossible for objective reasons.
>
> Consequently, those operations may continue to be undertaken only when they are the sole means of ensuring the public safety of persons in the immediate vicinity of transport routes or other significant infrastructure where it is impossible to ensure such safety, for objective reasons, by taking other, less radical measures, such as adequate signposting of the danger or a temporary ban, backed up, where necessary, by appropriate penalties, on public access to the immediate vicinity.

The Court fully shared the EC's views on the merits, finding that the Polish authorities undertook very active forest management operations despite the spread of bark beetles not being a threat to the Forest. The CJEU additionally noted that the Polish Government expressly ignored concerns and opposition from scientists and NGOs. It seems therefore that the disregard of the culture of dialogue with civil society, demonstrated by the Polish authorities, was one of the arguments which convinced the Court. In the light of the imminent threat to the forest, even the fact that Poland submitted a scientific opinion contradicting the one deposited by the EC did not prevent the imposition of interim measures.

Legally, it is interesting that the CJEU for the first time interpreted Article 279 and Article 260 TFEU as allowing periodic penalty payments for non-compliance with the interim measures order. The Court shared the EC's views in so doing and noted that Article 279 TFEU allows measures which will guarantee the full effectiveness of the final decision in a case.[44] Given the expedient character of interim measures, the penalty may be imposed by the adjudicating judge without an additional procedure under Article 260 TFEU.[45] In other words, the objective of interim measures stipulated in Article 279 TFEU overrides the procedural requirements of Article 260 TFEU. According to the Court, the ancillary nature of interim measures does not preclude means which will safeguard their efficacy. Poland's previous non-compliance with the order of the Vice-President was a direct trigger of the Court's decision.[46] Ultimately, the CJEU determined that if Poland were to violate the order, it would be liable to pay at least €100,000 per day for non-compliance.

In this regard the Court's order was innovative. Article 260 TFEU in its literal wording allowed for such an interpretation. Article 260(2) TFEU states

---

[44] ibid, paras 94, 100.
[45] ibid, paras 100–05.
[46] ibid, paras 109–13.

that a penalty may be imposed after a Member State fails to comply with the earlier declaratory judgment of the Court, while this judgment may concern a non-specified disrespect of any norms of the Treaties, therefore also violating Article 279 TFEU.[47] The unprecedented attitude of the Polish Government pushed the CJEU to declare this possibility openly for the first time.

C. Disruption of Dialogue

The Polish authorities reacted to the order with the approach already demonstrated earlier: they issued a series of contradictory statements which altogether fuelled the information chaos and disturbance of dialogue with the EC and the CJEU. Immediately after the order was delivered, Minister Szyszko stated in a press conference that 'just as we did previously, we are going to conform in 100% to the *suggestions* contained in the interim motion [*sic*] of the Court of the EU [*sic*]' (emphasis added).[48] Apart from the incorrect terminology, the Minister's words diminished the Court's order as he claimed that no penalty was imposed on Poland, which allegedly proved that the Polish authorities had complied entirely with EU law. Indeed, the CJEU did not impose the penalty through this order. However, the finding that the penalty itself was possible was already a consequence of Poland's previous non-compliance with the Vice-President's order. During the same press conference, the Director General of the Forestry Office claimed that all the forest management activities had been halted, thereby admitting that they had been carried out. Both the Minister and the Director General claimed the exact opposite: on the one hand, they effectively admitted that EU law had been breached and, on the other hand, they claimed that Poland had acted in accordance with the Vice-President's order. Therefore, the Polish authorities effectively *took no stance*: owing to internal contradiction, it was impossible to establish what they indeed claimed. There was no dialogue – and not even a true dispute between the parties – because they effectively did not speak the same language. Even though the EC and the CJEU played different roles in the case, both used the language of facts and effective actions which was confronted with the Polish authorities' muddy language simultaneously confirming and denying the accusations.

These proceedings before the Court demonstrated that Poland may not only be willing to disrespect the Court's order, but also to refuse to undertake any dialogue with the EC on the basis of common views and fact-checking. The problem was far more acute than the ordinary opposition of the two parties'

---

[47] See also R Geiger, DE Khan and M Kotzur, *European Union Treaties* (Munich and Oxford, CH Beck and Hart Publishing, 2015) 867–71.

[48] M Orłowski, *Harwestery wstrzymane. Szyszko: Spełnimy sugestie Trybunału UE*, Gazeta Wyborcza (21 November 2017), available at wyborcza.pl/7,75398,22675643,szyszko-spelnimy-sugestie-trybunalu-ue.html.

statements in a case. The Polish authorities opposed all the EC's scientific findings, but did not present any persuasive arguments to demonstrate their fallacy.[49] On the contrary, as if echoing the EC's statements, Poland claimed that halting the forest management activities would threaten the existence of the forest. The initial reaction of the Ministry for the Environment to the 27 July 2017 order showed that the Polish authorities had created an information bubble which partly referred to the CJEU's decisions (as demonstrated by the abuse of the public safety clause) but was self-founded and deliberately eluded a common platform to weigh up arguments. To each scientific opinion submitted by the EC, the Polish Government produced its own, as is natural in litigation; however, the government openly defied any kind of scientific universality and turned scientific arguments into mere opinions.[50] The echoing strategy was also manifested by Poland's request for compensation from the EC for halting the activities. The government demanded an exorbitant sum of around €757 million, claiming that this represented the value of the forest's damaged areas and the cost of disrupting economic activities in it, such as collecting understorey and producing honey.[51] Simultaneously, the Polish Government pretended to restore dialogue with the European Commission in areas when it would serve its goals. The government pointed out that it had allegedly adopted conservation measures in greater parts of the forest whereas the parts affected by the active operations constituted only 5.4 per cent of the Natura 2000 site.[52]

Simultaneously, Minister Szyszko contributed to the confusion around Poland's stance in the case by claiming that the Polish authorities had acted in concordance with EU law. Soon after the order was delivered and the main hearing in the case was being prepared, the Minister went as far as to claim that, in fact, 'Poland had defended EU law'.[53] This statement was made to a group of international scientists who came to the Białowieża Forest to assess the scope and results of the management activities. Moreover, the Minister claimed that the CJEU was badly informed about what happened in the forest. Finally, he identified the positions of the EC and the CJEU and concluded that their assessments of the case were essentially flawed, 'because the Białowieża Forest is not a great natural heritage [of humankind]. It is a great cultural-natural heritage of the local population, the local foresters, the local hunters, the local school of nature protection.'[54] With this pseudo-argument, he attempted to negate the

---

[49] Given that the government's arguments were presented at closed-door sessions, it is difficult to determine their exact content. It must be deduced from the Court's assessment and comments of government officials.

[50] *cf* Order of 20 November 2017, para 51.

[51] ibid, paras 70–71.

[52] ibid, para 52.

[53] M Chołodowski, *Szyszko: Puszcza Białowieska to nie jest wielkie dziedzictwo przyrodnicze*, *Gazeta Wyborcza* (3 December 2017), available at bialystok.wyborcza.pl/bialystok/7,35241,22730860, szyszko-puszcza-bialowieska-to-nie-jest-wielkie-dziedzictwo.html.

[54] ibid.

EC's claim that the Białowieża Forest was the last of the untouched primeval forests in Europe. As he claimed,

> It is not [primeval], because it is a human work. We will stand before the Court of Justice, defending honour and knowledge, but we also want to treat the Białowieża Forest as an object, so that there should be no such mistakes in relation to Poland and other objects [*sic*] within the EU Natura 2000 network. We are leaders in terms of creating, shaping biodiversity through use. It means that we use these resources naturally, so that they serve human beings and simultaneously in order to protect them. This is a typical example of the principle of sustainable growth which is currently so fashionable in the EU: use natural resources in order to make them serve human beings and, simultaneously, in order to rehabilitate, restore, multiply.[55]

As regards the future CJEU's ruling, he claimed to sincerely hope that 'normality and truth would return'.[56] At another public meeting, Minister Szyszko stated that,

> Also on the Polish territory there are people who bring charges against Poland. They think that Poland destroys natural resources and believe that this object is untouched by human hand, that it must be protected against humans at any price. In this manner they breach EU law.[57]

These enigmatic statements – apart from their inconsistency – demonstrate that the Polish authorities once again changed their defence contradicting their previous position. They attempted to oppose the EC's claim about the Białowieża Forest being a primeval forest, thus manifestly denying the classification of the Forest as a Natura 2000 site. The fallacy of such claims was not the pivotal problem. Rather, the permanent inconsistency of Poland's statements was a major source of chaos and misinterpretation. At no point did Minister Szyszko acknowledge the contradiction inherent in his stances. Seemingly, he kept all his previous arguments at hand to juggle between them. Before the CJEU, he once again returned to claiming that all the activities undertaken in the forest had the goal of protecting biodiversity and public safety.[58]

Before the final judgment, on 9 January 2018, Minister Szyszko was discharged from his position together with the entire government of Prime Minister Beata Szydło. This move, alongside more moderate statements from members of the new cabinet (including the new Prime Minister), was received by the EU as a conciliatory gesture. Nevertheless, the future of the forest management activities remained uncertain as the new Minister for the Environment was still ambiguous about the matter.

---

[55] ibid. Author's translation.
[56] ibid.
[57] M Chołodowski, *Szyszko w drodze przed Trybunał. Próba generalna przed procesem*, Gazeta Wyborcza (8 December 2017), available at bialystok.wyborcza.pl/bialystok/7,35241,22754237,szyszko-w-drodze-przed-trybunal-proba-generalna-przed-procesem.html.
[58] M Chołodowski, 'Rzeź w Puszczy Białowieskiej przed Trybunałem Sprawiedliwości UE', Gazeta Wyborcza (11 December 2017), available at bialystok.wyborcza.pl/bialystok/7,35241,22769200,rzez-w-puszczy-bialowieskiej-przed-trybunalem-sprawiedliwosci.html.

D. The Final Judgment and Sour Reconciliation

On 20 February 2018, Advocate General Bot issued his opinion on the case,[59] recommending the CJEU to declare failures to fulfil obligations by Poland in all four complaints (see footnote 28 above). Assessing whether the operations undertaken by the Polish authorities may be deemed conservation measures, Advocate General Bot noted that

> it follows from the terms of the dispute that scientific controversy remains as to whether the measures thus undertaken, on the one hand, will have an effect on the spread of the spruce bark beetle and, on the other hand, constitute an appropriate method of conserving the protected habitats.[60]

Nonetheless, he did not consider it to be an argument in favour of the Polish Government, because undertaking massive sanitary operations whose effects were not sufficiently established violated the precautionary principle.[61] Thus, the scientific controversy, which was artificially fuelled by Poland, backfired on the Polish Government.

The CJEU delivered its final judgment on 17 April 2018.[62] Unsurprisingly, the Court followed the Advocate General and found that Poland had violated EU law as specified in the EC's application. Based on the evidence adduced by the Commission, it dismissed the arguments of the Polish Government. Among others, the CJEU stated that

> [the] line of argument based on the fact that the Białowieża Forest cannot be regarded as a 'natural' or 'primal' forest since it has always been the subject of active human exploitation that has determined its characteristics is irrelevant, since the Habitats and Birds Directives, regardless of the classification of that forest, provide the framework for forest management in it.[63]

The Court was equally unpersuaded by the Polish authorities' claim that the actions undertaken were aimed at protecting the forest against the bark beetle as well as guaranteeing public safety. The CJEU noted that the activities were carried out against all trees, not only against spruces, which were supposedly endangered by the beetle.[64] Consequently, these measures entailed potential danger for the fauna population protected under Natura 2000 and thus violated EU law.[65] The Court identified some of the internal contradictions contained in Poland's stance. It pointed out, among others, that the Polish Government

---

[59] Opinion of Advocate General Bot delivered on 20 February 2018, *Commission v Poland (Forêt de Białowieża)*, C-441/17, EU:C:2018:80.
[60] ibid, para 145.
[61] ibid, para 169.
[62] Judgment of 17 April 2018, *Commission v Poland (Forêt de Białowieża)*, C-441/17, EU:C:2018:255.
[63] ibid, para 155.
[64] ibid, para 163.
[65] ibid, paras 164–69.

compared the activities undertaken in the Białowieża Forest with operations in other EU countries, but at the same time claimed that the forest was unique in Europe.[66] Moreover, Poland contradicted itself by claiming that spruces were not natural habitats for some saproxylic beetles, even though it was a basic assumption of the forest's 2015 management plan adopted by the Polish authorities.[67] However, the Court just briefly noted or ignored other contradictory statements of the Polish Government, effectively confirming that Poland had been engaged in meaningful dialogue.[68]

In the aftermath of the CJEU's ruling, the new Polish Minister for the Environment, Henryk Kowalczyk, stated publicly that Poland would respect the judgment.[69] Despite that, some operations (logging and transport of wood) continued to be carried out in the Forest[70] until on 15 May 2018, Decision No 51 authorising the increase in logging from February 2017 was repealed.[71]

III. BEYOND THE *BIAŁOWIEŻA* CASE: THE POPULIST (UN)REASON IN LAW

The C-441/17 R case was both factually and legally quite simple. The possibility of applying sanctions under Article 261 TFEU for non-compliance with interim measures was an unquestionable novelty, but it was uncontroversial given the combined wordings of Articles 261 and 279 TFEU. Neither were Poland's violations of the two environment directives a matter of serious dispute. As far as scientific evidence for the allegedly precautionary measures is concerned, Poland did not back its claims with any credible sources, which made the CJEU accept the EC's expertise without much consideration. The Polish Government, however, attempted to derail the very channels of communication with the CJEU. In this work of populist (un)reasoning, four main strategies can be discerned.

A. A Disinformation War

First, the government waged what may be called a disinformation war on the CJEU and the EC, treated as parts of the same bloc.[72] Poland defended its actions

---

[66] ibid, para 180.
[67] *cf* ibid, para 260.
[68] *cf* for example ibid, para 234.
[69] M Chołodowski, 'Polska uszanuje wyrok w sprawie Puszczy Białowieskiej, ale wycinki są możliwe', *Gazeta Wyborcza* (15 April 2018) available at bialystok.wyborcza.pl/bialystok/7,35241, 23274257,polska-uszanuje-wyrok-w-sprawie-puszczy-bialowieskiej-ale-wycinki.html.
[70] M Chołodowski, 'Kowalczyk wstrzymuje wycinkę', *Gazeta Wyborcza* (15 May 2018), available at wyborcza.pl/7,134154,23404649,kowalczyk-wstrzymuje-wycinke.html.
[71] ibid.
[72] On contemporary disinformation and fake news see generally A Alemanno, 'How to Counter Fake News? A Taxonomy of Anti-fake News Approaches' (2018) 9 *European Journal of Risk Regulation* 1.

with a series of pretexts (the imminent danger of the beetle's spread, and, after the first interim order, the protection of public safety) which manifest fallacy was proportionate to the degree of self-belief of government officials. The epistemological status of these statements is comparable to conspiracy theories: through refusal to acknowledge criticism, they function as infallible, even if some of them are clearly unreasonable – like the claim that hunting contributes to saving and multiplying populations of animals. Additionally, the Minister for the Environment used elements of already existing and widespread far-right conspiracy theories on the dangers of 'ecoterrorism'. In order to combat the defenders of the forest, he launched propaganda actions which included inviting hunters for school lessons. He also haphazardly concocted an ideology of Poland's specific environmental approach which allegedly had been tested for centuries. Simultaneously, the government attempted to use elements of the rule of law's discourse to its advantage. It claimed that Poland was respecting EU law (although the infringement procedure precisely put this in doubt) and accused the EC of violating it by supressing the alleged precautionary measures of logging and pruning. At some point, it even denied that Białowieża Forest was a primeval forest, while boasting about its natural treasures.

Particularly conspicuous in the *Białowieża* case is the fact that the inconsistency of the Polish Government's statements in the proceedings was not a matter of mistake or poor preparation, but part of a deliberate strategy aimed at confusing the general public and, unsuccessfully, the CJEU and the EC. In this sense, the government was more intent on sowing disinformation to make its actions appear legitimate than winning the case.

B. The Deliberate Undermining of Judicial Authority

The second strategy, closely linked to the disinformation war, consisted in deliberate downgrading of the Court's rulings as mere opinions. According to this perspective, all opinions are of the same value except for the fact that one party's opinions must be defended by this particular party. Consequently, accepting another institution's view is tantamount to losing the dispute. No standards of veracity or objectivity can be applied in this epistemological universe because all opinions are necessarily biased. It is for this reason that the Minister for Environment did not even recognise the judicial character of the Court's rulings: the CJEU appeared as yet another EU institution, alongside the European Commission.

This situation echoes an old foreboding of Jürgen Habermas, who denounced postmodernism as a form of reactionary undermining of the Enlightenment project.[73] The populist reason demonstrated in the *Białowieża* case draws from

---

[73] J Habermas, 'Modernity: An Unfinished Project' in M Passerin d'Entrèves and S Benhabib (eds), *Habermas and the Unfinished Project of Modernity* (Cambridge MA, The MIT Press, 1997) 54.

a vulgarised version of postmodern belief in lack of objective truth and great narratives.[74] As is often pointed out, the contemporary wave of populism benefits from new channels of communication which weaken hierarchies of information and put expertise and lay opinion on the same level.[75] Such a situation evidently eats away at judicial authority, which appears to produce only yet another biased set of opinions without more universal standards of reasoning and justification. The populist discourse, as evidenced by the *Białowieża* case, is eager to fuel this tendency in its struggle for power.

C. The Politicisation of the Judiciary and the Creation of an Enemy

Third, the populist discourse disrupts the legal order by presenting it as political, which liberal democracies have attempted to curb within the rule of law.[76] In this regard, it clearly resorts to the originally leftist manoeuvre against liberal democracy which consists in re-politicising what previously was held as apolitical and shielded by the guarantees of judicial independence and the sanctity of the judicial office.[77] To use Gramsci's, Laclau's and Mouffe's terms,[78] the hitherto hegemonic discourse of the rule of law, which had attempted to restrain political positions within a certain circumscribed field, was revealed in its particularity, namely as a discourse of domination. Thus, the law was clearly demarcated in its relation to the political outside.

The re-politicisation of the legal field could have a refreshing effect for democracy, if some matters were excluded from political discussion through judicialisation – (for example, fundamental questions about distribution of wealth or globalisation-induced inequality). Nonetheless, cases such as *Białowieża Forest* nip this effect in the bud because the political line of division was drawn simply between the two camps which were constructed so as to embody either the rule of law or the political outside. The EU (including the CJEU and the EC) were thrown into the first camp, whereas populists presented themselves as representatives of a second, distinct camp. As Jan-Werner Müller convincingly demonstrated, these tactics allow populists to reinvigorate the difference between two constructs: 'the elites' and 'the people'.[79] The defenders

---

[74] JF Lyotard, *The Postmodern Condition: A Report on Knowledge* (Minneapolis, University of Minnesota Press, 1984).

[75] A Ágh, 'The EU polycrisis and hard populism in East-Central Europe: From the Copenhagen dilemma to the Juncker paradox' (2017) 13 *Politics in Central Europe* 9.

[76] *cf* G Palombella, 'Illiberal, Democratic and Non-Arbitrary? Epicentre and Circumstances of a Rule of Law Crisis' (2018) 10 *Hague Journal of the Rule of Law* 8.

[77] *cf* M Stone, I Rua Wall and C Douzinas (eds), *New Critical Legal Thinking. Law and the Political* (Abingdon, Routledge, 2012) 1.

[78] See generally E Laclau and C Mouffe, *Hegemony and Socialist Strategy: Towards a Radical Democratic Politics* (New York, Verso, 2001).

[79] JW Müller, *What Is Populism?* (Philadelphia, University of Pennsylvania Press, 2016).

of the rule of law, the resistant judiciary and the EU are thus welded into one chain of equivalence and fought as representatives of alienated elites which have nothing to do with the interests of the silent majority, allegedly represented by populists. This division recalls Carl Schmitt's concept of the enemy: there can be no negotiation or communication between the two camps, because they are at odds in their very essence.[80]

D. Nationalism in the Dismantling of the Rule of Law

Fourth, populists put a dangerous, nationalistic spin on the political division. As was demonstrated even more tellingly in the attempt at dialogue between the EC and the Polish Government under the Rule of Law Framework, the rule of law was presented by Polish populists as an imposition of foreign mechanisms, allegedly motivated by foreign interests. In this perspective, the law taken autotelically is a device whose aim is to serve other, not national, interests. The Polish ruling majority resorted to nationalistic and xenophobic discourses in response to the criticisms of international organisations and institutions after the crisis concerning the Constitutional Court.[81] These agents, whose concerns were raised by the unconstitutional manoeuvres of the far-right coalition, were presented as following their own interests and imposing mechanisms on Poland which did not serve the Polish nation.

With this discursive trick, the law loses its demand for universal comprehensibility. The law cannot be interpreted by foreign actors, who are by definition opposed to Polish sovereignty, unless they support the far-right revolution (like Hungary). In other words, the law is always supplemented by its outside, in which – this time – the national badge of the interpreter is located. The autotelic legal order is ripped open by an extra-legal reference to the nationality of those who interpret and apply the law. Therefore, the dismantling of the rule of law may be presented as a reaffirmation of the national identity. In the classic nationalistic short circuit, a conjuration between liberals and international agents is assumed: whoever defends the rule of law stands against the nation. Moreover, the law becomes an artificial, value-abstracting tool, which is meant to carry out objectives in the interest of the nation. Values encoded in the legal text as well as the inner dynamics of the interpretation process of law are disregarded; the law is portrayed as a transparent means to realise (national) goals.

---

[80] C Schmitt, *The Concept of the Political: Expanded Edition* (Chicago, The University of Chicago Press, 2007) 26.
[81] cf 'Beata Szydło o Komisji Weneckiej: Polska sama poradzi sobie ze swymi sprawami' (13 July 2017), available at www.polskieradio.pl/5/3/Artykul/1642837,Beata-Szydlo-o-Komisji-Weneckiej-Polska-sama-poradzi-sobie-ze-swymi-sprawami.

Nevertheless, upon closer analysis, even this national interest as defined by the populist government is extremely vague and changeable, as evidenced by the *Białowieska* case. Indeed, the government claimed that logging a primeval forest suited the national interest only to withdraw from this position after the CJEU's judgement. What remains unchanged is that this supposed national interest always conflates with the interest of the populist majority.[82] If we ignore the self-interested nature of this national interest, it would be as if the populist reason had gone into a postmodern spiral of equivalent signifiers which follow one another at a fast pace and can never produce a stable meaning communicable to the other party to the dialogue – this was clearly demonstrated by Minister Szyszko's subsequent contradictory arguments. It is for this reason that in the negotiations with the EC in the Rule of Law Framework and in the *Białowieża* case before the CJEU the dialogue could never be effectively established. The Polish Government as a partner of communication produced a relentless stream of contradictory and fallacious statements which could not be coherently referred to the other party.

To sum up, it is important to consider the *Białowieża* case within the process of dismantling of the rule of law which had been taking place since 2015. Even if the rule of law has never had an unambiguous definition,[83] it is always presented as having for its elements at least some of the following:[84] (1) generality of norms,[85] (2) stability and transparency of law,[86] (3) coherence of law, (4) lack of arbitrary and unmotivated decisions,[87] (5) non-retroactivity, (6) promulgation in advance,[88] (7) supremacy of law,[89] (8) independence and effectiveness of the judiciary, and (9) accountability of those in power for violating the law.

---

[82] In this respect Poland is a model example of Müller's observation about the populists usurping an almost total overlap between their movement and the entire nation.

[83] *cf* RH Fallon, Jr, '"The Rule of Law" as a Concept in Constitutional Discourse' (1997) 97 *Columbia Law Review* 1; D Desai, R Wagner and M Woolcock, 'The Missing Middle: Reconfiguring Rule of Law Reform as if Politics and Process Mattered' (2014) 6 *Hague Journal on the Rule of Law* 231; R McCorquodale, 'Defining The International Rule Of Law: Defying Gravity?' (2016) 65 *International Comparative Law Quarterly* 278.

[84] *cf* L Fuller, *Morality of Law* (New Haven, Yale University Press, 1969) 39–90; SE Skaaning, 'Measuring the Rule of Law' (2010) 63 *Political Research Quarterly* 452; JE Lane, 'A Theory of Rule of Law (RL)' (2016) 16 *Romanian Journal of Political Science* 36; European Commission for Democracy through Law (Venice Commission), 'Report on the Rule of Law, adopted at its 86th plenary session' (Venice, March 2011), available at www.venice.coe.int/webforms/documents/?pdf=CDL-AD(2011)003rev-e.

[85] C Murphy, 'Lon Fuller and the Moral Value of the Rule of Law' (2005) 24 *Law and Philosophy* 240.

[86] TAO Endicott, 'The Impossibility of the Rule of Law' (1999) 19 *Oxford Journal of Legal Studies* 1.

[87] E Mak and S Taekema, 'The European Union's Rule of Law Agenda: Identifying Its Core and Contextualizing Its Application' (2016) 8 *Hague Journal on the Rule of Law*, 28; TAO Endicott, 'The Impossibility of the Rule of Law' (1999) 2.

[88] L Fuller, *Morality of Law* (1969) 42–44; RH Fallon, Jr, '"The Rule of Law" as a Concept in Constitutional Discourse' (1997) 3.

[89] R McCorquodale, 'Defining the International Rule Of Law: Defying Gravity?' 288.

Protection against anarchy has also been described as a crucial value of the rule of law, at least from the perspective of state power.[90] Besides the internal split of the Polish legal system due to the so-called constitutional crisis, the rule of law is undermined also insofar as EU law, being part of the Polish legal system, is openly defied. The Polish ruling majority's approach to judicial authority and EU law, most clearly demonstrated by its disregard for the CJEU's rulings, is a direct threat to the stability, coherence, supremacy and hierarchy of the EU legal system and to the authority of the EU's judiciary.

IV. CONCLUSIONS

The *Białowieża* case is first and foremost an environmental catastrophe, perpetrated for the sake of material interest and in blatant disregard of the modern approach to the protection of nature. However, the important legal nature and precedent of this case should not be ignored. Obviously, the case will be remembered in future records of EU law as the first act of open disrespect by a Member State of a CJEU's ruling on interim measures which met with the Court's innovative reaction – admitting the possibility of imposing a financial penalty for violating the interim measures order.

Yet behind the strictly legal layer of the case lies another important aspect concerning the very foundation of the legal discourse and the possibility of dialogue. For 11 months between February 2017 and January 2018, the Polish authorities undertook a deliberate campaign to dismantle the very possibility of dialogue with and the judicial authority of the CJEU. Owing to the information chaos, a seemingly easy case stumbled upon a complex web of contradictory claims from the government. Recourse to nationalism presented the EU as essentially foreign to Poland and Polish interests.

For all those who investigate the challenges to EU law the *Białowieża* case is an ominous augur of what may need to be confronted in future attacks on the rule of law in the EU: not tacit non-compliance with EU law and the CJEU's judgments (which has a long history), not even an argued opposition to EU law, but the muddy waters of populist (un)reasoning that turn courts into parties and dialogue into an echo of unlinked and contradictory statements. In this sense, European populism consists not (only) in open confrontation with the EU and its norms, but with the very form of discourse that underpins contemporary liberal democracies.

Simultaneously, this case displays the limits of EU law's effectiveness. While the case ended with Poland's complying with the CJEU's judgment, the compliance was to a great extent forced by political circumstances. As a consequence, the *Białowieża* case should be studied as a warning of what may soon happen

---

[90] RH Fallon, Jr, '"The Rule of Law" as a Concept in Constitutional Discourse' (1997) 7.

in populist-ruled European countries. The system of sanctions established by Part 6, Title 1, Section 5 TFEU is efficient, but as long as penalties imposed by the Court are willingly paid by the state. If, however, the Member State decides to disregard the CJEU's judgments and EC's decisions altogether, there is no actual means of enforcing sanctions. Resort to the sanctions of Article 7 TEU is now effectively blocked by the requirement of unanimity. For this reason, it is of utmost urgency to introduce new mechanisms which would make payment of structural funds dependent on Member States' respect for the rule of law and, even more importantly, EU law.[91]

The current populist upsurge in Europe, especially in Central and Eastern Europe, is a major challenge to the EU's functioning, if not its existence. It is not just a new wave of euro-scepticism, but a profound disruption of the Enlightenment tradition on which post-war liberal democracies have been built.

---

[91] Pech and Scheppele, 'Illiberalism Within' (2017) 45; G Halmai, 'The Possibility and Desirability of Rule of Law Conditionality' (2018) 1 *Hague Journal on the Rule of Law* 10 h; V Vita, 'Revisiting the Dominant Discourse on Conditionality in the EU: The Case of EU Spending Conditionality' (2017) 19 *Cambridge Yearbook of European Legal Studies* 1.

5

Hungarian Economic Patriotism and Internal Market Law: Questioning Fundamental Freedoms and Disregarding Fundamental Rights

MÓNIKA PAPP AND MARTON VARJU

I. INTRODUCTION: THE HUNGARIAN IMAGE BEFORE THE CRISIS

SINCE ACCESSION TO the European Union in 2004, Central and Eastern Europe (CEE), including Hungary, had been viewed by the public and also by academia as one of the frontrunners in legal and policy compliance in the EU.[1] National judiciaries in these countries were also perceived as competent institutional actors capable of ensuring the successful reception of EU law.[2] However, this positive assessment of Central and Eastern European membership changed significantly after the global financial and economic crisis.

---

[1] On compliance see TA Börzel and U Sedelmeier, 'Larger and More Law Abiding? The Impact of Enlargement on Compliance in the European Union' (2017) 24 *Journal of European Public Policy* 197; U Sedelmeier, 'After Conditionality: Post-Accession Compliance with EU Law in East Central Europe' (2008) 15 *Journal of European Public Policy* 806; A Zhelyazkova, C Kaya and R Schrama, 'Notified and Substantive Compliance with EU Law in Enlarged Europe: Evidence from Four Policy Areas' (2017) 24 *Journal of European Public Policy* 216. See also the European Commission's Report on Monitoring the Application of Union Law (2018) COM 540, available at ec.europa.eu/info/publications/2017-commission-report-monitoring-application-eu-law_en, according to which Hungary has the 9th highest score on the number of open infringement cases.

[2] On the constitutional and judicial reception of EU law in Hungary, see M Varju and E Várnay (eds), *The Law of the European Union in Hungary: Institutions, Processes and the Law* (Budapest, HVG-ORAC, 2014); M Varju, 'The Reception of European Union Law in Hungary: The Constitutional Court and the Hungarian Judiciary' (2011) 48 *Common Market Law Review* 1945. On the judicial transformation, see M Bobek (ed), *Central European Judges Under the European Influence* (Oxford, Hart Publishing, 2015).

In Hungary, the crisis led to a change in government which brought profound changes in the domestic political, constitutional and economic system. The constitutional transformation is well documented, together with the backsliding in the implementation of democratic principles and the rule of law.[3] The 'national interest', whatever its meaning, has become the dominant factor invoked by authorities in policy making and regulation. This has led to evident conflicts with EU obligations and shed doubts as to the commitments of Hungarian institutions to comply with EU law.[4]

In our view, the tensions, and sometimes open conflicts, between Hungarian and EU policies can be linked to a general and more profound clash between Member States' policy of patriotism and the EU's allegedly neoliberal policy agenda.[5] On the one hand, some Member States and their governments, as demonstrated also by the case of post-2010 Hungary, seek to pursue local interests and gain or maintain the support of the local electorate. On the other, the European Union, as defined in the Treaties, aims to realise objectives which characteristically transcend national borders and which, necessarily, rest on some form of alignment of and/or compromise between the respective interests of the Member States. More importantly, core EU policies, such as the Internal Market, favour – although far from exclusively – market-based responses to achieve the Treaties' socio-economic objectives. Additionally, one core EU policy is the obligation of treating nationals and individuals from other Member States equally. This creates an obvious problem for national policy making which, following the government's assumed political mandate, aims to restructure national markets in favour of domestic economic operators as well as keeping foreign competition away from opportunities in the national market. In the case of Hungarian economic policy since 2010, the directions followed have already

---

[3] A von Bogdandy and P Sonnevend (eds), *Constitutional Crisis in the European Constitutional Area: Theory, Law and Politics in Hungary and Romania* (Oxford, Hart Publishing, 2015); N Chronowski and M Varju, 'Two Eras of Hungarian Constitutionalism: From the Rule of Law to Rule by Law' (2016) 8 *Hague Journal on the Rule of Law* 271; G Halmai, 'An Illiberal Constitutional System in the Middle of Europe' in W Benedek, F Benoit-Rohmer, W Karl, MC Kattemann and M Nowak (eds), *European Yearbook of Human Rights* (Vienna, Neuer Wissenschaftlicher Verlag, 2014); G Halmai, 'How the EU Can and Should Cope with Illiberal Member States' (2018) 2 *Quaderni costituzionali* 313; A Jakab and D Kochenov (eds), *The Enforcement of EU Law and Values: Ensuring Member State Compliance* (Oxford, Oxford University Press, 2017); AL Pap, *Democratic Decline in Hungary: Law and Society in an Illiberal Democracy* (Abingdon, Routledge, 2017).

[4] On the role of national interest in EU law, see M Varju, The national interest in European Union law. Paper prepared for the HPOPs Research Group, Hungarian Academy of Sciences, Centre for Social Sciences, available at https://hpops.tk.mta.hu/uploads/files/EUNatIntELJ.pdf.

[5] On neoliberalism, see VA Schmidt and M Thatcher, *Resilient Liberalism in Europe's Political Economy* (Cambridge, Cambridge University Press, 2013). The term neoliberalism is used in line with Schmidt and Thatcher as a commitment to certain core principles focused on market competition, open markets across borders, while the state should have a limited political economic role; see Schmidt and Thatcher, *Resilient Liberalism* 3–7. Orenstein defines neoliberalism in similar terms as a synonym 'economic freedom'; MA Orenstein, 'Reassessing the Neo-Liberal Development Model in Central and Eastern Europe' in Schmidt and Thatcher, *Resilient Liberalism* (2013) 8–10.

been observed as representing 'a major shift, rejecting core elements of the neoliberal policy agenda'.[6]

This contribution examines certain economic policy developments in Hungary after the global financial and economic crisis and takes stock of the measures introduced in some sectors of the Hungarian economy aiming to reshape the economic landscape and implement 'patriotic' policy objectives. This chapter focuses on Hungarian compliance with EU internal market rules, especially the freedom to provide services and the freedom of establishment.[7] We will not analyse in detail the Hungarian Government's expressed goal to increase state ownership in strategic sectors, like banking and energy. This so-called statist turn, meaning more state involvement in the economy, will only be addressed when pertaining to the regulatory policies covered by the chapter.[8]

Our analysis is structured as follows. Section II sketches out the historical and economic context of the patriotic turn in Hungary. Section III defines the concept of economic patriotism as understood by two leading scholars, Cornelia Woll and Ben Clift. Section IV introduces briefly the instruments of EU enforcement. Sections V to VIII critically examine the assumedly patriotic measures recently introduced in Hungary, by looking in turn at the monopolisation of service markets; the change of market conditions through direct taxation; the targeting of big commercial retail chains; and agricultural reforms.

II. THE CRISIS AND MORE PROACTIVE NATIONAL ECONOMIC POLICY MAKING

Economic policy in CEE Member States is organised according to a particular combination of objectives and priorities. After the collapse of communism and the planned economy, CEE national economies were starving for foreign direct investment (FDI) to rebuild, integrate local firms into the global value chain, and secure employment and growth. In the 1990s, attracting FDI was, therefore, a central and dominant objective of domestic economic and industrial policies. It continues to remain so today. As a result, CEE market economies have been classified neither as liberal market, nor as co-ordinated market economies,

---

[6] MA Orenstein, 'Reassessing the Neo-Liberal Development Model' in Schmidt and Thatcher, *Resilient Liberalism* (2013) 391.

[7] The authors discussed Hungary's stance on EU economic governance in another paper; see M Varju and M Papp, 'The Crisis, National Economic Particularism and EU Law: What Can We Learn from the Hungarian Case?' (2016) 53 *Common Market Law Review* 1647.

[8] On this topic, see M Szanyi, 'The Reversal of the Privatisation Logic in Central European Transition Economies' (2016) 66 *Acta Oeconomica* 33. See also the increase of public ownership as a strategic goal in, eg, A Byrne, 'Hungary Seeks Rapprochement with Bruised Foreign Investors' *Financial Times* (12 May 2016), available at www.ft.com/content/e0c44550-0ad2-11e6-b0f1-61f222853ff3.

but rather as FDI-dependent market economies.[9] Some sectors of the national economy, such as car manufacturing or consumer electronics, became dominated and dependent on transnational corporations.[10] Domestic firms remained the main market participants in other globally or regionally less relevant sectors. In this dualised system, highly productive foreign-owned companies exist in spaces parallel to those occupied by low-productivity, under-developed and under-invested domestic firms.[11] This structure caused Hungary and other CEE countries to be severely hit by the global financial and economic crisis, especially when inward capital flows dried out and the borrowing in international capital markets became very expensive.

Policy patriotism, as evidenced in Hungary, largely grew out of these circumstances. Nevertheless, patriotic tendencies had also characterised Hungarian policy making in earlier, more prosperous, times. Its place in the pre-crisis policy mix has been explained with reference to the prevailing ideological considerations and also to the interests of the post-1989 business elite.[12] After 2010, a clear patriotic turn became observable, characterised by commentators as representing 'the greatest departure from the neo-liberal development model yet attempted in Central and Eastern Europe'.[13] Hungary is not the only country in the world or even Europe where economic patriotism emerged as a distinctly identifiable policy direction in a post-crisis environment.[14] In fact, patriotism had long been influencing national policy making before the crisis; it only become more visible to stakeholders, the international institutions, and the general public in the turmoil after the crisis hit national economies. The crisis was labelled as a 'game changer' which brought to light 'the vulnerability of the hitherto dominant developmental model' (ie, free trade and open national economies) and which pushed national governments towards experimenting

---

[9] For varieties of capitalism, see PA Hall and D Soskice, *Varieties of Capitalism: The Institutional Foundations of Comparative Advantage* (Oxford, Oxford University Press, 2001); A Nölke and A Vliegenhart, 'Enlarging the Varieties of Capitalism, The Emergence of Dependent Market Economies in East Central Europe' (2009) 61 *World Politics* 670; B Farkas, *Models of Capitalism in the European Union* (Basingstoke, Palgrave, 2016).

[10] H Appel and MA Orenstein, *From Triumph to Crisis. Neoliberal Economic Reform In Postcommunist Countries* (Cambridge, Cambridge University Press, 2018) 166–67.

[11] B Galgóczi and J Drahokoupil, 'Abandoning the FDI-Based Economic Model Driven by Low Wages' in B Galgóczi and J Drahokoupil (eds), *Condemned to be Left Behind? Can Central and Eastern Europe Emerge from its Low-wage Model?* (Brussels, European Trade Union Institute, 2017); M Sass, 'Is a Live Dog Better than a Dead Lion? Seeking Alternative Growth Engines in the Visegrad Countries' in Galgóczi and Drahokoupil (eds), *Condemned to be Left Behind* (2017).

[12] Szanyi, 'The Reversal of the Privatisation Logic' (2016); M Szanyi, 'Impacts of the Crisis on the FDI-Led Development Model in Hungary: Emergence of Economic Patriotism or Shift from the Competition State to Patronage?' in P Havlik and I Iwasaki (eds), *Economics of European Crises and Emerging Markets* (Basingstoke, Palgrave Macmillan, 2017).

[13] Orenstein, 'Reassessing the Neo-Liberal Development Model' (2013) 395.

[14] See, eg, U Bernitz and WG Ringe (eds), *Company Law and Economic Protectionism: New Challenges to European Integration* (Oxford, Oxford University Press, 2010) and B Clift and C Woll (eds), 'Special Issue on Economic Patriotism: Political Intervention in Open Economies' (2012) 19 *Journal of European Public Policy* 307.

with alternatives.[15] Policy patriotism has also been attractive to the populist and extreme ethnocentric nationalist ideological and political agendas which have come to the fore in the past decade.[16] Politically, patriotism, as will be explained in the next section, constitutes an obvious choice for national governments.

III. NATIONAL ECONOMIC PATRIOTISM

In Clift and Woll's conceptualisation, economic patriotism is closely linked to democratic national politics and the legitimacy derived from it by national governments when they develop and implement policies for the national economy.[17] The notion is not anti-European per se; it merely reflects and reinforces the obvious fact for EU integration that the interests realised in the framework of common policies come from the national polities, just as the political mandate which keeps the Union in place. According to Clift and Woll, economic patriotism stands for national governments adopting and pursuing economic policies in the national territory which are put to the service of concerns and interests emerging in 'one's homeland'.[18] They hardly have other options: they have 'spatially limited political mandates' and their political responsibility is similarly territorially framed.[19] Put simply, the national electorate wants national governments to act in the 'national economic interest'. Furthermore, national policy-making may ignore one highly crucial circumstance at its own risk, namely that despite the impacts of globalisation and regionalisation national economies remain constructed within the confines of the State and continue to be exposed to socio-economic considerations that are locally determined.[20]

The evolution of EU integration has, however, revealed that the interests of the national economy may demand policy responses which transgress national boundaries and which do not favour exclusively domestic economic participants. EU membership, together with the domestic implementation of EU policies under binding legal obligations, may be acts of economic patriotism if that is what follows from the 'national interest'. Participation in the EU necessarily excludes certain forms of patriotism, or rather places significant institutional-legal constraints on their implementation. The EU's core policy of market

---

[15] M Naczyk, 'Budapest in Warsaw: Central European Business Elites and the Rise of Economic Patriotism Since the Crisis' (2014) available at ssrn.com/abstract=2550496 6.

[16] S Auer, 'New Europe': Between Cosmopolitan Dreams and Nationalist Nightmares' (2010) 48 *Journal of Common Market Studies* 1163.

[17] B Clift and C Woll, 'Economic Patriotism: Reinventing Control over Open Markets' (2012) 19 *Journal of European Public Policy* 307, and B Clift, 'Economic Patriotism, the Politics of Market Making, and the Role of the State in 21st Century Capitalism' in T Gerőcs (ed), *Rising Tensions between Market-Liberalism and Economic Patriotism in Capitalist Systems* (forthcoming, Palgrave Macmillan, 2019).

[18] Clift and Woll, 'Economic Patriotism' (2012) 308.

[19] ibid 310.

[20] ibid 311–12.

integration prohibits the introduction of national measures which undermine – actually or potentially – the integration of national economies and the freedom of activity and competition in the integrating market space. Its fundamental economic freedoms, like the free movement of goods, persons, services and capital, together with the rules on unrestrained competition, specifically exclude that Member States unlawfully differentiate in the formulation and implementation of policies and regulations between nationals and non-nationals or disadvantage non-nationals in other ways in the national economy.

In this framework, EU membership entails a constant conflict for national governments between their previously established European commitments, made in the national interests, and their actual political mandates and the measures introduced under those mandates. In Clift and Woll's words, there is a 'profound if not self-evident contradiction' between the actions expected from them domestically and the membership of their states in the EU, especially in the Internal Market.[21] Because they operate under territorially bound political mandates and seek re-election in the national political arena, they are under constant pressure to disengage from their EU obligations in case these prevent or excessively constrain the adoption of policy responses to legitimate local interests and needs.[22] Member State governments must also address the dilemma inherent in EU membership that the more constraints they undertake under a common policy framework, the more creative they need to be in designing and implementing local policies that satisfy both EU obligations and the relevant local interests and needs.[23]

As already indicated, economic patriotism does not have to be protectionist or exclusionary towards non-national economic actors and interests. Patriotic economic policies range from neo-liberal to illiberal and their policy tools may also range from pro-competitive and pro-FDI to protectionist, discriminatory and selective.[24] It is the national economic interest served by those policies and instruments that determines the approach taken, which can vary from sector to sector (eg, high value-added manufacturing versus tourism) and even between the different segments of a specific sector (eg, energy for private households versus energy for industrial or commercial operators). Conflicts with EU obligations may, therefore, arise only when and where the direction of economic patriotism contradicts that pursued by the relevant EU policy. Where EU obligations allow the introduction of different national policy models, permit general

---

[21] ibid 308.

[22] B Clift, 'Economic Patriotism, the Clash of Capitalisms, and State Aid in the European Union' (2013) 13 *Journal of Industry, Competition and Trade* 101, 104–05; see also AM Weaver, 'Convergence through the Crisis: State Aid Modernization & West European Varieties of Capitalism' (2015) 21 *Columbia Journal of European Law* 587, 607–08.

[23] Clift and Woll, 'Economic Patriotism' (2012) 311–12; on creative compliance, see A Batory, 'Defying the Commission: Creative Compliance and Respect for the Rule of Law in the EU' (2016) 94 *Public Administration* 685.

[24] Clift and Woll, 'Economic Patriotism' (2012) 316–18.

derogations from the main thrust of an EU policy, or regulate only minimum requirements, the chance for a significant conflict may be low. The Member States must, however, ensure that, beyond national policies and regulation, the actual practices pursued by the administration also meet EU obligations. The unrestrained or arbitrary use of public powers by national agencies, as well as the lack of effective legal redress against their decisions, may prevent entry in the domestic market or raise the costs and risks of continuing presence there in the same way as general policy and legal measures.

The following section illustrates that since 2010, Hungarian economic policy measures have often clashed with EU internal market rules requiring open, competitive markets and the non-discrimination of market players. We will first examine the formal compliance record of Hungary, as published by the European Commission, which shows a clearly worsening performance. We will then introduce short case summaries which will shed more light on the causes of Hungary's compliance performance. But first, we introduce briefly the different avenues available to the Union to monitor and enforce compliance, as the EU enforcement system also plays a role in how Member States frame their conduct under EU obligations.

IV. SCRUTINISING COMPLIANCE

The responsibility for monitoring and enforcing compliance with EU law and, in this case specifically with the Internal Market obligations, rests with the European Commission. Enforcement by the Commission is probably the most convenient for individuals as they are relieved from paying national court charges and do not bear the burden of proving the Member State's infringement.[25] However, the Commission is not obliged to proceed in infringement cases, and in case it does not, the individual is left with the option of enforcing the rights provided by the infringed EU measure before national courts. Additionally, with infringements declared by the national court, the individual can also claim damages. This can ensure that the individual is able to operate further in the national market affected.[26]

The Commission regularly publishes its Single Market Scoreboard, which shows important figures on the late transposition of directives, conformity deficit with EU internal market law, and the number of infringement procedures launched by the Commission. Hungary had traditionally been performing well with regard to the timely transposition of directives. At the end of 2017, its score

---

[25] Generally, on infringement proceedings, see L Prete, *Infringement Proceedings in EU Law* (Alphen aan den Rijn, Wolters Kluwer, 2016); K Lenaerts, I Maselis and K Gutman, *EU Procedural Law* (Oxford, Oxford University Press, 2014).

[26] Judgment of 5 March 1996, *Brasserie du Pêcheur* and *Factortame*, C-46/93 and C-48/93, EU:C:1996:79.

was three times higher than the EU average.[27] It is now among the three Member States with the lowest transposition deficit score. Regarding the correct transposition of directives, Hungary had always had a low conformity deficit compared to the EU average. This has changed since 2015 and now Hungary's conformity deficit is higher than average.[28] Its number of active infringement cases used to indicate a better performance than the EU average. Since 2017, Hungary's record has slipped slightly below average.[29] The sector most affected by infringement is services, which has overall been less integrated into the Internal Market than other sectors.[30]

The services sector infringement cases, as will be seen below in detail, concern either the monopolising of a formerly competitive market or changing market regulation to strengthen the position of domestic economic operators. Faced with the challenging task of questioning the lawfulness of national legislation, the companies affected invoked a variety of legal instruments available in EU and international law (the EU Treaties, fundamental rights, secondary law, bilateral investment treaties, etc.). They have to use these instruments strategically as EU law may not be the most appropriate tool for the protection of rights. Other avenues of redress, especially investment arbitration, may be more effective than litigation before Hungarian courts. Full compensation ordered in international arbitration may also be more effective than the remedies available in national law. The European Court of Human Rights may offer another avenue for legal redress when the right to property needs to be protected outside the scope of EU law. From the perspective of domestic litigants, it is unfortunate that EU law has been gradually squeezing out these alternative avenues of legal redress.[31] We share the concerns of Sadowski that currently in certain CEE countries the Court of Justice of the EU (CJEU) should instead broaden possibilities for legal protection and should, in particular, 'view investment treaty tribunals as potential partners, and not as foes or competitors, for the protection and promotion of the rule of law in the EU'.[32]

---

[27] See 'EU Single Market: Single Market Scoreboard' (2019) available at ec.europa.eu/internal_market/scoreboard/performance_by_member_state/hungary/index_en.htm.

[28] On Hungary's performance on compliance with EU law generally (not only internal market law), see E Várnay, 'The Hungarian Government before the Courts of the European Union: Rationales and Results' in M Varju and E Várnay (eds), *The Law of the European Union in Hungary: Institutions, Processes and the Law* (Budapest, HVG-ORAC, 2014).

[29] We also have to recognise that this change is largely due to the EU average falling sharply since 2006.

[30] According to the Single Market Scoreboard, Hungary's integration into the EU trade in goods is more than 60 per cent, while in services it is only 11 per cent, see ec.europa.eu/internal_market/scoreboard/performance_by_member_state/hungary/index_en.htm#maincontentSec11. Statistics also show that openness to trade in services is worsening.

[31] See Opinion of the Court of 18 December 2014, *Accession of the European Union to the European Convention on Human Rights*, EU:C:2014:2454 and judgment of 6 March 2018, *Slovak Republic v Achmea BV*, C-284/16, EU:C:2018:158.

[32] W Sadowski, 'The Protection of the Rule of Law in the European Union through Investment Treaty Arbitration: Is Judicial Monopolism the Right Answer?' (2018) 55 *Common Market Law Review* 1025, 1027.

Besides infringement procedures, preliminary ruling procedures have been used by national courts and litigants to enforce compliance with EU law. The number of references from Hungary indicate the willingness as well as the ability of Hungarian judges to detect possible violations of EU law, including the law of the Internal Market. Indeed, as will be evident from the case studies below, several potential mismatches of Hungarian law with the Internal Market law have been discovered and litigated before national courts.[33] The number of Hungarian preliminary references is relatively higher than those from other CEE countries.[34] As pointed out by Bobek, taking into account the size of its population, Hungary, together with Latvia, Bulgaria, Estonia and Lithuania, is the leader in terms of the total number of references sent to Luxembourg.[35] Active engagement with EU law and the open-mindedness of judges to initiate preliminary references have been crucial to the actual and effective application of EU law in Hungary.[36]

V. PATRIOTISM AND MONOPOLISING SERVICES MARKETS IN HUNGARY

This chapter's first case study on economic patriotism in Hungary is the monopolising of service markets. This section looks in turn at the restructuring of the tax-free remuneration voucher market; the creation of a national mobile payment monopoly; the establishing of gambling and betting monopolies; and the monopolisation of national school book distribution.

A. Restructuring the Tax-Free Remuneration Voucher Market

One of the first changes introduced in the Hungarian economy after the change of government in 2010 was the restructuring of the lucrative market for issuing and managing tax-free remuneration vouchers. Under the previous framework, employers could pay non-salaried, therefore tax-free, allowances in the form

---

[33] These potential infringements are evidently formulated in the preliminary questions neutrally as questions on the interpretation of EU law, see the text of Art 234 TFEU.

[34] *Annual Report 2017 on Judicial Activity* (Luxembourg, Court of Justice of the European Union, 2018) 122, available at https://curia.europa.eu/jcms/upload/docs/application/pdf/2018-04/_ra_2017_en.pdf. Hungarian courts have initiated 158 preliminary ruling procedures since accession. The figures for Bulgaria are 117 and for Poland 127: considerably lower, although the size of the countries is bigger.

[35] M Bobek, 'Talking Now: Preliminary Rulings in and from the New Member States' (2014) 21 *Maastricht Journal of European and Comparative Law* 782. Note that Hungarian lower courts, which do not have the obligation to refer, are also active in referring cases.

[36] On judges' attitudes see Z Kühn, M Matczak and M Bencze, 'EU Law and Central European Judges: Administrative Judiciaries in the Czech Republic, Hungary and Poland Ten Years after the Accession' in M Bobek (ed), *Central European Judges Under the European Influence: The Transformative Power of the EU Revisited* (Oxford, Hart Publishing, 2015).

of paper or electronic vouchers. Undertakings operating under normal market conditions organised the distribution and management of these vouchers. In 2011, the market was erased with the establishment of a State monopoly for the paper voucher market, at the same time imposing a 51 per cent tax on the vouchers issued by the market incumbents. This change was introduced without an adequate transitional period. The European Commission criticised the set-up of the new market for electronic vouchers as de facto reserved market entry for the three large banks domiciled in Hungary. The rationale of the change was openly discussed in Parliament, where the State Secretary of the Ministry of Justice asserted: 'This segment was in the hands of foreign companies. The 10 per cent profit of the market, which has a turnover of approximately 200 billion HUF, served the interests of non-Hungarian companies. With the amendment, this profit stays 100 per cent in Hungary'.[37]

Later, the CJEU struck down the Hungarian rules for violating freedom of establishment rules and the free movement of services.[38] The conditions introduced for entry into the electronic vouchers market were considered by the Court as indirectly discriminatory. In the paper vouchers market, the exclusive right granted to the State monopoly was ruled unjustified.

The foreign market incumbents, pushed completely out of the market, sought remedy through international arbitration under the French-Hungarian Bilateral Investment Treaty.[39] In this case, the arbitration tribunal of the International Centre for Settlement of Investment Disputes found that Hungary was responsible for the substantial dispossession of property (indirect expropriation) and awarded significant damages.[40]

B. The Creation of a National Mobile Payment Monopoly

The state monopoly for mobile payment for certain public services, such as public parking, was established under national law in 2011. The state-controlled undertaking has the task of establishing and operating a uniform and universal payment system, the use of which is mandatory in the case of road toll

---

[37] Our translation. See the minutes of the Hungarian National Assembly, available at www.parlament.hu/orszaggyulesi-naplo-elozo-ciklusbeli-adatai?p_auth=Vpv77frs&p_p_id=pairproxy_WAR_pairproxyportlet_INSTANCE_9xd2Wc9jP4z8&p_p_lifecycle=1&p_p_state=normal&p_p_mode=view&p_p_col_id=column-1&p_p_col_count=1&_pairproxy_WAR_pairproxyportlet_INSTANCE_9xd2Wc9jP4z8_pairAction=%2Finternet%2Fcplsql%2Fogy_naplo.naplo_fadat%3Fp_ckl%3D39%26p_uln%3D152%26p_felsz%3D90%26p_szoveg%3D%26p_felszig%3D90.

[38] Judgment of 23 February 2016, *Commission v Hungary*, C-179/14, EU:C:2016:108.

[39] ICSID Case No ARB/13/21, *Edenred SA v Hungary*; ICSID Case No ARB/13/35, *Le Chèque Déjeuner v Hungary*, ICSID Case No ARB/14/20, *Sodexo*.

[40] Only the Decision in ARB/13/35 is final: the Arbitration Tribunal did not accept the Respondent's claim to keep the profit previously realised by foreign-owned companies within Hungary as justified, para 414.5.

charges, public parking, or certain forms of public transportation. It replaced a competitive market where multiple companies offered mobile payment services contracted at local government level.

In the infringement procedure, the Court examined whether the payment service constituted a service of general economic interest (SGEI) and whether the creation of the monopoly was compatible with the Services Directive[41] and the free movement of services.[42] Hungary succeeded in part as the Commission failed to establish that the government had used its discretion erroneously when it established a uniform, continuously available and universally accessible public mobile payment system. The violation of the Services Directive was, however, established. Based on the principles of non-discrimination, necessity and proportionality, Hungary was condemned for not following a less restrictive, and, therefore, more market-friendly, solution when setting up the state monopoly, namely the granting of a concession in a competitive process.[43]

C. Establishing Gambling and Betting Monopolies

Gambling itself as an economic activity and the regulation of gambling are contentious issues not only in Hungary, but all over Europe. The national regulation of gambling activities has triggered numerous legal cases under EU law, including several infringement cases.[44] In 2017, the Commission introduced a new policy of self-restraint in this domain and announced that it would close all infringement proceedings against Member States, on the grounds that complaints can be more efficiently handled by national courts.[45] Hence, the claimants' bear the (excessive) burden of proving infringements before national courts. This recent development does not mean, however, that the changes introduced in the Hungarian market and the way they were introduced were uncontroversial or demonstrate that patriotic national policies and their implementation do not raise serious concerns about their legality.

The first step in transforming the Hungarian gambling market was the practical ban on slot machines outside licensed casinos. The legislation adopted in 2011 revoked the licences of these slot machines on the day following its entry into force. In the preliminary ruling procedure initiated by the national court

---

[41] Directive 2006/123/EC of the European Parliament and of the Council of 12 December 2006 on services in the internal market, OJ L 376, 27.12.2006.
[42] Judgment of 7 November 2018, *European Commission v Hungary*, C-171/17, EU:C:2018:881.
[43] ibid para 82.
[44] See, eg, judgment of 16 February 2012, *Marcello Costa and Ugo Cifone*, C-72/10 and C-77/10, EU:C:2012:80; judgment of 13 September 2007, *Commission v Italy*, C-260/04, EU:C:2007:508; judgment of 6 March 2007, *Placanica*, C-338/04, EU:C:2007:133.
[45] European Commission, 'Press Release: Commission closes infringement procedures and complaints in the gambling sector' (7 December 2017), available at http://europa.eu/rapid/press-release_IP-17-5109_en.htm.

dealing with the damages claim put forward by economic operators, the Court noted the basic rule of law requirement that 'if the national legislature revokes licences that allow their holders to exercise an economic activity, it must provide a transitional period of sufficient length to enable them to adapt or reasonable compensation system'.[46] It also noted that

> a trader who has made costly investments in order to comply with the scheme adopted previously by the legislature could see his interests considerably affected by the withdrawal of that scheme before the date announced, all the more so if that withdrawal takes place suddenly and unforeseeably, without leaving him enough time to adapt to the new legal situation.[47]

The referring court and later the Hungarian Supreme Court established the right to damages for a breach of freedom to provide services of the economic operators affected, the precise amount of which is still under litigation.[48]

The restructuring of the online betting market was scrutinised in more than one judgment by the CJEU. In *Sporting Odds*, the referring Hungarian court asked whether the free movement of services excludes a national provision under which the grant of a licence for the organisation of online gaming is reserved exclusively to operators of games of chance operating a casino under a concession in a national territory.[49] The Court responded that such reservation of access to the market for online games of chance constitutes an unjustified discriminatory condition contrary to EU law.

The system of granting concessions and licences for the organisation of online games of chance was also problematic. Under the current legal framework, concessions and licences can be obtained either under a call for tenders organised by the Minister for the Economy or by making an offer to the Minister for the conclusion of a concession contract. The latter possibility is open only to so-called 'trustworthy' operators. In *Unibet*, the CJEU made clear that such a system will only be justified as a proportionate and appropriate instrument of market regulation when the means used are consistent and systematic.[50] It added that the conditions for granting concessions and licences must be based on objective, non-discriminatory criteria which are known in advance and which are able to exclude the arbitrary exercise of the discretion available to the granting public authority. Additionally, the granting authority must comply with the obligation of transparency and the principle of legal certainty and its corollary, the protection of legitimate expectations. It is particularly important that the

---

[46] Judgment of 11 June 2015, *Berlington and others v Hungarian State*, C-98/14, EU:C:2015:386, para 85. The Court has also referred to the judgment of the European Court of Human Rights (ECtHR) in *Vékony v Hungary* (2015) ECHR 5.

[47] *Berlington*, C-98/14, para 87.

[48] Kúria (Supreme Court) Pfv.IV.20.211/2017/13.

[49] Judgment of 28 February 2018, *Sporting Odds Ltd*, C-3/17, EU:C:2018:130.

[50] Judgment of 22 June 2017, *Unibet International*, C-49/16, EU:C:2017:491.

conditions and the detailed rules of the award procedure are drawn up in a clear, precise and unequivocal manner. The Hungarian rules, in particular the fact that it created 'trustworthy' operators, did not satisfy any of these conditions.

D. The Monopolisation of National School Book Distribution

EU law proved to be of limited impact when the Hungarian authorities monopolised the national distribution of school books because the restriction did not involve an obvious inter-state element. As in the previously mentioned cases, a multi-operator flourishing distribution market was abolished without compensating the incumbents in the interest of establishing a state-owned distributor operating in what was to become a strictly not-for-profit market.[51]

The national avenues of legal redress proved to be ineffective. The claim to the Hungarian Constitutional Court was thrown out on admissibility grounds without an examination of the merits.[52] The damages action against the State also failed when the Supreme Court held that Hungarian law does not provide for such a remedy and that it had no jurisdiction to create one.[53]

The applicants were, however, more successful before the European Court of Human Rights, which established the violation of their right to property and awarded just satisfaction.[54] The Court of Human Rights was not persuaded by the public interest justifications raised by Hungary. The Court asserted that it is crucial in such circumstances that measures be put in place by the Contracting States to protect individuals against arbitrary State interventions, as required by the rule of law in a democratic society. The lack of judicial redress or financial

---

[51] A similar case was already decided by the ECtHR in *Vékony v Hungary* Application no 65681/13 (ECtHR 13 January 2015). The ECtHR found that Hungary had violated Convention rights by excluding economic operators from the reorganised tobacco market. The legal preparation and the actual execution of the concession process raised doubts as to whether the selection of concession holders was based on objective, transparent and relevant criteria. Para 34: 'the procedure appears to have been devoid of elementary transparency and of any possibility of legal remedies.' Para 36: 'The Court found that the measure did not offer a realistic prospect to continue the possession because the process of granting of new concessions was verging on arbitrariness, given that (i) the existence of the previous licence was disregarded; (ii) the possibility of a former licence-holder to continue tobacco retail under the changed conditions accommodating the policy of protection of minors was not considered in the new scheme; (iii) the concession system enabled the granting of five concessions to one tenderer which objectively diminished the chances of an incumbent licence holder, in particular of those individuals, such as the applicant's family, whose livelihood had depended for many years on the possibility of tobacco sale, now lost and, finally, (iv) the lack of transparent rules in the awarding of the concessions, which took place (v) without giving any privilege to a previous licence-holder, such as limiting the scope of the first round of tendering to such persons.'

[52] 3108/2014. (IV.17) Constitutional Court Order (14 April 2014).

[53] This ruling originates from another prior case and Kúria is using it as a reference in its judgments adopted later. See judgment of the Kúria no Pfv.IV.20.602/2017/5.

[54] *Könyv-Tár Kft and others v Hungary* Application no 21623/13 (ECtHR, 16 October 2018). Please note that, at the time of writing, this judgment had not yet become final.

compensation under Hungarian law meant that the applicants were exposed to an individual and excessive burden in violation of their rights under the European Convention of Human Rights.[55]

VI. PATRIOTISM AND CHANGING MARKET CONDITIONS BY TAX LAW

Direct taxation has been extensively used in implementing the patriotic turn in Hungarian economic policy. It offered a fast, effective, and controversially used tool – available to be introduced in retained national competences – for the government. The authorities set their mind on expelling foreign economic operators from certain markets and distorting competition in favour of nationals when that was dictated by the national economic interest. The applicable tax rules in EU law are mainly Treaty-based, where limited EU direct tax harmonisation takes place. Hence, it is more difficult for the Commission to detect infringements as the Commission is usually more focused on the correct implementation of secondary law. Any challenge by wronged economic operators treated as 'outsiders' comes ex post facto and remedies are served by national courts only a long time after the introduction of the tax, the negative discriminatory effects of which take place immediately.

A. Introducing an Indirectly Discriminatory Retail Tax

Sector-specific direct taxes and surtaxes were initially introduced during the crisis years as means for raising additional revenues.[56] They later became part of the Hungarian patriotic economic policy repertoire as selective components favoured domestic undertakings over their 'non-national' competitors.[57] The economic sectors affected are indicative of the inclinations of these measures: financial services, telecommunications, energy, marketing and advertisement, and retail, where markets had been opened to foreign investment relatively early on after the regime change. Evidently, there was no domestic economic interest in expelling foreign economic operators from the export-orientated high added value sectors, such as car manufacturing, the presence of which in Hungary is crucial for national employment policy.

Retail was one of the sectors where selective taxation was used to restructure a market dominated by foreign-owned large retail chains present in Hungary

---

[55] ibid paras 50 and 58.
[56] OECD, 'Economic Survey of Hungary' (2016) available at www.oecd.org/hungary/economic-survey-hungary.htm.
[57] Lendület-HPOPS Research Group, 'The Legal and Regulatory Environment for Economic Activity in Hungary: Market Access and Level Playing-field in the Single Market: A Legal Expert Review Report' (2017) available at hpops.tk.mta.hu/uploads/files/HLEE_HPOPs_2017_final-1.pdf.

via their subsidiaries. Their domestic competitors are smaller in size and rely on franchises to build up their chains. This organisational difference (single subsidiary of an international group versus a franchise network of small and medium sized undertakings) was directly exploited when drafting patriotic sector-specific tax measures. The retail tax introduced was a steeply progressive tax applied on the turnover of companies linked to each other. The tax base was calculated on the basis of the turnover of a group of companies.

When challenged before national courts, a reference was made to the CJEU raising the question of whether the calculation method indirectly discriminated between non-national retailers (usually belonging to a group of companies and having, as a result, a larger tax base) and their national competitors (organised through the franchise format in such a way that the new law provided a considerably smaller tax base).

In *Hervis*, the Grand Chamber of the CJEU accepted the possibility of indirect tax discrimination and instructed the referring national court to verify whether the taxable persons belonging to a group of companies and covered by the highest band of the special tax were, in the majority of cases, linked to companies which have their registered offices in other Member States.[58] The Court noted that the application of the steeply progressive scale of the retail tax to a consolidated tax base consisting of turnover is liable to disadvantage taxable persons linked to companies which have their registered office in another Member State.[59] Hungary abolished the tax before the Court gave its preliminary ruling. The referring national court, based on the Court's ruling, established that the retail tax was liable to give rise to indirect discrimination and squashed the tax authority's prior decision ordering the payment by the claimant of the tax.[60]

B. State Aid and Selective Sectoral Taxation

The selective nature of Hungarian sector-specific taxes has also been investigated by the Commission under EU state aid law. The Commission found that their selective application was incompatible with Internal Market rules. The tax introduced in the advertising industry was struck down by the Commission on the ground that it provided unjustified advantages to smaller undertakings producing low turnovers in the Hungarian market.[61] The Commission

---

[58] Judgment of 5 February 2014, *Hervis Sport- és Divatkereskedelmi*, C-385/12, EU:C:2014:47.
[59] ibid para 39.
[60] Judgment of the Székesfehérvári Közigazgatási és Munkaügyi Bíróság (7 November 2014), available at szekesfehervaritorvenyszek.birosag.hu/sajtokozlemeny/20141107/itelet-szuletett-hervis-ugyben.
[61] Commission Decision 2017/329 of 4 November 2016 on the measure SA.39235 (2015/C) (ex 2015/NN) implemented by Hungary on the taxation of advertisement turnover [2017] OJ L49/36–49.

also found that the general interest aims raised in defence of the measure were unable to justify its steeply progressive nature which, in effect, singled out one of the major, foreign-owned players in the national media market. The similarly progressive tax introduced in the tobacco industry and in the food retail sector received, on analogous grounds, a similar legal treatment from the Commission.[62]

VII. PATRIOTISM AND TARGETING BIG COMMERCIAL RETAIL CHAINS

As part of the government's strategy, Hungarian legislation prohibited retailers selling rapid turnover goods, such as groceries, to operate at a loss for two consecutive years.[63] This provision effectively prevented expanding retailers to deduct expansion costs from their profit. The Commission launched an infringement procedure on this matter. Hungary modified the measure after the adoption of the reasoned opinion which asserted that the ban was contrary to the freedom of establishment and the free movement of capital.[64]

Large retailers also have a vital interest in building further large-size retail outlets. Legislation introduced to restrict the size of outlets gave the responsible minister complete discretion to grant planning licences in individual cases as an exemption from the restriction.[65] The minister's decision could not be

---

[62] Commission Decision (EU) 2016/1846 of 4 July 2016 on the measure SA.41187 (2015/C) (ex 2015/NN) implemented by Hungary on the health contribution of tobacco industry businesses [2016] OJ L282/43 and Commission Decision (EU) 2016/1848 of 4 July 2016 on the measure SA.40018 (2015/C) (ex 2015/NN) implemented by Hungary on the 2014 Amendment to the Hungarian food chain inspection fee [2016] OJ L282/63. Another pending case concerns the particular sanctions of failure to register in the national register established for the purposes of paying the advertising tax. See request for a preliminary ruling from the Fővárosi Közigazgatási és Munkaügyi Bíróság (Hungary) lodged on 24 July 2018, *Google Ireland*, C-482/18 (pending). One of the questions raised by the national court (beside rule of law questions) is whether the free movement of services provision and the prohibition on discrimination can be interpreted as precluding a Member State's tax legislation in which the penalty provisions require, for breach of the obligation to register for the purposes of an advertisement tax, the imposition of a fine for failure to comply, the total amount of which, for companies not established in Hungary, can be 2,000 times greater than the amount of the fine for companies established in Hungary. Discriminatory taxation of goods is the subject of a pending Commission infringement case in which reasoned opinion challenged the Hungarian tax exemption from the public health tax to fruit distillates as well as to herbal drinks where national production is dominant. As similar goods are not exempted, Hungary is deemed to be in violation of its obligations under Article 110 TFEU, see European Commission, 'Fact Sheet: May Infringement Package' (17 May 2018) available at europa.eu/rapid/press-release_MEMO-18-3446_en.htm.

[63] Act CXII of 2014 on the amendment of Act CLXIV of 2005 on commerce. The ban applied only to retailers having a net turnover higher than 15 billion HUF. Low turnover retailers were not subject to the ban.

[64] European Commission, 'Fact Sheet: July Infringement Package' (13 July 2017), available at europa.eu/rapid/press-release_MEMO-17-1935_en.htm. Hungary modified the Act on Commerce and the compulsory suspension of the commercial activity was deleted from the Act. All proceedings based on this ban ceased. See Act LXVIII of 2018 on the amendment on the Act of Commerce.

[65] Act LXXVII of 1997 on the construction of built environment and its protection.

challenged before the courts in judicial review. Public records obtained after freedom of information litigation revealed that licences had only been granted to nationals and that applications by foreign-owned undertakings had all been rejected.

Based on complaints, the Commission investigated the minister's licensing practice and asked for information from the Hungarian authorities. Quickly afterwards, Hungary amended the licensing framework so that licensing decisions made by an administrative authority can be challenged in judicial review.[66] As in the previous cases, the problem with the planning restriction was not that it aimed to impose limitations on economic activity in the general interest, but that the powers granted were open to be, and may have been, used to favour national economic operators. As the minister's decisions were taken in complete secrecy, it took years to gain reliable information on the discriminatory use of administrative competences and for the Commission to investigate the issue.

VIII. PATRIOTISM AND AGRICULTURAL LAND

The ownership and use of agricultural land are sensitive social and political issues in Hungary. The protection of the interests of nationals from the undesirable consequences of freedom of movement had been on the political agenda since the beginning of accession talks. The 2013 legislation was introduced with the clear intention of keeping non-nationals out of the domestic agricultural property market. It introduced strict conditions on the acquisition and use of agricultural land, under the declared aim of protecting farmers.[67] It retained earlier legislation's complete ban on the acquisition of land by legal entities and imposed the strict condition that the owner must farm the land themselves.[68] The measure also regulated the right of usufruct, which can no longer be created by contract, and provided – controversially – that any existing right of usufruct shall be extinguished by law unless the usufructuary is a close family relation of the land owner. This latter requirement meant that previously held usufruct rights by non-nationals were almost completely extinguished without any

---

[66] Under the new framework, the administrative agency must ask the Opinion of a Ministerial Committee, see Government Decree 5/2015 (I.29.).

[67] Act CXXII of 2013 on transactions in agricultural and forestry land.

[68] The European Commission triggered infringement proceedings against Hungary in 2016. In its reasoned opinion, it stated that the complete ban on the acquisition of land by legal entities and the obligation to farm the land by the farmers themselves are not necessary and proportionate under the freedom of establishment and free movement of capital rules; see European Commission, 'Press Release – Financial services: Commission requests Bulgaria, Hungary, Latvia, Lithuania and Slovakia to comply with EU rules on the acquisition of agricultural land' (26 May 2016), available at europa.eu/rapid/press-release_IP-16-1827_en.htm. The European Commission has triggered proceedings against four other CEE countries.

legislation requiring the payment of compensation. In the Hungarian Constitutional Court's view, this legislative hiatus did not raise any constitutional problem since the general rules of civil law are available to claimants to secure any compensation due.[69]

The CJEU had a distinctively more negative legal opinion of Hungary's treatment of holders of usufruct rights. Its Grand Chamber held that the national measure placed foreign nationals at a disadvantage compared to Hungarian nationals.[70] It further rejected that the requirement of 'having close family ties' constituted a necessary and proportionate restriction supported by public interest aims. It emphasised in particular that the Hungarian measure places on those usufructuaries the burden of having to pursue the recovery, by means of procedures that may prove lengthy and expensive, of any compensation which might be payable to them by the landowner. Indeed, those rules of civil law, which are moreover not mentioned by the legislation at issue in the main proceedings, do not make it easy to determine whether compensation will in fact be obtainable at the end of such procedures or disclose the nature of the compensation. Nor do the usufructuaries have the assurance that they will be able to obtain full compensation for the loss that they have sustained, in particular in the event of insolvency of the owner of the land to which the usufruct relates.[71]

The Commission also launched an infringement procedure to investigate whether the Hungarian measure, beside the free movement of capital, also violated the right to property protected in the EU Charter of Fundamental Rights.[72] The CJEU's forthcoming ruling on this matter is likely to be the first case when a Charter's violation is examined separately from a violation of the fundamental freedoms.[73]

---

[69] Hungarian Constitutional Court decision 25/2015 (21.VII).

[70] Judgment of 6 March 2018, *'SEGRO' and Günther Horváth*, C-52/16 and C-113/16, EU:C:2018:157. Public policy goals are frequently invoked by Member States. In this case, the Hungarian Government relied on the goals of supporting viable and competitive agriculture, preventing depopulation, preventing fraud and on the fact that the land is owned by the farmer themselves.

[71] ibid para 91. The restrictions are still in force at the time of writing. The Parliament has adopted an amendment under which registration into the land registry of the debated usufruct rights is subject to a national court ruling. Furthermore, should the national court positively decide on the existence of the usufruct right, the land registry has the obligation to inform the public prosecutor before registering the right. The Attorney General has the obligation to investigate in each case whether the usufruct right was lawfully obtained under the law in force at the time of filing the original land registry application. See Act CXXXVI of 2018, sections 108(4) and (5).

[72] In *'SEGRO' and Günther Horváth*, C-52/16 and C-113/16, the Court did not find it necessary to answer the national court's question in this regard, para 128. See also the Commission's infringement procedure in *Commission v Hungary*, C-235/17 (pending), in which the Commission requested the Court to rule on the compatibility of the Hungarian legislation with the right to property guaranteed by Article 17 of the Charter of Fundamental Rights of the European Union.

[73] Opinion of AG Saugmandsgaard of 29 November 2018, *Commission v Hungary*, C-235/17, EU:C:2018:971.

IX. CONCLUSIONS

Hungarian economic policy patriotism must be assessed – in law and in other disciplines – while bearing in mind that the national economy has an essentially dualised structure and, correspondingly, the national economic interest pursues two opposing directions. First, in the segment of the Hungarian economy where investment, production and employment are provided by foreign-owned enterprises, the government has striven to keep markets and competition open and to proactively promote free economic activity. Second, outside this domain, where foreign investment does not promise such strategic advantages, the government has been keen to promote national ownership and national economic presence, often through heavy state involvement, and has intervened to restructure the markets affected accordingly. Both of these approaches are patriotic in the broad sense as they give effect to the local economic interest under the territorially bound political mandate of the government. It is mostly the latter type of exclusionary and discriminatory patriotism which raises a problem in the light of EU Internal Market law. This has led to several legal challenges under the different avenues available for monitoring and enforcing EU obligations.

Hungary's transparent aims – of promoting national champions, keeping certain markets national, and expelling non-nationals or restricting their market positions otherwise – have brought to light deep-rooted ideological divisions between the Internal Market as a core EU policy and the economic policy of one of the Member States. There is a stark contrast between the neoliberal ideas of free movement and competition fostered by the EU internal market rules and the vision of a more nationalised and inward-looking economy in Hungary, as dictated by the national economic interest in specific segments of the national economy.[74] In the affected markets, patriotic Hungarian economic policy does not allow the invisible hand of the competitive process to select winners and losers, rather it is the State which makes that choice. In this regard, the government seems to have taken decisions while being conscious of the prevailing EU legal framework: it intervened more readily and intensively in sectors, where Treaty prohibitions provide the only legal constraint, than in harmonised sectors. The authorities seemingly anticipated that EU enforcement would be more sluggish or less guarded in non-harmonised sectors.

The EU's response to undesirable economic policy patriotism in Hungary has been mixed. A lapse of time was necessary to establish that instead of bumping into EU restraints in isolated cases, Hungary – a Member State with a

---

[74] On the resilience of neoliberalism, see VA Schmidt and M Thatcher, *Resilient Liberalism*. On the other hand, Hungary expressly embraced unorthodox economic policies coupled with illiberalism. On illiberalism and society, see AL Pap, *Democratic Decline in Hungary* (Abingdon, Routledge, 2018).

formerly exemplary general compliance record – was following a general policy direction in stark contrast with its EU obligations in the Internal Market. More importantly, EU enforcement appears to be more effective and confident where the implementation of national policy involves obvious violations of rule of law requirements, such as legal certainty, judicial redress and the denial of compensation for wronged individuals, or where it involves arbitrary and potentially abusive use of public powers. The national enforcement of EU obligations is markedly more effective when the violation of EU law also entails the breach of fundamental rights, protected in the EU Charter and in the European Convention of Human Rights, or the violation of bilateral investment treaties. Under these separate legal frameworks, additional avenues of legal redress may be available to individuals for whom the national legal order does not provide access to remedy.

Part III

Case Studies on Migration and Free Movement of People

6

Schengen, Migration – and the Resurrection of the Westphalian Nation-State?

PETER THALMANN*

I. INTRODUCTION

A. Fashion and Function of Border Control

OVER THE PAST few years, border control has again become a reality not just beyond or on the outskirts of the European continent, but at the geographical heart of the European Union (EU) and the Schengen Area. A couple of years ago widespread reinstatement of border control would have seemed almost unimaginable.[1] However, in the wake of the 2015–16 migration crisis, a substantial number of EU Member States, as well as Schengen-associated states, have reintroduced temporary controls along their borders with other Member States. These states are Austria, Belgium, Denmark, France, Germany, Hungary, Norway, Slovenia and Sweden. Borders are thus very much *en vogue* these days, or so it seems.

From a sober legal perspective, state borders demarcate the territorial limits of a state's enforcement jurisdiction.[2] As such, they embody the spatial confines – and allow for the existence – of distinct political entities.[3] Borders and their control or even physical fortification may serve as customs or other

---

*The author is grateful to the editors, Anna Khalfaoui, Dr Evangelia (Lilian) Tsourdi and an anonymous reviewer for their most helpful comments received on earlier versions of this chapter.
[1] K Groenendijk, 'Reinstatement of Controls at the Internal Borders of Europe: Why and Against Whom?' (2004) 10 *European Law Journal* 150, 169.
[2] See generally, from the perspective of public international law, J Crawford, *Brownlie's Principles of Public International Law*, 8th edn (Oxford, Oxford University Press, 2012) 456 ff (478 ff); from a German constitutional law perspective, see DE Khan, *Die deutschen Staatsgrenzen* (Tübingen, Mohr Siebeck, 2004) 28 ff.
[3] *cf* already G Jellinek, *Allgemeine Staatslehre*, 5th reprint of 3rd edn (Berlin, Springer, 1929) 394 ff (395 f).

110 *Peter Thalmann*

trade barriers, as well as provide protection against acts of military aggression, against cross-border crime, or against irregular outward or inward migration. Border control and fortification make existing[4] state borders and their essentially obstructive function more visible.

B. A Clash of Cultures of Sorts: Westphalia vs Schengen

Historically, while the Peace of Westphalia (1648) has been said to have 'made the territorial [or nation] state the cornerstone of the modern state system',[5] European states only started to attach greater value to overseeing their borders and establish systematic barriers to inward migration around the end of the nineteenth century.[6] Accordingly, if there has ever been a 'Westphalian culture of border control',[7] it certainly has to be a comparatively young phenomenon. This phenomenon arguably reached its zenith in the decades after World War II.[8] Its gradual decay then found expression, in particular, in the 1985 Schengen Agreement and the 1990 Schengen Implementing Convention.[9]

More generally, the Westphalian model posits that every sovereign state should, within its defined territorial boundaries, exercise governmental powers, without interference by external (ecclesiastical or secular) authority.[10] This model is hardly compatible with the emergence of supranational entities and, therefore, with the process of post-World War II European integration.[11]

---

[4] See R Zaiotti, *Cultures of Border Control* (Chicago, The University of Chicago Press, 2011) ix, according to whom 'talk of the *rebordering* of world affairs … can be misleading, for they imply that borders have … disappeared from the political map. But clearly they have not. While globalising processes might have rendered them less visible and politically salient, borders have maintained a pivotal role in defining who can move what, where, and when around the world.'

[5] HJ Morgenthau, *Politics Among Nations: The Struggle for Power and Peace*, 4th edn (New York, Knopf, 1967) 264, cited after B Fassbender, 'Westphalia, Peace of (1648)' in R Wolfrum (ed), *The Max Planck Encyclopedia of Public International Law* (Oxford, Oxford University Press, 2012) para 18.

[6] F Pastore, 'Visas, Borders, Immigration: Formation, Structure, and Current Evolution of the EU Entry Control System' in N Walker (ed), *Europe's Area of Freedom, Security and Justice* (Oxford, Oxford University Press, 2004) 89 f; Zaiotti, *Cultures* (2011) 46 ff. Compare also Jellinek, *Staatslehre* (1929) 395 ('keine Staatsdefinition vom 16. bis ins 19. Jahrhundert hinein etwas von einem den Staate wesentlichen festen Gebiet weiß').

[7] Zaiotti, *Cultures* (2011) 45 ff.

[8] *cf* Zaiotti, *Cultures* (2011) 47.

[9] Agreement between the Governments of the States of the Benelux Economic Union, the Federal Republic of Germany and the French Republic on the gradual abolition of checks at their common borders [2000] OJ L239/13 and Convention implementing the Schengen Agreement of 14 June 1985 between the Governments of the States of the Benelux Economic Union, the Federal Republic of Germany and the French Republic on the gradual abolition of checks at their common borders [2000] OJ L239/19.

[10] See generally on the epochal religious, territorial and other constitutional arrangements established by the Peace of Westphalia, Fassbender, 'Westphalia, Peace of (1648)' (2012) and R Grote, 'Westphalian System' in R Wolfrum (ed), *The Max Planck Encyclopedia of Public International Law* (Oxford, Oxford University Press, 2012).

[11] In the same vein Grote, 'Westphalian System' (2012) para 3; see also Zaiotti, *Cultures* (2011) 58 ff.

By means of the founding or accession treaties and the series of revision treaties up until the 2009 Lisbon Treaty, every Member State has conferred political powers of remarkable scope and scale onto the EU. As early as 1963 and 1964,[12] the Court of Justice made very clear that the law of (what today is) the EU is directly effective and supreme over conflicting provisions of domestic law.[13] What began with market integration gradually affected other, politically more sensitive, areas such as economic and monetary policy, partially foreign affairs and defence, and not least justice and home affairs (including the eventual supranationalisation of border control). Accordingly, commentators have described the process of European integration as having brought the Westphalian era to an end.[14]

Against this background, the recent re-establishment of border controls within – and effectively (partially) suspending – the Schengen Area may be perceived as a resurrection of the essentially state-centred 'Westphalian culture of border control'. Yet more fundamentally, it may also be understood as a resurrection of the Westphalian territorial (or nation) state *as such* and also as evidence of a, momentary or perhaps permanent, weakening of the European integration process *as a whole*. Member States may no longer be willing to trust and unquestioningly accept the EU's political authority on border control. Consequently, law and order as well as internal security as traditional core functions of the nation-state come into play.[15]

C. Aim and Structure of the Chapter

This chapter addresses the question of whether the widespread departure from open EU internal borders in the wake of the 2015–16 migration crisis has been a suitable and necessary response to 'a serious threat to public policy or internal security', as provided in the Schengen Borders Code[16] (SBC) – or rather populist, and unlawful, national politicking at the expense of integration.

---

[12] Judgment of 5 February 1963, *van Gend en Loos*, 26/62, EU:C:1963:1; judgment of 15 July 1964, *Costa/ENEL*, 6/64, EU:C:1964:66.

[13] Here and subsequently, 'Court of Justice' means (what today is) the 'Court of Justice of the European Union', as established by Art 19(1) TEU (n 25 below).

[14] Grote, 'Westphalian System' (2012) para 3; *cf* also J Monar, 'The Area of Freedom, Security and Justice' in A von Bogdandy and J Bast (eds), *Principles of European Constitutional Law*, 2nd rev edn (Oxford, Hart Publishing, 2009) 552 f.

[15] Monar, 'Area of Freedom, Security and Justice' (2009) 552 f; N Walker, 'In Search of the Area of Freedom, Security and Justice: A Constitutional Odyssey' in N Walker (ed), *Europe's Area of Freedom, Security and Justice* (Oxford, Oxford University Press, 2004) 16. On state functions/tasks generally, see M Brenner, 'Staatsaufgaben' in O Depenheuer and C Grabenwarter (eds), *Verfassungstheorie* (Tübingen, Mohr Siebeck, 2010) paras 11 f, 52 f.

[16] Regulation (EU) 2016/399 of the European Parliament and of the Council of 9 March 2016 on a Union Code on the rules governing the movement of persons across borders (Schengen Borders Code) [2016] OJ L77/1.

I first outline the political and legal status of open internal borders. I argue that open internal borders are not just a minor supplement to the free movement (internal market) rights, but an achievement of distinct constitutional value that must not be sacrificed easily (section II). I then turn to the requirements for the lawful reintroduction of internal border control. Here I indicate that the Member States have been given – or, more accurately, have retained for themselves – ample scope for action as a consequence of particularly broad and vaguely defined terms in the SBC (section III). I assess whether the migration crisis (section IV) and its actual or potential ramifications – such as an administrative or financial overload of individual Member States, a frustration of their efforts in the management of irregular migration, or a threat of terrorism or other serious crime – may have fulfilled the legal requirements for the reintroduction of internal border control. Does the migration crisis constitute a serious threat to public policy or internal security (section V)? Does the re-establishment of internal border control comply with the principle of proportionality (section VI)? Conclusions end the chapter. Here, I offer a succinct assessment of whether the suggested signs of a resurrection of the Westphalian nation-state have some merit (section VII).

II. LEGAL AND POLITICAL STATUS OF OPEN INTERNAL BORDERS

Pursuant to Article 22 SBC, 'Internal borders may be crossed at any point without a border check on persons, irrespective of their nationality, being carried out.' Article 22 SBC thus, in principle, abolishes all controls[17] at the internal borders of the Schengen Area, of which most Member States,[18] as well as, due to their respective association agreements, Iceland, Liechtenstein, Norway and Switzerland[19] are part.[20] Article 23 SBC adds important clarifications regarding,

---

[17] Pursuant to Art 2(10) SBC, 'border control' consists of both 'border checks' and 'border surveillance'. Art 2(11) SBC clarifies that border checks 'means the checks carried out at border crossing points, *to ensure that persons*, including their means of transport and the objects in their possession, *may be authorised to enter the territory* of the Member States' (emphasis added). Border surveillance, in contrast, 'means the *surveillance of borders between border crossing points* ... in order to prevent persons from circumventing border checks' (Art 2[12] SBC, emphasis added).
[18] While 'the Schengen *acquis* ... shall be regarded as an *acquis* which must be accepted in full by all States candidates for admission [into the EU]' (Art 7 of Protocol [No] 19 on the Schengen Acquis [2016] OJ C202/290), a number of Member States still are not part of the Schengen Area. For different reasons, an exemption applies to Bulgaria, Croatia, Cyprus, Ireland, Romania and the UK, see S Peers, *EU Justice and Home Affairs Law, Volume I: EU Immigration and Asylum Law*, 4th edn (Oxford, Oxford University Press, 2016) 26–37, 87–91.
[19] Peers, *EU Justice* (2016) 37–39, 90 f.
[20] Art 22 SBC is complemented by Art 24(1) SBC, according to which 'Member States shall remove all obstacles to fluid traffic flow at road crossing-points at internal borders, in particular any speed limits not exclusively based on road-safety considerations'. According to Art 24(2) SBC, 'Member States shall [at the same time] be prepared to provide for facilities for checks in the event that internal border controls are reintroduced'.

in particular, police controls in (internal) border areas. The latter are permissible as long as they do not have effects equivalent to border checks.[21]

While the internal market programme had served as a catalyst,[22] the removal of internal border control initially had to be established outside the Community legal system by means of the 1985 Schengen Agreement and the 1990 Schengen Implementing Convention.[23] In contrast, the SBC as it stands today is validly based upon Article 77 TFEU.[24] Article 77 TFEU explicitly confers onto the EU the task – and the corresponding legislative competence – to 'develop a policy with a view to … ensuring the absence of any controls on persons, whatever their nationality, when crossing internal borders'. Additionally, Article 3 TEU, which sets out the EU's overarching objectives, provides that the 'Union shall offer its citizens an area of freedom, security and justice without internal frontiers, in which the free movement of persons is ensured'.[25] It is certainly not fortuitous, as stressed by Craig, 'that mention of the area of freedom, security, and justice has moved up the list to become Article 3(2) TEU, thereby signifying its centrality to EU policy' as a whole.[26] Importantly, open internal borders today are not presented as being just accessory to the internal market, but as self-sufficient legal value in their own right.[27] Internal border checks are prohibited as such; regardless of whether they may undermine the fundamental economic freedoms of the Treaty.[28]

---

[21] Art 23(a) SBC specifies four criteria to that end. The Court of Justice provided clarification in judgment of 22 June 2010, *Melki and Abdeli*, C-188/10 and C-189/10, EU:C:2010:363 and in judgment of 19 July 2012, *Adil*, C-278/12 PPU, EU:C:2012:508. For comment, see G Cornelisse, 'What's Wrong with Schengen? Border Disputes and the Nature of Integration in the Area without Internal Borders' (2014) 51 *Common Market Law Review* 741, 761–63; Peers, *EU Justice* (2016) 106–08. See also the more recent judgment of 21 June 2017, *A*, C-9/16, EU:C:2017:483 and section VI.C below.

[22] *cf* Commission, 'Completing the Internal Market: White Paper from the Commission to the European Council' COM (85) 310 final, paras 24 f. See also J Monar, 'The Dynamics of Justice and Home Affairs: Laboratories, Driving Factors and Costs' (2001) 39 *Journal of Common Market Studies* 747, 754–56; Pastore, 'Visas' (2004) 94 f.

[23] See n 9 above. It was not until the entry into force of the Amsterdam Treaty in May 1999 that the Member States conferred onto the (then) European Community explicit legislative competence over internal border issues; *cf* Peers, *EU Justice* (2016) 72–74.

[24] Consolidated Version of the Treaty on the Functioning of the European Union [2016] OJ C202/47.

[25] Consolidated Version of the Treaty on European Union [2016] C202/13.

[26] P Craig, *The Lisbon Treaty: Law, Politics, and Treaty Reform* (Oxford, Oxford University Press, 2010) 337; in a similar vein Monar, 'Area of Freedom, Security and Justice' (2009) 554. In contrast, since the entry into force of the Lisbon Treaty, the tasks of establishing an internal market and an EMU feature only after in Art 3(3) and (4), respectively.

[27] *cf* also D Thym, 'Legal Framework for Entry and Border Controls' in K Hailbronner and D Thym (eds), *EU Immigration and Asylum Law: A Commentary*, 2nd edn (Munich, CH Beck, 2016) para 3.

[28] This being said, checks at internal borders to ensure that persons are authorised to enter the territory of a Member State (see n 17) may not only run counter to Art 22 SBC, but at the same time make the exercise of the fundamental freedoms less attractive. As long as checks follow the rules set out in the SBC (see section III below), it can only be the substance of the latter – and not the individual Member State measure – that may be checked for compliance with the internal market rules.

Seen in perspective, Article 22 SBC constitutes both the starting point and the nucleus of all efforts of integration made within the Area of Freedom, Security and Justice (AFSJ),[29] which, taken as a whole, is also responsible for the present-day EU showing traits not only of an economic, but a broader political union. Having regard to the 2015–16 migration crisis and the resulting reinstatement of border checks by a substantial number of Member States, the political (and symbolic) value of open internal borders has explicitly been emphasised not only by the supranational European Commission,[30] but also by the intergovernmental European Council.[31] Similarly, the European Parliament and the Council in the preamble to the SBC proclaim that the 'creation of an area in which the free movement of persons across internal borders is ensured is one of the main achievements of the Union'.[32]

III. LEGAL REQUIREMENTS FOR REINTRODUCING INTERNAL BORDER CONTROL

A. Common Denominator and Constitutional Embedding

In spite of the paramount legal and political status of open borders within the Schengen Area, Member States are not entirely prohibited from reintroducing internal border control.[33] Articles 25–30 SBC set out three exceptions to the basic rule that is Article 22 SBC.[34] In any of these three constellations, outlined subsequently,[35] a fundamental and overarching precondition for the reintroduction of internal border control is that there must be 'a serious threat to public policy or internal security in a Member State'.[36] The precise meaning of that phrase, as well as the various proportionality requirements established by Articles 25–30 SBC, are respectively discussed in sections V and VI.

See D Ehlers, 'Allgemeine Lehren der Grundfreiheiten' in D Ehlers (ed), *Europäische Grundrechte und Grundfreiheiten*, 4th edn (Berlin, de Gruyter, 2014) para 108; also *cf* T Kingreen, 'Fundamental Freedoms' in A von Bogdandy and J Bast (eds), *Principles of European Constitutional Law*, 2nd revised edn (Oxford, Hart Publishing, 2011) 543.

[29] Monar, 'Dynamics' (2001) 750–52; Pastore, 'Visas' (2004) 95; also *cf* Cornelisse, 'What's Wrong with Schengen?' 741, 748.

[30] See Commission, 'Back to Schengen – A Roadmap', COM (2016) 120 final.

[31] *cf* the conclusions of the European Council meeting of 19 October 2017, EUCO 14/17, 4 ('commitment to the Schengen system and … intention to get "Back to Schengen" as soon as possible').

[32] Recital 22 SBC.

[33] On the notion of 'border control' and 'border checks', respectively, see n 17 above.

[34] Arts 31–35 SBC contain additional rules on information, reporting and confidentiality.

[35] Subsections B, C, and D below.

[36] Slightly differently, Art 29(1) SBC (see below, subsection D) requires there to be 'a serious threat to public policy or internal security within the area without internal border control or within parts thereof'.

On the level of primary law, the exemption clauses within Articles 25–30 SBC are supported by Article 72 TFEU. According to Article 72, 'This Title' – namely the tasks and competences conferred on the EU as regards the AFSJ – 'shall not affect the exercise of the responsibilities incumbent upon Member States with regard to the maintenance of law and order and the safeguarding of internal security.' Similarly, Article 4(2) TEU demands that the EU 'shall respect [Member States'] essential State functions, including … maintaining law and order and safeguarding national security. In particular, national security remains the sole responsibility of each Member State.'[37] Taken together, these primary as well as secondary law provisions appear as carefully placed 'safeguard clauses' in support of the – perhaps not *that* dated – Westphalian nation-state and its continuing ability to perform its core functions within its own territorial boundaries.[38]

B. Foreseeable Cases

Under Article 25(1) SBC, a 'Member State may exceptionally reintroduce border control at all or specific parts of its internal borders for a limited period of up to 30 days'. While the Member State has to assess the proportionality of the measure envisaged (Article 26 SBC),[39] no authorisation by the EU institutions is needed. Article 27(1) SBC only requires the Member State to notify and submit relevant information to the Commission and the other Member States at the latest four weeks before the planned reintroduction. Concurrently, the information shall be submitted to the European Parliament and the Council.[40] Where proportionate, controls may be prolonged for renewable periods of up to 30 days, up to a total of six months.[41]

Prior to the migration crisis, Member States had used the 'general framework for the temporary reintroduction of border control at internal borders' – now Article 25 SBC – with regard to, in particular: political summit meetings (such as G7/G8 summits, NATO summits, or the visit of the US President to Estonia) and major sports events (European Football Championships), but also Nobel Peace Prize ceremonies or visits of the 'Hells Angels' to the Icelandic Motorcycle Club.[42]

---

[37] Art 72 TFEU and Art 4(2) TEU are further discussed in sections V and VI below.
[38] See text at and references in n 15 above. Also see Y Pascouau, 'The Schengen Governance Package: The Subtle Balance between Community Method and Intergovernmental Approach' (2013) available at www.epc.eu/pub_details.php?cat_id=1&pub_id=4011 3 ('sovereignty clause').
[39] On proportionality, see section VI below.
[40] Art 27(2) SBC.
[41] Art 25(3) and (4) SBC, respectively.
[42] Commission, 'Member States' notifications of the temporary reintroduction of border control at internal borders pursuant to Article 25 *et seq.* of the Schengen Borders Code' (ec.europa.eu/home-affairs/sites/homeaffairs/files/what-we-do/policies/borders-and-visas/schengen/reintroduction-border-control/docs/ms_notifications_-_reintroduction_of_border_control_en.pdf).

C. Cases Requiring Immediate Action

Article 28(1) SBC sets out that where 'immediate action [needs] to be taken, the Member State concerned may ... immediately reintroduce border control at internal borders, for a limited period of up to 10 days.' Again no authorisation by the EU institutions is needed, but Article 28(2) SBC adds that the Member State 'shall at the same time notify the other Member States and the Commission'. If deemed proportionate, controls may be prolonged for renewable periods of up to 20 days, up to a total of two months.[43]

Prior to the migration crisis, internal border control was only rarely based on (what is now) Article 28 SBC. A prominent example is the checks carried out by France along its border with Italy in April 2011. The checks were a response to Italy issuing temporary residence permits on humanitarian grounds to some 25,000 mostly Tunisian migrants who had arrived in Italy in the wake of the Arab Spring. The Italian residence permits gave an automatic right to move freely within the Schengen Area.[44] (Importantly, the dispute between Italy and France exhibited a lack of clarity as to the criteria under which temporary border control could be reintroduced more generally and eventually led to significant amendments of the SBC through Regulation 1051/2013.[45] The amendments are discussed elsewhere in this chapter.[46]) Another notable example of urgent action is the reactions of Norway and Sweden to the bomb explosion in Oslo and the shooting on the island of Utøya in July 2011.[47]

D. Cases Where the Overall Functioning of the Area Without Internal Border Control is Put at Risk

Article 29(1) SBC enables the Member States to reintroduce internal border control in 'exceptional circumstances, where the overall functioning of the area without internal border control is put at risk as a result of persistent serious

---

[43] Art 28(3) and (4) SBC. On proportionality, see section VI below.
[44] S Carrera, E Guild, M Merlino and J Parkin, 'A Race against Solidarity: The Schengen Regime and the Franco-Italian Affair' (2011) available at www.ceps.eu/system/files/book/2011/04/The%20Franco-Italian%20Affair.pdf.
[45] Regulation (EU) 1051/2013 of the European Parliament and of the Council of 22 October 2013 amending Regulation (EC) No 562/2006 in order to provide for common rules on the temporary reintroduction of border control at internal borders in exceptional circumstances [2013] OJ L295/1. See Cornelisse, 'What's Wrong with Schengen?' (2014) 741, 757–60; E Guild et al, 'Internal Border Controls in the Schengen Area: is Schengen Crisis-Proof?' (Brussels, European Parliament Policy Department for Citizens' Rights and Constitutional Affairs, 2016) available at www.europarl.europa.eu/thinktank/en/document.html?reference=IPOL_STU(2016)571356, 23–31; Pascouau, 'Schengen Governance Package' (2013) 1 f.
[46] The amendments concerned the new 'serious deficiencies' ground that (now) is Art 29 SBC (subsection D below), and more detailed rules on proportionality (section VI below) and time limits more generally.
[47] Commission (n 42) 6.

deficiencies relating to external border control'. The serious deficiencies must either have been established by a Commission evaluation report in line with Article 21 SBC,[48] or be the result of a Member State's non-compliance with a Council decision referred to in Article 19(1) of the 'Frontex Regulation'.[49] In any case, the serious deficiencies must 'constitute a serious threat to public policy or internal security' within the Schengen Area or parts thereof.[50] Border control may at first be reintroduced for a period of up to six months. If the exceptional circumstances persist, that period may be prolonged for further three periods of up to six months, up to a total of two years.[51] In contrast to foreseeable cases or cases requiring immediate action, Member States under Article 29 SBC may reintroduce, or prolong, border control based only upon a prior Council recommendation.[52] Before making a recommendation, which itself must be based upon a Commission proposal,[53] the Council pursuant to Article 30(1) SBC must assess the proportionality of the measure envisaged.[54]

The exception clause in (what is now) Article 29 SBC was newly introduced by Regulation 1051/2013 in November 2013.[55] Article 29(1) SBC was further amended by Article 80 of the revised Frontex Regulation in October 2016.[56]

IV. THE MIGRATION CRISIS AND MEMBER STATES' REACTIONS

A. The Migration Crisis (and the Frailties of the Common European Asylum System)

The 'Dublin III Regulation',[57] one of the current pillars of the Common European Asylum System (CEAS), allocates responsibility for handling applications for

---

[48] In essence, Art 21(3) SBC mandates that 'Where an evaluation report ... has concluded that the evaluated Member State is seriously neglecting its obligations ... and where, following [a] three-month period, the Commission finds that the situation persists, it may trigger the application of the procedure provided for in Article 29' SBC. See also Pascouau, 'Schengen Governance Package' (2013) 7–11.

[49] Regulation (EU) 2016/1624 of the European Parliament and of the Council of 14 September 2016 on the European Border and Coast Guard and amending Regulation (EU) 2016/399 of the European Parliament and of the Council and repealing Regulation (EC) 863/2007 of the European Parliament and of the Council, Council Regulation (EC) 2007/2004 and Council Decision 2005/267/EC [2016] OJ L251/1. In essence, Art 19(1) of the Frontex Regulation reads as follows: 'Where control of the external borders is rendered ineffective to such an extent that it risks jeopardising the functioning of the Schengen area because' a Member State does not take the necessary measures or has not requested sufficient support from Frontex, 'the Council ... may adopt without delay a decision ..., identifying measures to mitigate those risks to be implemented by [Frontex] and requiring the Member State concerned to cooperate'.

[50] Art 29(1) SBC. See already subsection A above.

[51] Art 29(1) SBC.

[52] Art 29(1) and (2) SBC.

[53] Art 29(2) SBC.

[54] On proportionality, see section VI below.

[55] Section III.C.

[56] Above n 49.

[57] Regulation (EU) 604/2013 of the European Parliament and of the Council of 26 June 2013 establishing the criteria and mechanisms for determining the Member State responsible for

and, as the case may be, eventually granting refugee or subsidiary protection status[58] pursuant to a hierarchical set of criteria.[59] In practice and in spite of a – hardly justiciable[60] – 'principle of solidarity and fair sharing of responsibility' set out in Article 80 TFEU, responsibility in many cases lies with the Member State through the territory of which the applicant first irregularly enters the EU (Article 13[1] of the Dublin III Regulation). This holds true also for applicants whose (irregular) entry is tolerated by the authorities of that Member State.[61] Should the applicant later move and seek protection in another Member State, they, following an examination to that end by the second Member State, in principle will have to be taken back to the first Member State.[62] In order to make the system viable, Member States are under an obligation under the 'Eurodac Regulation' to take and share fingerprints of third-country nationals within 72 hours after an application for international protection has been made or after apprehension in connection with irregular crossing of an external border.[63]

Against this legal background, starting in late summer 2015 and throughout 2016, the EU faced an unprecedented influx of 2.5 million third-country nationals seeking international protection, many of them fleeing armed conflict or other conditions hostile to life in their African, Asian or Middle Eastern countries of origin.[64] In Greece alone, already shaken by a sovereign debt crisis

examining an application for international protection lodged in one of the Member States by a third-country national or a stateless person (recast) [2013] OJ L180/31.

[58] *cf* Art 2(d–g) of Directive 2011/95/EU of the European Parliament and of the Council of 13 December 2011 on standards for the qualification of third-country nationals or stateless persons as beneficiaries of international protection, for a uniform status for refugees or for persons eligible for subsidiary protection, and for the content of the protection granted [2011] OJ L337/9.

[59] Arts 7–15 of the Dublin III Regulation. Arts 16–17 contain further rules regarding dependent persons as well as discretionary clauses (*cf* n 70 below), respectively.

[60] See, eg, K Hailbronner and D Thym, 'Legal Framework for EU Asylum Policy' in K Hailbronner and D Thym (eds), *EU Immigration and Asylum Law: A Commentary*, 2nd edn (Munich, CH Beck, 2016) para 43 ('broad political discretion').

[61] Judgment of 26 July 2017, *A.S.*, C-490/16, EU:C:2017:585, paras 36–42, and judgment of 26 July 2017, *Jafari*, C-646/16, EU:C:2017:586, paras 93–102.

[62] Art 18(1) of the Dublin III Regulation. Responsibility of the Member State of first irregular entry may cease or be transferred to another Member State subject to the criteria set out in Art 19 leg cit.

[63] Arts 9(1) and 14(2) of Regulation (EU) 603/2013 of the European Parliament and of the Council of 26 June 2013 on the establishment of 'Eurodac' for the comparison of fingerprints for the effective application of Regulation (EU) 604/2013 establishing the criteria and mechanisms for determining the Member State responsible for examining an application for international protection lodged in one of the Member States by a third-country national or a stateless person and on requests for the comparison with Eurodac data by Member States' law enforcement authorities and Europol for law enforcement purposes, and amending Regulation (EU) 1077/2011 establishing a European Agency for the operational management of large-scale IT systems in the area of freedom, security and justice [2013] OJ L180/1.

[64] Member States received 1.257 million first-time applications for international protection in 2015, and another 1.206 million applications in 2016. In 2017, there was a significant drop to a still remarkable 649,900 first-time asylum applications. See Eurostat, 'Asylum applications (non-EU) in the EU-28 Member States, 2006–2017' available at ec.europa.eu/eurostat/statistics-explained/index.php/Asylum_statistics.

for years, 856,723 migrants arrived by sea in 2015, and a further 173,450 in 2016.[65] Italy witnessed 153,842 sea arrivals in 2015, and a further 181,436 in 2016.[66] While a substantial fraction of arrivals remained, or were forced to remain, in the Member State of first entry, the greater part moved on and filed applications for international protection elsewhere in the EU. From 2015 through 2017, the highest aggregate number of first-time asylum applications was registered in Germany (1,362,320), followed by Italy (330,565), France (239,325), Hungary (205,765), Sweden (200,630), Austria (147,835) and Greece (118,185).[67]

The reasons for this – illegal[68] – 'secondary migration' taking place to such an extent, and being successful in law or fact, are manifold and complex. First, Greek and some other Member States' authorities reportedly did not manage – or want – to properly fingerprint the remarkable number of sea arrivals in line with the Eurodac Regulation and waved many third-country nationals through.[69] Second, early on during the crisis Germany signalled its intention to deviate from the CEAS by temporarily waiving its right to transfer Syrian nationals back to the Member State of irregular first entry.[70] Third, if a person requests asylum in or at the border of a Member State, that Member State must grant the individual access to the asylum procedure.[71] The procedure, which is often lengthy, in turn establishes, in line with the Dublin III Regulation, whether the particular Member State is responsible for the handling of the application.[72] Fourth, transferring migrants back to Greece may have regularly run counter to Article 3(2) of the Dublin III Regulation. The latter provision provides for the responsibility of the Member State where an asylum application has been made if

> there are substantial grounds for believing that there are systemic flaws in the asylum procedure and in the reception conditions for applicants in [the Member State of

---

[65] UNHCR, 'Operational Data Portal: Mediterranean Situation' (last updated 21 September 2018) available at data2.unhcr.org/en/situations/mediterranean.
[66] ibid.
[67] Eurostat, 'Asylum and first time asylum applicants by citizenship, age and sex' (last updated 24 August 2018) available at ec.europa.eu/eurostat/en/web/products-datasets/-/MIGR_ASYAPPCTZA.
[68] D Thym, 'The "Refugee Crisis" as a Challenge of Legal Design and Institutional Legitimacy' (2016) 53 *Common Market Law Review* 1545, 1548 (at n 17).
[69] cf Commission (n 30) 7 f; Thym, 'The "Refugee Crisis"' (2016) 1547 f. See also C Hruschka and F Maiani, 'Dublin III Regulation' in K Hailbronner and D Thym (eds), *EU Immigration and Asylum Law: A Commentary*, 2nd edn (Munich, CH Beck, 2016) Art 13 para 1 ('Article 13[1] ends up encouraging lax border controls').
[70] But cf Art 17(1) of the Dublin III Regulation. See also U Koehler, *Praxiskommentar zum Europäischen Asylzuständigkeitssystem* (Berlin, BWV, 2018), Dublin III-VO Artikel 3 para 4; G Blume et al, 'The Night Germany Lost Control' *Die Zeit* (Hamburg, 30 August 2016), available at www.zeit.de/gesellschaft/2016-08/refugees-open-border-policy-september-2015-angela-merkel/komplettansicht.
[71] See below, text at n 166.
[72] Art 6 of the Directive 2013/32/EU of the European Parliament and of the Council of 26 June 2013 on common procedures for granting and withdrawing international protection [2013] OJ L180/60.

irregular first entry], resulting in a risk of inhuman or degrading treatment within the meaning of Article 4 [CFR].[73]

Fifth, once arrived, transfers to the responsible Member State of first entry often proved as ineffective as returns of applicants to their home country following a negative asylum decision.[74] Reasons for take charge (or take back) requests[75] or return decisions[76] being ineffective include resistance by the individuals concerned (such as concealment of identity or absconding)[77] and lack of co-operation from countries of origin or transit.[78]

B. Member States' Reactions

'Countermeasures' against what was perceived as a major crisis were, on the one hand, taken at EU level, such as two (rather ineffective) 'Relocation Decisions' for the benefit of Italy and Greece,[79] and a (highly effective) 'EU-Turkey Statement'.[80] On the other hand, a number of Member States as well as Schengen-associated states reintroduced temporary controls at their borders with other Member States. The number of reintroductions and prolongations of internal border checks has tripled compared to the October 2006 to August 2015 period to stand at 108 as of 14 January 2019.[81]

---

[73] Charter of Fundamental Rights of the European Union [2016] OJ C202/389. Art 3(2) of the Dublin III Regulation implements judgments handed down by the ECtHR (*MSS v Belgium and Greece* App no 30696/09, 21 January 2011) and the Court of Justice (judgment of 21 December 2011, *NS and ME*, C-411/10 and C-493/10, EU:C:2011:865), respectively. For a meticulous account of the situation in all Member States, see Koehler, *Praxiskommentar* (2018) paras 89 ff.

[74] Thym, 'The "Refugee Crisis"' (2016) 1548 f.

[75] Arts 21, 23 and 24 of the Dublin III Regulation.

[76] Art 6 of Directive 2008/115/EC of the European Parliament and of the Council of 16 December 2008 on common standards and procedures in Member States for returning illegally staying third-country nationals [2008] OJ L348/98.

[77] *cf* already Commission, 'Communication to the Council and the European Parliament on EU Return Policy' COM (2014) 199 final.

[78] Commission, 'Communication from the Commission to the European Parliament and the Council on a more effective return policy in the European Union – A renewed Action Plan' COM(2017) 200 final.

[79] Council Decision (EU) 2015/1523 of 14 September 2015 establishing provisional measures in the area of international protection for the benefit of Italy and of Greece [2015] OJ L239/146 and Council Decision (EU) 2015/1601 of 22 September 2015 establishing provisional measures in the area of international protection for the benefit of Italy and Greece [2015] OJ L248/80. See generally B De Witte and E Tsourdi, 'Confrontation on relocation – The Court of Justice endorses the emergency scheme for compulsory relocation of asylum seekers within the European Union: Slovak Republic and Hungary v. Council' (2018) 55 *Common Market Law Review* 1457.

[80] European Council, 'EU-Turkey Statement', Press Release 144/16 [Brussels, 18 March 2016] available at www.consilium.europa.eu/en/press/press-releases/2016/03/18/eu-turkey-statement/pdf. As regards the effectivity of the Statement, *cf* n 83 below.

[81] See Commission (n 42). See also E Guild et al, 'What is Happening to the Schengen Borders?' (2015) available at www.files.ethz.ch/isn/195352/No%2086%20Schengenland_0.pdf, 5–8; E Guild et al, 'Internal Border Controls?' (2016) 42–45, 94–112.

At certain times Hungary and Slovenia (in 2015) and Belgium (in 2016) had internal border checks in place, but for no longer than a couple of weeks.[82] In spite of a significant drop in sea arrivals as of 2017,[83] border checks have been carried out continuously since 2015 until the present day – and have been notified mostly until 11 May 2019 – by, in alphabetical order:

- Austria (land borders with Hungary and Slovenia);
- Denmark (all internal borders, with an initial focus on the land border with Germany and ports with connection to Germany);
- France (all internal borders, notified until 30 April 2019);
- Germany (land border with Austria);
- Norway (all internal borders, with an initial focus on ferry connections with Denmark, Germany and Sweden); and
- Sweden (all internal borders, notified until 11 February 2019).[84]

Reasons put forward by the Member States include the 'security situation in Europe and threats resulting from the continuous significant secondary movements [of migrants]'.[85] France is carrying out checks due to 'terrorist threats, [and the] situation at the external borders'.[86] Earlier during the crisis, Member States usually invoked as a justification for – at times spatially more extensive – border controls a 'big influx of persons seeking international protection' or, as in the case of Norway 2016, a 'continued *threat* of big influx of persons seeking international protection' (emphasis added).[87]

Formally, the reintroduction of border checks took place in stages under all three headings outlined above. In the initial days of the crisis, checks were based on Article 28 SBC (cases requiring immediate action).[88] Next, they were based on Articles 25–27 SBC (foreseeable cases).[89] From May 2016 through November 2017, even longer checks were based on Articles 29–30 SBC (cases where the overall functioning of the area without internal border control is put at risk) and corresponding Council recommendations.[90] In each of its four consecutive recommendations, the Council found a serious threat to public policy or internal security

---

[82] Commission (n 42).
[83] In 2017, there were 29,718 sea arrivals in Greece and 119,369 in Italy (n 65).
[84] See n 81 above.
[85] Commission (n 42).
[86] ibid.
[87] ibid.
[88] See Commission, 'Opinion of 23.10.2015 on the necessity and proportionality of the controls at internal borders reintroduced by Germany and Austria pursuant to Article 24(4) of Regulation No 562/2006 (Schengen Borders Code)' C (2015) 7100 final.
[89] Commission (n 30) 10.
[90] Council Implementing Decision (EU) 2016/894 of 12 May 2016 setting out a recommendation for temporary internal border control in exceptional circumstances putting the overall functioning of the Schengen area at risk [2016] OJ L151/8; Council Implementing Decision (EU) 2016/1989 of 11 November 2016 setting out a recommendation for prolonging temporary internal border control in exceptional circumstances putting the overall functioning of the Schengen area at risk [2016]

due to a 'persistent risk of secondary movements' of unregistered migrants from Greece to the Member States listed above.[91] Since November 2017, border checks have – again – been based on Articles 25–27 SBC (foreseeable cases).[92] This may be somewhat 'creative' in the light of the six-month time limit established under Article 25(4) SBC.[93] Doctrinally, it cannot be ruled out that even longer border checks necessary for 'the maintenance of law and order and the safeguarding of internal security' could also be based directly upon – the procedurally less constrictive – Article 72 TFEU and Article 4(2) TEU, respectively.[94]

V. A SERIOUS THREAT TO PUBLIC POLICY OR INTERNAL SECURITY?

This section first discusses the concepts of public policy and internal security in general, before turning to the core question of whether the migration crisis constitutes a serious threat to public policy or internal security.

A. Public Policy

Neither primary nor secondary EU law offers a definition of 'public policy' (or 'public order'[95] or 'law and order',[96] as the terms are sometimes used interchangeably). The Court of Justice as early as in the 1974 *van Duyn* case emphasised that the concept 'must be interpreted strictly, so that its scope cannot be determined unilaterally by each Member State'.[97] At the same time, the Court held that

> the particular circumstances justifying recourse to the concept of public policy may vary from one country to another and from one period to another and [that] it is

---

OJ L306/13; Council Implementing Decision (EU) 2017/246 of 7 February 2017 setting out a Recommendation for prolonging temporary internal border control in exceptional circumstances putting the overall functioning of the Schengen area at risk [2017] L36/59; and Council Implementing Decision (EU) 2017/818 of 11 May 2017 setting out a Recommendation for prolonging temporary internal border control in exceptional circumstances putting the overall functioning of the Schengen area at risk [2017] L122/73.

[91] Other than France. See, eg, Council Implementing Decision (EU) 2016/894 (n 90) recitals 14 ff.
[92] According to the website of the Commission's DG Migration and Home Affairs, border checks in place until 11 May 2019 are 'controls in the context of *foreseeable events*' available at ec.europa.eu/home-affairs/what-we-do/policies/borders-and-visas/schengen/reintroduction-border-control_en.
[93] Section III.B above. Also *cf* J Jasiewicz, 'A Not-So-Temporary Reinstatement of Internal Border Controls' (2018) available at leidenlawblog.nl/articles/a-not-so-temporary-reinstatement-of-internal-border-controls.
[94] See above section III.A. Also *cf* PC Müller-Graff, 'Artikel 72 AEUV' in M Pechstein et al (eds), *Frankfurter Kommentar zu EUV, GRC und AEUV* (Tübingen, Mohr Siebeck, 2017) paras 1–6.
[95] See, in the context of Art 36 TFEU, judgment of 9 December 1997, *Commission v France (Spanish strawberries)*, C-265/95, EU:C:1997:595, para 33.
[96] See, eg, Art 4(2) TEU and Art 72 TFEU.
[97] Judgment of 4 December 1974, *van Duyn*, 41/74, EU:C:1974:133, para 18. See also S Enchelmaier, 'Article 36 TFEU: General' in P Oliver (ed), *Oliver on Free Movement of Goods in the European*

therefore necessary in this matter to allow the competent national authorities an *area of discretion* within the limits imposed by the Treaty (emphasis added).[98]

The Court soon after in *Bouchereau* clarified that 'the perturbation of the social order which *any infringement of the law* involves' is not sufficient for public policy to be affected (emphasis added).[99] Instead, 'recourse ... to the concept of public policy presupposes ... the existence ... of a genuine and sufficiently serious threat to ... *one of the fundamental interests of society* (emphasis added)'.[100]

The Court developed its interpretation of public policy mainly in light of restrictions to the fundamental freedoms.[101] In this context, the justification has rarely been invoked successfully. The concept does *not* include, for instance, *Cassis* 'mandatory requirements',[102] not even fundamental rights.[103] Among the few legitimate grounds for justification accepted by the Court under Article 36 TFEU are 'the need to protect the right to mint coinage'[104] and 'the prevention of fraud with regard to the quality and composition of goods qualifying for export refunds'.[105] While dismissed on grounds of necessity, the Court accepted as a matter of public policy the detection or prevention of dealing in stolen vehicles, ie criminal prosecution.[106] In the same vein, the Court has seemingly confirmed that in principle averting public unrest may as well be a concern of public policy.[107] Member States must *not* enact trade 'restrictions which are explained primarily by a concern to lighten the administration's burden or reduce public expenditure', but Article 36 TFEU may be invoked if 'this burden or expenditure clearly would exceed the limits of what can reasonably be required'.[108]

While there may be some disparities due to the inherent distinctiveness of internal market law,[109] it is likely that the same meaning should be given to the

---

Union, 5th edn (Oxford, Hart Publishing, 2010) para 8.72, who suggests that the French *ordre public* and the German *öffentliche Ordnung* are inherently narrower in scope.

[98] *van Duyn*, 41/74, para 18.

[99] Judgment of 27 October 1977, *Bouchereau*, 30/77, EU:C:1977:172, para 35.

[100] ibid; *cf* also judgment of 23 November 1978, *Thompson*, 7/78, EU:C:1978:209, para 34 ('involving the fundamental interests of the State').

[101] Art 36, 45, 52, and 65 TFEU.

[102] Judgment of 6 November 1984, *Ringelhan*, 177/83, EU:C:1984:334, para 19 (consumer protection).

[103] *cf* judgment of 12 June 2003, *Schmidberger*, C-112/00, EU:C:2003:333, para 92. In judgment of 14 October 2004, *Omega*, C-36/02, EU:C:2004:614, the Court did, however, qualify human dignity as a public policy concern (at para 41). For lucid commentary, see C Barnard, *The Substantive Law of the EU: The Four Freedoms*, 5th edn (Oxford, Oxford University Press, 2016) 155; Enchelmaier, 'Article 36 TFEU: General' (2010) para 8.63.

[104] *Thompson*, 7/78, para 34.

[105] Judgment of 22 June 1994, *Deutsches Milchkontor*, C-426/92, EU:C:1994:260, para 44.

[106] Judgment of 17 June 1987, *Commission v Italy*, 154/85, EU:C:1987:292, paras 13 f. Also *cf* judgment of 30 April 1991, *Boscher*, 239/90, EU:C:1991:180, paras 22 f.

[107] Judgment of 29 January 1985, *Centre Leclerc*, 231/83, EU:C:1985:29, para 32 f. Also *cf Commission v France (Spanish strawberries)*, C-265/95, para 50.

[108] See, albeit in the context of the health-and-life defence under Art 36 TFEU, judgment of 20 May 1976, *de Peijper*, 104/75, EU:C:1976:67, para 18; judgment of 12 July 1990, *Commission v Italy*, C-128/89, EU:C:1990:311, para 22.

[109] *cf* text at n 28 above.

notion of public policy in Articles 25–30 SBC (or 'law and order' in Article 4[2] TEU and Article 72 TFEU, respectively.)[110] This view is supported by the EU legislator itself stating in recital 27 of the preamble to the SBC that

> in accordance with the case-law ... a derogation from the fundamental principle of free movement of persons must be interpreted strictly and the concept of public policy presupposes the existence of a genuine, present and sufficiently serious threat affecting one of the fundamental interests of society.

The Court has used very similar wording regarding the Returns Directive[111] in *Zh and O*.[112] In the realm of migration law more generally, the Court has acknowledged Member States' responsibilities for the maintenance of public policy (or law and order), for instance, combating drug trafficking[113] or other serious[114] crime, such as theft-related offences.[115] The application of Articles 25–27 SBC to cases preceding the migration crisis also suggests that the same logic applies to the goal of preventing violence among foreign and local demonstrators.[116] Moreover, the Court has expressly confirmed that 'combating illegal immigration and unauthorised residence' serves 'the maintenance of law and order and the safeguarding of internal security'.[117] In a similar vein, the Court qualified 'human smuggling by securing entry into German territory of third-country nationals holding visas obtained by fraud' as undermining public order.[118]

B. Internal Security

The SBC also does not define 'internal security'. Although the concept is at times coupled with or relied upon together with public policy, internal security is a ground for justification in its own right.[119] The Court has held that internal security is an integral part of 'public security' which, as a broader term, also covers external security.[120] External security is frequently understood as referring, in particular, to military security (which is also dealt with under

---

[110] C Franzius, 'Artikel 4 EUV' in M Pechstein et al (eds), *Frankfurter Kommentar zu EUV, GRC und AEUV* (Tübingen, Mohr Siebeck, 2017) para 52.
[111] See n 76.
[112] Judgment of 11 June 2015, *Zh and O*, C-554/13, EU:C:2015:377, paras 48–50.
[113] Judgment of 29 April 2004, *Orfanopoulos*, C-482/01 and C-493/01, EU:C:2004:262, para 67.
[114] *cf Zh and O*, C-554/13, para 65.
[115] *cf* judgment of 15 February 2016, *JN*, C-601/15 PPU, EU:C:2016:84, paras 22, 64.
[116] See section III.B above.
[117] *Adil*, C-278/12 PPU, para 66. Also see judgment of 6 December 2011, *Achughbabian*, C-329/11, EU:C:2011:807, paras 30, 33.
[118] *cf* judgment of 10 April 2012, *Vo*, C-83/12 PPU, EU:C:2012:202, para 2.
[119] Judgment of 10 July 1984, *Campus Oil*, 72/83, EU:C:1984:256, para 33.
[120] Judgment of 4 October 1991, *Richardt*, C-367/89, EU:C:1991:376, para 22.

Article 346 TFEU).[121] However, a self-contained positive interpretation of internal security is still lacking.[122] Making sense of the case law developed in the context of the fundamental freedoms,[123] public security generally seems to cover the *existence of the State, its institutions and essential services* on the one hand, and the *survival of its inhabitants* on the other.[124] It was successfully invoked, in particular, with regard to trade restrictions on dual-use goods,[125] as well as obligations to maintain essential oil supplies.[126]

C. A Serious Threat?

i. Instinct vs Evidence

In line with the Court's judgment in *Bouchereau*,[127] Articles 25–30 SBC, as a critical precondition for the reintroduction of internal border control, require there to be a genuine and sufficiently *serious threat* to public policy or internal security.[128] Typically, the satisfaction of this requirement will have to be assessed *ex ante*.[129]

Against this background, the EU legislator in recital 26 of the preamble to the SBC expressly states that 'migration and the crossing of external borders by a large number of third-country nationals should not, per se, be considered to be a threat [at all] to public policy or internal security.' This statement is supported by the EU's declared commitment to a set of fundamental values. Per Article 2 TEU, the Union is founded on values such as 'respect for human dignity … the rule of law and respect for human rights', which 'are common to the Member States in a society in which pluralism, non-discrimination, tolerance, justice [and] solidarity … prevail'.[130] Instinctively, it is also doubtful that an influx of 2.5 million third-country nationals seeking international protection[131] could actually ever pose serious problems to a sophisticated Union of 28 states and more than 500 million citizens.

There is limited empirical data to assess whether or not the 2015–16 migration crisis constituted a serious threat – for which the Member States and the

---

[121] cf *Richardt*, C-367/89, para 22 ('goods capable of being used for strategic purposes may affect the public security'); judgment of 13 July 1000, *Albore*, C-423/98, EU:C:2000:401, para 18 (regarding an obligation to seek an administrative authorisation for any purchase of real property in an area of the country designated as being of military importance).
[122] See Enchelmaier, 'Article 36 TFEU: General' (2010) paras 8.77 and 82.
[123] C Franzius, 'Artikel 4 EUV' (2017) para 52.
[124] *Campus Oil*, 72/83, para 34.
[125] *Richardt*, C-367/89.
[126] *Campus Oil*, 72/83.
[127] Text to n 100 above.
[128] See already above section III.A.
[129] PC Müller-Graff, 'Artikel 72 AEUV' (2017) para 5.
[130] As far as fundamental rights are concerned, see also Art 67(1) TFEU.
[131] Section IV.A.

Commission are to blame at any rate.[132] However, from the perspective of the Member States which reinstated border checks, the migration crisis, and secondary migration within the EU more specifically,[133] may still have brought about the required serious threat to public policy or internal security.[134]

ii. Administrative Overload

First, the historically high numbers of asylum applications may have caused a serious threat to public policy and internal security by way of an actual or imminent administrative overload experienced by (some of) the Member States and their police or asylum authorities.[135] The Commission, in its Opinion on the necessity and proportionality of the controls at internal borders reintroduced by Germany and Austria,[136] found that

> the Austrian authorities need to deal with this high number of arrivals, and this, irrespective of whether the persons stay on Austrian territory, can indeed, at least for a certain period of time, cause a serious threat to public policy and internal security.[137]

According to the Commission, it 'needs to be acknowledged that the reintroduction of border control may contribute to avoid a continuous overstressing of police forces, rescue services and public infrastructure'[138] (but also see below)[139]. In line with the Commission's statement it seems at least likely, though, that this type of threat, while perhaps being genuine and serious enough in late 2015 and early 2016, may have been of a more temporary nature only.

iii. Frustration of Migration Management

Member States have a legitimate, fundamental and lawful interest in regulating, and having information about, the entry and stay of refugees as well as other migrants in their territory.[140] The above case law[141] and the discretion afforded to Member States[142] suggest that a second serious threat to public policy could

---

[132] E. Guild et al, 'Internal Border Controls?' (2016) 42–45; Jasiewicz, 'A Not-So-Temporary Reinstatement' (2018). Also see text at n 173 below.
[133] Section IV.A.
[134] Also see section IV.B above.
[135] *cf* above text at n 108.
[136] Commission, 'Opinion of 23.10.2015 on the necessity and proportionality of the controls at internal borders reintroduced by Germany and Austria pursuant to Article 24(4) of Regulation No 562/2006 (Schengen Borders Code)' C (2015) 7100 final.
[137] ibid, para 42.
[138] ibid, para 43.
[139] Section VI.C.
[140] See generally Peers, *EU Justice* (2016) 319 (as regards legal migration) and 443 (as regards irregular migration); D Thym, *Migrationsverwaltungsrecht* (Tübingen, Mohr Siebeck, 2010) *passim*.
[141] See text at n 117.
[142] See text after n 97.

have been associated with a partial frustration of Member States' legitimate interest and legislative efforts in managing regular and irregular migration, due to deficient external border controls and – sufficiently substantial – illegal secondary migration of often unregistered migrants.[143] As cited above, the Council, in its recommendations adopted under Articles 29–30 SBC, found a serious threat to public policy or internal security due to the 'persistent risk of secondary movements' of unregistered migrants.[144] It did not give any additional reasons. A perhaps related serious threat to public policy may also be discerned in the long-term effects of unmanaged migration of third-country nationals. Such migration could impact, for instance, on the domestic labour market (access to which is a prerogative of each Member State),[145] or the prospects of successful integration of migrants within their host communities. Unmanaged migration may perhaps also impose financial strains on national social security systems which 'would exceed the limits of what can reasonably be required'.[146]

Importantly, the 'conceptual asymmetry of the Dublin system' established by the Council (together with the Parliament),[147] even in the face of large streams of migration cannot be regarded as a declaration of consent on the side of Member States to secondary migration. Neither does it amount to a waiver of Member States' far-reaching, perhaps even absolute, right under Article 72 TFEU and Article 4(2) TEU, to invoke a correlated serious threat to public policy or internal security.[148] The seriousness of this point is not diminished by the attempted temporary adjustment of this conceptual asymmetry in the light of Article 80 TFEU[149] by means of the Council's two Relocation Decisions of September 2015,[150] or by the lack of implementation of these Decisions by most Member States.[151] It is also not diminished by Germany's temporary waiver, in the early days of the migration crisis, of its right to transfer Syrian nationals back to the Member State of irregular first entry,[152] or by the Member State of first entry itself experiencing a serious threat to public policy or internal security. It is suggested that Member States are also entitled to invoke a serious

---

[143] Section IV.A; *cf* text at n 118. See also recital 6 of the preamble to SBC, according to which effective external border control 'should help to combat illegal immigration and trafficking in human beings and to prevent any threat to the Member States' internal security, public policy, public health and international relations.'
[144] Text at n 91 above.
[145] Art 79(5) TFEU.
[146] *cf* n 108 above.
[147] K Hailbronner and D Thym, 'Legal Framework for EU Asylum Policy' (2016) para 41; Thym, 'The "Refugee Crisis"' (2016) 1549 ff. See also text after n 59 above.
[148] *cf* below section VI.D.
[149] On the limited justiciability of Art 80 TFEU, see n 60 above.
[150] Above n 79.
[151] See Commission, 'Relocation: EU solidarity between Member States' (15 November 2017) available at ec.europa.eu/home-affairs/sites/homeaffairs/files/what-we-do/policies/european-agenda-migration/20171114_relocation_eu_solidarity_between_member_states_en.pdf.
[152] See text at n 70.

threat to public policy in the face of substantial secondary migration due to 'systemic flaws in the asylum procedure and in the reception conditions for applicants' in the Member State of irregular first entry, as addressed by Article 3(2) of the Dublin III Regulation.[153] The fact that there is a serious threat to public policy or internal security elsewhere cannot exonerate a Member State, even if perhaps partly politically responsible for the emergence of the former, from its own domestic core tasks and responsibilities with regard to the maintenance of law and order and the safeguarding of internal security. The situation may have to be reappraised when external border control and the registration of immigrants in line with the Eurodac Regulation become fully effective.

iv. Terrorism or Other Serious Crimes

A third serious threat to public policy and internal security may have resulted from a potentially increased threat of, or complication in the prevention and detection of, terrorism or other serious crimes against health or life, exceptionally to be committed either by migrants who may be unregistered, or by domestic or EU citizens. While, again, limited empirical data prohibits a definitive finding, recital 25 of the preamble to the SBC explains that the 'reintroduction of internal border control might exceptionally be necessary in the case of a serious threat to public policy or to internal security … in particular *following terrorist incidents or threats, or because of threats posed by organised crime*' (emphasis added). Even very rare incidents of terrorism or other serious crime severely encroach upon public policy or internal security. In view of the *ex ante* assessment to be made by Member States,[154] it is arguable that the standard applied to the concept of *serious* threat should not be overstretched. Again, this view is supported by the discretion afforded to the Member States in line with the jurisprudence of the Court. On the other hand, a possible, yet not likely, terrorist attack will not qualify as a serious threat; this would otherwise be the end of the Schengen Area.

VI. PROPORTIONALITY OF INTERNAL BORDER CONTROL

A. Normative Foundations

As has been pointed out above, a final verdict as to whether the migration crisis actually caused a serious threat to public policy or internal security within the Schengen Area is impossible given the limited availability of determinative empirical data. If we assume that the migration crisis did constitute such a threat, it is important to ask whether the reinstatement of border control

---

[153] See text at n 73.
[154] *cf* above text to n 129.

by several Member States, as repeatedly recommended by the Council under Article 29 SBC,[155] actually helped relieve the serious threat in question – or whether it was just symbolism and, hence, national politicking at the expense of EU integration. Articles 25–26, 28 and 29–30 SBC set out a proportionality test to that end. In essence, the measure must be both suitable and necessary.[156] In large part, the pertinent criteria, including detailed time limits,[157] were added to the SBC by Regulation 1051/2013.[158]

Importantly, the CJEU is not precluded from checking the suitability and necessity of a Member State measure, such as temporary internal border control, even if the latter may fall within the scope of Article 72 TFEU or Article 4(2) TEU.[159] This is straightforward when the adopted measures are not suitable to maintain law and order or safeguard internal security. The Court of Justice is, however, also entitled to check whether other courses of action were available to the Member State in question which, while also effective and thus suitable, would have been less restrictive on the free movement of persons. If the Court finds that the measure is either not suitable or necessary, or both unsuitable and unnecessary, the measure is unnecessarily restrictive. As a result, prohibiting such a disproportionate measure would not adversely 'affect the exercise of the responsibilities incumbent upon Member States with regard to the maintenance of law and order and the safeguarding of internal security'.[160] Proportionality *stricto sensu*,[161] in contrast, may have a limited scope of application.[162]

B. Suitability

On suitability, Article 26 SBC explicitly mandates that the Member State in question 'shall assess the extent to which [temporary control at internal borders] is likely to adequately remedy the threat to public policy or internal security'. Article 30(1) SBC contains an analogous clause addressed to the Council.

---

[155] Sections III.D and IV.B.
[156] See also recitals 21–24 of the preamble to the SBC.
[157] *cf* section III above.
[158] Section III.C.
[159] *cf* section III.A above; in the same vein PC Müller-Graff, 'Artikel 77 AEUV' in M Pechstein, C Nowak and U Häde (eds), *Frankfurter Kommentar zu EUV, GRC und AEUV* (Tübingen, Mohr Siebeck, 2017) para 31. Also *cf*, albeit based on pre-Lisbon treaty law, D Thym, 'The Schengen Law: A Challenge for Legal Accountability in the European Union' 8 *ELJ* (2002) 218, 233 f.
[160] Art 72 TFEU.
[161] Proportionality *stricto sensu* requires balancing the benefits gained by the public by a – suitable and necessary – state measure and the harm the state measure may cause to the restricted legal position (here, the free movement of persons). See more generally A Barak, *Proportionality: Constitutional Rights and their Limitations* (Cambridge, Cambridge University Press, 2012) 340 ff.
[162] *cf* P Craig, *EU Administrative Law*, 2nd edn (Oxford, Oxford University Press, 2012) 615, who argues that one 'should be aware in this respect of the need for careful identification of the positive law and of the normative foundations on which it is based'.

Generally, one may assume that checks on persons at internal borders will in fact enable the Member State at least to gather essential information about the (sufficiently substantial) streams of – potentially unregistered – persons wishing to enter its territory.[163] This may be in the interest of migration management more broadly, and also constitute a suitable remedy to an increased threat, or complication in the prevention or detection, of terrorism or other serious crime.

On the other hand, the reintroduction of internal border control may not constitute a suitable means to effectively fight a serious threat to public policy or internal security caused either by the administrative overload of a Member State's police or asylum authorities or coming from Member States' frustrated efforts to manage migration flows. In principle, any (Member) State may – and, from an EU law perspective, must – refuse entry to a third-country national who does not satisfy the entry conditions in Article 6 SBC.[164] The situation changes entirely when a third-country national files an application for international protection. Here, international law, in particular Articles 2–3 of the European Convention on Human Rights and the principle of *non-refoulement*,[165] 'dictates that state responsibility for applicants at the border is the same as for those in the country.'[166] Crucially, a serious threat to public policy or internal security experienced by a Member State will not render its responsibilities under the Convention moot.[167] This is reinforced by Article 3(b) of the SBC, which states that the SBC 'shall apply to any person crossing the internal or external borders of Member States, without prejudice to … the rights of refugees and persons requesting international protection, in particular as regards *non-refoulement*.' The Commission also points out that

> Legally, in accordance with Article 6 of the Asylum Procedures Directive, if a third-country national requests asylum in a Member State, *including when the application is made at the border*, the Member State must grant that person access to the asylum procedure (emphasis added).[168]

The 'question of whether that particular Member State will remain responsible for the handling of the particular application [and eventually for granting international protection] will … be decided in accordance with the … Dublin Regulation'.[169] During this determination, the third-country national will

---

[163] *cf* Art 8 SBC.
[164] Commission, 'Back to Schengen – A Roadmap' (2016) 8.
[165] On the principle of *non-refoulement*, see Peers, *EU Justice* (2016) 247 ff.
[166] C Costello, 'The Asylum Procedures Directive in Legal Context: Equivocal Standards Meet General Principles' in A Baldaccini, E Guild and H Toner (eds), *Whose Freedom, Security and Justice? EU Immigration and Asylum Law and Policy* (Oxford, Hart Publishing, 2007) 161. See also Thym, 'Legal Framework for Entry and Border Controls' (2016) paras 36 ff.
[167] C Grabenwarter and K Pabel, *Europäische Menschenrechtskonvention*, 6th edn (Munich, CH Beck, 2016) § 2 para 8 ff (as regards Art 15 ECHR) and § 20 para 87 (as regards Art 3 ECHR).
[168] Commission, 'Back to Schengen – A Roadmap' (2016) 7; Directive 2013/32/EU of the European Parliament and of the Council of 26 June 2013 on common procedures for granting and withdrawing international protection [2013] OJ L180/60.
[169] Commission, 'Back to Schengen – A Roadmap' (2016) 7 f.

already be present in the territory, often for a long time. Article 3(2) of the Dublin III Regulation provides that, in case of 'systemic flaws' in the Member State of irregular first entry, the Member State where the asylum application was made will remain permanently responsible.[170]

C. Necessity

Articles 25–26 SBC provide for a necessity test. Article 25(1) SBC stresses the exceptional and temporary character of, and imposes specific time limits[171] for, internal border control. Article 25(1) also mandates that the 'scope and duration of the temporary reintroduction of border control … shall not exceed what is strictly necessary to respond to the serious threat.' Article 26 SBC adds to[172] the necessity requirement by stating that 'Border control at internal borders shall only be reintroduced as a last resort', that is only if – and to the extent that – all else fails. Articles 29–30 SBC are analogously worded.

Naturally, whether the reinstatement of internal border control will pass the necessity test depends on the facts of each case individually – and is therefore not least a matter of empirical evidence. Here, one may also be sceptical of the nature and quality of information provided by the Member States in question. The Commission may also have been overly generous in approving the Member States' statements.[173] As a general proposition, however, one would have to consider whether police checks within the territory of the Member State may be sufficient to adequately combat a given serious threat to public policy or internal security, in line with Article 23(a) SBC.[174] Here, the Court recently clarified that

> the objective … of preventing or terminating illegal entry into the … territory [of a Member State] or to prevent certain criminal offences [such as crimes which undermine border security or which are to be prosecuted under the provisions of passport, residence of asylum laws] does *not* in itself mean that the [police] checks … have an equivalent [effect] to border checks [prohibited by Article 23(a) SBC]' (emphasis added).[175]

---

[170] See text at n 73 above.
[171] See section III above.
[172] In the same vein Peers, *EU Justice* (2016) 113 ('suggests a stronger application of the proportionality requirement').
[173] E Brouwer, 'Migration Flows and the Reintroduction of Internal Border Controls: Assessing Necessity and Proportionality' (2015) available at eumigrationlawblog.eu/migration-flows-and-the-reintroduction-of-internal-border-controls-assessing-necessity-and-proportionality; E Guild et al, 'What is Happening to the Schengen Borders?' (2015); E Guild et al, 'Internal Border Controls?' (2016) 38–58.
[174] *cf* text at n 21 above. This option was used, eg, by the Netherlands. See E Brouwer, 'Migration Flows' (2015).
[175] *A*, C-9/16, para 51.

In comparison to border checks, the effectiveness of police measures may be limited for, to comply with Article 23(a) SBC, they must be applied selectively – ie based on knowledge of the situation or border police experience and on the basis of spot-checks only.[176] Therefore, a strong case for the necessity of internal border control may be made, in particular, on the legitimate interest of a Member State to systematically gather essential information about potentially large streams of unregistered persons wishing to enter its territory. The necessity of internal border control to face an increased threat, or complication in the prevention or detection, of terrorism or other serious crime may be more a matter of discretion, and of empirical evidence.

Article 30(1)(a) SBC further recalls the possibility that technical or financial support measures may be (or may have been) available at national or Union level to strengthen external border control. In the face of a present serious threat to public policy or internal security, these measures will lack short-term effectiveness and, thus, will be unsuitable in the first place.

D. Proportionality *Stricto Sensu*

Article 26 SBC states that the Member State 'shall assess the proportionality of the measure in relation to that threat'. Moreover, Article 26(b) SBC, and similarly Article 30(1)(c) SBC, require the affected Member State or the Council, respectively, to consider 'the likely impact of such a measure on free movement of persons within the area without internal border control'.

These clauses, and the requirement of proportionality *stricto sensu* set out therein, may be ultra vires. Article 4(2) TEU and Article 72 TFEU[177] arguably establish a Member State's reserve, which is absolute insofar as the Member State's essential state functions[178] may not be outweighed by any goals of EU integration whatsoever.[179] This is reminiscent of the German domestic constitutional requirements articulated by the *Bundesverfassungsgericht* in its 2009 Lisbon Judgment.[180] Accordingly, once it is established that border checks are both suitable and necessary to face a serious threat to public policy or internal security, the Court of Justice must *not* further examine whether these checks may have disproportionately encroached upon the free movement of persons. Article 4(2) TEU, in particular, is very clear on this regarding internal security.[181]

---

[176] A, C-9/16, paras 74–75. See further E Guild et al, 'Internal Border Controls?' (2016) 55–57.
[177] Section III.A.
[178] *cf* above, text at n 15.
[179] In the same vein PC Müller-Graff, 'Artikel 72 AEUV' (2017) paras 1 ff.
[180] BVerfG, 2 BvE 2/08, DE:BVerfG:2009:es20090630.2bve000208, para 249 ('essential areas of [German] democratic formative action comprise, *inter alia* … the civil and the military monopoly on the use of force').
[181] See above section III.A.

Applying a less radical reading to Article 4(2) TEU and Article 72 TFEU, proportionality *stricto sensu* may play a minor role with regard to seriously threatened, though perhaps somewhat less essential, concerns of public policy.[182] It can be doubted, however, whether frustration of a Member State's efforts to manage regular or irregular migration, in particular, could constitute a less essential concern.

VII. CONCLUSIONS

The SBC solemnly declares that one of the main achievements of the Union is the creation of an area in which the free movement of persons across internal borders is ensured. Against this background, the long-term 'temporary' reintroduction of checks on persons at the Schengen internal borders in the wake of the 2015–16 migration crisis seriously calls this achievement into question. While the case law provides some orientation, it is difficult to pin down the concept of 'serious threat to public policy or internal security' on a doctrinal level. There are, however, reasons to argue that the crisis in fact caused such a serious threat to public policy or internal security in a number of Member States. In particular, such a threat may have materialised as:

— a temporary administrative overload of some Member States' police or asylum authorities;
— a partial frustration of Member States' efforts to manage regular or irregular migration due to substantial secondary movements of often unregistered third-country nationals;
— and a concurrent threat of, or a complication in the prevention or detection of, terrorism or other serious crimes, committed by migrants or by domestic or EU citizens.

Empirical evidence is limited – for which the Member States in question and the Commission are to blame. This again prevents a final verdict as to whether border control may have been a suitable and necessary means to address the said serious threats. It may have helped Member States to collect critical information on third-country nationals who wished to enter, and perhaps stay, in their respective territory as a means of migration management, and to address a perhaps increased threat of terrorism or other serious crime.

Arguably, the 'conceptual asymmetry of the Dublin system' is at least partly responsible for the first two of the serious threats listed above.[183] While further integration is not the likeliest of all options politically, there is still a chance that the Union will eventually alleviate the said asymmetry by legislative means,

---

[182] *cf* C Franzius, 'Artikel 4 EUV' (2017) para 53 ff.
[183] *cf* above at n 147.

together with the possible threats to public policy or internal security that may come with it. The Commission did its part by presenting in 2016 a proposal for a 'Dublin IV Regulation'.[184] The proposal aims to 'ensure fair sharing of responsibility between Member States by complementing the current system with a corrective allocation mechanism' in cases of disproportionate pressure, and to 'discourage abuses and preventing secondary movements of the [asylum] applicants within the EU'.[185] Even prior to this, the SBC itself could be amended, including on extended time limits,[186] so as to 'legalise existing practices of Member States which [in terms of duration] are not anymore in line with the current provisions of the SBC'.[187]

As regards the question of whether the reinstatement of border control in the wake of the migration crisis signifies a resurrection of the Westphalian nation-state at the expense of EU integration, the answer is ambiguous. On the one hand, Member States tend to apply the SBC's exception clauses without much ado, thereby effectively suspending the Schengen Area and its default mode of operation. On the other hand, only a relatively small fraction of Member States had and still have internal border checks in place, and in only specific limited sections of their respective borders.[188] By having internal border checks in place, Member States strive to complement, or offset, ineffective legal rules regarding the registration of migrants and the allocation of asylum applications as envisaged by the supranational Eurodac and Dublin III Regulations. In doing so, Member States, at least in principle, rely on common rules provided in the SBC and in the EU Treaties themselves. While featuring prominently over the past few years, the Westphalian nation-state as a guardian of essential state functions, thus, has never entirely been a thing of the past.[189] It rather appears to be encoded into the EU's very DNA and the curious *Staatenverbund* the EU displays.

---

[184] Commission, 'Proposal for a Regulation of the European Parliament and of the Council establishing the criteria and mechanisms for determining the Member State responsible for examining an application for international protection lodged in one of the Member States by a third-country national or a stateless person (recast)' COM (2016) 270 final.

[185] ibid 4.

[186] See Commission, 'Proposal for a Regulation of the European Parliament and of the Council amending Regulation (EU) 2016/399 as regards the rules applicable to the temporary reintroduction of border control at internal borders' COM (2017) 571 final.

[187] Jasiewicz, 'A Not-So-Temporary Reinstatement' (2018). See also text at n 93 above.

[188] In the same vein E Guild et al, 'What is Happening to the Schengen Borders?' (2015) 8–9.

[189] Also *cf* E Evrard et al, 'The Temporary Reintroduction of Border Controls Inside the Schengen Area: Towards a Spatial Perspective' (2019) *Journal of Borderlands Studies* (forthcoming), who conclude that 'borders remain a marker of identity and security which reveals them to be an essential component in the contemporary definition of European states'.

7
'Euroreluctance' at the Heart of Europe? Challenges to the Free Movement of People in Luxembourg

CATHERINE WARIN

I. INTRODUCTION

THE GRAND-DUCHY OF Luxembourg proudly self-describes as a deeply European state,[1] with good reason. In addition to being one of the founding members of the European Economic Community and home to several EU institutions, the country of Schengen hosts numerous nationals from all EU Member States. Most notably, its dynamic job market provides employment and income to many residents of all three neighbouring EU countries: Belgium, France and Germany. Luxembourg hardly comes to mind when thinking of the rising challenges to the fundamental values of the Union. Yet, the free movement of persons has been recurrently challenged in the Grand Duchy, as demonstrated by many cases in the Luxembourgish courts.

This chapter sheds light on the forms and possible motivations of the Luxembourgish 'Euroreluctance' that manifests itself in litigation over the free movement of people before the Court of Justice of the EU (CJEU) and before the Luxembourgish domestic courts. The chapter first recalls the key rules and principles of the EU rights to free movement of persons and their implementations by Luxembourg. It then successively analyses three categories of persons who are affected by this phenomenon: the frontier worker; the frontier worker's grown-up child; and the qualified lawyer. These characters

---

[1] In 2015 the Luxembourg Government launched a heavily funded nation-branding plan: 'The Grand Duchy has always fought for a united open Europe, a Europe characterized by tolerance and solidarity', 'a cosmopolitan crossroads at the centre of Europe', 'an international meeting place where integration is an everyday reality.' This description and other materials are available at inspiringluxembourg.public.lu.

embody Luxembourg's problematic policy restrictions to the fundamental freedom of movement of persons. Many of these restrictions are relatively subtle. Yet, overall, they give rise to substantial issues, all the more acute in a small EU Member State surrounded by other Member States. The analysis suggests that the observed Euroreluctance corresponds to a defensive reflex in anticipation of the potential domestic consequences of the full free movement of EU citizens.

II. LUXEMBOURG AND THE EU RIGHT TO FREE MOVEMENT OF PERSONS

The free movement of persons was first protected in the Treaty of Rome as the free movement of workers and the freedom of establishment.[2] The Treaty provisions were complemented, in particular, by the 1968 Regulation on freedom of movement for workers.[3] Since the Treaty of Maastricht, the fundamental freedom of movement of persons covers a broader reality, ie the freedom of movement and residence for Union citizens.[4] The common theme across this evolution is that, concerned with ensuring the effectiveness of the free movement of persons, EU law (and case law) takes discrimination on the ground of nationality very seriously.

Article 18 TFEU unambiguously provides that 'Within the scope of application of the Treaties, and without prejudice to any special provisions contained therein, any discrimination on grounds of nationality shall be prohibited'.[5] This prohibition gives rise to a concrete right to equal treatment for the individuals concerned.[6] Over several decades, the CJEU has developed and consolidated a very generous interpretation of this right,[7] especially insofar as EU citizens

---

[2] Arts 48 and 52 of the EEC Treaty (Treaty Instituting the European Economic Community, 1957 294 UNTS 17).

[3] Regulation (EEC) No 1612/68 of 15 October 1968 on freedom of movement for workers within the Community (Official Journal, English Special Edition 1968 (II) 475).

[4] Art 8a of the Treaty on European Union, OJ 1992 191/1.

[5] Formerly Art 12 EC, formerly Art 7 EEC.

[6] *Van Gend en Loos* already made clear that a Treaty provision phrased as a prohibition on the Member States (the *telos* of which is the realisation of an internal market characterised by free movement – ie the four fundamental freedoms) gives rise to a correlative individual right. The same approach applies not only to provisions relating to the free movement of goods, but also to other fundamental freedoms enshrined in the Treaty and especially the free movement of workers. Judgment of 5 February 1963, *Van Gend en Loos*, C-26/62, ECLI:EU:C:1963:1.

[7] See especially the *Baumbast* case, in which the Court held that the right to reside within the territory of the Member States is 'conferred directly on every citizen of the Union by a clear and precise provision of the EU Treaty [ie Article 21(1) TFEU] purely as a national of a Member State, and consequently a citizen of the Union'. Judgment of 17 September 2002, *Baumbast and R*, C-413/99, EU:C:2002:493, para 84. See also Judgment of 20 September 2001, *Grzelczyk*, C-184/99, EU:C:2001:458, para 31, in which the Court famously stated that 'Union citizenship is destined to be the fundamental status of nationals of the Member States'.

are concerned.[8] The rights of EU workers and citizens are, in turn, mirrored by correlative obligations binding on national authorities, and these rights must be effectively respected by the legislation and administrative practice of the Member States.[9] This also has financial implications for individuals and Member States, for instance when it comes to family allowances and other social assistance benefits.[10]

Following this long and consistent evolution, direct discrimination by public authorities against EU citizens on grounds of nationality no longer raises significant problems and, therefore, does not constitute the main concern in the case law on the free movement of people.[11] Indirect discrimination on the same grounds, however, constitutes a more complex and more persistent challenge. As observed by Advocate General Jacobs, 'discrimination on the basis of residence has been a recurrent theme in the Court's case law as a form of indirect discrimination on grounds of nationality'.[12] As we shall see, this observation applies very well to Luxembourg.

The Grand Duchy has a rather atypical population structure. Its total resident population includes 48 per cent of foreigners (86 per cent of whom are EU citizens). The proportion of foreigners in the labour force amounts to 71 per cent (45 per cent of the labour force is composed of frontier workers, the other 26 per cent are foreign residents). The proportion of frontier workers has increased spectacularly between 1961 (3 per cent) and 2010 (45 per cent, with one in two commuting from France).[13] The Luxembourgish economy, perhaps more than any other EU Member State,[14] undoubtedly thrives on the free movement of persons.

---

[8] The issue of free movement of third-country nationals is outside the scope of this study. On the distinction and difference of approach see, eg, C Hublet, 'Some foreigners more equal than others under EU law' in S Bonjour, A Rea and D Jacobs (eds), *The Others in Europe: Legal and Social Categorization in Context* (Brussels, Editions de l'Université de Bruxelles, 2011); S Morano-Faodi, 'Third Country Nationals Versus EU Citizens: Discrimination Based on Nationality and the Equality Directives' (2010) available at ssrn.com/abstract=1729141; E Muir, 'Enhancing the Protection of Third Country Nationals against Discrimination: Putting EU Anti-Discrimination Law to the Test' (2011) 18 *Maastricht Journal of European and Comparative Law* 136.

[9] eg judgment of 23 March 2006, *Commission v Belgium*, C-408/03, EU:C:2006:192, which invalidated the conditions for granting residence permits and orders to leave Belgian territory issued to citizens of the Union.

[10] See, eg, judgment of 12 May 1998, *Martínez Sala v Freistaat Bayern*, C-85/96, EU:C:1998:217; judgment of 7 September 2004, *Trojani*, C-456/02, EU:C:2004:488.

[11] R Plender, 'Equality and Non-Discrimination in the Law of European Union' (1995) 7 *Pace International Law Review* 57; see also E Ellis and P Watson, *EU Anti-Discrimination Law* (Oxford, Oxford University Press, 2012).

[12] Opinion of Advocate General Jacobs delivered on 20 November 2003, *Pusa*, C-224/02, EU:C:2003:634, para 17.

[13] Grand-Duché de Luxembourg, 'Population et multiculturalité', available at www.luxembourg.public.lu/fr/le-grand-duche-se-presente/luxembourg-tour-horizon/population-et-multiculturalite/.

[14] R Mironescu, 'Luxembourg Has Largest Proportion of Mobile Workers In EU', *Luxembourg Times* (28 February 2018), available at luxtimes.lu/european-union/32974-luxembourg-has-largest-proportion-of-mobile-workers-in-eu.

138 Catherine Warin

Nevertheless, Luxembourg is not at the forefront of implementing the EU requirements deriving from this fundamental freedom. This is not necessarily an expression of bad will: after all, for a country with a legislature proportionate to its size, and therefore with smaller capacity than that of other EU Member States, the work of transposing and implementing the abundant EU legislation is a particularly acute challenge. This is perhaps why the 1972 law on the entry and residence of foreigners[15] stayed in force, essentially unchanged, until the late 2000s, when it was finally abrogated and replaced by a new law[16] to comply with the evolution of EU legislation allowing for the free movement of EU citizens, especially Directive 2004/38.[17] On the other hand, the advantage of the Luxembourgish legal order is that it is profoundly monist and has no major conceptual issue in receiving and applying international and European norms,[18] such as the Regulation on freedom of movement for workers.

This did not prevent at least one infamous case of blatant direct discrimination of workers on grounds of nationality, which was brought before the CJEU in 1990.[19] Up to this date, only Luxembourgish nationals had a right to vote in occupational guilds, even though foreign workers also paid a membership fee for these bodies, which had a consultative function in the national legislative process. One organisation employing many foreign nationals refused to pay the contribution and took the matter to court. The CJEU found that the freedom of movement of workers precluded this discrimination, at least in so far as it applied to European citizens.[20] The law was modified following

---

[15] Loi du 28 mars 1972 concernant 1. l'entrée et le séjour des étrangers; 2. le contrôle médical des étrangers; 3. l'emploi de la main-d'œuvre étrangère, Mémorial A – No 24, 13 April 1972.

[16] Loi du 29 août 2008 1) portant sur la libre circulation des personnes et l'immigration; 2) modifiant: la loi modifiée du 5 mai 2006 relative au droit d'asile et à des formes complémentaires de protection; la loi modifiée du 29 avril 1999 portant création d'un droit à un revenu minimum garanti; le Code du travail; le Code pénal; 3) abrogeant: la loi modifiée du 28 mars 1972 concernant 1. l'entrée et le séjour des étrangers; 2. le contrôle médical des étrangers; 3. l'emploi de la main-d'œuvre étrangère; la loi du 26 juin 1953 portant fixation des taxes à percevoir en matière de cartes d'identité pour étrangers; la loi du 28 octobre 1920 destinée à endiguer l'affluence exagérée d'étrangers sur le territoire du Grand-Duché (Mémorial A – No 138, 10 September 2008).

[17] Directive 2004/38/EC of the European Parliament and of the Council of 29 April 2004 on the right of citizens of the Union and their family members to move and reside freely within the territory of the Member States, OJ L 158, 30.4.2004, pp 77–123. See F Moyse, 'Grand-Duchy of Luxembourg: Report on the free movement of workers', European Commission (2006).

[18] Conseil d'État, *Le Conseil d'État, gardien de la Constitution et des Droits et Libertés fondamentaux* (Luxembourg, 2006) 567; P Schmit with E Servais, *Précis du droit constitutionnel* (Luxembourg, Saint-Paul, 2009) 86; P Kinsch, 'L'application du droit international public par les tribunaux luxembourgeois' (1993) 3 *Annales du droit luxembourgeois* 183, 190; C Sauer-Rappe, 'Le contrôle juridictionnel de conventionnalité et de constitutionnalité des lois au Grand-Duché de Luxembourg' (PhD thesis, University of Luxembourg, 2018).

[19] Judgment of 4 July 1991, *ASTI v Chambre des employés privés*, C-213/90, EU:C:1991:291.

[20] S Kollwelter and S Pauly, 'Entretien avec Monsieur Jean-Claude Juncker, ministre du Travail et des Finances, Président du Parti chrétien-social' (October 1991) 130 *Forum für Politik, Gesellschaft und Kultur in Luxemburg* 3.

this judgment.[21] Apart from this notable but already ancient case, most issues recently taken to court show that the free movement of persons is mainly being challenged through indirect forms of discrimination. Because of the proportion of the working population that they potentially impact upon, these court cases often attract important domestic media coverage.[22]

III. THREE PROTAGONISTS, THREE LUXEMBOURGISH CHALLENGES TO THE FUNDAMENTAL FREEDOM OF MOVEMENT

A. The Frontier Worker: Discriminatory Income Taxation of Non-Resident Workers

Most frontier workers in Luxembourg pay their income tax in the Grand-Duchy. Consequently, they have been repeatedly exposed to discrimination by the Luxembourgish tax authorities, compared to another category of taxpayers, ie resident workers.

This has been an issue ever since the phenomenon of frontier workers developed as a characteristic of the Luxembourgish economy, as illustrated already in the CJEU's 1990 ruling in *Biehl*.[23] Mr Biehl had been working and residing in the Grand-Duchy and moved to Germany, to discover that the income tax which had been anticipatorily deducted from his salary was not refundable, even though the situation that justified the tax (ie, residence in Luxembourg) no longer existed. Upon reference from the Luxembourgish administrative tribunal,[24] the CJEU highlighted the close connection between the free movement of workers and the prohibition on discrimination based on nationality under Article 48(2) EC,[25] so that the principle of equal treatment of workers with regard to remuneration 'would be rendered ineffective if it could be undermined by discriminatory national provisions on income tax'.[26] The Court

---

[21] Loi du 13 juillet 1993 portant modification a) de la loi modifiée du 4 avril 1924 portant création de chambres profesionnelles à base élective (…), Mémorial A – No 50 – 13 juillet 1993. Art 5 was abrogated and replaced by a new Art 5 providing that all members of a professional chamber aged over 18 have the right to vote. Luxembourgish nationality is required only for voters within certain specialised chambers (chambre des métiers, chambre de commerce et chambre des fonctionnaires et employés publics). Other provisions were amended so that Luxembourgish and EU nationals could vote and be elected in the same conditions (specific conditions remained for third country nationals, although much more favourable than under the previous regime).

[22] These types of case also represent the majority of those referred to the CJEU for preliminary rulings by the Luxembourgish courts – although the small total number of cases makes statistics irrelevant, as already observed in JM Goerens, 'Le renvoi préjudiciel à la Cour de justice des Communautés européennes. Rapport luxembourgeois' *ACA Europe* (2002).

[23] Judgment of 8 May 1990, *Biehl v Administration des contributions*, C-175/88, EU:C:1990:186.

[24] The administrative tribunal (*tribunal administratif*) is the administrative court of first instance in Luxembourg. Its judgments may be appealed before the administrative appeal court (*Cour administrative d'appel*).

[25] Now Art 45(2) TFEU.

[26] *Biehl v Administration des contributions*, C-175/88, paras 11–12.

insisted that the Treaty prohibited 'all covert forms of discrimination which, by the application of other criteria of differentiation, lead to the same result' as open discrimination.[27] In the case in point, the criterion of permanent residence entailed 'a risk that it [would] work in particular against taxpayers who [were] nationals of other Member States'.[28] The concern for the effectiveness of the prohibition on discrimination overrode the justification advanced by the Luxembourgish authorities, ie protecting the progressivity of the domestic tax system.[29]

The Court maintained this position in its 1995 *Schumacker* judgment.[30] Still, the Luxembourgish legislator did not amend its law to comply with this interpretation. In view of this inertia, the European Commission launched an infringement procedure and the CJEU held in 1995 that Luxembourg had failed to fulfil its obligations under Article 48 EC.[31]

This sequence of litigation before the CJEU had far-reaching consequences in Luxembourg, where other taxpayers realised they could rely on Article 48 EC to protect their financial interests. In a later case, both the administrative tribunal and the administrative appeal court diligently applied the CJEU's case law and concluded that the challenged provisions of the Luxembourgish tax legislation were indeed contrary to Community law and, therefore, had to be disapplied.[32] All in all, a textbook illustration of the primacy of EU law over domestic law as well as of loyal co-operation from the Luxembourgish judges – who willingly referred preliminary questions to the CJEU in two cases and then consistently applied the relevant case law.

The story, however, does not end on this positive note, as the Luxembourgish legislator was not so diligent in drawing conclusions from the CJEU's interventions. By the end of 1997, it had introduced a new provision in its law on income tax (Article 157ter LIR), which was supposed to ensure compliance with EU law.[33] This proved insufficient. Before long the matter was back before

---

[27] *Biehl v Administration des contributions*, C-175/88, para 13 and case law cited.

[28] *Biehl v Administration des contributions*, C-175/88, para 14.

[29] As explained by the Luxembourgish authorities during the proceedings before the CJEU: *Biehl v Administration des contributions*, C-175/88, para 15.

[30] The Court held that Art 48 EC was 'capable of limiting the right of a Member State to lay down conditions concerning the liability to taxation of a national of another Member State and the manner in which tax is to be levied on the income received by him within its territory' because it did not allow a Member State to treat a national of another Member State less favourably than its own nationals in the same situation, Judgment of 14 February 1995, *Finanzamt Köln-Altstadt v Schumacker*, C-279/93, EU:C:1995:31, para 24.

[31] Judgment of 26 October 1995, *Commission v Luxembourg*, C-151/94, EU:C:1995:357.

[32] Judgment of the administrative appeal court of 23 December 1999, n°11352C, confirming a judgment of the administrative tribunal of 17 May 1999, No 10918.

[33] Article 157ter of the Loi du 4 décembre 1967 concernant l'impôt sur le revenu, Mémorial A – No 79, 6 décembre 1967, introduced by the Loi du 23 décembre 1997 modifiant certaines dispositions de la loi concernant l'impôt sur le revenu, de la loi sur l'évaluation des biens et valeurs et de la loi générale des impôts, Mémorial A – No 104, 30 décembre 1997.

the CJEU in the 2000 *Zurstrassen* case. The Court again stated that the Luxembourgish income tax legislation was contrary to Article 48(2) EC and Article 7(2) of the Regulation on freedom of movement for workers.[34]

In the wake of *Zurstrassen*, the Luxembourgish courts have again shown their goodwill in applying the EU prohibition of national rules on income tax that would hinder the free movement of workers. In a 2005 case, German spouses residing in Germany but having earned most of their annual income in Luxembourg asked to be taxed jointly in Luxembourg, so that their personal situation would be taken into account in the same way as for Luxembourg residents.[35] They had negative rental income from properties in Germany and wanted this to be considered when determining the applicable tax rate on their Luxembourgish income. The tax administration, based on Luxembourgish law, refused to take this negative income into account. The claimants argued that this created a discrimination since Luxembourgish residents could include negative income from foreign rented property in the calculation of the tax rate. This, they argued, constituted a violation of Article 39 EC (former Article 48 EC) as the newly introduced Article 157ter LIR allowed for discrimination against non-resident workers to persist.

The administrative tribunal cited the CJEU's relevant case law (ie *Schumacker* and *Zurstrassen*) and recalled that the CJEU had admitted that not granting certain tax advantages to non-residents was not necessarily discriminatory. The tribunal added, still following the CJEU's reasoning, that the situation of residents and non-residents becomes comparable when the resident earns a negligible proportion of their income in their State of residence, meaning that the latter State cannot grant them advantages corresponding to their personal situation.[36] The tribunal pointed out that, in designing the new Article 157ter, the Luxembourgish legislator had failed to take into account a Commission's recommendation which suggested that the total global income should be considered when calculating the tax rate for non-residents taxed in Luxembourg.[37] The system hindered the free movement of workers by discriminating against non-residents. The tribunal concluded that this amounted to indirect discrimination based on residence, prohibited by Article 39 EC.

Still not giving up, the government appealed the judgment and the administrative appeal court referred the case to the CJEU. The latter, through a very similar reasoning, reached the same conclusion as the administrative tribunal.[38]

---

[34] Judgment of 16 May 2000, *Zurstrassen*, C-87/99, EU:C:2000:251.
[35] Judgment of the administrative tribunal of 10 October 2005, Nos 19039 and 19664.
[36] Judgment of the administrative tribunal of 10 October 2005, Nos 19039 and 19664, p 9; citing *Finanzamt Köln-Altstadt v Schumacker*, C-279/93, para 38.
[37] C (1993) 3702: 94/79/EC: Commission Recommendation of 21 December 1993 on the taxation of certain items of income received by non-residents in a Member State other than that in which they are resident, OJ L 39, 10 February 1994.
[38] Judgment of 18 July 2007, *Lakebrink and Peters-Lakebrink*, C-182/06, EU:C:2007:452.

The administrative appeal court followed the CJEU and held that Article 157ter LIR was contrary to EC law.[39] Eventually the Luxembourgish tax authorities complied with the case law through an administrative circular in 2008 which adjusted their administrative practice to the requirements of EU law.[40] At last, a law passed in 2010 modified the problematic provision.[41]

Despite the judicial interventions and legislative adaptations, the compliance of Luxembourgish tax authorities with EU law remains an ongoing challenge and the domestic courts have repeatedly proved crucial in enhancing compliance. In 2015, the administrative tribunal followed a reasoning similar to that of 2005 and invalidated a distinction between, on the one hand, separated couples where one resides in Luxembourg and the other in another Member State and, on the other, separated couples residing in Luxembourg who received a more favourable treatment.[42] In another case, pensioners challenged a condition for obtaining tax credit, ie the condition that they possess a tax deduction form issued by national authorities. They argued that this condition discriminated against non-resident workers, some of whom were not issued such a form. The administrative tribunal referred the issue to the CJEU. The Luxembourgish Government argued that this restriction was justified by the need to avoid an excessive burden of work for the administration and thus, in the long run, to preserve the functioning of the whole taxation system.[43] However, the Court was not satisfied by the justification and held that the challenged provision violated EU free movement law. The line of argument developed by Luxembourg in this case is nevertheless interesting because it suggests that the compliance challenge for Luxembourg is of a practical nature, ie that the concern lies with the practical functioning of the country's taxation system.

Looking at the restrictions imposed on the free movement of frontier workers through the Luxembourgish income tax policies, some features consistently characterise the approach of the Luxembourgish authorities – namely, delayed reactions and minimalist adaptations to the requirements of EU law, even when clarified by the CJEU. This lack of reactivity from the legislator and the administration contrasts with the approach of the domestic courts which refer questions to the CJEU when relevant and, if necessary,

---

[39] Judgment of the Administrative appeal Court of 28 February 2008, No 20675C. However, the Court agreed with the Luxembourgish tax administration that the negative rental income had to be taken into account following Luxembourgish law, not German law, which in the end did not bring a positive outcome for the plaintiffs.

[40] Gouvernement du Grand-Duché de Luxembourg, Administration des contributions directes, Circulaire du directeur des contributions, L.I.R. No 157ter/1 du 27 juin 2008.

[41] Loi du 26 juillet 2010 modifiant les articles 157, 157bis et 157ter de la loi modifiée du 4 décembre 1967 concernant l'impôt sur le revenu, Mémorial A – No 120, 28 July 2010.

[42] Judgment of the administrative tribunal of 5 January 2015, No 33979.

[43] Judgment of 26 May 2016, *Kohll and Kohll-Schlesser*, C-300/15, EU:C:2016:361, paras 45–59. E Traversa and A Maitrot de la Motte, 'Droit fiscal européen' (2017) 6 *Journal de droit européen* 233.

disapply domestic provisions to ensure that the fundamental freedom of workers (including frontier workers) is protected. The pattern is a recurring one, so that it may be described as an ongoing challenge to the free movement of people rather than a recently emerged challenge. This phenomenon will most likely deserve attention in the coming years because of the constant increase in the number and proportion of frontier workers in the country.

B. The Frontier Worker's Child: The Decade-Long Saga of Higher Education Financial Aid

As already observed, financial considerations are at stake in people's exercise of the freedom of movement – a key issue besides taxation is the question of rights to social benefits. Unsurprisingly, Luxembourg has been the stage of many court cases on social benefits for frontier workers and their families.[44] We shall focus on one emblematic saga which illustrates the Luxembourgish authorities' 'trial and error' approach: attempting to comply with EU law on fundamental freedoms while still applying a form of residence protectionism.

Up to 2010, the law of 22 June 2000 guaranteed family benefits to frontier workers whose children aged over 18 were registered in higher education programmes.[45] On 26 July 2010, a new law was voted in the Chambre des Députés, suppressing this right.[46] This law introduced a new system of financial support for students, to which only residents (or children of residents) were eligible. Although the higher education aid reform was enacted in the context of a deficit-reduction programme and was concomitant with the suppression of certain family benefits to which all children of frontier workers had been eligible, the CSV government[47] officially denied that there was any connection between its social policy and its higher education policy.[48] The official explanation

---

[44] In addition to those discussed here, see, eg, Judgment of 3 October 2000, *Ferlini*, C-411/98, EU:C:2000:530, where the CJEU held that application by a healthcare provider to EC officials of scales of fees for medical and hospital care which were higher than those applicable to residents affiliated to the national social security scheme constituted discrimination on the ground of nationality prohibited under the Treaty. See also judgment of 13 December 2012, *Caves Krier Frères*, C-379/11, EU:C:2012:798 concerning discrimination of job seekers on grounds of residence.
[45] Loi du 22 juin 2000 concernant l'aide financière de l'Etat pour études supérieures, Mémorial A – No 49, 28 juin 2000.
[46] Loi du 26 juillet 2010 modifiant: 1. la loi modifiée du 22 juin 2000 concernant l'aide financière de l'Etat pour études supérieures (…), Mémorial A – No 118, 27 juillet 2010.
[47] The CSV is Luxembourg's Social Christian Party, a right-wing party following a Christian Democratic ideology.
[48] 'Nous n'avons pas transformé les allocations familiales en bourses d'études' (we did not transform family benefits into scholarships), said François Biltgen, then Higher Education Minister. P Thery, 'Nous n'allons pas financer sans fin un étudiant', *L'essentiel* (26 July 2014), available at www.lessentiel.lu/fr/news/story/30223869. See also Luxembourg's Chamber of Deputies, Report on Session 43, 13 July 2010.

for the reform was the government's ambition to increase the proportion of Luxembourg residents holding a higher education degree.[49]

The law was drafted in urgency to be applicable for the academic year 2010–2011. The Conseil d'Etat, pressed to observe this time constraint when reviewing the law, showed little enthusiasm for the new approach but did not elaborate on its reluctance.[50] During the discussion in the Chambre des Députés prior to the vote, several opposition parties pointed out that the democratic process had been shaken up: in addition to the Council of State being pressed to deliver its opinion, no time had been granted for the country's professional chambers to provide their own opinions.[51] An in-depth assessment prior to the vote could have perhaps avoided the long saga that followed. Indeed, the newly voted law was met with harsh criticism from opposition parties,[52] associations of frontier workers,[53] and trade unions.[54]

The law's immediate consequence was that children of frontier workers above 18 years old were no longer entitled to family benefits nor to student financial support.[55] The European Commission considered this a violation of the freedom of movement of workers and considered initiating infringement proceedings against the Grand Duchy.[56] It was also not long before the administrative tribunal faced about 600 actions challenging the refusal of financial aid for higher education to children of Belgian, French and German frontier workers. The claimants argued before the administrative courts that this new law instituted indirect discrimination and asked that the following question be referred to the CJEU: was such discrimination precluded in light of Article 7(2) of the Regulation on freedom of movement for workers or was it justified in light of the aim?

---

[49] As explained by François Biltgen in a letter to the Commission dated 26 May 2011, available at www.europaforum.public.lu/fr/dossiers-thematiques/2011/loi-etudes-sup/Mise_en_demeure2011-4032_lettre_COMM_reponse_FB.pdf.

[50] Chambre des Députés, document No 6148/01, Avis du Conseil d'Etat du 29.6.2010.

[51] Chambre des Députés, rapport sur la séance 43, 13 July 2010.

[52] See, eg, the Green party's comments: 'Claude Turmes dénonce dans une lettre ouverte adressée à Viviane Reding la politique "anti-européenne et donc totalement inacceptable" du gouvernement luxembourgeois' *Europaforum* (15 September 2010), available at www.europaforum.public.lu/fr/actualites/2010/09/turmes-lettre-reding/index.html.

[53] 'Allocations familiales et aides aux études supérieures: la commission des frontaliers belges du LCGB appelle le gouvernement à revoir sa position au nom de l'arrêt de la CJCE dit Meeusen', *Europaforum* (9 September 2010), available at www.europaforum.public.lu/fr/actualites/2010/09/lcgb-arret-meeusen/index.html.

[54] 'Lors de la manifestation syndicale contre la loi sur l'aide financière de l'Etat pour études supérieures, le droit communautaire et le projet européen ont été les références essentielles pour une solution politique', *Europaforum* (16 September 2010), available at www.europaforum.public.lu/fr/actualites/2010/09/manif-aide-etudes/index.html.

[55] P Peuvrel, 'L'affaire des aides financières' (5 March 2013), available at www.jurislux.eu/laffaire-des-aides-financières/.

[56] Formal notice of the European Commission, 2011/4032, C(2011) 2227 final, 6 April 2011.

This aim, as the Luxembourgish Government explained before the CJEU in *Giersch*,[57] was to increase the proportion of residents holding a higher education degree. This in turn was meant to promote the development of the domestic economy. The CJEU unsurprisingly confirmed that making the grant of financial aid for higher education studies conditional upon residence by the student in the Member State granting the aid gave rise to a difference of treatment. This amounted to indirect discrimination between residents of the Member State and the children of non-resident frontier workers carrying out an activity in that Member State. The Court admitted that increasing the proportion of holders of higher education degrees in the resident population is an objective of general (both economic and social) interest that could justify indirect discrimination.[58] In addition, a frontier worker is not necessarily integrated in the Member State of employment in the same way as a worker residing in that state. The Member State of employment is therefore entitled to ask them to demonstrate their attachment to this state.[59] However, the Court held that the condition of residence imposed by the new law was disproportionate.

This time, both the Luxembourgish lawmakers and courts quickly reacted to the judgment. One solution hinted at in the judgment was that the host state could require a minimal duration, a 'significant period of time', possibly of five years of employment in Luxembourg.[60] Based on this, a new law was precipitously adopted on 9 July 2013, before the start of the 2013/14 academic year.[61] In the meantime, the cases argued before the CJEU were back before the administrative tribunal which delivered a series of judgments on 14 October 2013 applying the *Giersch* judgment (and dismissing the Luxembourgish Government's argument that this solution should not be applied retroactively).[62]

Again, however, the legislative adaptation to the CJEU's case law was to prove inadequate.[63] The requirement of a minimal duration of five uninterrupted

---

[57] Judgment of 20 June 2013, *Giersch and others*, C-20/12, EU:C:2013:411.

[58] E Neframi, 'Principe d'intégration et pouvoirs de l'Etat membre' (2013) 4 *Revue des affaires européennes* 709.

[59] *Giersch and others*, C-20/12, paras 64–65.

[60] This solution has been criticised in that it may put frontier workers at a disadvantage compared to other EU workers. J Gerkrath, 'Des aides financières discriminatoires? L'arrêt de la Cour de justice de l'Union européenne dans l'affaire Elodie Giersch et autres contre Etat du Grand-Duché de Luxembourg' (2014) 337 *Forum für Politik, Gesellschaft und Kultur in Luxemburg*, 10; JY Carlier, 'La marge d'appréciation du juge national en matière de libre circulation des travailleurs, une figure à géométrie variable' in E Neframi (ed), *Renvoi préjudiciel et marge d'appréciation du juge national* (Brussels, Larcier, 2015); A Iliopoulou-Penot, 'Citoyenneté de l'Union, mobilité et intégration dans l'espace européen' (2014) 3 *Revue de l'OFCE* 29.

[61] See the Giersch story narrated by the President of the Administrative appeal court F Delaporte, 'Juges luxembourgeois et juges de la CJUE', interviewed by C Warin for *Blogdroiteuropeen* (17 November 2016), available at blogdroiteuropeen.com/2016/11/17/juges-luxembourgeois-et-juges-de-la-cjue-interview-de-francis-delaporte-partie-3/.

[62] Judgment of the administrative tribunal of 14 October 2013, Nos 27576, 27679, 27689 and 28442.

[63] A Lagoutte, 'Bourses d'études pour non-résidents: une histoire sans fin' (December 2015) 12 *Legimag*.

years of work in Luxembourg for parents of non-resident students applying for financial aid was challenged in court and the issue was referred to the CJEU. The latter held that the requirement of continuity was indeed too restrictive because it excluded workers who had been working in the Grand-Duchy for periods of time that amounted to possibly much more than five years, but with brief periods of interruption.[64] In parallel, another issue was raised before the courts. The Ministry of Education interpreted the law as meaning that children of the spouse or partner of a frontier worker were not eligible to the financial aid scheme. The CJEU held, however, that those children had to be included within the beneficiaries of the law when they were being supported by their (frontier worker) step-parent.[65] The Luxembourgish Ministry of Education reacted promptly to the judgment by issuing two press statements within a few hours, announcing that the law would be modified accordingly.[66] This case thus illustrates the key role that domestic courts play (especially when they trigger a dialogue with the CJEU) in encouraging legislative compliance with the EU requirements on free movement.[67]

By contrast, the last high-profile judicial episode to date has been described in the media as a huge setback for frontier workers and their families.[68] The Ministry of Education used to deduct the housing aid and family benefits received by young adults in France or Belgium from the amount which they could be granted through the higher education financial aid scheme. The claimants suggested that the question of whether and how to take into account the aids received in the Member State of residence should be referred to the CJEU. In its judgment of 16 February 2017, however, the administrative appeal court refused to refer the question and confirmed the approach of the Ministry of Education.[69] It held that, even though the aids perceived in the state of residence did not constitute financial aid for higher education in the strict sense, they practically served the same function and, therefore, should indeed be deducted from the education aid. This is a questionable conclusion, given the previous case law of the CJEU on similar issues, which suggests instead that benefits granted in different Member

---

[64] Judgment of 14 December 2016, *Bragança Linares Verruga and Others*, C-238/15, EU:C:2016:949; G Friden and A Germeaux, 'Chronique – Cour de justice de l'Union européenne 2016' (2016) 26 *Annales du droit luxembourgeois*.

[65] Judgment of 15 December 2016, *Depesme and Kerrou*, C-401/15 to C-403/15, EU:C:2016:955.

[66] Available at www.gouvernement.lu/6582250/15-aides-financieres and www.gouvernement.lu/6578776/14-ue-enseignement.

[67] M Pena Pinon, *La fonction juridictionnelle au service de l'intégration sud-américaine: Regards croisés sur la contribution des juges régionaux à la construction d'un espace intégré: Europe et Amérique du Sud* (Baden-Baden, Nomos, 2017) 270.

[68] C Damiani, 'Bourses d'études pour les frontaliers: la bataille judiciaire se poursuit' *Le Quotidien* (10 March 2017), available at www.lequotidien.lu/politique-et-societe/bourses-detudes-pour-les-frontaliers-la-bataille-judiciaire-se-poursuit; C Frati, 'Jeudi noir pour les frontaliers' *Paperjam* (26 April 2017), available at paperjam.lu/news/jeudi-noir-pour-les-frontaliers.

[69] Judgment of the administrative appeal court of 16 February 2017, No 38154C.

States cannot systematically be compared.⁷⁰ In any case, the length of the judgment, mirroring the complexity of the issue, raises in itself serious doubts as to whether the decision not to refer the matter to the CJEU was wise.⁷¹ Thus, in addition to the legal justification that is contained in the judgment itself, it cannot be excluded that political factors may also have been considered by the appeal court. After all, many studies have emphasised that 'courts may make the strategic choice not to submit a reference to the CJEU if the outcome of the preliminary ruling procedure is expected to have a negative effect on national policy'.⁷² One can here only speculate as to whether the appeal court's judgment was influenced by such considerations – perhaps a fear of pushing too far in an already long and complicated saga, and of ending up with a counterproductive result (ie a financially unsustainable higher education aid scheme)?

In the higher education financial aid story, the Luxembourgish legislator oscillates between precipitation in adjusting to recent developments in EU law and reluctance to draw full conclusions from these developments. The administration, meanwhile, performs a conservative reading of the law. As we have seen in the previous example on taxation, the necessary adjustments eventually happen thanks to judicial processes with the administrative tribunal being consistently willing to give full effect to the fundamental freedom of movement of persons. Time will tell whether the administrative appeal court, which so far readily referred relevant issues to the CJEU, will continue doing so or whether the February 2017 judgment indicates a shift in its perception of the duty of sincere co-operation⁷³ – if the latter it would become more difficult for frontier workers and their children to rely on litigation in response to restrictions to their freedom of movement.

C. The European Lawyer: The Language Barrier to Free Establishment

Luxembourg employs many lawyers, most of whom are not Luxembourg nationals and/or have been trained outside the country for at least part of their curriculum (unsurprisingly, since the Faculty of Law of the University

---

⁷⁰ eg judgment of 8 May 2014, *Wiering*, C-347/12, EU:C:2014:300: for the purpose of calculating the supplementary allowance to which a migrant worker may be entitled in their Member State of employment, all the family benefits received by the worker's family under the legislation of the Member State of residence should not be systematically taken into account since the family benefits granted by the different States are not necessarily of the same kind.

⁷¹ See the strict criteria laid down by the CJEU for not referring a question in a last instance case: judgment of 29 February 1984, *CILFIT*, C-77/83, EU:C:1984:91.

⁷² JMR Van Casteren, 'Who Is Watching the Courts? Supervising the Preliminary Ruling Procedure' (Master's thesis, Tilburg University, 2016) 29. See also G Tridimas and T Tridimas, 'National Courts and the European Court of Justice: A Public Choice Analysis of the Preliminary Reference Procedure' (2004) 24 *International Review of Law and Economics* 125.

⁷³ Concerning the duty of sincere co-operation see, eg, E Neframi, 'Le principe de cooperation loyale comme fondement identitaire de l'Union européenne' (2012) 556 *Revue du Marché Commun et de l'Union européenne* 197.

of Luxembourg was created only 15 years ago). Issues in relation to the free movement of lawyers therefore provide an interesting example of obstacles to the freedom of establishment in Luxembourg. Over the years, the multiple restrictions have impacted on both lawyers qualified in other Member States and EU citizens obtaining their lawyer's qualification in Luxembourg.

From the onset, Luxembourg actively and consistently opposed the free movement of lawyers,[74] and especially the adoption of Directive 98/5/EC, the 'home title' directive organising the freedom of establishment in a Member State for lawyers who have obtained their qualification in another Member State.[75] The Grand-Duchy first challenged the validity of the directive through an action for annulment – this failed.[76] Pressured by an action for failure to fulfil obligations initiated by the Commission,[77] the country eventually transposed the directive into its domestic legislation in 2002.[78] The transposition was, however, minimalistic as it maintained some of the key restrictions of the previous legislation.[79] In addition, the reform introduced a strict requirement that lawyers practising in Luxembourg must master all three national languages (German, French and Luxembourgish). Since this condition did not exist before 2002,[80] it could reasonably be understood as an attempt to mitigate the directive's effects by limiting the influx of foreign-trained lawyers in the country.

The new law was promptly challenged in court and this led to the famous 2006 case of *Wilson*, where the CJEU held that a lawyer who has obtained their qualification in an EU Member State cannot be subjected to language examinations prior to registering in another Member State where they want to practise

---

[74] An old but important case is judgment of 21 June 1974, *Reyners v Belgian State*, C-2/74, EU:C:1974:68, in which a Dutch national had been denied registration to the Belgian bar. Luxembourg had vigorously intervened to defend this discrimination on grounds of nationality, although the Court eventually ruled against it.

[75] Directive 98/5/EC of the European Parliament and of the Council of 16 February 1998 to facilitate practice of the profession of lawyer on a permanent basis in a Member State other than that in which the qualification was obtained, OJ L 77, 14.3.1998, pp 36–43.

[76] Judgment of 7 November 2000, *Luxembourg v Parliament and Council*, C-168/98, EU:C:2000:598.

[77] Case C-142/02 initiated by the Commission on 17 May 2000 and removed on 24 January 2002 (following adoption of the transposition law).

[78] Loi du 13 novembre 2002 portant transposition en droit luxembourgeois de la Directive 98/5/CE du Parlement européen et du Conseil du 16 février 1998 visant à faciliter l'exercice permanent de la profession d'avocat dans un Etat membre autre que celui où la qualification a été acquise et portant: 1. modification de la loi modifiée du 10 août 1991 sur la profession d'avocat; (…), Mémorial A – No 140, 17 décembre 2012. The Council of State had emphasised that the linguistic condition (all three languages) would likely be held contrary to freedom of establishment. Nevertheless, the Chambre des Députés maintained this condition in the final text. F Biltgen, 'La libre circulation des avocats au Luxembourg', *Annales du droit luxembourgeois: Volume 22 – 2012* (2014) Bruylant.

[79] Notably, the prohibition to provide company domiciliation services.

[80] M Thiewes, *La profession d'avocat au Grand-Duché de Luxembourg* (Brussels, Larcier, 2015) 70.

under their home-country professional title.[81] Simultaneously, an action for failure to fulfil obligations had been launched by the Commission and led to another CJEU judgment, delivered on the same day as *Wilson*, establishing that there was indeed failure on all counts.[82] Right after the two judgments, the Conseil de l'Ordre[83] applied the CJEU's position on the language issue and agreed to register lawyers under their home-country title without subjecting them to language examinations. However, it took the Grand-Duchy no less than seven years, and the added pressure of an infringement procedure initiated by the European Commission in October 2011,[84] along with informal consultations with the Commission and intense debates within the Chambre des Députés, to fully adapt its legislation and allow EU lawyers who had practised for three years under their home-country title to register on the bar's list of Luxembourg-qualified lawyers without having to take language exams.[85]

Within the present framework, language restrictions remain for young aspiring lawyers who must prove their abilities in all three national languages if they want to train and practise in Luxembourg.[86] Following a complaint of an applicant to the bar, who did not have the required competences in the German language, the Conseil de l'Ordre confirmed that it did not consider the linguistic requirements for accessing the bar as a trainee lawyer to be discriminatory.[87] The council stressed the need for lawyers to understand all three languages in order to ensure the proper functioning of the justice system (which indeed works in

---

[81] Judgment of 19 September 2006, *Wilson*, C-506/04, EU:C:2006:587. A Heniqui, 'Droit d'établissement des avocats – Mir verstinn eis' *D'Lëtzebuerger Land* (15 February 2007), available at www.land.lu/page/article/302/302/FRE/index.html; S Bois, 'Le non-respect par le Luxembourg de la liberté d'établissement des avocats au sens la directive 98/5', Centre d'Etudes Juridiques européennes (4 October 2006) available at www.ceje.ch/fr/actualites/citoyennete-et-libre-circulation-des-personnes/2006/10/le-non-respect-par-le-luxembourg-de-la-liberte-detablissement-des-avocats-au-sens-la-directive-985/.

[82] ie the language condition, the exclusion from domiciliation activity, and the composition of the conseil disciplinaire d'appel. Judgment of 19 September 2006, *Commission v Luxembourg*, C-193/05, EU:C:2006:588.

[83] This institution exercises administrative, disciplinary and regulatory powers over lawyers registered at the Luxembourg Bar.

[84] Infringement procedure 2010/4241, mise en demeure du 27 October 2011, C. (2010)7528, avis motivé du 27 September 2012, C. (2012) 6610.

[85] Loi du 13 juin 2013 modifiant la loi du 10 août 1991 sur la profession d'avocat, Mémorial A – No 102, 21 juillet 2013. F Biltgen, 'La libre circulation des avocats au Luxembourg' (2012) 22 *Annales du droit luxembourgeois*; C Frati, 'Semi-révolution linguistique au barreau' *Paperjam* (22 July 2016), available at paperjam.lu/news/semi-revolution-linguistique-au-barreau; C Frati, 'Un barreau remis en ordre' *Paperjam* (12 July 2017), available at paperjam.lu/news/un-barreau-remis-en-ordre.

[86] More specifically, levels required: B2 in French, B2 for oral understanding and B1 for spoken production in Luxembourgish, B2 for written production and oral understanding and B1 for spoken production in German.

[87] Conseil disciplinaire et administratif des avocats du Grand-Duché de Luxembourg, 18 juin 2014. As pointed out by Thewes, the issue might have usefully been referred to the Constitutional Court. Thewes, *La profession d'avocat au Grand-Duché de Luxembourg* 70.

three languages and needs lawyers who can keep up). This justification had already been advanced by the Luxembourgish authorities in the abovementioned cases before the CJEU. The argument makes sense provided it constitutes a reasonable restriction and not a disproportionate one.

An additional argument advanced by the council was more surprising (at least from the perspective of an EU lawyer). It emphasised that the applicant had not been prevented from entering or staying in Luxembourg while following the courses leading up to the qualification, so that her freedom of movement had not been affected in any way.[88] This was a very literal and restrictive understanding of this principle, far from the CJEU's interpretation which takes into account not only physical restrictions (which are the easiest to spot and remove) but also various indirect disincentives. At the very least, one can reasonably doubt whether such an approach would stand before the CJEU. Denying that the language condition imposes any kind of restriction to the free movement of EU citizens is bold given that Luxembourgish in particular is taught and learned almost exclusively in Luxembourg. Moreover, few EU citizens outside Luxembourg are raised speaking three languages. The language requirements, thus, give a clear advantage to lawyers born and raised in Luxembourg and they could thus well be labelled a restriction to the freedom of movement – although this could be justified by the needs of the domestic justice system.

However, even this argument is not met with unanimous approval. As Biltgen observes, there were about 100 lawyers in Luxembourg 30 years ago.[89] Now, following the surge in banking and financial activities in the country, the number has been multiplied by 25 and most of them are not Luxembourgers. The majority also do not have to deal with Luxembourgish issues in their daily work. The stringent language requirements are perhaps becoming less justifiable. The president of the Bar himself has publicly called for new, more flexible legislation, arguing that the current system prevents highly qualified lawyers from accessing the bar.[90] So far, he has not been heard by lawmakers. At any rate, the slowness with which the restrictions to the free establishment of lawyers, especially the language barriers, are being adapted to the requirements of EU law again demonstrates a form of (legislative and perhaps also corporatist[91]) 'euroreluctance' in the Grand-Duchy.

---

[88] 'La requérante n'a en rien été empêchée ni à entrer au Grand-Duché, ni à y séjourner pendant les Cours complémentaires, de sorte que le principe de la liberté de circulation n'est en rien affecté'.
[89] F Biltgen, 'La libre circulation des avocats au Luxembourg'.
[90] M Chevrier, 'On se prive d'avocats qui ont les compétences', *L'essentiel* (26 September 2017), available at www.lessentiel.lu/fr/luxembourg/story/On-se-prive-d-avocats-qui-ont-les-competences--13183760. The Minister of Justice has expressed the view that no such reform is necessary: C Frati and F Aulner, 'Un gouvernement qui débat beaucoup en son for' *Paperjam* (4 April 2018), available at paperjam.lu/news/un-gouvernement-qui-debat-beaucoup-en-son.
[91] ie specific to the lawyer profession.

IV. CONCLUSIONS: VARIABLE BUT PERSISTING EURORELUCTANCE

Our three protagonists have all been (and are still, to a certain extent) restrained in their freedom of movement by the Luxembourgish authorities. These recurring issues, mainly indirect forms of discrimination on grounds of residence or nationality, arise from a misunderstanding by the Luxembourgish lawmakers of the far-reaching implications of the fundamental freedom of movement and the EU prohibition on discrimination.

Whether this misunderstanding is intentional is not fully clear, although some (possibly cumulative) explanations may be suggested. In the public debate and before the courts, the justifications advanced by the authorities for measures restricting the free movement of EU citizens are generally a systemic argument. It is about ensuring the proper functioning of the taxation system, the social benefits system, or the justice system – with the implication that full free movement would have harmful effects on these systems at the domestic level. This is consistent with neorationalist accounts, according to which Member States' governments 'are less likely to acquiesce in adverse ECJ decisions when the country gains little (at least in the short run)' from implementing EU policies.[92] Additionally, the legislator and administration's defensive reflex could be understood as a strategy to pull the rug out from under Eurosceptics, present – for now marginally – on both ends of the Luxembourgish political spectrum. These figures have expressed views that have been described as 'soft' Euroscepticism, ie criticising not so much the principle of a European Union but rather its policies, including those relating to free movement.[93]

In any case, the domestic legislative framework and the corresponding administrative practice retain features that are incompatible with the Union's policy of fostering the free movement of people. Compliance often occurs only after a judicial sanction and often in a minimalistic way. The judicial branch appears so far to be the most consistent in observing its duty of sincere co-operation and carrying out its responsibility of protecting the rights conferred on individuals by EU law, most notably by using the preliminary reference mechanism. It remains to be seen whether the reluctance of the administrative appeal court to use this mechanism in the latest episode of the higher education financial aid story will remain an isolated case or whether it announces a shift in the appeal court's conception

---

[92] G Garrett, 'The Politics of Legal Integration in the European Union' (1995) 49 *International Organization* 171.
[93] ie, the ADR (Alternativ Demokrateësch Reform Partei, the Alternative Democratic Reform Party) on the far right, which used the slogan '*Manner Europa, Méi Lëtzebuerg*' (Less Europe, More Luxembourg) in its 2013 election campaign, and déi Lenk ('the Left') on the far left. Together these two parties account for about 10 per cent of the seats at the Chambre des Députés. See C Decroux, 'Analyse de la présence, de l'influence et de la rhétorique de partis politiques eurosceptiques dans les pays fondateurs de l'Union européenne' (Master's thesis, University of Geneva, 2017).

of its own function.[94] The CJEU itself, after all, has been described as not only a judicial actor but also a political actor which takes into account extra-legal factors, including the potential political impacts of a judgment.[95] The same may apply to national courts, including the Luxembourgish courts.

Thus, the Grand-Duchy, a country that thrives on the free movement of people, paradoxically illustrates persisting domestic-level challenges to the freedom of movement. Nevertheless, the small-scale laboratory on this fundamental freedom that is Luxembourg may still overcome the paradox and come to see the free movement of persons (especially frontier workers) as an objective of national interest and not a constraint.[96] After all, with its specific demographic and economic profile, Luxembourg is ideally equipped to become a model pupil in the realisation of the Union's free movement principles.

---

[94] It must however be conceded that, in terms of adhesion to the European integration process, the frequency of decisions to refer is only one indicator of how national courts position themselves: this was argued in the British context by J Golub, 'Rethinking the Role of National Courts in European Integration: A Political Study of British Judicial Discretion', Paper prepared for the Fourth Biennial International Conference of the European Community Studies Association, Charleston, South Carolina (11–14 May 1995).

[95] CJ Carruba and M Gabel, 'Do Governments Sway European Court of Justice Decision-making? Evidence from Government Court Briefs' IFIR Working Paper No 2005–06, available at martin.uky.edu/sites/martin.uky.edu/files/IFIR/Pub/IFIR-WP-2005-06.pdf.

[96] J Gerkrath, 'Les acquis et spécificités en matière de libre circulation des travailleurs et des citoyens au Luxembourg: "'Le laboratoire luxembourgeois'" (La libre circulation des travailleurs et des citoyens. Colloque belgo-luxembourgeois, University of Luxembourg and Université catholique de Louvain, Louvain-la-Neuve, 12 November 2013).

Part IV

Resistance Within and Against the Preliminary Reference Procedure

8

Who is the National Judge? A Typology of Judicial Attitudes and Behaviours Regarding Preliminary References

ANNA WALLERMAN*

I. THE NATIONAL JUDGE: MAN OR MYTH?

NATIONAL JUDGES HAVE the power to make or break the peaceful coexistence of legal subjects in the European Union (EU). At the request of national judges, the Court of Justice of the European Union (CJEU) has ruled on contentious issues such as the Polish judicial reforms[1] and the UK's withdrawal procedure from the EU.[2] National judges have exposed and reversed national legislatures' non-compliance with EU law obligations and have triggered far-reaching changes in the Member States' legal systems. However, they have also resisted EU law, challenged its authority and rejected the Court's judgments.

Still, little is known about the national judge. While national courts' behaviours have been subject to considerable analysis in European legal and political scholarship, the national judge remains an almost mythical figure. The national judge is not a person but a class. The national judge has no name or identity, merely a role to play. Like the ancient deities of Norse or Greek mythology, national judges are rarely spotted by mortals, yet they are ever present and relied upon as guardians of justice, protectors of the righteous and revengers of wrongdoing – in short, enforcers of law. And considering the mandate and

---

*I am grateful to Clara Rauchegger and Ola Zetterquist for valuable comments on an earlier draft. All shortcomings remain, of course, my own responsibility.
[1] See, eg, judgment of 25 July 2018, *LM*, C-216/18 PPU, EU:C:2018:586; C-522/18, *Zakład Ubezpieczeń Społecznych* (pending).
[2] Judgment of 10 December 2018, *Wightman*, C-621/18, EU:C:2018:999.

responsibilities ascribed to them in the case law of the CJEU, one wonders if they do not have superhuman powers.[3]

Drawing on, but expanding, nuancing and diversifying the mythical status of the national judge, this chapter seeks to initiate a discussion about EU law judicial decision making in a personal, rather than institutional or national, context. Based on existing literature on judges and judicial behaviours, as well as a previous study of national courts' requests for preliminary references,[4] the chapter addresses the question of when and under what circumstances national judges' behaviours challenge the authority of EU law in the Member States' legal systems. In particular, the chapter focuses on national judges' use, or non-use, of the preliminary reference procedure laid down in Article 267 of the Treaty on the Functioning of the European Union (TFEU). It argues that national judges are not a homogeneous group, but that their motivations for referring, as well as for refraining from referring, differ based not only on specialisation and nationality but also on personal preferences and world views.[5] Furthermore, it argues that these motivations matter in assessing the national judge's (dis)loyalty to EU law. Interaction with the CJEU does not necessarily entail approval, and, conversely, not all non-referrals signal indifference or resistance.

The argument proceeds as follows. Section II describes the conventional narrative on the role of national courts in European integration, showing how its depiction of the preliminary reference procedure conflates national court activity with national court support. Thereafter, section III gives an overview of previous European scholarship on national courts' use of the preliminary reference procedure, noting that little attention has so far been devoted to individual judges. Section IV therefore outlines three judicial archetypes and their likely motivations and behaviour in the preliminary reference procedure. Finally, section V discusses whether and how the typical behaviours of each of the three judicial characters may constitute or contribute to Eurosceptic challenges to EU law.

II. THE PRELIMINARY REFERENCE PROCEDURE: A SUCCESS STORY?

It is part of the EU's core historical narrative that national courts have not only been empowered by, but also contributed to the empowerment of, the CJEU,

---

[3] cf, eg, U Jaremba, 'At the Crossroads of National and European Union Law. Experiences of National Judges in a Multi-level Legal Order' (2013) 6 *Erasmus Law Review* 196; M Bobek, 'On the Application of European Law in (Not Only) the Courts of the New Member States: Don't Do as I Say?' (2008) 10 *Cambridge Yearbook of European Legal Studies* 1.

[4] A Wallerman, 'Can Two Walk Together, Except They Be Agreed? Preliminary References and (the Erosion of) National Procedural Autonomy' (2019) 44 *European Law Review* 159.

[5] cf O Wiklund, 'Taking the World View of the European Judge Seriously – Some Reflections on the Role of Ideology in Adjudication' in O Wiklund (ed), *Judicial Discretion in European Perspective* (Stockholm, Norstedts/Kluwer, 2003).

particularly through the preliminary reference procedure.[6] According to the Court itself, the procedure forms an integral part of the 'complete system of legal remedies and procedures'[7] and is a 'keystone' in the judicial system of the Union.[8]

Among scholars, the preliminary reference procedure has also been highlighted as pivotal in the Union's judiciary and hailed as a success story of European integration.[9] Dissenting, critical voices have been raised, but mostly drowned out by the chorus of acclaim.[10] Member State courts are perceived as the 'linchpins'[11] of the EU's system of judicial protection and

---

[6] GF Mancini, 'The Making of a Constitution for Europe' (1989) 26 *Common Market Law Review* 595, 597; AM Burley and W Mattli, 'Europe Before the Court: A Political Theory of Legal Integration' (1993) 47 *International Organization*, 64 f; JHH Weiler, 'A Quiet Revolution: The European Court of Justice and Its Interlocutors' (1994) 26 *Comparative Political Studies* 510, 518–20; M Pollack, *The Engines of European Integration: Delegation, Agency, and Agenda Setting in the EU* (Oxford, Oxford University Press, 2003) 178 ff; D Chalmers, 'The Much Ado about Judicial Politics in the United Kingdom: A Statistical Analysis of Reported Decisions of United Kingdom Courts Invoking EU Law 1973–1998' (2000) *Harvard Jean Monnet Working Paper* 1/00, 3; G Davies, 'Activism Relocated: The Self-Restraint of the European Court of Justice in its National Context' (2012) 19 *Journal of European Public Policy* 76, 88; S Nyikos, 'The Preliminary Reference Process: National Court Implementation, Changing Opportunity Structures and Litigant Desistment' (2003) 4 *European Union Politics* 397, 410; T Tridimas, 'Knocking on Heaven's Door: Fragmentation, Efficiency and Defiance in the Preliminary Reference Procedure' (2003) 40 *Common Market Law Review* 9, 11; JA Mayoral, 'In the CJEU Judges Trust: A New Approach in the Judicial Construction of Europe' (2017) 55 *Journal of Common Market Studies* 551, 552.

[7] See, eg, judgment of 25 July 2002, *Unión de Pequeños Agricultores*, C-50/00 P, EU:C:2002:462, para 40; judgment of 23 April 1986, *Parti écologiste "Les Verts"*, 294/83, EU:C:1988:94, para 23.

[8] Opinion 2/13, EU:C:2014:2454, para 176.

[9] JHH Weiler, 'The Transformation of Europe' (1992) 100 *Yale Law Journal* 2403, 2420 ff; CJ Carrubba and L Murrah, 'Legal Integration and Use of the Preliminary Ruling Process in the European Union' (2005) 59 *International Organization* 399; M Broberg and N Fenger, 'Variations in Member States' Preliminary References to the Court of Justice – Are Structural Factors (Part of) the Explanation?' (2013) 19 *European Law Journal* 488; A Gerbrandy, 'The Dual Identity of National Judges in the EU and the Implausibility of Uniform and Effective Application of European Law throughout the European Union' (2014) 7 *Review of European Administrative Law* 33, 59; Mayoral, 'In the CJEU Judges Trust' (2017) 551 f.

[10] See, eg, P Allott, 'Preliminary Rulings – Another Infant Disease' (2000) 25 *European Law Review* 538; J Komarek, 'In the Court(s) We Trust? On the Need for Hierarchy and Differentiation in the Preliminary Ruling Procedure' (2007) 32 *European Law Review* 467; G Davies, 'Abstractness and Concreteness in the Preliminary Reference Procedure: Implications for the Division of Powers and Effective Market Regulation' in N Nic Shuibhne (ed), *Regulating the Internal Market* (Cheltenham, Edward Elgar Publishing, 2006), 210. It is telling that concerns over the functioning of the preliminary reference system are often framed in the positive terms of the Court falling 'victim of its own success'; see, eg, K Lenaerts, 'The Unity of European Law and the Overload of the ECJ – The System of Preliminary Rulings Revisited' in I Pernice, J Kokott and C Saunders (eds), *The Future of the European Judicial System in a Comparative Perspective* (Baden-Baden, Nomos, 2006), 211, 212; DU Galetta, 'European Court of Justice and Preliminary Reference Procedure Today: National Judges, Please Behave!' in U Becker, A Hatje, M Potacs and N Wunderlich (eds), *Verfassung und Verwaltung in Europa. Festschrift für Jürgen Schwarze zum 70. Geburtstag* (Baden-Baden, Nomos, 2014) 674; N Wahl and L Prete, 'The Gatekeepers of Article 267 TFEU: On Jurisdiction and Admissibility of References for Preliminary Rulings' (2018) 55 *Common Market Law Review* 511, 543 f.

[11] K Lenaerts, I Maselis and K Gutman, *EU Procedural Law* (Oxford, Oxford University Press, 2014) 3; K Alter, *Establishing the Supremacy of European Law* (Oxford, Oxford University Press, 2001) 33.

'willing partners'[12] in a 'symbiotic relationship'[13] with the CJEU under the 'genius process'[14] of preliminary references. In particular, they are credited with having functioned as engines of the Union's legal development and deepening integration, often achieved through what has been seen as lower court activism in landmark preliminary reference cases, such as *Costa v ENEL*,[15] *Simmenthal*,[16] and *Francovich*.[17],[18] Furthermore, national courts' support has been considered vital for the enforcement of Union law against national legislatures and governments, with one influential commentator asserting that the threat of non-compliance with the CJEU is 'largely gone' '[b]ecause of national court support'.[19]

The depiction of the preliminary reference procedure as a success story relies on two assumptions: first, the extensive participation of national courts[20] and, second, the national courts' support for EU law and particularly for the CJEU.[21] These assumptions have acquired a status close to established truths in European legal scholarship. Consequently, much of the literature asks not whether national courts support European integration, but why or how they support it.[22]

---

[12] Weiler, 'A Quiet Revolution' (1994) 518.

[13] E Stein, 'Lawyers, Judges, and the Making of a Transnational Constitution' (1981) 75 *American Journal of International Law* 1.

[14] JHH Weiler, 'The Political and Legal Culture of European Integration: An Exploratory Essay' (2011) 9 *International Journal of Constitutional Law* 678, 690.

[15] Judgment of 15 July 1964, *Costa/ENEL*, 6/64, EU:C:1964:66.

[16] Judgment of 9 March 1978, *Simmenthal*, 106/77, EU:C:1978:49.

[17] Judgment of 19 November 1991, *Francovich and Bonifaci*, C-6/90 and C-9/90, EU:C:1991:428.

[18] Mancini, 'The Making of a Constitution for Europe' (1989) 597; Alter, *Establishing the Supremacy* (2001) 33; Pollack, *The Engines of European Integration* (2003) 190 f; A Stone Sweet and TL Brunell, 'Constructing a Supranational Constitution: Dispute Resolution and Governance in the European Community' (1998) 92 *American Political Science Review* 62, 65.

[19] K Alter, 'Explaining National Court Acceptance of European Court Jurisprudence: A Critical Evaluation of Theories of Legal Integration' in AM Slaughter, A Stone Sweet and JHH Weiler (eds), *The European Court and National Courts: Doctrine and Jurisprudence: Legal Change in Its Social Context* (Oxford, Hart Publishing, 1998) 227, 228. *cf* also Weiler, 'The Transformation of Europe' (1992) 2421 and 'A Quiet Revolution' (1994) 51. Recent cases, however, have shown this to have been overly optimistic, see M Steinbeis, 'Law Rules!' (*Verfassungsblog*, 24 November 2018) available at verfassungsblog.de/law-rules/; M Rask Madsen, H Palmer Olsen and U Šadl, 'Competing Supremacies and Clashing Institutional Rationalities: The Danish Supreme Court's Decision in the Ajos Case and the National Limits of Judicial Cooperation' (2017) 23 *European Law Journal* 140; M Bobek, '*Landtová, Holubec*, and the Problem of an Uncooperative Court: Implications for the Preliminary Rulings Procedure' (2014) 10 *European Constitutional Law Review* 54.

[20] See, eg, Burley and Mattli, 'Europe before the Court' (1993) 58 f; U Šadl and G Butler, 'The Preliminaries of a Reference' (2018) 43 *European Law Review* 120, 122.

[21] See, eg, M Wind, 'The Nordics, the EU and the Reluctance Towards Supranational Judicial Review' (2010) 48 *Journal of Common Market Studies* 1039, 1041, who sets out to 'challenge the dominant view in the literature that lower national courts (always) willingly take part in the judicial dialogue with the ECJ'. See also M Shapiro, 'The European Court of Justice' in AM Sbragia (ed), *Euro-politics: Institutions and Policymaking in the New European Community* (Washington, Brookings Institution, 1991) 123, 127.

[22] See, eg, Alter, *Establishing the Supremacy* (2001) 36; Carrubba and Murrah, 'Legal Integration' (2005) 415; M Claes, *The National Courts' Mandate in the European Constitution* (Oxford, Hart Publishing, 2006) 246.

However, both assumptions are problematic. First, participation is in fact not extensive. Although the number of references has consistently increased,[23] it remains low compared to the number of courts in the Union.[24] Many important courts long resisted interacting with the CJEU altogether.[25] Most cases concerning EU law – which presumably includes most cases before courts covered by the obligation to refer under Article 267(3) TFEU[26] – never come before the CJEU.[27] Furthermore, many of the references come from repeat-player courts, whereas the majority of courts – not to mention the majority of judges – may never refer a single question.[28]

Second, even if these participation rates appeared substantial, participation is a poor proxy for co-operation or even approval.[29] Challenges and co-operation in the interaction between the national and European judiciaries cannot be reduced to a question of participation or non-participation. Just as participation does not necessarily indicate acceptance, non-participation does not necessarily amount to a challenge.[30]

Questioning the use of the number of references as a proxy for the loyalty of national courts with the CJEU and with EU law, this chapter expands the discussion by analysing the questions of not only *when* and *how often* but also *how* and *to what effects* national judges enter into dialogue with the CJEU. The next section shows that while previous scholarship has contributed to significant insight on court behaviour, particularly at the Member State level, further nuance can be achieved by focusing on those who actually make (or refrain from making) the reference: the individuals on the bench.

---

[23] See, eg, Carrubba and Murrah, 'Legal Integration' (2005) 402; Stone Sweet and Brunell, 'Supranational Constitution' (1998) 67.

[24] M Bobek, 'Of Feasibility and Silent Elephants: The Legitimacy of the Court of Justice Through the Eyes of National Courts' in M Adams et al (eds), *Judging Europe's Judges: The Legitimacy of the Case Law of the European Court of Justice Examined* (Oxford, Hart Publishing, 2013) 197, 208; M Glavina, chapter 10 in this volume.

[25] eg, the Spanish Constitutional Court sent its first request for a preliminary reference in 2011 (*Melloni*, C-399/11, EU:C:2013:107), its French counterpart in 2013 (*Jeremy F*, C-168/13, EU:C:2013:358) and the German Federal Constitutional Court only in 2014 (*Gauweiler*, C-62/14, EU:C:2015:400).

[26] Bobek, 'On the Application of European Law' (2008) 26.

[27] L Conant, *Justice Contained: Law and Politics in the European Union* (Ithaca, Cornell University Press 2002) 81–83; Alter, *Establishing the Supremacy* (2001) 34; F Ramos Romeu, 'Law and Politics in the Application of EC Law. Spanish Courts and the ECJ 1986–2000' (2006) 43 *Common Market Law Review* 395; DC Hübner, 'The Decentralized Enforcement of European Law: National Court Decisions on EU Directives With and Without Preliminary Reference Submissions' (2018) 25 *Journal of European Public Policy* 1817.

[28] M Bobek, 'Talking Now? Preliminary Rulings in and from the New Member States' (2014) 21 *Maastricht Journal of European and Comparative Law* 785; Glavina, this volume.

[29] A Hofmann, 'Resistance against the Court of Justice of the European Union' (2018) 14 *International Journal of Law in Context* 264; *cf* also K Alter and J Vargas, 'Explaining Variation in the Use of European Litigation Strategies: European Community Law and British Gender Equality Policy' (2000) 33 *Comparative Political Studies* 452, 470 f in fn 27.

[30] *cf* Nyikos, 'The Preliminary Reference Process' (2003); Davies, 'Activism Relocated' (2012).

III. THE STATE OF THE ART

An extensive literature focuses on explaining why judges refer questions to the CJEU. Among the theories developed, the judicial empowerment theory has most successfully withstood the test of time. According to this theory, national court behaviour is guided by a desire to expand the courts' own powers.[31] A particularly influential development of this thesis is the inter-court competition theory promoted by Alter: lower instance courts would be more prone to interact with the CJEU to strengthen their position vis-à-vis national superiors, whereas higher courts would be more reluctant towards Europeanisation.[32]

Beyond this general explanation, scholars have relied on inter-state differences in referral rates to hypothesise as to the factors that cause national courts to refer cases to the CJEU. Stone Sweet and Brunell argued that national courts' propensity to refer is higher in areas highly influenced by EU law, particularly where inter-state trade is high.[33] Wind contended that constitutional cultures have a significant effect on reference frequency.[34] Both of these theories imply that national judges do not act strategically but, in Stone Sweet and Brunell's theory, rationally from a legal perspective (referring more questions where there is more to be asked and a higher efficiency gain from increased knowledge) or, in Wind's theory, based on domestic legal culture. Extra-legal factors, such as the level of public support for European integration,[35] or structural factors, such as population size and litigation rate,[36] have also been claimed to influence Member States' referral rates.

These works compellingly show that national legal cultures and institutional logic influence national courts' behaviour. However, Member States do not make decisions to refer, judges do.[37] As already noted, the majority of references come from a small number of courts. This indicates that intra-state

---

[31] Burley and Mattli, 'Europe Before the Court' (1993); Weiler, 'The Transformation of Europe' (1992), W Mattli and AM Slaughter, Revisiting the European Court of Justice' (1998) 52 *International Organization* 177; W Mattli and AM Slaughter, 'The Role of National Courts in the Process of European Integration: Accounting for Judicial Preferences and Constraints' in Slaughter et al (eds), *The European Court and National Courts* (1998) 253.

[32] Alter, 'Explaining National Court Acceptance' (1998); Alter, *Establishing the Supremacy* (2001).

[33] A Stone Sweet and TL Brunell, 'Supranational Constitution' (1998); A Stone Sweet and TL Brunell, 'The European Court and the National Courts: A Statistical Analysis of Preliminary References, 1961–95' (1998) 5 *Journal of European Public Policy* 66. See also Carrubba and Murrah, 'Legal Integration' (2005).

[34] M Wind, D Sindbjerg Martinsen and G Pons Rotger, 'The Uneven Legal Push for Europe: Questioning Variation when National Courts go to Europe' (2009) 10 *European Union Politics* 63; M Wind, 'The Nordics, the EU' (2010).

[35] Carrubba and Murrah, 'Legal Integration' (2005).

[36] Broberg and Fenger, 'Variations in Member States' Preliminary References' (2013).

[37] With the possible exception of Denmark, where orders for reference have to be approved by the Ministry of Justice before being submitted, see M Wind, 'The Scandinavians: The Foot-Dragging Supporters of European Law?' in M Derlén and J Lindholm (eds), *The Court of Justice of the European Union: Multidisciplinary Perspectives* (Oxford, Hart Publishing, 2018), 191, 194.

variations between courts and judges may be at least as significant as interstate variations.[38] Research into the attitudes of individual judges thus offers a valuable complement.

Some more recent studies have indeed turned their attention to judges. These studies point to the importance of personal factors such as attitudes towards the Court of Justice,[39] education in and knowledge of EU law,[40] and perceptions of the everyday relevance of Union legislation.[41] However, these studies have tended to move beyond the question of (non-)referrals and discussed other indicators of judicial behaviours in relation to national courts' EU law mandate (such as ex officio application and the use of European precedent).[42] This chapter brings the conclusions from these wider studies – which breathe new air into the discussions of the role of national judges in the EU judiciary – back to the preliminary ruling context. It discusses how judge-centred insights can help refine our understanding of judicial behaviour regarding the (non-)use of the preliminary reference procedure.

IV. THREE NATIONAL JUDGES

The various reasons for referring (or not) questions to the CJEU may be equal in effect, but they are by no means equal in motivations or attitudes. When considering whether national courts' reluctance or willingness to engage with the Court constitutes a challenge to EU law, it is essential to differentiate between not only the binary outcomes of these considerations – reference or non-reference – but also between the different motivations of individual judges.

I have invented, for this purpose, three lawyers with different and somewhat exaggerated, although by no means superhuman, qualities. I shall call them Daphne, Ariadne, and Hera.[43] They are judges in representative national courts in EU Member States and, consequently, are more or less frequently presented with cases pertaining to EU law. They will then have to contemplate – or, possibly, not even contemplate – whether or not to procure the assistance of

---

[38] Similarly, see RD Kelemen and T Pavone, 'The Political Geography of Legal Integration: Visualizing Institutional Change in the European Union' (2018) 70 *World Politics* 358.

[39] Mayoral, 'In the CJEU Judges Trust' (2017).

[40] JA Mayoral, U Jaremba and T Nowak, 'Creating EU law Judges: The Role of Generational Differences, Legal Education and Judicial Career Paths in National Judges' Assessment Regarding EU Law Knowledge' (2014) 21 *Journal of European Public Policy* 1120.

[41] T Nowak, F Amtenbrink, M Hertogh and M Wissink, *National Judges as European Union Judges: Knowledge, Experiences and Attitudes of Lower Court Judges in Germany and the Netherlands* (The Hague, Eleven International Publishing, 2011); Jaremba, 'At the crossroads' (2013).

[42] See U Jaremba and JA Mayoral, 'The Europeanization of National Judiciaries: Definitions, Indicators and Mechanisms' (2018) 26 *Journal of European Public Policy* 386.

[43] On female judges, myths and storytelling see E Rackley, 'Representations of the (Woman) Judge: Hercules, the Little Mermaid, and the Vain and Naked Emperor' (2002) 22 *Legal Studies* 602.

the CJEU. By outlining not only how they act in the application of Article 267 TFEU but also and more importantly why they act in this way, I illustrate three different national attitudes or approaches to the EU judiciary.[44] In the subsequent discussion, I reflect upon the Eurosceptic qualities and challenging implications of each of the attitudes' behaviours and motivations.

A. Judge Daphne: The Economical Judge

Judge Daphne practises economy in her professional activities, with time and effort. She strives to achieve her desired goal as efficiently and with as little wasted resources as possible.[45] In this sense, Daphne is the very opposite of her Dworkinian colleague Hercules, the super-judge who strives and is able to base all his decisions on a coherent theory of law.[46] Daphne is not concerned with whether her solution is the most elegant or correct solution; she is satisfied that the case has been resolved, the parties can move on, and she can get to work on the next case (or go home to dinner, depending on the hour).[47] This is not to be taken as criticism. If all our courts were full of Herculeses, we might get excellent judgments, but we would get very few of them. Daphne's qualities are highly useful or indeed indispensable, particularly in lower courts.[48]

Reasons for Daphne's attitude, discussed in the literature, include both institutional and personal factors. Among the former, efficiency measurements at her court can play a particularly strong role, as many national judiciaries measure judicial performances in quantitative output.[49] Among personal factors, her perception of the judicial role vis-à-vis the parties as well as the legislator is likely to influence her behaviour.[50] She might most often – although not necessarily nor exclusively – be found at first or lower instance courts. As a lower

---

[44] The three approaches are based on the three categories of preliminary references discussed by L Coutron, 'La motivation des questions préjudicielles' in E Neframi (ed), *Renvoi préjudiciel et marge d'appreciation du juge national* (Brussels, Éditions Larcier, 2015) 101.

[45] In Greek mythology, Daphne was a nymph whose beauty caught the eye of Apollo. Trying to escape Apollo's advances, Daphne pleaded with the river god to save her and he responded by turning her into a laurel tree.

[46] See R Dworkin, *Taking Rights Seriously* (New York, Bloomsbury, 1997) 105 ff.

[47] On leisure time as a goal of judicial behaviour see RA Posner, 'What Do Judges and Justices Maximize? (The Same Thing Everybody Else Does)' (1993) 3 *Supreme Court Economic Review* 1; GR Foxall, 'What Judges Maximize: Toward an Economic Psychology of the Judicial Utility Function' (2004) 25 *Liverpool Law Review* 177; A Dyevre, 'European Integration and National Courts: Defending Sovereignty under Institutional Constraints?' (2013) 9 *European Constitutional Law Review* 153 f.

[48] Bobek, 'Of Feasibility and Silent Elephants' (2013) 201.

[49] European Commission for the Efficiency of Justice, 'European Judicial systems – Edition 2014 (2012 data): Efficiency and Quality of Justice' (2014) available at rm.coe.int/european-judicial-systems-edition-2014-2012-data-efficiency-and-qualit/1680785d95, 135.

[50] U Jaremba, *Polish Civil Judges as European Union Law Judges: Knowledge, Experiences and Attitudes* (Rotterdam, Erasmus Universiteit Rotterdam, 2012), 329 f.

court judge, she does not conform to Alter's competition theory as Daphne has no interest in using her role to induce change.[51]

Daphne presumably does not request preliminary references very frequently. The studies discussed in section II provide several possible explanations for her reluctance to refer. She may find the preliminary reference procedure time-consuming and cumbersome, and thus difficult to fit into her daily schedule.[52] She may not find it to be her responsibility to clarify EU law and its national implications, preferring to leave such responsibilities to the higher levels of the judiciary and perhaps, once they have fulfilled this function, maybe even preferring to rely on their case law over that of the CJEU.[53] Relatedly, she may, particularly if she sits in a private law court, consider it impertinent to raise the matter unless prompted by the parties.[54]

When she does refer, Daphne conforms to the expectations articulated by Bobek; she is not particularly interested in entering into debate to develop the law, but expects the CJEU to return a concise and accessible answer that will be of immediate use in the case before her, hopefully directly leading to its conclusion.[55] It is likely that she will refer following requests from at least one of the parties to the dispute,[56] and that the reference and the questions referred will then be closely influenced by the parties, or possibly even drafted by (one of) them.[57]

What characteristics can we expect from an order for reference authored by judge Daphne? An illustrative example is the reference sent by the Western Court of Appeal (*Vestre Landsret*) in Denmark in *Danfoss*.[58] The case concerned the well-rehearsed theme of taxes levied but not due, and the order for reference contained lengthy descriptions of the CJEU's previous case law concerning remedies for such charges, showing the referring court to be neither ignorant nor lazy. The characteristics of judge Daphne transpire in the completely descriptive

---

[51] See fn 32 above.
[52] Nowak et al, *National Judges as European Union Judges* (2011) 52–56; Chalmers, 'The Much Ado about Judicial Politics' (2000). *cf* G Tridimas and T Tridimas, 'National Courts and the European Court of Justice: a Public Choice Analysis of the Preliminary Reference Procedure' (2004) 24 *International Review of Law and Economics* 125, 135 f, who note that the procedure is costly in terms of time, effort and materials, but appear only to consider the time, effort and materials spent by the CJEU.
[53] *cf* M Derlén and J Lindholm, 'Serving Two Masters: CJEU Case Law in Swedish First Instance Courts and National Courts of Precedent as Gatekeepers' in M Derlén and J Lindholm (eds), *The Court of Justice of the European Union: Multidisciplinary Perspectives* (Oxford, Hart Publishing, 2018), 79.
[54] Chalmers, 'The Much Ado about Judicial Politics' (2000); Coutron, 'La motivation des questions préjudicielles' (2015) 128.
[55] Bobek, 'Of Feasibility and Silent Elephants' (2013) 204. *cf* also Mayoral, 'In the CJEU Judges Trust' (2017) 557, who argues that trust in the CJEU increases if national judges believe that they will receive an answer that is easily applicable in the national context.
[56] Nyikos, 'The Preliminary Reference Process' (2003).
[57] Coutron, 'La motivation des questions préjudicielles' (2015) 128.
[58] Order for reference of 17 February 2010 in *Danfoss A/S and Sauer-Danfoss ApS v Skatteministeriet*, C-94/10, EU:C:2011:674.

approach taken in this order for reference, with no attempt at interpretation or analysis of the legal sources referenced, and no argumentation except for that provided by the parties. Furthermore, the reference is typical of her in that the referring court completely refrains from offering its own perspective or opinion on the matters referred, merely pointing out that the referral fulfils the admissibility criteria in Article 267 TFEU. Under the heading 'The *Vestre Landsret's* assessment' stands only one sentence: 'Seeing that the outcome of the case depends on the interpretation of Community law on repayment and Member State liability, the *Landsret* finds it necessary to refer the following questions to the CJEU with a request for a preliminary ruling.'[59]

B. Judge Ariadne: The Conscientious Judge

Judge Ariadne believes that a judge's first loyalty is to the law. She does not seek the easiest way out or look to somebody else to change the position of the law, but uses her skills and the legal tools available to her to devise solutions to the problems that come before her court, guiding the parties to the most suitable outcome.[60] Ariadne represents the legalist judge in the theories discussed in section II.[61] She does not give preference to the wishes of the parties, and she resists both arguments of convenience and career-optimising decisions. Her judicial decisions are based only on (her best interpretation of) the law. Where the law affords her discretion, she endeavours to exercise it coherently and rationally, basing her reasoning on interests recognised by the legal order.[62]

As with national laws enacted by a political party she did not vote for, judge Ariadne accepts the EU and its legislation as legal reality, regardless of her personal policy preferences. This means that she accepts EU law as an integral part of the legal system that she is charged to uphold, embraces the doctrines of

---

[59] ibid 16.

[60] In Greek mythology, Ariadne was a princess and guardian of the labyrinth of Crete, where the Minotaur dwelled. Before Theseus was sent into the labyrinth as a sacrificial offering to the monster, Ariadne provided him with a sword and a ball of thread, instructing him to fasten one end of the thread to the door of the labyrinth in order to find his way out again once he had slain the Minotaur with the sword.

[61] While Joseph Weiler, in his seminal work *The Transformation of Europe*, considered the content and authority of the established sources of law an 'obvious' answer with 'considerable force' as to why national courts cooperate with the CJEU (p 2425), the legalist account has been discarded in much of the literature as a naïve or at best unsubstantiated theory (see, eg, Burley and Mattli, 'Europe Before the Court' (1993) 44; Alter, 'Explaining National Court Acceptance' (1998) 230 ff). Legal scholars have, however, largely continued to argue that the law constitutes a central factor in understanding the causes of judicial behaviour in relation to the preliminary reference procedure (see, eg, M Claes, *The National Courts' Mandate in the European Constitution* (Oxford, Hart Publishing, 2006) 246 f).

[62] cf A Molander, H Grimen and EO Eriksen, 'Professional Discretion and Accountability in the Welfare State' (2012) 97 *Journal of Applied Philosophy* 214–230.

supremacy and direct effect, and considers herself to be both a national and a European judge.[63] While judge Ariadne may have opinions of her own as to the degree of harmonisation desirable, these views will be constrained in her professional activities by what she considers to be the most compelling interpretation of EU law. In the same vein, Ariadne may well be critical of the CJEU, when she finds its rulings less convincing or inconsistent with previous case law. Such criticism is then based, however, on an interpretation of the law rather than on her personal preferences.

This is not to say that she is immune to those external or internal influences that have caused behaviouralist scholars to discard the legalist theory of judicial behaviour. Ariadne is but a human being. However, she strives to resist such influences as far as possible and seeks to base herself to the greatest extent possible on compelling legal argumentation and logic.

Being guided to the greatest extent imaginable by the law, judge Ariadne's use of the preliminary reference procedure is that which most closely follows the functions and requirements set out in the case law and guidelines of the Court of Justice.[64] Ariadne enters into dialogue with the CJEU as she considers herself bound by Article 267 TFEU: by obligation if she sits in a court of final appeal, and as a matter of discretion in other cases. When she refers, it is not solely to seek the CJEU's assistance in resolving the legal problem. Ariadne considers herself a capable judge and is as such willing to take on any problem that comes before her. Her main criterion for referring to the CJEU is instead whether it is in the interest of the legal system, and particularly of uniform interpretation and development of precedent, that the matter be brought before the CJEU. Only where she serves at a court against whose decisions there is no remedy in the meaning of Article 267(3) TFEU may she also refer cases she considers herself capable of resolving, in order to comply with the *CILFIT* criteria (although complete fulfilment of those requirements can arguably be achieved only by her colleague, judge Hercules[65]). Where Ariadne does not refer, she is not less likely to apply EU law to the dispute, on her own motion if required, and she strives to integrate Union law into her rulings to the extent she finds warranted by the law.[66]

An incarnation of judge Ariadne could be responsible for the Estonian Supreme Court's (*Riigikohus*) reference in *Sintax Trading*.[67] The background of the case was the seizure by national customs authorities of goods imported

---

[63] Gerbrandy, 'The Dual Identity of National Judges' (2014) 62.
[64] See, eg, judgment of 16 January 1974, *Rheinmühlen*, 166/73, EU:C:1974:3, para 2; judgment of 6 October 1982, *CILFIT*, 283/81, EU:C:1982:335, para 7; judgment of 16 December 2008, *Cartesio*, C-210/06, EU:C:2008:723, para 90.
[65] Bobek, 'On the Application of European Law' (2008) 2 ff.
[66] cf Chalmers, 'The Much Ado about Judicial Politics' (2000), who in a British context points out that courts appear to be able to successfully apply EU law even in areas where references are rare.
[67] Order for reference of 12 December 2012 in *Sintax Trading OÜ*, C-583/12, EU:C:2014:244.

into Estonia on suspicion that the packaging of the products – a mouthwash – infringed upon the intellectual property rights of a third party. By the time the dispute reached the referring court, it concerned whether the national customs authorities had handled the issue correctly from a procedural perspective.

The order for reference clearly indicates that the ruling was requested not only at the court's initiative, but actually against the express wishes of both parties. This bears witness to the referring court's involvement and dedication to the correct legal solution, typical of judge Ariadne. Furthermore, compared to the judge Daphne reference discussed above, the order for reference in *Sintax Trading* is notable for its analytical ambition. The referring court first discussed the possible interpretations of the relevant national provisions. Finding that both parties had presented viable but conflicting arguments, the court then analysed the applicable Regulation.[68] Here, it noted that the matter had been discussed by Advocate General Cruz Villalon, in *Philips* and *Nokia*, who had reached a conclusion coinciding with that argued by the applicants in the case before the national court. However, the referring court also noted that the Regulation was silent on the crucial issue, and that the points brought forward by the Advocate General had not been commented upon by the Court. In conclusion, it found it impossible to reach any 'firm conclusions' on the matter. Considering this and that Union law was to inform the interpretation of the equally ambiguous national legislation, the court held that the opinion of the CJEU must be sought.

The order for reference in *Sintax Trading* is characteristic of Ariadne by displaying her meticulous approach. It pinpoints exactly the legal questions at issue and the conflicting and/or indeterminate legal sources and arguments. Still, it does so without containing any value statements, other than those going to the clarity of the legislation ('The administrative law division considers that the Regulation does not clearly stipulate the competence of the customs authority'[69]) and the aims sought by it ('One could also accept the position of the [defendant], that it would better conform with the aims laid down in recital 2 of the Regulation, i.e. the health and safety of consumers, if the customs authorities had competence to declare an infringement of intellectual property'[70]). No position or agenda of the referring court, other than finding the correct meaning of the law, can be discerned in the national court's communication with its European counterpart. It is precisely in this regard that judge Ariadne differs from her colleague judge Hera, whose acquaintance we are about to make.

---

[68] Council Regulation (EC) No 1383/2003 of 22 July 2003 concerning customs action against goods suspected of infringing certain intellectual property rights and the measures to be taken against goods found to have infringed such rights.
[69] Order for reference in *Sintax Trading OÜ*, para 23.
[70] Order for reference in *Sintax Trading OÜ*, para 21.

C. Judge Hera: The Activist Judge

Judge Hera holds strong opinions and is willing to use her position and the powers it affords her to further (her understanding of) justice and social development.[71] Her actions are ultimately based on her own policy preferences, in the words of Mattli and Burley, using the law as a mask and a shield – hiding her promotion of policy objectives and shielding herself from accusations of political bias.[72] Unlike Ariadne, who considers the enforcement of the law as her highest duty, Hera considers courts and judges to be moral actors. The law is for her not a goal in its own right, but a means for achieving social goods.[73] Hera is, however, not necessarily committed to a particular set of opinions; she may be a hard-line integrationist or a Eurosceptic, and she may also hold differing views on the EU depending on the subject matter.

Hera's use of the preliminary reference mechanism is equally instrumental. Her questions are, unlike her colleague Ariadne's, not expressions of true queries on her part; she knows which answer she believes to be the best and is looking for confirmation or agreement rather than explanations or solutions. When she refers questions to the CJEU, she composes her references strategically to promote her agenda and try to influence the CJEU to rule in her favoured direction. This may include explicitly arguing for a preferred outcome in the case, but it may also be done in more subtle ways. Importantly, Hera is not necessarily a protectionist judge: she can also be a proponent of deeper EU integration and harmonisation.[74] When she refrains from referring, this will most often be an expression of the *don't ask and the CJEU can't tell* strategy – namely she considers it unlikely that the CJEU will deliver the desired answer.[75] The situation presumably will arise more often when she wishes to pursue a protectionist or otherwise state autonomy-orientated agenda.

An example of an order for reference originating from a national judge Hera is *Sánchez Morcillo and Abril García*.[76] The case concerned the enforced sale of mortgaged property (which was also the defendants' home) after the defendants failed to meet their obligations under a credit agreement with the applicant. Spanish law put some limitations on the defendants' right of appeal and also

---

[71] In Greek mythology, Hera was the wife of Zeus and queen of the gods. Her husband's frequent infidelities often left her jealous and vengeful, and many myths about her concern her plots to torment Zeus' lovers and extramarital children. However, being the complex woman that she was, Hera was also worshipped as the goddess of marital unions.

[72] Burley and Mattli, 'Europe before the Court' (1993).

[73] While in European literature this type of optimising judge has not been extensively explored, she is well known in American scholarship. See, eg, JA Segal and HJ Spaeth, *The Supreme Court and the Attitudinal Model Revisited* (Cambridge, Cambridge University Press, 2002); RA Posner, *How Judges Think* (Cambridge, MA, Harvard University Press, 2008).

[74] Other studies by this author indicate that the latter stance is indeed the most common; see Wallerman, 'Can Two Walk Together' (2019).

[75] KJ Alter, 'The European Court's Political Power' (1996) 19 *West European Politics* 458, 465 f.

[76] Order for reference of 7 April 2014, *Sánchez Morcillo and Abril García*, C-169/14, EU:C:2014:2099.

entailed that ongoing adjudication concerning the debt did not temporarily prevent the enforced sale of the property. The CJEU on describing the dispute noted that the 'referring court entertains doubts as to whether this national law is compatible with' EU consumer protection law.[77] Reading the order for reference, this description is an understatement.

First, in setting out the relevant national provisions, the referring court repeatedly remarked upon and evaluated their consequences for the dispute at hand, noting inter alia that the law 'precludes an appeal regardless of the strength of the debtor's reasons', entailing that the debtor 'cannot effectively assert these reasons in the enforcement procedure'. Second, the order for reference contained a section entitled 'The deficient adjustment to EU law and the CJEU criteria'. There the referring court discussed legislative reforms aimed at bringing national law in conformity with Union law, noted that the provision at issue here had not been amended, and observed that the referring court's 'assessment that this provision may be incompatible with [EU law] motivates this request for a preliminary ruling'. Third, and most clearly, the order for reference included, for both questions, a section entitled 'The referring court's view' where the referring court explicitly stated that it considered the national legislation at issue to be contrary to Union law.

V. THE (NON-)REFERRING JUDGE: ANGEL OR DEMON?

The three judges described above are, of course, caricatures. Most national judges harbour elements of all three, with circumstances of the case or perhaps themselves deciding which of these inner goddesses is to gain the upper hand in a given situation. However, setting out their differences clearly illustrates that referrals, as well as non-referrals, may have a multitude of different motivations. Previous studies indicate that the prevalence of these motivations may vary between, for instance, Member States, levels of the judiciary, types of courts, legal fields, or constitutional culture. They may, however, also vary *within* these groups, depending on micro-level factors pertaining to the case or the judge. The factors which actually motivate judges to refer (or not) must be investigated empirically among limited groups – this is precisely the object of some of this volume's contributions.[78]

A. The Challenge of Non-Referrals

The essential question here is why and under what circumstances our three judges' behaviours regarding preliminary references constitute challenges to the

---

[77] ibid para 18.
[78] See the contributions of Glavina, Claassen and Mayoral to this volume.

European ideal. Hera's passivity, and her actions, clearly cannot be equated with Ariadne's or Daphne's. The above analysis seems to suggest that only Hera's non-referrals are to be interpreted as Eurosceptic challenges to EU legal authority in the normative sense, whereas Daphne's non-referrals constitute at most challenges in the sense of unintended hurdles and Ariadne's do not constitute challenges at all.

Judge Daphne's non-referrals are, as noted above, dictated more by a lack of time, resources or interest than by normative reluctance towards European integration. Thus, interpreting Daphne's non-referrals as signs of Euroscepticism or a lack of trust in the Union and its judiciary is probably unfair – at least at the level of individual judges. However, on a more systemic and institutional level, Daphne's passivity is problematic since it may lead to lesser enforcement of Union law. In particular, uniform application may suffer and points of EU law may go undetected. In this sense, it is an obstacle to be overcome for the promotion of legal integration. Education could presumably lessen this risk – the more knowledgeable a judge is about EU law, the easier is it for her to apply it – as could increased resources, such as libraries and other sources of expertise.[79] Failure to provide these resources may be a symptom of a negative or at least disinterested attitude towards EU law within the judiciary at large and/or among those who administer it. Judging by Glavina's contribution to this volume, such challenges are emanating from Slovenia and Croatia, and perhaps also from other Member States.

Decisions not to refer, when made by judge Ariadne, speak a quite different language – one of confidence and loyal co-operation. This is arguably not a challenge at all, but on the contrary a sign of a more advanced, and even desirable, state of integration. This approaches the ideal of EU law as an integral part of the legal systems of the Member States, as set out in *van Gend en Loos*.[80] According to this logic, the CJEU's function as an 'assistant', as it likes to put it,[81] to national courts would be another infant disease of EU law.[82] As national judges grow more confident and experienced in EU law, the Court could transition into a more traditional court of precedence.[83] Yet, Ariadne's passivity can be construed as an obstacle to the full and effective development to EU law, as it entails that opportunities to develop the law may be kept from the CJEU.[84]

---

[79] *cf* Nowak et al, *National Judges as European Union Judges*, 87 f.
[80] Judgment of 5 February 1963, *van Gend en Loos*, 26/62, EU:C:1963:1.
[81] See, eg, judgment of 5 June 2018, *Relu Adrian Coman*, C-673/16, EU:C:2018:385, para 22; judgment of 20 October 2016, *Evelyn Danqua*, C-429/15, EU:C:2016:789, paras 36–37; judgment of 10 September 2014, *Monika Kušionová*, C-34/13, EU:C:2014:2189, para 71.
[82] *cf* P Pescatore, 'The Doctrine of "Direct Effect": An Infant Disease of Community Law' (1983) 40 *European Law Review* 135.
[83] *cf* in this regard Wahl and Prete, 'The Gatekeepers of Article 267 TFEU' (2018).
[84] This point is discussed in the Dutch context by Claassen in his contribution to this volume.

Lastly, non-reference decisions from judge Hera are likely to be votes of mistrust or lack of confidence in the EU and/or the CJEU. Largely in conformity with Alter's inter-court competition theory or Weiler's empowerment hypothesis, judge Hera's non-references must be interpreted as a means of seeking to contain judicial powers at the national level, effectively and perhaps intentionally resisting harmonisation and integration. This is clearly disruptive from an EU law perspective and may also lead to lower levels of protection of EU legal rights.

B. Challenging Orders for Reference

Naturally, a reference can also contain or constitute a challenge of the CJEU's previous stances or even its competence.[85] While such references can be seen as warnings or invitations to the CJEU to take a step back, they are challenges of a different, friendlier kind. Here, the very act of referring indicates that the referring court is interested in the CJEU's opinion and willing to 'play by the rules' (although this, as the Danish Supreme Court's ruling in the *Ajos* case demonstrates, is no guarantee that the referring court will ultimately prove itself willing to follow the CJEU).[86]

Additionally, the design of the order for reference does not necessarily correspond to the motivation or character of the referring judges. The examples provided in the previous section illustrate how each judge would compose such an order under circumstances as oversimplified as the judges themselves. To give but two examples: if a conscientious analysis of the legal sources leads judge Ariadne to form a view on the questions she refers, she may well state that view in the order for reference, thus rendering it identical to that which judge Hera would compose out of ideological conviction. Judge Hera herself may well compose a completely neutral order for reference in the minimalist style of judge Daphne, if she considers that this strategy would be more likely to yield the desired result.

When the national judge does refer, it may therefore be more interesting to look at *how* she refers. Hera-style orders for reference are again easily classified as either approvals or challenges. The latter, clearly, puts the CJEU on the defensive and may be considered Eurosceptic.

On the other side of the spectrum, a Daphne-style order for reference – regardless of who composed it – typically offers little constraint for the CJEU. If the function of national courts in the EU legal order is first and foremost to provide the CJEU with cases and opportunity to develop its

---

[85] T Tridimas, 'Bifurcated Justice: The Dual Character of Judicial Protection in EU Law' in A Rosas, E Levits and Y Bot (eds), *The Court of Justice and the Construction of Europe: Analyses and Perspectives on Sixty Years of Case-law* (The Hague, Asser Press, 2013) 367, 378.
[86] Judgment of 19 April 2016, *Dansk Industri*, C-441/14, EU:C:2016:278.

now (in)famous *certaine idée de l'Europe*,[87] Daphne-style references appear ideal; they provide the Court with a blank canvas. However, the lack of contextualised information may also lead the CJEU to develop an insufficient understanding of the problem, so that the ruling may ultimately be less compatible with or easily transposable to the national context or may have to be set aside or re-referred by the national courts. Such actions not only take time and accrue costs, but may also contribute to the CJEU losing respect and legitimacy. This risk may be mitigated by an Ariadne-style order for reference which helps the Court understand the problem from the perspective of the national judge and thereby facilitates constructive dialogue between the two courts.

C. National Judges and Eurosceptic Governments

In a society based on the rule of law, courts and thereby ultimately judges also fulfil the role of guardians of the law by supervising the activities of other public actors. In this respect, the judges act as supervisors or enablers, constraining or accelerating the Eurosceptic policies of other actors. Given growing Euroscepticism in many Member States' parliaments and governments, judicial actions mitigate or intensify such tendencies. Against this backdrop, how should we understand the three national judges' decisions as regards the preliminary reference procedure?

As for judge Hera, her personal position will clearly be crucial. If she is generally pro-Europe, she will be able to petition the CJEU and presumably be an effective counterbalance to a Eurosceptic regime. If, on the other hand, she sides with the regime, she may become an equally effective agent for Euroscepticism. In this regard, judicial reforms such as court-packing or other threats against the independence of the judiciary may increase both the number of Hera judges in the national judiciary and their inclination towards Euroscepticism.[88]

Judge Daphne is at least equally liable to become an enabler of a Eurosceptic government, as her reluctance to engage with difficult questions leaves her liable to act only against blatant violations of Union law. However, Daphne may, to a greater extent than her colleague Hera, subscribe to the party autonomy principle. As a result, and also because of her lack of own (substantive) agenda, she may be more open to party initiative. Thus, in a judiciary largely populated by Daphne judges, civil society groups may have a better opportunity to advance their causes through the courts, thereby gaining access to the CJEU.[89]

---

[87] Pescatore, 'The Doctrine of Direct Effect' (1983) 157.
[88] The further implications of such developments are discussed by Mayoral in his contribution to this volume.
[89] For a thorough account on the interaction of civil society groups and the CJEU, see R Cichowski, *The European Court and Civil Society: Litigation, Mobilization and Governance* (Cambridge, Cambridge University Press, 2007).

Judge Ariadne may, alongside the pro-Union judge Hera, be least likely to be corrupted by Eurosceptic tendencies. This is, however, only valid in relation to developments contrary to Union law. Where Eurosceptic policies are enacted in conformity with the Treaties, such as the Brexit negotiations, judge Ariadne is unlikely to put any major stumbling blocks in her government's way – whereas her colleague Hera might.

D. Nature or Nurture: Questions for Future Research

The purpose of this exposé has been to nuance the debate on national courts' use of the preliminary reference procedure by adding the personal dimension of the judge. However, judges are part of the legal system and culture of their legal community, which even in Europe most often remains that of their Member State.[90] This insight brings the matter of the personality of the judge back to the discussion on national reference patterns. Can the judges we have been acquainted with in this chapter be attributed nationalities?

It seems that the Polish and Hungarian governments and legislatures are presently striving to fill their national courts with Eurosceptic or nationalist versions of judge Hera, or at the very least to keep other judges out – the opposite incarnation of Hera as well as the incorruptible judge Ariadne.[91] But even less drastic measures, or the lack of any measures except the everyday reinforcement of judicial culture through, inter alia, legal education, may encourage the development of certain judicial traits. Do common law traditions as regards judicial style spill over into the composition of orders for reference, so that we could, for instance, expect more Ariadne-style references from an Irish judge than from her French counterpart? Does a majoritarian constitution with little or no room for judicial review foster more Daphnes than Heras?[92] Is the intuition of the present volume's editors – that Swedish courts are largely populated by Daphne judges, whereas many Austrian judges seem to embody judge Ariadne – correct, and if so, why?

These questions cannot be answered in the present chapter, but should be pursued in further studies on national judiciaries. In a Europe where the independence of the judiciary can no longer – if it ever could – be taken for granted, the integrity of the national judge and her relationship with the Court of Justice appear more important than ever. This chapter has shown that although, by and

---

[90] Gerbrandy, 'The Dual Identity of National Judges' (2014) 58.
[91] See K Kovács and K Lane Scheppele, 'The Fragility of an Independent Judiciary: Lessons from Hungary and Poland – and the European Union' (2018) 51 *Communist and Post-Communist Studies* 189.
[92] Cf fn 34 above.

large, the national judge is more of an ally than a rebel in the endeavour towards the ever closer Union, her loyalty should not, as perhaps it has been, be overstated. Nor should the judge's loyalty be reduced to a matter of nationality. A thorough and nuanced understanding of who the national judge is, how she thinks and acts, and what made her what she is, may help us understand her role in both contributing to and countering the current Eurosceptic challenge.

9

Attitude or Aptitude? Explaining the Lack of Preliminary References in Dutch Competition Law Cases

JESSE CLAASSEN

I. INTRODUCTION

'JUDGES, REFER MORE preliminary questions to the CJEU!' That was the message of Sacha Prechal, the Dutch Judge at the Court of Justice of the European Union (CJEU), during the presentation of the CJEU's 2016 annual report.[1] The annual report established that the Netherlands no longer belonged to the top three Member States making the most preliminary references. Apparently, this was reason for concern. In general, the importance of the preliminary ruling procedure is indeed undisputed. The procedure is essential to ensure the uniform application of European Union (EU) law throughout the Member States.[2] It forms the cornerstone of the EU's system of judicial protection.[3] Additionally, the preliminary references of the national courts have enabled the CJEU to spur on EU integration.[4]

However, a first response to Judge Prechal's call for more preliminary questions could be to question whether this relatively lower number of preliminary references by Dutch courts really constitutes a reason for concern. In times where Euroscepticism and nationalism are gaining ground, it is tempting to interpret declining numbers of preliminary references as a negative trend attributable to these kinds of sentiments. And indeed, the literature has widely argued that, for national courts, the clarity of an EU law provision is not the only factor when deciding whether to refer preliminary questions. Several studies support the

---

[1] 'Rechters, stel vragen aan Europees Hof!', *Mr. Online*, 23 May 2017, available at www.mr-online.nl/rechters-stel-vragen-aan-europees-hof/.
[2] Judgment of 9 September 2015, *Van Dijk*, C-72/14 and C-197/14, EU:C:2015:564, para 54.
[3] Judgment of 28 April 2015, *T&L Sugars*, C-456/13 P, EU:C:2015:284, para 45.
[4] M Broberg and N Fenger, *Preliminary References to the European Court of Justice*, 2nd edn (Oxford, Oxford University Press, 2014) 2.

idea that sentiments that could be qualified as Eurosceptic may result in lower numbers of preliminary references. For example, in Denmark, dissuasion by the executive branch was found to be an important reason for Danish judges not to refer preliminary questions.[5] In the Netherlands, national authorities prevented preliminary questions from being answered by the CJEU in asylum cases by granting a favourable decision to the asylum seeker in question, thereby ending the dispute.[6] Furthermore, several quantitative studies have found support for a relation between a lack of public support for EU integration and declining numbers of preliminary references.[7]

In most cases, however, more positive alternative explanations for lower numbers of preliminary references seem to receive less attention. Instead of an unwillingness to co-operate with the CJEU, an explanation could also very well be that, for example, the national courts are perfectly able to correctly apply EU law on their own. This raises the following question: what can we derive from the number of preliminary references in a certain field or Member State? This chapter is a step in answering this question. The central question is the following: what are the motives of the Dutch courts when deciding whether or not to refer preliminary questions in competition law cases? To answer this question, the chapter first provides a brief overview of the situations that can lead to preliminary references by Dutch courts on EU competition law (section II). Thereafter, it will be shown that Dutch courts have been generally unwilling to refer such questions to the CJEU (section III). After describing its methodology (section IV), this chapter's central part focuses on the motives of Dutch courts which explain the low numbers of references (section V). Finally, a conclusion lays down the challenges that the practice of Dutch courts poses to the EU (section VI).

II. EU COMPETITION LAW BEFORE DUTCH COURTS

In this chapter, the field of competition law is narrowed down to the cartel prohibition of Article 101 of the Treaty on the Functioning of the European Union (TFEU). Together with the prohibition on abuse of a dominant position,

---

[5] M Wind, D Sindbjerg Martinsen and G Pons Rotger, 'The Uneven Legal Push for Europe: Questioning Variation when National Courts go to Europe' (2009) 10 *European Union Politics* 63.

[6] K Groenendijk, 'Waarom rechters niet naar Luxemburg gaan: politieke structuur of rechtscultuur?' in R Baas et al (eds), *Rechtspleging en rechtsbescherming. Liber amicorum voor prof. dr. Leny E. de Groot-van Leeuwen* (Deventer, Kluwer, 2015) 202–03.

[7] See, eg, CJ Carrubba and L Murrah, 'Legal Integration and Use of the Preliminary Ruling Process in the European Union' (2005) 2 *International Organization* 399; M Vink, M Claes and C Arnold, 'Explaining the Use of Preliminary References by Domestic Courts in EU Member States: A Mixed-Method Comparative Analysis', Paper presented at the 11th Biennial Conference of the European Union Studies Association, 24 April 2009, available at aei.pitt.edu/33155/1/vink._maarten.pdf. Against: A Dyevre and N Lampach, 'The Choice for Europe: Judicial Behaviour and Legal Integration in the European Union', 2 March 2017, available at ssrn.com/abstract=2926496.

this prohibition has been at the heart of the EU's competition law policy from the start. All aspects of Articles 101 and 102 TFEU can be applied by the national courts. For reasons of conciseness, the focus here will be on Article 101 TFEU, since this provision leads to the majority of cases before national courts.[8] Merger control and state aid are thus also excluded. The role of national courts, and consequently of the preliminary ruling procedure, is more limited in these areas. In merger control and state aid, the majority of the procedure falls under the jurisdiction of the European Commission: in merger control due to the one-stop shop principle,[9] and in state aid because the national court is only confined to the standstill obligation.[10] In such a case, the procedure comes directly under the judicial review of the CJEU.

There are essentially three situations in which national courts can refer preliminary questions on the cartel prohibition of Article 101 TFEU. First, Reg 1/2003 has introduced a decentralised enforcement system for EU competition law.[11] Article 101 TFEU is not only centrally enforced by the Commission under the scrutiny of the CJEU. It is also enforced by the National Competition Authorities (NCAs). In fact, Reg 1/2003 stipulates that the NCAs must apply Article 101 TFEU, in addition to the national cartel prohibition, when there may be an effect on trade between Member States (Article 3(1)). In the Netherlands, the Dutch competition rules are laid down in the *Mededingingswet* (Competition Act, Mw). Article 88 Mw assigns the Autoriteit Consument & Markt (Consumers & Market Authority, ACM), as the Dutch competition authority, the competence to apply Article 101 TFEU and the regulations based thereon. Therefore, the ACM can impose sanctions for infringements of Article 101 TFEU. The decisions of the NCAs can be challenged before the national courts. The national courts are competent to apply Article 101 TFEU (Article 6 of Reg 1/2003) and can thus refer preliminary questions in doing so. In the Netherlands, the competent court in these proceedings is the Rechtbank Rotterdam (Rotterdam District Court, Rb Rotterdam).[12] On appeal, the College van Beroep voor het bedrijfsleven (Administrative Court for Trade and Industry, CBb) is competent.[13]

Second, Article 101 TFEU is not applicable in cases where there is no effect on trade between Member States. NCAs, however, can still apply the national competition rules to an alleged cartel. In many Member States, the national

---

[8] Abuse of dominance cases comprised only 32 per cent of the enforcement decisions of the national competition authorities in the first 10 years after Reg 1/2003 came into force; see Communication from the Commission to the European Parliament and the Council, *Ten Years of Antitrust Enforcement under Regulation 1/2003: Achievements and Future Perspectives*, COM(2014) 453, p 4.

[9] R Wish and D Bailey, *Competition Law* (Oxford, Oxford University Press, 2018) 849.

[10] JLB Sierra and MAB Ferruz, 'State Aid Assessment: What National Courts Can Do and What They Must Do' (2017) 16 *European State Aid Law Quarterly* 408, 411; JW van de Gronden, *Mededingingsrecht in de EU en Nederland* (Uitgeverij Paris, Zutphen, 2017) 437.

[11] Council Regulation (EC) No 1/2003 of 16 December 2002 on the implementation of the rules on competition laid down in Articles 81 and 82 of the Treaty, [2003] OJ L 1/1.

[12] *Bijlage* 2, Art 7 *Algemene wet bestuursrecht*.

[13] *Bijlage* 2, Art 11 *Algemene wet bestuursrecht*.

competition rules have been voluntarily harmonised with the EU competition rules.[14] In the Netherlands, Article 101 TFEU is faithfully reproduced in Article 6 Mw. The Dutch legislature expressly purported to harmonise national competition law with EU law, requiring Article 6 Mw to be interpreted strictly in accordance with Article 101 TFEU.[15] In these situations, the CJEU has jurisdiction to answer preliminary questions on the interpretation of Article 101 TFEU in cases dealing with the Dutch Article 6 Mw, even though Article 101 TFEU, strictly speaking, is not directly applicable.[16]

The two prior situations both concern public enforcement of EU competition law. In the third situation, EU competition rules are enforced by private parties. Article 101 TFEU has direct effect and can thus be relied upon before national courts.[17] Therefore, this provision may be invoked to annul an agreement,[18] or to receive compensation for damages resulting from a violation,[19] in which cases preliminary questions may also be referred to the CJEU. In the Netherlands, there is no specialised jurisdiction in these proceedings. The claims fall under the general civil law jurisdiction. The Rechtbank (District court, Rb) is competent in first instance. The Gerechtshof (Court of appeal, Gh) has jurisdiction on appeals. Finally, the Hoge Raad (Supreme Court, HR), the highest court, rules on appeal in cassation.

III. THE LACK OF DUTCH COMPETITION LAW REFERENCES

Despite the possibilities of referring preliminary questions in competition law cases, Dutch courts have seemed hesitant to do so. Since the late 1990s, when the Mw entered into force, only three preliminary references have been sent to the CJEU by the Dutch courts relating to the cartel prohibition. Of these references, just one contained classic competition law questions, one contained only subsidiary questions relating to the cartel prohibition which were not addressed by the CJEU, and one was on the intersection between competition and labour law. The first reference, on classic competition law, was sent by the CBb in 2007 in the well-known *T-Mobile* case.[20] This reference's importance was highlighted by Advocate General Kokott, who, in her opinion, stated that '[t]he significance of these questions ... cannot be underestimated.'[21]

---

[14] Van de Gronden, *Mededingingsrecht* (2017), 34.

[15] The interpretation should not be stricter, nor more lenient ('*Niet strenger en niet soepeler*') according to the legislative history: MvT Tweede Kamer 1995–1996, 24707, No 3, 10.

[16] Judgment of 14 March 2013, *Allianz Hungária*, C-32/11, EU:C:2013:160, para 20. See further J Krommendijk, 'Wide Open and Unguarded Stand our Gates: The CJEU and References for a Preliminary Ruling in Purely Internal Situations' (2017) 18 *German Law Journal* 1359.

[17] Art 101(1) TFEU: Judgment of 30 January 1973, *BRT*, 127/73, EU:C:1974:6, para 16; Art 101(3) TFEU: Judgment of 13 October 2011, *Pierre Fabre*, C-439/09, EU:C:2011:649, para 49.

[18] Art 101(2) TFEU.

[19] Judgment of 20 September 2001, *Courage & Crehan*, C-453/99, EU:C:2001:465, para 26.

[20] Judgment of 4 June 2009, *T-Mobile*, C-8/08, EU:C:2009:343.

[21] Opinion of AG Kokott of 19 February 2009, *T-Mobile*, C-8/08, EU:C:2009:110, para 3.

The second reference came from the Gh Amsterdam in *UPC Nederland* in 2011. Four questions were referred on the regulatory framework for the telecoms sector, followed by four questions on the cartel prohibition. Having answered three of the first four questions, the CJEU held that it was not necessary to answer the remaining questions.[22] Finally, a third reference followed in 2013 by the Gh 's-Gravenhage in *FNV*. These preliminary questions, dealing with the applicability of the cartel prohibition to collective labour agreements, will be discussed further later in this chapter.[23]

Of course, these three instances, on their own, cannot suffice to conclusively determine that Dutch courts refer few preliminary questions on the cartel prohibition. However, two observations do support this claim. First, in the 2013–2017 period that this chapter focuses on, the total number of preliminary references by all Dutch courts together was 180.[24] As became clear, only one of those 180 references related to Article 101 TFEU. The 2013–2017 period is quite representative, because over the last 20 years, only three preliminary references were made relating to Article 101 TFEU. Thus, in the 2013–2017 period, of all preliminary references sent to the CJEU by Dutch courts, only 1 in 180 – approximately 0.56 per cent – related to the cartel prohibition. When compared to the EU-wide ratio, the share of competition law references compared to other subjects is low among Dutch courts. In the same period of 2013–2017, all EU Member States together referred 2,316 cases to Luxembourg.[25] Thirty-two[26] of these cases pertained to Article 101 TFEU.[27] This means that in the whole EU, a significantly higher share of 1 in 72 – approximately 1.39 per cent – of all preliminary references related to the cartel prohibition.

Second, as will be elaborated upon in the following sections, Dutch courts have had many opportunities to refer preliminary questions in competition law cases over the period 2013–2017. The cases discussed illustrate the motives driving the decision to refer or not refer. The objective is not to provide an exhaustive

---

[22] Judgment of 4 June 2009, *T-Mobile*, C-8/08, EU:C:2009:343, para 64.
[23] Judgment of 4 December 2014, *FNV*, C-413/13, EU:C:2014:2411.
[24] CJEU, Annual Report 2017: Judicial Activity, p 122, available at www.curia.europa.eu/jcms/upload/docs/application/pdf/2018-04/_ra_2017_en.pdf.
[25] ibid.
[26] Joined cases that are referred on the same day by the same court are considered as one reference. Cases that are joined but are referred by different courts and/or on different dates are considered as separate references.
[27] A first search was conducted with Curia's search form (curia.europa.eu/juris/recherche.jsf?language=en) with the following parameters: 'Period or date: Date of the lodging of the application initiating proceedings: from 01/01/2013 to 31/12/2017'; 'Procedure and result: "Reference for a preliminary ruling", "Preliminary reference – urgent procedure"'; 'References to case-law or legislation: "Category: Treaty, Treaty: TFEU (Lisbon), Article: 101".' However, this search seems to omit pending cases. Therefore, a second search was conducted with the following parameters: 'Case status: Cases pending'; 'Text: "101 TFEU"'; 'Period or date: Date of the lodging of the application initiating proceedings: from 01/01/2013 to 31/12/2017'; 'Procedure and result: "Reference for a preliminary ruling", "Preliminary reference – urgent procedure".' The search results were then manually checked to see whether the hit on Art 101 TFEU related to one of the preliminary questions, or whether Art 101 TFEU was mentioned for other reasons.

list of competition law cases in which Dutch courts could potentially have made a preliminary reference.[28] Nonetheless, at least 51 cases have been identified in which a Dutch court could have referred preliminary questions. Twelve of these cases (four before the HR and eight before the CBb) were before a court against whose decision there was no judicial remedy under national law in the sense of Article 267(3) TFEU, meaning that there was in principle an obligation to refer. It is striking that this number of referable cases only resulted in one actual reference.

IV. METHODOLOGY

The following section examines the motives of Dutch courts (not) to refer preliminary questions in competition law cases. This is based on an analysis of case law over the period 2013–2017 combined with interviews with judges who have been involved in Dutch competition law cases in that same period. In addition to the referred question, cases were identified in which preliminary questions *could* have been referred. These cases were compiled in three ways. First, the Dutch competition law journal *Markt & Mededinging* provides yearly overviews of competition law judgments from Dutch courts. These overviews have been browsed for new developments on the cartel prohibition. These Dutch cases were compared against questions that were referred by courts from other Member States over the same time period to determine whether the same questions also stood before Dutch courts. Second, the Dutch case law search engine, *Rechtspraak.nl*, was used to search for judgments containing an explicit consideration of the court or a request by one of the parties to refer preliminary questions. Third, all interviewees were asked for specific cases or questions in general which could have led to a preliminary reference.

This case law analysis is supplemented by 17 interviews (see Table 9.1). Thirteen judges and one senior staff lawyer[29] were interviewed. The aim in selecting interviewees was to provide a complete picture by including a wide variety of judges. Judges in two different district courts and two courts of appeal were selected. Furthermore, the selection included judges with varying experience with the preliminary ruling procedure: repeat players, one-shotters and non-referrers. The interviews were conducted at the location of each interviewee. Each interview started with open questions about motives when deciding whether or not to refer. Thereafter, judges were asked about their opinion on specific motives identified in the literature, about factors which would make the

---

[28] Creating a complete overview would be impossible, as a significant number of cases, especially before lower courts, are not published.

[29] In the Netherlands, staff lawyers support the judges in the preparation and drafting of the judgments; see, eg, NL Holvast, *In the Shadow of the Judge: the Involvement of Judicial Assistants in Dutch District Courts* (The Hague, Eleven International Publishing, 2017).

decision to refer in the field of competition law different from other fields of law, and about competition law questions which could be or might be referred by Dutch courts. In addition, interviews were conducted with two lawyers of the ACM and one specialised competition lawyer, representing the repeat players in this type of proceedings. These interviews mainly focused on their impression of Dutch courts' referral practice, lawyers' own interests in having preliminary questions referred, and the way by which lawyers try to influence courts' decision to refer.

Table 9.1 Overview of interviewees

Public enforcement		Private enforcement	
ACM	2 lawyers	District Court	3 judges
Rb Rotterdam	1 judge, 1 senior lawyer	Court of Appeal	4 judges
CBb	4 judges	Supreme Court	1 judge
Law firms	1 attorney at law		

The anonymity of interviewees must be guaranteed for them to speak freely. Each interviewee therefore was assigned a random number between 1 and 99. No reference was made in situations where certain statements can easily be traced back to individual persons. The motives provided in the interviews were used to find possible explanations for the decision (not) to refer the identified 'referable' questions. The motives mentioned for specific cases are thus not necessarily the motives of (one of) the judge(s) who decided the case. To ensure anonymity, no distinction was made between statements by (one of) the deciding judge(s) and other, non-involved judges.

V. THE MOTIVES (NOT) TO REFER

A. The Procedural Context of the Question

The only Dutch preliminary reference on competition law in the selected timeframe concerns a question on the scope of Article 101 TFEU on the intersection with labour law. The question's background is a reflection document of the ACM's predecessor, the NMa. This document stated that self-employed persons should be seen as undertakings. Therefore, collective labour agreements in which self-employed persons are bound, should not be excluded from the scope of the cartel prohibition, although collective labour agreements in principle are excluded.[30] This statement in the reflection document was challenged

---

[30] NMa, *Cao-tariefbepalingen voor zelfstandigen en de Mededingingswet*, 5 December 2007.

by FNV, a Dutch trade union, and came before the Gh 's-Gravenhage on appeal. Because the dispute revolved exclusively around the scope of the cartel prohibition, and because there were doubts about the correct interpretation, the Gh 's-Gravenhage referred preliminary questions.[31] The decision to refer may have been influenced by FNV's explicit request for a preliminary reference. The dispute's context, focusing exclusively on one question of law, coupled with an explicit request to refer, seemingly significantly enhances the chances of referral, especially before lower civil courts. These courts' proceedings are characterised by a relatively informal approach where the main aim is simply to find the best solution to the dispute between the parties.[32]

The *Zilveruien* case is a good example to show that a request for referral in itself, without the procedural context, will usually not be sufficient. In this case, the ACM for the first time included the turnover in other Member States than the Netherlands to calculate a fine. This decision was challenged by the fined parties who argued that there was no legal basis for extraterritorial fining under EU law. The Rb Rotterdam upheld the decision on appeal with a summary reasoning.[33] When the question came up again in *Eerstejaars plantuien*, the Rb Rotterdam referred to its earlier judgment.[34] The CBb upheld the conclusion of the Rb Rotterdam in both cases. In *Zilveruien*, the CBb extensively detailed its reasoning.[35] Nevertheless, the fined parties elaborately argued thereafter in *Eerstejaars plantuien* that the judgment of the CBb was incorrect and explicitly requested the CBb to refer preliminary questions on the matter. The CBb, however, saw no reason to do so.[36]

Thus, a substantiated request to refer preliminary questions (the only one that was reported in a judgment within the selected timeframe) did not convince the CBb. An important difference with the *FNV* case is, of course, that *Zilveruien* is an administrative procedure in which this question was one of many, as opposed to *FNV*. However, in general most judges recognise that a well-reasoned request for referral forces them to have a second, thorough, look at the issue. But they do indicate that the decision to refer will always remain their own and does not require a request by one of the parties. Usually, the other party also disagrees about the necessity to refer preliminary questions.[37] When both parties request a referral, some judges indicate that they will most likely co-operate, assuming that the question is relevant for the dispute.[38]

---

[31] Gh 's-Gravenhage 9 July 2013, NL:GHDHA:2013:5381, paras 3.5–3.6 (*FNV Kunsten Informatie en Media*).
[32] Interview 5, 31, 56, 61, 63, 73, 96.
[33] Rb Rotterdam 20 March 2014, NL:RBROT:2014:2045, paras 79–80 (*Zilveruien*).
[34] Rb Rotterdam 24 July 2014, NL:RBROT:2014:5930, paras 7.9–7.10 (*Eerstejaars plantuien*).
[35] CBb 24 March 2016, NL:CBB:2016:56, para 4.9.3 (*Zilveruien*).
[36] CBb 6 October 2016, NL:CBB:2016:272, paras 7.1.1–7.3.9 (*Eerstejaars plantuien*).
[37] Interview 5, 31, 40, 56, 61, 63, 70, 73, 76, 79, 86, 96, 97.
[38] Interview 5, 31, 56, 96.

B. The Clarity of the General Framework

As stated, the *FNV* case was the only actual preliminary reference. All the following questions were *not* referred by the Dutch courts. A first important reason not to refer these questions is that competition law is a very mature field of law. The foundations of the current framework were laid down already in the 1970s and 1980s. Even though new questions do arise, most judges consider that the answers can usually be derived from the existing rich case law.[39]

This point of view is illustrated by the issue of qualifying restrictions as 'by object'. One of the conditions for finding an infringement of the cartel prohibition is that a restriction must either have the object or the effect of restricting competition. The qualification as an object restriction has given rise to several difficulties of interpretation. The CJEU has been moving between, on the one hand, a broader, effects-based approach, and on the other hand, a stricter interpretation based on the traditional list of 'hardcore restrictions'.[40] This question has arisen in particular on the conduct of cover pricing. Cover pricing entails the sharing of information by an undertaking about its bid in a tender procedure with other undertakings that are actually not interested in winning the tender. This enables the non-interested undertakings to submit a competitive but unsuccessful bid, thereby remaining in the picture without the risk of winning an undesired contract. The conduct differs from hard-core bid-rigging, where the information is shared between undertakings that are interested in winning the tender, but have agreed to a certain outcome. Since cover pricing is less serious conduct, the question is whether it can be qualified as an object restriction, or whether the effects on competition must be examined.

The Rb Rotterdam was confronted with this question in *Gemeentewerken Rotterdam*. Referring to the general definition of an object restriction in *T-Mobile*, the Rb Rotterdam held that cover pricing falls within this category.[41] When the question came back in *Limburgse Wegenbouw*, the Rb Rotterdam referred to its own judgment in *Gemeentewerken Rotterdam*, but also provided much more detailed reasons for its finding, including a reference to the British Competition Appeal Tribunal.[42] On appeal in *Gemeentewerken Rotterdam*, the CBb also elaborated on its application of the general case law of the CJEU leading it to the same conclusion.[43] Thus, although the question was not answered by the CJEU, the Dutch courts considered that similar CJEU case law provided them with sufficient guidance to tackle this issue on their own.

---

[39] Interview 2, 5, 40, 61, 63, 70, 73, 76, 79, 86, 96, 97.
[40] eg M Herz and J Lindeboom, 'Art. 101(1) TFEU: A Bitter Pill for Hoffmann-La Roche' *European Law Blog*, 26 February 2018, available at www.europeanlawblog.eu/2018/02/26/art-1011-tfeu-a-bitter-pill-for-hoffmann-la-roche/.
[41] Rb Rotterdam 26 November 2015, NL:RBROT:2015:8610, para 15.5 (*Gemeentewerken Rotterdam*).
[42] Rb Rotterdam 23 June 2016, NL:RBROT:2016:4738, para 7.1 (*Limburgse wegenbouw*).
[43] CBb 12 October 2017, NL:CBB:2017:325, paras 5.3.8–5.3.12 (*Gemeentewerken Rotterdam*).

An interesting alternative explanation circulates among Dutch competition lawyers. The rumour is that the earlier attempt in *T-Mobile* to receive guidance on the qualification of object restrictions has deterred Dutch judges from referring new questions because of the CJEU's tone in its ruling.[44] However, this suggestion has explicitly been rejected by judges in interviews. The judges asked about this rumour admitted that the tone of the CJEU in *T-Mobile* could be interpreted as a bit crusty, but this would not deter them from referring new questions on this issue.[45]

C. The Practical Relevance of the Question

Although competition law is indeed a very mature field of law, the CJEU case law is still widely debated by academics. A focus point within this timeframe was the condition that restrictions of competition must be appreciable. This topic has been debated particularly since the judgment of the CJEU in *Expedia*.[46] For several years, administrative and civil courts have had a different view on the matter. Whereas the administrative courts assumed that object restrictions by their nature constituted an appreciable restriction of competition, the civil courts examined the appreciability condition separately, also in case of a restriction by object.[47]

Since *Expedia*, the Rb Rotterdam and the CBb have been consistent in their approach.[48] The approach of the civil courts, on the other hand, has

---

[44] Interview 13. A similar explanation has been given for the lack of preliminary references by the Spanish Constitutional Court after its reference in *Melloni*: M García, 'Cautious Openness: The Spanish Constitutional Court's Approach to EU law in Recent National Case law' *European Law Blog*, 7 June 2017, available at www.europeanlawblog.eu/2017/06/07/cautious-openness-the-spanish-constitutional-courts-approach-to-eu-law-in-recent-national-case-law/.

[45] Interview 86, 97.

[46] eg A Ortega González, 'Restrictions by Object and the Appreciability Test: The *Expedia* Case, a Surprising Judgment or a Simple Clarification' (2013) 34 *European Competition Law Review* 457.

[47] A Outhuijse, 'Wat doet de Nederlandse rechter met het merkbaarheidsvereiste na Expedia?' (2014) *SEW* 391.

[48] Vzr Rb Rotterdam 1 August 2013, NL:RBROT:2013:5927, para 26 (*Executieveilingen*); Rb Rotterdam 20 March 2014, NL:RBROT:2014:2045, para 53 (*Zilveruien*); Rb Rotterdam 12 June 2014, NL:RBROT:2014:4689, para 14.5 (*Paprika's*); Rb Rotterdam 17 July 2014, NL:RBROT:2014:5830, para 6.45 (*Meel*); Rb Rotterdam 17 July 2014, NL:RBROT:2014:5849, para 6.41 (*Meel*); Rb Rotterdam 17 July 2014, NL:RBROT:2014:5884, para 6.45 (*Meel*); Rb Rotterdam 17 July 2014, NL:RBROT:2014:5822, para 7.4 (*Meel*); Rb Rotterdam 18 December 2014, NL:RBROT:2014:10129, paras 10.1–10.6 (*Executieveilingen*); Rb Rotterdam 18 December 2014, NL:RBROT:2014:10173, paras 10–10.3 (*Executieveilingen*); Rb Rotterdam 18 December 2014, NL:RBROT:2014:10174, paras 10–10.2 (*Executieveilingen*); Rb Rotterdam 30 April 2015, NL:RBROT:2015:2912, para 7.3 (*De Friese Wouden*); Rb Rotterdam 23 June 2016, NL:RBROT:2016:4738, para 7.2 (*Limburgse wegenbouw*); CBb 24 March 2016, NL:CBB:2016:56, para 4.6.3. (*Zilveruien*); CBb 14 July 2016, NL:CBB:2016:185 (*Meel*); Rb Rotterdam 13 October 2016, NL:RBROT:2016:7659; Rb Rotterdam 13 October 2016, NL: RBROT:2016:7660; Rb Rotterdam 13 October 2016, NL:RBROT:2016:7661; Rb Rotterdam 13 October 2016, NL:RBROT:2016:7662; Rb Rotterdam 13 October 2016, NL:RBROT:2016:7663;

changed significantly. The starting point was the *Batavus/X* case, where the HR annulled the decision of the Gh Leeuwarden, stating that the finding of an object restriction in general did not warrant the conclusion that the requirement of appreciability did not apply anymore.[49] Consequently, it referred the case back to the Gh Arnhem-Leeuwarden. However, a year later, the CJEU held in *Expedia* that object restrictions constitute by their nature an appreciable restriction on competition.[50] In *Confectie/Setpoint*, the Gh 's-Hertogenbosch nevertheless followed the HR.[51] In the continuation of *Batavus/X*, the Gh Arnhem-Leeuwarden stated that *Expedia* had raised questions regarding the requirement of appreciability in case of object restrictions relevant to this case. However, it refrained from referring, because the Gh Arnhem-Leeuwarden considered that referral was not necessary, since the requirement of appreciability *in casu* had been fulfilled anyway.[52] In subsequent cases, most civil courts stuck to the HR case law,[53] even though, as the Vzr Rb Gelderland explicitly stated, there was no unanimity about the answer to this question.[54] The HR twice had the opportunity to provide clarity,[55] but omitted to do so.[56] It was not until six years after *Batavus/X* that the HR changed its approach. In *Geborgde dierenarts/Agib*, following the opinion of Advocaat-Generaal (Advocate General before the HR) De Bock,[57] the HR held that after the qualification as an object restriction, the appreciability is given, which is in accordance with the administrative courts.[58]

Despite the scholarly discussion and the apparent divergence in the national case law on the topic, it is surprising that the majority of the judges interviewed

---

Rb Rotterdam 13 October 2016, NL:RBROT:2016:7664 (*Contractueel taxivervoer*); CBb 11 January 2017, NL:CBB:2017:1, para 6.2.8 (*De Friese Wouden*); CBb 3 July 2017, NL:CBB:2017:204 (*Executieveilingen*).

[49] HR 16 September 2011, NL:HR:2011:BQ2213, para 3.9.3 (*Batavus/X*).

[50] Judgment of 13 December 2013, *Expedia*, Case C-226/11, EU:C:2012:795, para 37.

[51] Gh 's-Hertogenbosch 12 February 2013, NL:GHSHE:2013:BZ1827, para 4.9 (*Confectie/Setpoint*).

[52] Gh Arnhem-Leeuwarden 22 March 2013, NL:GHARL:2013:BZ5188, paras 3.2–3.3 (*Batavus/X*).

[53] Rb Amsterdam 21 August 2013, NL:RBAMS:2013:6591, para 4.12 (*Drachten Storage/City Box*); Rb Rotterdam 23 April 2014, NL:RBROT:2014:3194, para 4.8 (*Koelhuis Dronten/The Greenery*); Rb Midden-Nederland 3 December 2014, NL:RBMNE:2014:6156, para 4.14 (*Vorne Koi/Oase*); Gh Den Haag 7 April 2015, NL:GHDHA:2015:910, para 8 (*Tronios/Dertronics*); Rb Limburg 27 July 2016, NL:RBLIM:2016:6268, para 4.11 (*Bakkerij/Supermarkt*); Gh 's-Hertogenbosch 11 July 2017, NL:GHSHE:2017:3114, para 4.6.6 (*Bakkerij/Supermarkt*). Exceptions are the cases Gh Arnhem-Leeuwarden 15 October 2013, NL:GHARL:2013:7702, para 4.10 (*Top 1 Toys/Vedes*); Gh Arnhem-Leeuwarden 4 October 2016, NL:GHARL:2016:7947, para 4.13 (*FHI/VGZ*); Gh Amsterdam 13 June 2017, NL:GHAMS:2017:2270, para 3.5.2 (*ML Tours/X*).

[54] Vzr Rb Gelderland 19 December 2014, NL:RBGEL:2014:8165, para 4.8 (*FHI/VGZ*).

[55] HR 25 October 2013, NL:HR:2013:CA3745, para 3.5.3 (*Mantje/Rab*); HR 20 December 2013, NL:HR:2013:2123, paras 3.5.3–3.5.4 (*BP/Benschop*).

[56] Conclusie A-G De Bock in HR 7 April 2017, NL:PHR:2017:290, para 3.6.7 (*Geborgde Dierenarts/Agib*).

[57] Conclusie A-G De Bock in HR 7 April 2017, NL:PHR:2017:290, para 3.6.12 (*Geborgde Dierenarts/Agib*).

[58] HR 14 July 2017, NL:HR:2017:1354, para 3.5.2 (*Geborgde Dierenarts/Agib*).

indicated that the issue of appreciability is mainly one of academic discussion.[59] One judge stated that the outcomes of the allegedly different approaches do not differ significantly. The exact steps leading to those outcomes then did not interest him particularly.[60] Another judge argued that the debate among scholars has come to a point where he is no longer able to follow it. According to him, the discussion should go back and focus on points that can actually be applied in concrete cases.[61] On the other hand, one judge stated that the CJEU case law develops so rapidly that he will only consult the latest CJEU judgment when he is confronted with the issue.[62] When asked about the need to ensure the uniform application of EU law, which seemed to have been endangered here, the judge at the HR was the only judge seeing a clear role for himself. However, this role is confined to the uniformity within the Netherlands; a goal which is primarily pursued through the HR's own judgments.[63] The uniform application of EU law across the EU was not mentioned as an objective pursued by any of the judges interviewed.

D. The Self-Perceived Task

The foregoing already touches upon another important factor: the judges' perception of their task. Dutch judges are not so much concerned with the uniformity and the broader development of EU law. Their main concern is to provide a solution to the disputes before them. Questions of EU law that come up in a dispute but can be evaded, will be evaded, even if the answer could clarify a broader issue of EU law. None of the judges interviewed consider it their task to contribute to the development or the uniformity of EU law.[64] Although it could be argued that questions that are not decisive for a dispute's outcome are inadmissible anyway, this seems to be a separate motive.[65] Several judges mentioned that the CJEU would probably not be aware of this fact anyway.[66] One judge stated that in less developed fields of law, such as intellectual property, judges are more keen to contribute to the development of EU law.[67]

The approach of the Dutch courts can be exemplified by a lasting question: must Article 101 TFEU be applied *ex officio*? In the context of private enforcement, the question was raised by the Gh Amsterdam in *UPC Nederland*. However, the CJEU could not answer due to the subsidiary context in which the

[59] Interview 2, 40, 73, 76, 79, 86, 97.
[60] Interview 73.
[61] Interview 40.
[62] Interview 76.
[63] Interview 2, 31, 40, 56, 61, 70, 73, 76, 79, 86, 97.
[64] Interview 5, 40, 56, 63, 70, 76.
[65] Judgment of 16 June 2015, *Gauweiler*, C-62/14, EU:C:2015:400, para 25.
[66] Interview 40, 76, 96.
[67] Interview 96.

question was asked.⁶⁸ *Brink/X* offered another opportunity to bring the question before the CJEU. Although the dispute did not revolve around the cartel prohibition, Advocaat-Generaal Van Peursem noticed in his opinion that the present agreement may in fact be contrary to Article 101 TFEU, although he stated this did not seem to be the case. If this would be examined, he deemed it necessary to refer preliminary questions on the *ex officio* application of Article 101 TFEU beyond the submitted grounds and documents.⁶⁹ However, the HR did not address the point at all in its judgment.⁷⁰

In the context of public enforcement, the question has been before the CBb in *Darthuizer*. The case concerned a decision of the ACM based on Article 6 Mw, because the ACM concluded that there was no effect on trade between Member States. On appeal before the Rb Rotterdam, the defendant argued that the relevant market was bigger than the national market. Consequently, the Rb Rotterdam applied Article 101 TFEU *ex officio* as well.⁷¹ This *ex officio* application was then challenged before the CBb. However, the CBb circumvented the question of whether Article 101 TFEU could or should have been introduced by the Rb Rotterdam, by concluding that Article 101 TFEU was inapplicable, since there was no effect on trade between Member States.⁷²

E. The Level of Specialisation

Finally, the decision not to refer preliminary questions may not always be a conscious decision. The decision of whether or not to refer only arises when there is doubt about the correct application of EU law. However, it seems that a lesser degree of EU law specialisation and a stronger orientation towards national law may result in unawareness of certain uncertainties at the EU level. Stronger orientation towards national law seems to be particularly typical for the lower civil judges. On the one hand, the judges widely indicate that competition law is a very complex field. However, on the other hand, there are relatively few competition law cases before civil courts. Consequently, it is difficult for the civil judges to keep their knowledge updated when they only encounter these cases occasionally.⁷³ Several judges mentioned informal practices of allocating relatively specialised judges to competition law cases. However, this approach does not seem uniform.⁷⁴ Some judges also stated that the idea of a specialised court for private enforcement is appealing.⁷⁵ The interviews, thus, provide

---

⁶⁸ Judgment of 7 November 2013, *UPC Nederland*, C-518/11, EU:C:2013:709.
⁶⁹ Conclusie AG Van Peursem in HR 26 June 2015, NL:PHR:2015:993, para 2.1 (*Brink/X*).
⁷⁰ HR 6 November 2015, NL:HR:2015:3237 (*Brink/X*).
⁷¹ Rb Rotterdam 1 July 2010, NL:RBROT:2010:BM9911 (*Darthuizer*).
⁷² CBb 10 April 2014, NL:CBB:2014:118, para 4.5.3 (*Darthuizer*).
⁷³ Interview 2, 5, 31, 56, 61, 76.
⁷⁴ Interview 2, 31, 56, 76.
⁷⁵ Interview 2, 56, 61.

support to previous quantitative studies that found a positive influence of EU law knowledge on the numbers of preliminary references.[76]

The lower degree of specialisation under civil judges may partially explain the divergent case law on the appreciability requirement. An issue where the difference between the specialised administrative courts and the non-specialised civil courts becomes even clearer is that of attribution of an infringement to undertakings. Once it has been established that an undertaking has infringed the cartel prohibition, the question may arise as to which undertakings this infringement can be attributed to. In *Akzo Nobel*, the CJEU clarified that when a parent undertaking owns 100 per cent of the shares of a subsidiary, there is a rebuttable presumption that decisive influence has been exercised. The undertakings then form a single economic unit, meaning that an infringement of the subsidiary can be attributed to the parent undertaking as well.[77] Within the public enforcement context, the question of attributability to parent undertakings seems clear. Several judges noted in interviews that the parties hardly ever raise any issues on the matter.[78]

In the civil law context, the situation is less clear. The civil courts apply national law here and do not automatically accept liability for parent undertakings in civil damage proceedings based on the *Akzo* presumption. A lenient approach was taken in *TenneT/ABB*, where the Rb Oost-Nederland found that a subsidiary could be held liable for an infringement of its parent undertaking, if the subsidiary is deemed to have been aware or should have been aware of the unlawful conduct.[79] On appeal, the Gh Arnhem-Leeuwarden also held the subsidiary liable, pointing to the influence of the parent undertaking, even if the subsidiary would not have been aware of the parent undertaking's conduct.[80] However, in *EWD*, the Rb Midden-Nederland was less lenient when it held that liability cannot be attributed to a parent undertaking without concrete facts or circumstances from which the liability of the parent undertaking can be derived.[81] It should be noted that these considerations *in casu* were actually obiter dicta because the claims had already been rejected on formal grounds.[82] At the end of 2017, the Finnish Supreme Court had referred preliminary questions which will enable the CJEU to give some clarification on the matter. This indicates that this issue has also led to difficulties in other Member States.[83]

---

[76] L Hornuf and S Voigt, 'Analyzing Preliminary References as the Powerbase of the European Court of Justice' (2015) 39 *European Journal of Law and Economics* 287; A Dyevre and N Lampach, 'The Choice for Europe: Judicial Behaviour and Legal Integration in the European Union', 2 March 2017, available at ssrn.com/abstract=2926496.

[77] Judgment of 10 September 2009, *Akzo Nobel*, C-97/08 P, EU:C:2009:536, para 61.

[78] Interview 40, 79, 86, 97.

[79] Rb Oost-Nederland 16 January 2013, NL:RBONE:2013:BZ0403, paras 4.9–4.11 (*TenneT/ABB*).

[80] Gh Arnhem-Leeuwarden 2 September 2014, NL:GHARL:2014:6766, para 3.17 (*ABB/TenneT*).

[81] Rb Midden-Nederland 20 July 2016, NL:RBMNE:2016:4284, paras 4.6–4.9 (*EWD*).

[82] Rb Midden-Nederland 20 July 2016, NL:RBMNE:2016:4284, para 4.11 (*EWD*).

[83] Case lodged on 22 December 2017, *Skanska Industrial Solutions*, C-724/17.

VI. CONCLUSIONS

The main objective of the preliminary ruling procedure is to ensure the uniform application of EU law. Looking at the motives (not) to refer of the Dutch judges in competition law cases, it could be argued that this objective is only partially shared by them. This mainly depends on how the objective of uniform application of EU law is interpreted. On the one hand, when confronted with questions of EU law, the Dutch courts do their best to apply EU law correctly to the present dispute. The reason why few questions are referred is mainly that the national courts consider themselves capable of applying EU law on their own, deriving the answers from the vast body of EU case law in this field. The less consistent case law of the civil courts is an indication of a slight uneasiness with EU law, which could be attributed to a lesser degree of specialisation. However, when a question of EU law is necessary to settle a dispute and leaves doubt about the correct interpretation, all judges indicate that they would have no problem to refer preliminary questions. There are no indications of hesitation or unwillingness towards the CJEU or EU legal order in this regard.

On the other hand, one could also include the broader development of EU law beyond the present dispute as an objective of the preliminary procedure, as Judge Prechal seems to do. This clearly does not align with the role that the Dutch judges see for themselves. Except for the HR that sees a role for itself in the development and uniformity of the national law, the judges generally do not seem overly concerned with issues of law transcending the present dispute. When in the proceedings a question of EU law arises which is relevant for the development of EU law, but which is not decisive for the outcome of the dispute, the question in principle will not be addressed. This mindset clearly contrasts with that of scholars who analyse possible answers and potential preliminary questions as soon as an issue comes up. If the broader development of EU law is considered as a task of the preliminary ruling procedure, one could conclude that Dutch judges lack a feeling of responsibility for this task. However, this has more to do with the perceived task of the judges in general than with Eurosceptic sentiments, since this attitude does not specifically relate to EU law. Although it is tempting to attribute declining numbers of references to these kinds of sentiments, it thus remains important to look beyond the figures.

10

Reluctance to Participate in the Preliminary Ruling Procedure as a Challenge to EU Law: A Case Study on Slovenia and Croatia

MONIKA GLAVINA*

I. INTRODUCTION

EVER SINCE THE preliminary ruling procedure was introduced by the Treaty of Rome, the Court of Justice of the European Union (CJEU) was supplied with a steady and rising stream of cases. As illustrated in Figure 10.1, the number of referrals has risen dramatically since the 1960s, allowing the CJEU to become presumably the world's most powerful international court.[1] The existence of the procedure had an impact on national courts too, giving them a new role as European Union (EU) courts with both the power and the duty to apply EU law in cases which appear before them.[2] Notwithstanding that the obligation to refer legal questions to the CJEU applies to top courts only,[3] many scholars still talk about the 'duty to refer', even in the case of lower courts.[4] This is mainly because the co-operation of national courts with the CJEU has been crucial for making the entire

---

* I am grateful for the financial support from ERC Starting Grant 638154 (EUTHORITY).
[1] KJ Alter, *The European Court's Political Power: Selected Essays* (Oxford, Oxford University Press, 2009) 5.
[2] PP Craig and G De Búrca, *EU Law: Text, Cases, and Materials*, 6th edn (Oxford, Oxford University Press, 2015) 501.
[3] See the wording of Article 267(3) TFEU.
[4] M Claes, *The National Courts' Mandate in the European Constitution* (Oxford, Hart Publishing, 2006); T Nowak, F Amtenbrink, M Hertogh and M Wissink, *National Judges as European Union Judges: Knowledge, Experiences and Attitudes of Lower Court Judges in Germany and the Netherlands* (The Hague, Eleven International Publishing, 2011); U Jaremba, 'Polish Civil Judges versus the EU Legal Order: Knowledge, Experiences and Attitudes' in U Jaremba (ed), *National Judges as EU Law Judges: The Polish Civil Law System* (Leiden, Martinus Nijhoff, 2013).

system work.⁵ The procedure became 'an essential guarantee of the coherence of the Community legal order and the uniform application of Community law'.⁶ Without Member States' courts acceptance of it, the constitutional transformation of Europe would have 'remained with all the systemic deficiencies of general public international law'.⁷

Over the last couple of decades, we have witnessed an increasing body of literature written on Article 267 of the Treaty on the Functioning of the European Union (TFEU). Scholars have devoted considerable attention to explaining why national judges send preliminary questions to the CJEU⁸ and cross-national variations in referral rates.⁹ Despite the overwhelming literature written on the preliminary ruling procedure, we still know very little about individual judges' motives to refer or not to refer legal questions to Luxembourg. This is because the research on Article 267 referral activity has focused too narrowly on country-level data. What is less appreciated is that preliminary questions are not the products of Member States' governments, nor courts, but rather of individual judges. Furthermore, scholars have concentrated on the number of preliminary questions while, in fact, preliminary questions are very rare. There are thousands of courts across the EU and they adjudicate millions of disputes every year. Yet, in 2017 the CJEU received merely 533 references from across the EU.¹⁰

---

⁵ Craig and De Búrca, *EU Law* (2015) 501.
⁶ European Parliament, Committee on Legal Affairs, 'Report on The Role of the National Judge in the European Judicial System, A6-0224/2008' (2008) 23.
⁷ JHH Weiler, 'The Transformation of Europe' (1991) 100 *Yale Law Journal* 2403, 2425.
⁸ Weiler, 'The Transformation of Europe' (1991); JHH Weiler, 'A Quiet Revolution: "The European Court of Justice and Its Interlocutors"' (1994) 26 *Comparative Political Studies* 510; KJ Alter, 'Explaining National Court Acceptance of European Court Jurisprudence: A Critical Evaluation of Theories of Legal Integration' in AM Slaughter (ed), *The European Court and National Courts: Doctrine and Jurisprudence: Legal Change in its Social Context* (Oxford, Hart Publishing, 1998); KJ Alter, *Establishing the Supremacy of European Law: The Making of an International Rule of Law in Europe* (Oxford, Oxford University Press, 2001); Claes, *The National Courts' Mandate in the European Constitution* (2006); M Vink, M Claes and C Arnold, 'Explaining the Use of Preliminary References by Domestic Courts in EU Member States: A Mixed-Method Comparative Analysis', Paper presented at the Biennial Conference of the European Union Studies Association, 24 April 2009, available at http://aei.pitt.edu/33155/1/vink._maarten.pdf.
⁹ A Stone Sweet and TL Brunell, 'The European Court and the National Courts: A Statistical Analysis of Preliminary References, 1961–95' (1998) 5 *Journal of European Public Policy* 66; AM Burley and W Mattli, 'Europe Before the Court: A Political Theory of Legal Integration' (1993) 47 *International Organization* 41; CJ Carrubba and L Murrah, 'Legal Integration and Use of the Preliminary Ruling Process in the European Union' (2005) 59 *International Organization* 399; Vink, Claes and Arnold, 'Explaining the Use of Preliminary References by Domestic Courts in EU Member States' (2009); M Wind, 'The Nordics, the EU and the Reluctance Towards Supranational Judicial Review' (2010) 48 *Journal of Common Market Studies* 1039; L Conant, 'Europeanization and the Courts: Variable Patterns of Adaptation among National Judiciaries' in MG Cowles, J Caporaso and T Risse (eds), *Transforming Europe: Europeanization and Domestic Change* (Ithaca, Cornell University Press 2001); T Pavone and RD Kelemen, 'The Political Geography of Legal Integration: Visualizing Institutional Change in the European Union' (2018) 70 *World Politics* 358; A Dyevre and N Lampach, 'The Choice for Europe: Judicial Behaviour and Legal Integration in the European Union', 2 March 2017, available at https://ssrn.com/abstract=292649.
¹⁰ CJEU, Annual Report 2017, available at https://curia.europa.eu/jcms/upload/docs/application/pdf/2018-04/ra_pan_2018.0421_en.pdf. The figure refers to preliminary questions submitted by EU-28 Member States' courts between 1 January and 31 December 2017.

The majority of national judges will never in their entire judicial career submit a preliminary question to Luxembourg.[11] The question, therefore, should be: why will some judges never turn to the CJEU? What drives the referral behaviour of national judges? What are the motives behind the decision to submit or not to submit a preliminary question to Luxembourg?

Figure 10.1 Preliminary questions submitted to the CJEU over time (1961–2017)

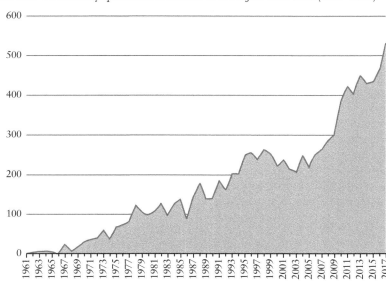

Source: CJEU annual reports.

This chapter addresses the shortcomings of the literature and focuses on the question of why national judges do not turn to the CJEU by means of the preliminary ruling procedure. It comes in a form of qualitative research which relies on interviews conducted among Slovenian and Croatian national judges. The relevance of this research is twofold. First, it tries to understand the referral behaviour by stepping away from country-level panel data and by focusing on the level of individual judges. Second, it moves away from the focus on the number of preliminary questions and it emphasises non-referrals as a possible challenge to EU law. Scholars and the CJEU itself have in several occasions expressed concerns over non-referrals. It has, for example, been argued that limiting access to the CJEU could jeopardise 'the uniform application and interpretation of [EU] law throughout the Union, and could deprive individuals

---

[11] M Glavina, '"To Submit or Not to Submit – That Is the (Preliminary) Question": Explaining National Judges' Reluctance to Participate in the Preliminary Ruling Procedure', 23 July 2018, available at https://ssrn.com/abstract=3218256.

of effective judicial protection and undermine the unity of the case-law'.[12] Not turning to the CJEU when its interpretation is crucial for delivering a judgment grants national judges the power to take the interpretation of EU law into their own hands. This could ultimately compromise the uniform application and interpretation of EU law across the EU, opposing the basic meaning of the procedure. Considering that the vast majority of judges will never turn to the CJEU with a preliminary question, it is crucial to understand judicial motives and how they shape judicial decisions to refer or not to refer legal questions to Luxembourg.

The chapter is structured as follows. Section II discusses key debates on referral behaviour of national judges and gives its own understanding of it. I argue that national judges are public sector workers who are motivated and constrained by different factors when deciding to submit or not to submit a preliminary question to the CJEU. Section III describes the choice of countries, the data and methodology. Section IV presents and discusses the results of in-depth interviews. Interviews conducted with Slovenian and Croatian national judges show that the decision not to submit a preliminary question to Luxembourg is shaped by a broader set of factors, from individual profiles of judges and litigation rates, to the institutional setting in which judges operate. The chapter concludes with main findings and suggestions for future research.

II. DISCUSSIONS ON JUDICIAL BEHAVIOUR AND THEORETICAL FRAMEWORK

Over more than three decades, scholars of different disciplines have tried to disentangle the question of why national courts 'go to Europe'. In the early 1990s, Weiler argued that the legal construction of Europe is a simple story of judicial empowerment. Domestic courts which do not hold the power of judicial review will, according to Weiler, be particularly eager to embrace the preliminary ruling procedure because it gives them the power to set aside parliamentary legislation.[13] Building on Weiler's Empowerment thesis, Alter argued that national courts seek to expand their power vis-à-vis higher courts in the national hierarchy. She argued that

> references to the ECJ have become a convenient means to circumvent higher courts. The ECJ is like a second parent in a battle where parental permission wards off a potential sanction for misbehaviour – if the lower court does not like what they think

---

[12] European Commission, 'Report of the Court of Justice of the European Communities', May 1995, available at www.cvce.eu/obj/report_of_the_court_of_justice_of_the_european_communities_luxembourg_may_1995-en-3644862f-2e8f-4170-9616-e573a41b61c5.html, 5; T Tridimas, 'Knocking on Heaven's Door: Fragmentation, Efficiency and Defiance in the Preliminary Reference Procedure' (2003) 40 *Common Market Law Review* 9.

[13] Weiler, 'The Transformation of Europe' (1991) 523.

one parent (the higher court) will say, they can ask the other parent (the ECJ) to see if they will get a more pleasing answer.[14]

It did not take long before scholars started relying on empirical data to support their theoretical claims. Ever since the 1990s, the European judicial politics literature has focused primarily on explaining cross-national variations in referral rates. Why, for example, are Italian courts so active in the preliminary ruling procedure and why do Danish courts send so few cases? Divergences in the number of questions submitted to the CJEU have been attributed to numerous factors such as years of membership;[15] differences in intra-EU trade;[16] legal culture;[17] litigation rates;[18] country size and population levels;[19] and public support for EU membership.[20] Correspondingly, non-referrals could be explained by, inter alia, a country's low transnational economic exchange; low public support for EU integration; the existence of judicial review; and majoritarian democracy.[21]

Although the non-referral argument has never fully captured scholars' attention, it has in some ways always been present in the European judicial politics literature. In 1989, Arnull wrote on the 'use and abuse' of Article 177 (current Article 256 TFEU).[22] He argued that CILFIT criteria would enable national top courts' judges 'to justify any reluctance they might feel to ask for a preliminary ruling' and encourage them to decide points of EU law for themselves, even in cases where they should be decided by the CJEU.[23] Furthermore, reluctance to submit a preliminary question has been attributed to previous (bad) experiences of national judges with the mechanism, where the CJEU's answer

---

[14] Alter, *Establishing the Supremacy of European Law* (2001) 48.
[15] N Lampach and A Dyevre, 'The Origins of Regional Integration: Untangling the Effect of Trade on Judicial Cooperation', 14 September 2017, available at https://papers.ssrn.com/abstract=3036797.
[16] Stone Sweet and Brunell, 'The European Court and the National Courts' (1998); Carrubba and Murrah, 'Legal Integration and Use of the Preliminary Ruling Process' (2005).
[17] W Mattli and AM Slaughter, 'Revisiting the European Court of Justice' (1998) 52 *International Organization* 177; Carrubba and Murrah, 'Legal Integration and Use of the Preliminary Ruling Process' (2005); Vink, Claes and Arnold, 'Explaining the Use of Preliminary References by Domestic Courts in EU Member States' (2009); M Wind, D Sindbjerg Martinsen and G Pons Rotger, 'The Uneven Legal Push for Europe: Questioning Variation When National Courts Go to Europe' (2009) 10 *European Union Politics* 63; Wind, 'The Nordics, the EU and the Reluctance Towards Supranational Judicial Review' (2010).
[18] Conant, 'Europeanization and the Courts' (2011); KJ Alter and J Vargas, 'Explaining Variation in the Use of European Litigation Strategies: European Community Law and British Gender Equality Policy' (2000) 33 *Comparative Political Studies* 452; Vink, Claes and Arnold, 'Explaining the Use of Preliminary References by Domestic Courts in EU Member States' (2009).
[19] Stone Sweet and Brunell, 'The European Court and the National Courts' (1998); Vink, Claes and Arnold, 'Explaining the Use of Preliminary References by Domestic Courts in EU Member States' (2009); Pavone and Kelemen, 'The Political Geography of Legal Integration' (2018).
[20] Carrubba and Murrah, 'Legal Integration and Use of the Preliminary Ruling Process' (2005).
[21] See nn 15–20.
[22] A Arnull, 'The Use and Abuse of Article 177 EEC' (1989) 52 *The Modern Law Review* 622.
[23] ibid 626; Tridimas, 'Knocking on Heaven's Door' (2003) 40.

was not helpful and could not be used in the national decision.[24] Bobek then talked about the so-called 'chilling effect'. He argued that the decision of the CJEU to reject the first wave of preliminary references coming from the CEE Member States was unfortunate as it created a chilling effect on the willingness of new Member States' courts to send preliminary questions,[25] suggesting that submitting preliminary questions entails reputational considerations.[26] Dyevre and Lampach further argued that, all things being equal, judges prefer policy outcomes which are closer to their ideological point. A pro-EU integration judge, for example, may want to refer a question to Luxembourg in order to 'promote deeper integration and greater compliance with EU law'.[27] An anti-EU integration judge, by contrast, would refrain from doing so.

This chapter places the research on Article 267 TFEU on more rigorous theoretical grounds, by focusing primarily on non-referrals. Contrary to the research discussed earlier in this section, I reject the view that the referral behaviour of national judges is shaped by merely one or a few factors. Instead, I start from the idea that a national judge is a labour market participant who, as any other worker, is motivated and constrained by costs and benefits, both pecuniary and non-pecuniary.[28] Judges care about their income, but also other benefits such as job tenure, bonuses, and the possibility of promotion. Working as a judge also includes other benefits such as power and prestige. Costs, by contrast, include the risk of losing one's job, limited time for leisure, professional and institutional rules, and expectations such as work quotas.[29]

The central concern for judges, according to the labour market model, is to find a balance between judicial work (conducting hearings, solving cases), non-judicial work (writing books, giving lectures) and leisure time.[30] Finding a balance, however, often leads to trade-offs which may have a direct bearing on the decision to send a preliminary question to the CJEU. Time, intellectual effort and resources a judge invested in drafting and submitting a reference are time,

---

[24] Vink, Claes and Arnold, 'Explaining the Use of Preliminary References by Domestic Courts in EU Member States' (2009) 8.
[25] M Bobek, 'Learning to Talk: Preliminary Rulings, the Courts of the New Member States and the Court of Justice' (2008) 45 *Common Market Law Review* 1611, 1618.
[26] See also Dyevre and Lampach, 'The Choice for Europe' (2017).
[27] ibid 8.
[28] L Epstein, WM Landes and RA Posner, *The Behavior of Federal Judges* (Cambridge, MA, Harvard University Press, 2013); L Epstein and J Knight, 'Reconsidering Judicial Preferences' (2013) 16 *Annual Review of Political Science* 11.
[29] Epstein, Landes and Posner, *The Behavior of Federal Judges* (2013) 5, 31.
[30] E Ash and WB MacLeod, 'Intrinsic Motivation in Public Service: Theory and Evidence from State Supreme Courts', June 2015, National Bureau of Economic Research Working Paper 20664, available at www.nber.org/papers/w20664.pdf 8. During the 1990s, Stone Sweet and Brunell argued that judges want to dispose of their case load efficiently and 'go home at the end of the day having disposed of more, rather than fewer, work-related problems': A Stone Sweet and TL Brunell, 'The European Court and the National Courts: Data Set on Preliminary References in EC Law', 1999, available at www.nuff.ox.ac.uk/Users/Sweet/codebook.htm 73.

effort and resources that cannot be used for something else such as managing one's workload or enjoying leisure time.[31] Vink, Claes and Arnold, for example, argued that 'in some countries more than others, judges work under time pressure and have to meet targets, which they cannot meet if they "lose time" making a reference'.[32] Stone Sweet and Brunell, similarly, wrote that 'national judges ... prefer to dispose of their cases efficiently, that is, they would like to go home at the end of the day having disposed of more, rather than fewer, work-related problems'.[33]

Thus, the higher the workload, the lower the opportunity costs of making a referral. Sufficient resources can, of course, lower these opportunity costs but not all judges have those at their disposal. Vink, Claes and Arnold further argued that 'one could think of the level of knowledge of European law, of practicing lawyers and advocates, and of judges, or the type of support the judges have with regard to research and documentation, and access to relevant materials'.[34] The higher the knowledge and understanding of EU law, the lower the opportunity costs of making a referral. Yet, not all judges have a sufficient knowledge of EU law or sufficient access to resources. Judges with limited EU law knowledge and without a law clerk will face a trade-off: devote less time and effort to other cases and to focus on making a preliminary question, or ignore the need to make a referral and continue managing their workload. Similar to the existence of law clerks, litigants, that is lawyers, can lower the opportunity costs of making a referral by pointing out the EU law element in a case or by suggesting that a preliminary question be referred to the CJEU. In some cases, lawyers even propose the wording of the preliminary question which ultimately (and very often unchanged) is referred to the CJEU.[35]

In this chapter I aim to understand the non-referral behaviour of national judges and judicial motives behind the decision to submit or not to submit a preliminary question to Luxembourg. Building on the labour market and resource management argument, I posit that there is no one single explanation of the referral behaviour of national judges. Instead, how national judges use

---

[31] A Dyevre, A Atanasova and M Glavina, 'Who Asks Most? Institutional Incentives and Referral Activity in the European Union Legal Order', 25 August 2017, available at https://ssrn.com/abstract=3051659.

[32] Vink, Claes and Arnold, 'Explaining the Use of Preliminary References by Domestic Courts in EU Member States' (2009) 22; European Parliament, Committee on Legal Affairs, 'Report on The Role of the National Judge' (2008).

[33] Stone Sweet and Brunell, 'The European Court and the National Courts' (1999) 73.

[34] Vink, Claes and Arnold, 'Explaining the Use of Preliminary References by Domestic Courts in EU Member States' (2009) 22.

[35] E Muir and S Kolf, 'Belgian Equality Bodies Reaching out to the CJEU: EU Procedural Law as a Catalyst' in E Muir, C Kilpatrick and B De Witte (eds), *How EU Law Shapes Opportunities for Preliminary References on Fundamental Rights: Discrimination, Data Protection and Asylum*, European University Institute, 2017, available at http://cadmus.eui.eu/bitstream/handle/1814/49324/LAW_2017_17.pdf?sequence=3&isAllowed=y.

the preliminary ruling procedure will be motivated and constrained by various factors, namely personal factors, factors pertaining to litigants, and factors deriving from the institutional set-up of the court they work in.

III. DATA AND METHODOLOGY

This chapter comes in the form of qualitative research which aims to understand non-referrals among national judges. It relies on the results of interviews conducted among Slovenian and Croatian judges in spring and autumn 2017. Interviews were not limited to the preliminary ruling procedure, but rather focused on the application of EU law in general. Yet, this chapter covers only those questions dealing specifically with the preliminary ruling procedure. Seventy-four judges were interested in participating in an interview. For practical reasons, a purposive sampling technique was used, selecting at least one judge per type and level of court. Ultimately, semi-structured in-depth interviews were conducted with 18 judges from Croatia and 13 judges from Slovenia.

Judges of first and second instance were interviewed. This was done for several reasons. First, lower instance judges are the largest group of judges in a country. Second, they adjudicate thousands of cases every year in which EU law occasionally plays a role.[36] Furthermore, lower court judges are not obliged to make a reference within the meaning of Article 267 TFEU, but rather enjoy considerable discretion in deciding how they apply EU law. Finally, lower instance judges have the best overview of all constraints which may hinder judicial participation in the preliminary ruling mechanism.

The research focuses on two of the newer EU Member States: Croatia and Slovenia. The choice of countries is justified by the small number of preliminary questions submitted by Slovenia and Croatia since their accession to the EU. The first Slovenian reference was submitted in 2009, five years after accession. By the end of 2017, Slovenian courts had sent a total of 19 preliminary questions. The majority, however, came from the Slovenian Supreme Court and the Administrative Court. An appeal court in Maribor 'broke the ice' by submitting the first Slovenian reference. Nonetheless, no further attempts had been made by any other lower court. The referral situation is slightly different in Croatia. Croatian courts, too, have used the procedure very sporadically, at least when compared to their counterparts from other newer Member States.[37] In the

---

[36] See also Nowak, Amtenbrink, Hertogh and Wissink, *National Judges as European Union Judges* (2011).

[37] Since their accession to the EU and until 2017, Hungarian judges have been the most active users of the preliminary ruling procedure compared to other newer EU Member States, sending as many as 158 references to the CJEU. Polish judges sent 128, Romanian judges 138, and Bulgarian judges 117 references. The lowest number of references came from Malta (3), Cyprus (7), Croatia (11), Slovenia (20), and Estonia (25). Source: CJEU annual report.

first four years of membership, Croatian courts sent 11 preliminary questions, all of them originating from lower courts (see Figure 10.2). Low numbers of referrals, thus, make Slovenia and Croatia interesting countries for explaining no-referrals and the reluctance of judges to participate in the preliminary ruling procedure.

Figure 10.2 Preliminary questions in selected newer Member States, 2004–2017

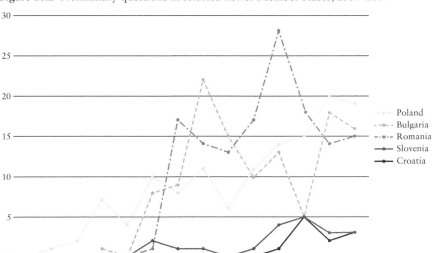

For analysing interview results, thematic content analysis – which aims to find common patterns across the data – was employed. After the interviews were transcribed, they were translated into the English language, while keeping the connotations of the original version. Questions pertaining to the preliminary ruling mechanism were manually coded and grouped into broader categories. In addition, text mining was performed in order to validate coding results (see Figure 10.5 in the Annex on word frequencies).

IV. RESULTS

This section explores the question of why national judges do not participate in the preliminary ruling procedure. The results of the qualitative interviews show that there is no one single explanation for non-referral. Instead, when deciding whether or not to make a referral, judges are influenced by their individual profiles and factors deriving from their institutional setting. Furthermore, their referral behaviour is also shaped by litigation rates and litigants' behaviour.

Table 10.1 Interview results: Summary of categories and codes

Category	Code	Coding example
Individual profiles of judges	Policy preferences	I do not see another way to end these local powers and the government. If the judges will not react. And Europe will give us some support (CRO judge 9)
	Knowledge	Too few judges know about it. When they need to refer, how to draft it, how to send it (CRO judge 12)
	Foreign languages skills	I speak Slovenian and Croatian. When I have to switch to English, this is slower, it takes a lot of time for me (SLO judge 4)
	Personal perception on the procedure	I know that it is a very demanding task. I never wrote one (CRO judge 6) In order for a court to make a referral it takes a lot of time and effort (SLO judge 8)
	Experience with the procedure	In these beginnings, now when we are still beginners, we still have no routine or experience (CRO judge 4)
	Reputational considerations	There is also ignorance, reservation. You are afraid you will look ridiculous (CRO judge 17)
	Fear of criticism	The preliminary question can be wise and can also be unwise. And if it is unwise, we Slovenians are boundlessly critical of our colleagues (SLO judge 4)
	Legal rules	I, in the first instance, am not obliged. I am not the last instance (SLO judge 3)
Institutional context	Workload	There are plenty of cases in our work and you just do not have time to deal with it to that extent, to go in depth (CRO judge 11)
	Court quotas	[J]udges spend a lot of time … on meeting these framework criteria. This is constantly pressuring you. You have to make the norm! (CRO judge 12)
	Court resources	Ultimately, the Supreme Court has the most resources in terms of professional help, people, staff. So they can solve this easier (SLO judge 8)
	Systematic education	We are not educated enough … There is not enough investment in us judges. (CRO judge 2)
	Initiative from the Supreme Court	We cling to the court practice of the Supreme Court. Preliminary questions could come from them, then maybe we might be more involved (CRO judge 2)
	No recognition or reward	I think that this is something that should be rewarded in a professional sense, in terms of some extra points for advancement (CRO judge 7)

(continued)

Table 10.1 *(Continued)*

Category	Code	Coding example
Litigation rates	Party initiative	[T]his should be the party's initiative. The party should initiate such a procedure. Everything comes from the party (CRO judge 8)
	Litigation volumes	I do not think there are many cases of such nature yet (CRO judge 10)
		[I]t is also because Slovenian judiciary is small. Because the state is small (SLO judge 6)

A. Individual Profiles of Judges

Interview results confirm the role of individual profiles of national judges on their referral behaviour. When deciding whether or not to submit a preliminary question, judges are motivated and constrained by (a) policy outcomes consistent with their ideological viewpoint, (b) knowledge considerations, (c) their experience with the procedure, (d) reputational costs, (e) fear of criticism, and (f) legal rules.

In line with Weiler's Empowerment thesis and Alter's Court Competition thesis, judges use the preliminary ruling procedure to get empowered and to bypass higher courts. In other words, they try to maximise **policy outcomes** which are closer to their ideological ideal viewpoint. One Slovenian judge argues:

> If the highest court would adopt a position with which I would not agree, I could think that the EU Court would help me … I would use the preliminary question. Preliminary questions give you more power. You are more important.[38]

Similarly, another Slovenian judge says:

> [If] the lower instance judge knows what is right, but the higher instance keeps deciding in a wrong way, [a lower court judge] could bypass the higher instance by making a referral to Luxembourg in order to get an answer which is compliant with his interpretation … With this, he could force the higher instance to accept his explanation. I think this is a trick … And the only way to change the position of the higher instance is through the Court in Luxembourg.[39]

Slovenian and Croatian judges report that they **lack the knowledge** of the procedure to be able to engage with such a complex issue. A lower court judge in Croatia argues that only '10% of judges in the entire system know … how this procedure works'.[40] Another Croatian county court judge emphasises

---

[38] Slovenian judge 3, district court, 1st instance.
[39] Slovenian judge 11, local court, 1st instance.
[40] Croatian judge 16, misdemeanour court, 1st instance.

that judges do not have 'the basic knowledge to recognise when they are in the zone of the application of EU law'.[41] Furthermore, he argues that judges sometimes do not know that it is 'not Strasbourg but rather the European Court in Luxembourg' to whom the preliminary question should be referred. Lack of knowledge of the procedure appears among Slovenian judges too, one argues that '[t]here is ignorance about the preliminary question. Ignorance about EU law'.[42]

Judges not only lack knowledge in the procedure, but also **lack foreign language skills**, which has a direct bearing on the willingness to submit. A Croatian municipal court judge says that 'a lot of judgments have not been translated into Croatian and the translations of some of the Regulations are catastrophic and have an array of mistakes'.[43] Judges, therefore, cannot rely on the Croatian version only. Yet, 'many judges are not proficient in the English language'.[44] Slovenian judges also emphasise the role of languages:

> If you want to ask [a preliminary question], you first need to see what the CJEU has decided. I do not mind if this is in English, but for someone else this could matter. The older generation is worse with [foreign] languages than the younger one.[45]

Furthermore, judges **lack experience with the procedure**. One Croatian judge says that '[w]hen a judge gets such a case, he cannot solve it on the basis of existing experience, knowledge and routine'.[46] A Slovenian judge compared the preliminary ruling mechanism with the national procedure for constitutional review: '[w]hen I first used the mechanism of constitutional review, it was time consuming. Already when I used it for the second time, I had the technique on how to do it'.[47] The same, according to him, goes for the preliminary question.

National judges also **perceive the procedure as too complicated** and argue that it requires **too much time and effort**. A Croatian municipal court judge says that judges are running away from it because

> you need to know how to draft [the reference] in a proper way, how to address it, invoke the relevant case law, already know the existing case law to not repeat the question. Maybe one more elegant solution is just to bypass it.[48]

Likewise, a Slovenian judge argues:

> I do not know now how much time it takes. Now it is 14 months. A few years ago, it was two–three years … This is a complicated, long-lasting procedure. It takes a lot of time to get the answer.[49]

---

[41] Croatian judge 17, county court, 2nd instance.
[42] Slovenian judge 3, district court, 1st instance.
[43] Croatian judge 1, municipal court, 1st instance.
[44] ibid.
[45] Slovenian judge 3, district court, 1st instance.
[46] Croatian judge 4, county court, 2nd instance.
[47] Slovenian judge 3, district court, 1st instance.
[48] Croatian judge, municipal court, 1st instance.
[49] Slovenian judge 8, local court, 1st instance.

An important and often cited reason for non-referral revolves around **reputational considerations**. Judges believe that they 'cannot ask something stupid'[50] and

> if the question has already been resolved ... then the man presents himself as someone who does not follow the case law. This would point out to some kind of sloppiness in work and that is probably something that nobody wants for himself.[51]

Two Slovenian judges similarly assert that it is 'a serious embarrassment if you ask a preliminary question to which the answer has already been given'[52] and '[n]obody wants to make a fool out of himself with a wrong or simply poorly posed preliminary question'.[53] These answers show that judges are well aware of the possibility that their preliminary questions be rejected by the CJEU, which entails reputational costs.

Judges further fear **criticism from their audience** which includes their colleagues, superiors and the public. A Slovenian judge says:

> Sending preliminary questions escalates judges into the public ... The preliminary question can be wise and can also be unwise. And if it is unwise, we Slovenians are boundlessly critical of our colleagues. If it is unwise, it is better not to stand out ... to avoid negative criticism from colleagues.[54]

The same judge further cites an example of criticism coming from academia:

> When the question was asked a couple of years ago in the *Detiček* case, then the legal profession criticised that this question was not necessary. Because it was clear ... So, I think that this judge will think very carefully before sending [a reference] again ... to avoid criticism.[55]

Unlike Slovenian judges who are mainly concerned with criticism from their superiors and their wider audience, Croatian judges care more about criticism coming from their colleagues. One judge recalls a personal experience when she had sent a preliminary question: '[t]here were [negative comments] like: what is she thinking? As if she would know how to ask a preliminary question'.[56] Another judge cites the negative experience experienced by a colleague:

> [Higher court judges] acted like some offended brides: who was she to go and ask for some opinion. And I think that she acted correctly and that she posed a crucial question ... It is taken as negative when you stand out with something. This has always been a problem in Croatia ... It is, somehow, best when you are average ... There is this sort of Croatian envy.[57]

---

[50] Croatian judge 9, municipal court, 1st instance.
[51] Croatian judge 16, municipal court, 1st instance.
[52] Slovenian judge 4, higher court, 2nd instance.
[53] Slovenian judge 6, higher court, 2nd instance.
[54] Slovenian judge 4, higher court, 2nd instance.
[55] Slovenian judge 7, higher court, 2nd instance.
[56] Croatian judge 9, municipal court, 1st instance.
[57] Croatian judge 17, misdemeanour court, 1st instance.

The last individual factor relates to the wording of Article 267 TFEU. Judges are aware that only last instance courts are under a **legal obligation to submit** a preliminary question to Luxembourg. Lower court judges, on the other hand, have the discretion to do so. Judges argue that '[a] first instance judge can but the court of last instance must ask a preliminary question if the need arises'.[58] A Slovenian district court judge says that he does not consider it 'bad that lower level judges do not refer. Why should they jump the gun if the matter is still not ripe'.[59] Highest courts are, therefore, the ones who should break the ice.

B. Institutional Context

Factors deriving from the institutional configuration of a particular court dominate interview results. In other words, references to the institutional context was found in almost all interviews. The decision not to refer questions to Luxembourg is prompted by court standards. Such standards include: (a) workload; (b) quotas and standards; (c) court resources; (d) EU law education; and (e) influence of the Supreme Court.

Judges cite **workload** as an important factor preventing them from engaging with the preliminary ruling procedure. A Slovenian judge says that 'the judge in first instance is so burdened that simply … it is hard to imagine that [the judge] would take one month's time to work only on [the preliminary reference]'.[60] Similarly, a Croatian judge on the municipal court discloses:

> I am overburdened. I think we all are … And this poses a problem if you want to dedicate yourself to something … I do not have time for this. I mean, it is a stupid apology. But actually, when you look at it, when you have 100 cases that you need to solve in a week because they just keep coming to you because you are overburdened, then losing three days on one case really seems like a waste of time.[61]

Similar to many other national judges, Slovenian and Croatian judges have certain standards, that is **quotas** that they need to fulfil. Croatian judges have numerical standards, meaning that they need to solve a certain number of cases in one year. Not fulfilling this quota results in a lower grade at the end of a year[62] but it can also result in sanctions such as lower salary or

---

[58] Croatian judge 4, county court, 2nd instance.
[59] Slovenian judge 3, district court, 1st instance.
[60] Slovenian judge 1, local court, 1st instance.
[61] Croatian judge 1, municipal court, 1st instance.
[62] Judges in Croatia receive a grade at the end of the calendar year which takes into account several factors such as: the number of solved cases, participation in extracurricular activities, the number of hours spent in education. A similar grade exists in Slovenia, yet it does not take into account the number of solved cases. See M Sesar and K Šustić, 'Ocjenjivanje rada sudaca u Hrvatskoj, Sloveniji, Austriji, SR Njemačkoj i Švicarskoj s posebnim osvrtom na okvirna mjerila za rad sudaca i metodologiju izrade ocjene sudaca' (2008) 45 *Zbornik radova Pravnog fakulteta u Splitu*.

even a dismissal.[63] One Croatian judge says that there is a heavy 'burden of mathematical, numerical indicators of work. [Judges] are burdened with numbers and not the quality of things [they] do.'[64] Another Croatian judge emphasised that sending preliminary questions is not being counted according to numerical standards. She says:

> And it does not even count according to the framework criteria that you worked on anything at all. And it may happen to you that – after you ask the question and the Court makes a ruling on the preliminary question – that your party withdraws the lawsuit. And then ... it counts as if you almost did not work on this case at all.[65]

Numerical standards have been abolished in Slovenia, yet Slovenian judges have different quotas to achieve. According to court rules, every case needs to be decided within prescribed time limits. These are so-called time standards. One Slovenian judge says:

> Time standards determine ... in what time you have to write your decision. Otherwise the case is marked as judicial backlog. Therefore, time standards have a major impact on [sending a preliminary question], because you are under pressure to work faster. Even faster.[66]

Sending a preliminary question under the time standards requires writing a special report where judges have to 'justify why [judges] think a case should be graded higher or should take longer time. And then the president of the senate as well as the president of the court have to agree with it. But this is all extra work.'[67]

Judges further emphasise poor **court resources** as a reason for not sending preliminary questions to Luxembourg. One Croatian judge says that 'judges in Croatia are left on their own. [They] have to dig up everything, look for everything. You do not even know who to contact if a problem emerges'.[68] Both Croatian and Slovenian judges stress the importance of law clerks in unburdening judges. A Slovenian judge of a higher court says:

> Not only [do] the [judges of the Supreme Court] have more time, but they also have something else and these are law clerks ... These are people who can be sent to investigate the legal situation, how to ask the preliminary questions, and who can also perform the administrative office tasks that need to be done ... And in this sense, they help and unburden a judge. The most of them are by far at the Supreme Court.

---

[63] Croatian judge 8 from a municipal court (1st instance) says: 'Sanctions do exist. Here and there we see [sanctions] for non-execution of framework measures. The procedure is being conducted before the State Judicial Council and I have heard [a judge has been sanctioned] for disorderly performing his judicial duties. And after three to four years he was given a sanction: his wages for the next three months were reduced by one third. And there could have been a dismissal.'
[64] Croatian judge 3, municipal court, 1st instance.
[65] Croatian judge 5, municipal court, 1st instance.
[66] Slovenian judge 2, labour and social court, 1st instance.
[67] Slovenian judge 13, administrative court, 1st instance.
[68] Croatian judge 2, county court, 2nd instance.

As compared to the number of judges. So the Supreme Court has the best opportunity to ask preliminary questions. [The Supreme Court] is the least burdened and it receives the most help.[69]

The existence of a department monitoring EU law is another important court resource which has an impact on the referral behaviour of national judges. When explaining the high number of preliminary questions coming from the Slovenian Administrative court, an Administrative court judge argues that:

With the accession of Slovenia to the EU, the Administrative court has established the department on EU law where there are judges who could be approached by their colleagues and asked any question regarding EU law … It is precisely the existence of this department and work of these individual judges who have been – already from the very beginning, since 2004 – incorporating these elements of international law into [Slovenian] case law. It might be … that our president, by already in 2004 establishing the department on EU law, in some way gave strong legitimacy to European law.[70]

Besides lack of resources, judges also emphasise the lack of a systematic and continuous **education on EU law**. A Croatian judge gives an interesting anecdote:

I always quote an example from a Slovenian colleague. The prosecution had started and the State had been exposed to serious damages. And then the minister threatened his judges … That the state might get regression from judges in such cases when the State had to pay damages for not applying European law. The judges told him … 'And what did you do to educate us?' Then the minister said to them: *jura novit curia*. And then his colleagues told him – because Jura is a common name in Slovenia – they said: 'that poor judge Jura, he must know everything and nobody cares about him, nobody prepares him or educates him'.[71]

The president of a misdemeanour court criticised the limited number of places for judges offered at EU law workshops. She said:

We do not have enough education … For example, they give you an introduction to the law of the European Union. And then for [our region] they foresee one workshop in one year. Our court at that time … had 11 judges. And we have the right to send one participant. It takes 10 years for all of us to get our turn to participate in the seminar on the introduction to the law of the European Union or on the preliminary question. Well, that just does not make sense.[72]

Another determinant of referral behaviour of Slovenian and Croatian judges relates to the **example set by the Supreme Court**. A Croatian judge says:

I do not know whether the Supreme Court has ever sent a question to the CJEU. See, they have not, so we have not either. So they need to be fixed first. You know how

---

[69] Slovenian judge 6, higher court, 2nd instance.
[70] Slovenian judge, administrative court, 1st instance.
[71] Croatian judge 4, county court, 2nd instance.
[72] Croatian judge 11, misdemeanour court, 1st instance.

they say, you start from the head. And they certainly have situations in which there is a need for that ... [W]e all listen and hear the Supreme Court ... [W]e have to accept their views and we have to accept their understandings ... And lower courts [judges] are not on the fence here. We are actually thirsty for the views of the Supreme Court because they are giving us guidelines.[73]

Another Croatian judge adds that the situation could be different:

If they start with asking preliminary questions. Or to hint at one of their decisions ... or if we would receive some sense from these lectures or in our contacts with ... the Supreme Court that it is sometimes good to solve [a case] with a preliminary question. Not to be afraid of it.[74]

Unlike the Croatian Supreme Court, the Slovenian Supreme Court has taken a lead in making referrals to Luxembourg. Out of 19 preliminary references sent by Slovenian courts between 2004 and 2017, 13 came from the Supreme Court. Lower court judges are well aware of this, as well as of the fact that none of the Supreme Court's references were dismissed by the CJEU. One Slovenian judge says:

I know that there were two preliminary references regarding ... the migration crisis made by our Supreme Court. I think these were good questions, they were not rephrased and there were no sarcastic remarks in the judgement, such as: why are you asking this?[75]

It is thus possible that the activity of the Supreme Court discourages lower court judges who believe that the Supreme Court should continue its good work with sending references to the CJEU. Another Slovenian judge focuses more on the fact-finding versus law finding specialisation and argues:

First of all, [the preliminary reference] goes to more legal issue. We at the first instance are somehow more concerned with the operative part [of the judgment]. [Dealing] with the legal theory is maybe not really a task for the first instance ... It seems to me that I would rather step aside some questions that are a bit more complicated, a bit more abstract, and let the Supreme Court deal with them.[76]

Finally, because judges work under time pressure and have numerical quotas to fulfil, they argue that an additional effort invested into drafting a preliminary question should be specially **recognised or rewarded**. A Slovenian judge illustrates this here: '[n]ot even in a situation such as asking a preliminary question. I am not even rewarded. Basically, you give yourself extra work'.[77] Croatian judges similarly point out that a more frequent use of the preliminary procedure could be encouraged by 'recognizing the case in which you use

---

[73] Croatian judge 13, county court, 2nd instance.
[74] Croatian judge 7, municipal court, 1st instance.
[75] Slovenian judge 11, local court, 1st instance.
[76] Slovenian judge 9, higher court, 2nd instance.
[77] Slovenian judge 9, labour court, higher court, 2nd instance.

EU law and spent a few days to ask the preliminary question [and] to evaluate it higher [in end-year assessment of judges]'[78] and that making a referral is 'something that should be rewarded in a professional sense, in terms of some extra points for advancement'.[79] One judge linked referrals to numerical standards in Croatia:

> Motivation is something that the judges are very fond of. [It would incentivise judges] to count [asking a preliminary question] as 10 solved cases. And this is the only way that the judge will start thinking that [sending preliminary questions] is really paying off. If, for the past 20 days that he dedicated to a preliminary question he does not decide a certain amount of cases, then no judge will ever opt for a preliminary question.[80]

Likewise, a Slovenian judge argues that

> as long as the system of assessment, promotion and the choice of judges will not give much more importance to the knowledge and understanding of EU law … That this is evident during the entry of a judge into the system, in his evaluation and promotion. As long as this system will not include this component of EU law, no essential steps [in making preliminary questions] will be taken. Rather, everything will be left at the level of individual judges.[81]

Yet, both Slovenian and Croatian judges agree that making a referral should not be rewarded in a monetary sense. A Croatian judge says: 'I am not sure whether monetary motivation for sending preliminary questions would be a good solution … It should not be rewarded financially because you can send preliminary questions for nothing.'[82]

C. Litigation Rates and Litigants' Initiatives

Finally, interview results show that the referral behaviour of national judges is influenced by **litigation rates** and **litigants' initiatives**. Judges argue that they do not have 'many cases of such a nature yet'[83] and that 'situations that require preliminary questions are very rare'.[84] They argue that 'other [Member States] have been longer in the EU'[85] and that 'over time, it will intensify'.[86] One Croatian

---

[78] Croatian judge 5, municipal court, 1st instance.
[79] Croatian judge 7, municipal court, 1st instance.
[80] Croatian judge 6, county court, 2nd instance.
[81] Slovenian judge 13, administrative court, 1st instance.
[82] Croatian judge 7, municipal court, 1st instance.
[83] Croatian judge 10, municipal court, 1st instance.
[84] Croatian judge 13, county court, 2nd instance. Likewise, Slovenian judge 5 says: '[t]here may be a small number of cases, where such a question might arise'.
[85] Croatian judge 7, municipal court, 1st instance.
[86] Croatian judge 13, county court, 2nd instance.

judge believes that '[i]t is essential that it kicks off, and once it kicks off, then it would rise to the level of some other average EU Member State'.[87]

A Croatian judge gave an interesting anecdote on the role of litigants:

> I always quote an example from a Slovenian colleague. We are geographically close to each other and we sometimes spend time together. I asked them what experience they have [with EU law]. They said that for the first couple of years […] they did not have a clue […] that there is some European law […] as long as lawyers did not scent European law.[88]

An interesting finding is that many judges believe that parties to the case are those which should request a preliminary question. One Croatian judge says:

> [T]his should be the party's initiative. The party should initiate such a procedure. Everything comes from the party. We, in civil law proceedings, are working in accordance with the parties' proposals. We cannot do anything without the positions of the parties. And there is no such thing on their side. Lawyers are probably uneducated.[89]

Other judges, nonetheless, believe that lawyers are more knowledgeable on the issue. One Croatian judge notes that what would encourage judicial participation in the preliminary ruling procedure is

> a party proposal. The parties, the lawyers now, they are young people who had [EU law] during university … I was born in 1963 and I have worked as a judge for 24 years. And I did not have EU law at university. But these younger generations have. They have already been trained at university to ask such preliminary questions and to point out to certain directives that I have never heard of.[90]

Furthermore, judges argue that it would 'certainly encourage [the judge] if the parties insisted on it; if the judge was compelled [to ask a preliminary question]; if there would be some external inputs; if the parties, the lawyers would insist on it'.[91]

V. CONCLUSIONS

This chapter has focused on the question of why national judges do not turn to the CJEU by means of the preliminary ruling procedure and, more specifically, explores factors which influence judges not to submit a preliminary question to the CJEU in case of interpretative doubts. The chapter contributes to the European judicial politics literature in several ways. First, it emphasises that

---

[87] Croatian judge 13, county court, 2nd instance.
[88] Croatian judge 11, misdemeanour court, 1st instance.
[89] Croatian judge 8, municipal court, 1st instance.
[90] Croatian judge 11, misdemeanour court, 1st instance.
[91] Croatian judge 7, municipal court, 1st instance.

submitting a preliminary reference is a rare event and that attention should be given to non-referrals and the reasons behind them. Second, it moves away from country-level data and focuses on judge-level data. Finally, contrary to the views of the previous scholarship, it rejects the idea that the referral behaviour of national judges is influenced by merely one factor. It rather argues that the decision to submit a preliminary question to Luxembourg depends on a wide range of factors: from the individual profiles of judges and litigants' input, to factors deriving from the wider setting in which judges operate.

Notwithstanding the variety of factors which influence the referral behaviour of national judges, factors pertaining to the institutional setting of a specific court were found to be one of the biggest constraints of the interviewed judges. These include, inter alia, time pressure, high workload, court quotas, and insufficient resources. This demonstrates that – contrary to what has been held across the legal and political science scholarship – Euroscepticism is not the biggest challenge to the application of EU law at the national level within the preliminary ruling procedure. Instead, the biggest concerns derive from the institutional structure of the national court itself. Faced with time constraints, quotas and sanctions, judges occasionally have to trade applying EU law or sending a preliminary question to the CJEU for the fast closure of the case before them. This chapter can only encourage future research in the same field. Although this would require large-scale data collection, future research should explore how divergences in workload and court resources among different courts affect the referral behaviour of national judges.

ANNEX

Figure 10.3 Court system in Slovenia

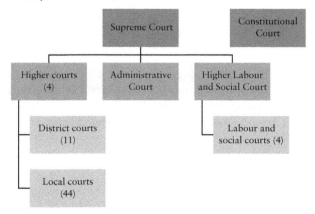

Figure 10.4 Court system in Croatia

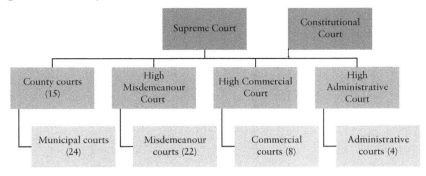

Figure 10.5 Word frequencies in interviews

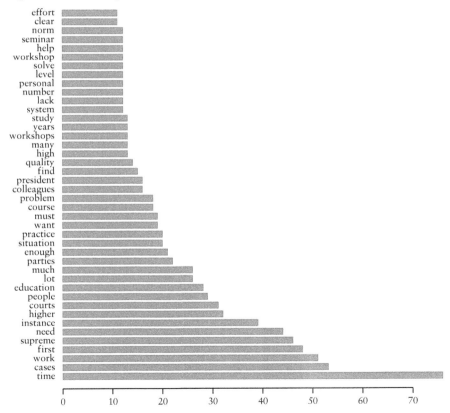

11

Game of Courts: The Effects of Constitutional Judicial Conflicts on Polish Judges' Co-operation with the CJEU

JUAN A MAYORAL[*]

I. INTRODUCTION

NATIONAL COURTS AND judges play key roles in the application, enforcement and legal integration of European Union (EU) law.[1] As members of the EU judiciary, courts serve as decentralised judicial enforcers responsible for ensuring the effectiveness of EU law and of the jurisprudence of the Court of Justice of the European Union (CJEU). The CJEU establishes and consolidates the position of EU law through the gradual dissemination of its jurisprudence, which directly impacts on national legal systems. National judges engage in legal integration, notably through the use of the preliminary ruling mechanism and by applying the CJEU's jurisprudence. In this regard, the CJEU successfully attracts the co-operation of domestic courts. Such co-operation allows the Court to effectively increase its power and fosters the functioning of the EU legal system.[2]

---

[*] The author wishes to thank Pola Cebulak, together with the editors and an anonymous reviewer, for their valuable suggestions and comments. This research was funded and conducted under the auspices of iCourts, the Centre of Excellence for International Courts (Danish National Research Foundation Grant No DNRF105).

[1] I Maher, 'National Courts as European Community Courts' (1994) 14 *Legal Studies* 226; U Jaremba, 'At the Crossroads of National and European Union Law. National Judges in a Multi-Level Legal Order – Legal and Empirical Perspective' (2013) 3/4 *Erasmus Law Review* 191; U Jaremba and JA Mayoral, 'The Europeanization of National Judiciaries: Definitions, Indicators and Mechanisms' (2018) 25 *Journal of European Public Policy* 1.

[2] LR Helfer, 'The Effectiveness of International Adjudicators' in CPR Romano, KJ Alter and C Avgerou (eds), *The Oxford Handbook of International Adjudication* (Oxford, Oxford University Press, 2013).

National courts in Member States empower the CJEU by requesting and implementing CJEU preliminary rulings on the interpretation or validity of EU law. The EU legal system, as a whole, has become a multi-level system of mutual enforcement and co-operation between courts, where the CJEU continuously needs to secure the collaboration of national judiciaries, acting as EU decentralised judges in the effective application of EU law. However, governments in Hungary and Poland have increasingly narrowed the independence of the judiciary and, particularly, of their constitutional courts. This recent rule of law crisis has raised concerns about the ability of national courts to perform their role as EU judges.

As a result of such political interventions, the constitutional courts may be instrumentalised by political powers to contradict or challenge the decisions of the CJEU.[3] This raises the risk of escalating judicial frictions between the CJEU and constitutional courts within the context of multi-level or heterarchical legal systems.[4] This would undermine the co-operation of national judges with the CJEU.

Although many academics have examined the co-operation between the national courts and the CJEU,[5] extremely little attention has been paid to the impact of contradictory judicial signals produced by clashes between top courts, with the notable exceptions of Kornhauser and Ramos.[6]

This chapter aims to contribute to the ongoing policy and legal debate by assessing how doctrinal conflicts between the CJEU and the Polish Constitutional

---

[3] L Pech and KL Scheppele, 'Illiberalism Within: Rule of Law Backsliding in the EU' (2017) 19 *Cambridge Yearbook of European Legal Studies* 3.

[4] A Dyevre, 'Domestic Judicial Defiance in the European Union: A Systemic Threat to the Authority of EU Law?' (2016) 35 *Yearbook of European Law* 106; A Dyevre, 'Domestic Judicial Defiance and the Authority of International Legal Regimes' (2016) 44 *European Journal of Law and Economics* 453; D Halberstam, 'Constitutional Heterarchy: The Centrality of Conflict in the European Union and the United States' in JL Dunoff and JP Trachtman (eds), *Ruling the World? Constitutionalism, International Law, and Global Governance* (Cambridge, Cambridge University Press, 2009).

[5] See, eg, MP Maduro, 'Contrapunctual Law: Europe's Constitutional Pluralism in Action' in N Walker (ed), *Sovereignty in Transition* (Oxford, Hart Publishing, 2003); N Walker, 'The Idea of Constitutional Pluralism' (2002) 65 *The Modern Law Review* 317; J Komárek, 'Czech Constitutional Court Playing with Matches: The Czech Constitutional Court Declares a Judgment of the Court of Justice of the EU Ultra Vires; Judgment of 31 January 2012, Pl. ÚS 5/12, Slovak Pensions XVII' (2012) 8 *European Constitutional Law Review* 323; M Claes, *The National Courts' Mandate in the European Constitution* (Oxford, Hart Publishing, 2006); KJ Alter, *Establishing the Supremacy of European Law: The Making of an International Rule of Law in Europe* (Oxford, Oxford University Press, 2001); JHH Weiler, 'A Quiet Revolution: The European Court of Justice and Its Interlocutors' (1994) 26 *Comparative Political Studies* 510; M Wind, 'The Nordics, the EU and the Reluctance Towards Supranational Judicial Review' (2010) 48 *Journal of Common Market Studies* 1039.

[6] LA Kornhauser, 'Adjudication by a Resource-Constrained Team: Hierarchy and Precedent in a Judicial System' (1995) 68 *Southern California Law Review* 1605; FR Romeu, 'Judicial Cooperation in the European Courts. Testing Three Models of Judicial Behavior' (2002) 2 *Global Jurist Frontiers* 1535.

Court (PCC) may affect the application of EU law by lower judges. The key question, more specifically, is whether a clash between the PCC and the CJEU would deter national Polish judges from applying EU law. To study this pattern, I make use of vignettes generated to study how Polish courts would react when a CJEU ruling would be incompatible with the PCC's doctrine on an EU law matter.[7] The objective is to test whether national judges would behave as EU judges and follow the CJEU when the national constitutional court contradicts the Court in Luxembourg. This study will help to address our lack of knowledge as to whether and how judicial conflicts impact on the willingness of judges to follow the CJEU, including in situations where the judiciary is under political pressure to side against the CJEU.

II. THE POLITICS OF THE CONSTITUTIONAL JUDICIARY AND THE RISK OF ESCALATION OF CONSTITUTIONAL JUDICIAL CONFLICTS ON EU LAW IN POLAND

Before the democratic and rule of law backsliding, the PCC, like many other constitutional courts in Central and Eastern Europe, was regarded as one of the main defenders of the idea of constitutional democracy in Poland.[8] The PCC actively promoted the process of democratisation and Europeanisation in co-operation with domestic and European actors, becoming a crucial actor in the Polish political landscape.[9] By intervening in inter-institutional disputes and curtailing the discretion of political institutions, the Constitutional Court built its legitimacy as an independent institution.[10]

This prominent role did not go unnoticed by populist politicians, who are often critical of constitutional courts' curtailing of political power.[11]

---

[7] Vignettes describe hypothetical situations in which judges choose to apply EU law or to follow any other course of action with regards EU law application. See J Finch, 'The Vignette Technique in Survey Research' (1987) 21 *Sociology* 105; T Nowak, F Amtenbrink, M Hertogh and M Wissink, *National Judges as European Union Judges: Knowledge, Experiences and Attitudes of Lower Court Judges in Germany and the Netherlands* (The Hague, Eleven International Publishing, 2011).

[8] B Bugarič and T Ginsburg, 'The Assault on Postcommunist Courts' (2016) 27 *Journal of Democracy* 69.

[9] J Komárek, 'National Constitutional Courts in the European Constitutional Democracy' (2014) 12 *International Journal of Constitutional Law* 525; D Piqani, 'Constitutional Courts in Central and Eastern Europe and Their Attitude towards European Integration' (2007) 1 *European Journal of Legal Studies* 213; M Kinander, 'Comparing Courts: The Accountability Function of the Constitutional Courts of Poland and Hungary' (2014) 39 *Review of Central and East European Law* 145.

[10] W Sadurski, 'Postcommunist Constitutional Courts in Search of Political Legitimacy' (1999) 6 *East European Case Reporter of Constitutional Law* 38.

[11] C Mudde, 'Are Populists Friends or Foes of Constitutionalism?' (2013) The Foundation for Law, Justice and Society Policy Brief, available at www.fljs.org/content/are-populists-friends-or-foes-constitutionalism.

Populists have frequently referred to constitutionalism and constitutional courts as adversaries of the will of the people. In Poland, the populist *Law and Justice* (PiS) government triggered a cascade of reforms and political strategies to curtail the power of the PCC.[12] They sought to pre-empt what they perceived as the difficulties that a powerful and autonomous constitutional court would create for their reform agenda. As a result, PiS successfully limited the power of the PCC, which became a new instrument for legitimising the transition to a new illiberal democracy and for dismantling the whole judicial system. The PCC became a necessary collaborator of the Polish populist government for neutralising the Supreme Court and the rest of the judiciary.[13] In the medium term, this strategy has ignored the possibility that individuals and opposition groups challenge the backlash against democracy and constitutional values through national and EU law before lower courts.[14]

The implications of the co-opting of the PCC for the enforcement of EU law does not end here. The Constitutional Court may also play an important role were the government to challenge EU legislations or policies. By questioning the principle of supremacy of EU law on the basis of the Polish constitution,[15] the Constitutional Court could be a powerful tool to limit the application of EU law and, particularly, for constraining the co-operation of Polish national judges with the CJEU. The PCC already questioned EU law's supremacy in its rulings on the Polish Accession Treaty and on the European Arrest Warrant.[16] Polish courts, like other Member States' courts, are required to co-operate by enforcing the doctrines established by the CJEU in a context of multi-level or heterarchical legal systems.[17] This is a consequence of the decentralised and interdependent structure of mutual enforcement and co-operation between courts, where the CJEU needs to secure the collaboration of national judiciaries. The potential escalation of 'constitutional judicial frictions or conflicts' between the CJEU and a co-opted constitutional court, such as the PCC, may distort the behaviour of lower courts as EU courts. In the next section, I will theoretically and empirically explore the implications of this clash of judicial powers for the application of EU law.

---

[12] K Kovács and KL Scheppele, 'The Fragility of an Independent Judiciary: Lessons from Hungary and Poland – and the European Union' (2018) 51 *Communist and Post-Communist Studies* 189.

[13] Pech and Scheppele, 'Illiberalism Within' (2017); Kovács and Scheppele, 'The Fragility of an Independent Judiciary' (2018).

[14] Kovács and Scheppele, 'The Fragility of an Independent Judiciary' (2018).

[15] W Sadurski, 'Solange, Chapter 3": Constitutional Courts in Central Europe – Democracy – European Union' (2008) 14 *European Law Journal* 1.

[16] Case K 18/4, 11 May 2005 and Case P 1/05, 27 April 2005.

[17] Dyevre, 'Domestic Judicial Defiance in the European Union' (2016); Dyevre, 'Domestic Judicial Defiance and the Authority of International Legal Regimes' (2016); Halberstam, 'Constitutional Hierarchy' (2009).

III. THE JUDICIAL SIGNALLING GAME OF COURTS: EXPLAINING JUDGES' REACTIONS TO CONSTITUTIONAL JUDICIAL CONFLICTS

Several theoretical models make different and mutually complementary predictions on how judges may behave when confronted with doctrinal conflicts between two judicial authorities. They identify different reasons as to why judges decide for one course of action or another.

Ramos Romeu's team model, inspired by Kornhauser's model of the United States legal system, emphasise the division of tasks between national judges and the CJEU.[18] National courts, as decentralised courts within the EU legal system, search for guidance from the CJEU because it stands at the apex of the EU legal system and because of its specialisation in EU law.[19] Under this assumption, national judges will consult the CJEU's jurisprudence to find an answer to the issues they have to rule on. Hence, in case of doubts about the application of EU law, national judges will follow EU guidance (Hypothesis 1). The CJEU's precedents are understood as a signal indicating the correct resolution of the case. However, this model also considers that the signal may be mixed with other signals provided by other courts (international, European and national courts). These signals may reinforce the application of EU law put forth by the CJEU but also contradict it, in which case the model predicts less adherence to the CJEU's interpretation (Hypothesis 2).

Realist/governmental models also account for situations of judicial doctrinal conflict in EU law. Such models detail that judicial actors are exposed to coercive influences from political actors who strive to shield their national power, policies or jurisdictions from the CJEU.[20] According to this model, faced with a judicial conflict, national judges will protect their own national legal system by being deferential to constitutional courts' positions and their constitutional and legal values. Scholars have highlighted that reputational and career threats can influence or constrain judicial decision making.[21] Judges, faced with these threats, will adapt their rulings to protect themselves from possible damage to their reputation and/or career perpetrated by judicial and political authorities.[22] Where judges are mindful of the judicial (and political) consequences of their judgments, they have an incentive to modify their behaviour when deciding on

---

[18] Kornhauser, 'Adjudication by a Resource-Constrained Team' (1995); FR Romeu, 'Law and Politics in the Application of EC Law: Spanish Courts and the ECJ 1986–2000' (2006) 43 *Common Market Law Review* 395.

[19] A Hinarejos, *Judicial Control in the European Union: Reforming Jurisdiction in the Intergovernmental Pillars* (Oxford, Oxford University Press, 2009).

[20] Jaremba and Mayoral, 'The Europeanization of National Judiciaries' (2018).

[21] L Epstein and J Knight, 'Reconsidering Judicial Preferences' (2013) 16 *Annual Review of Political Science* 11.

[22] L Epstein, 'Some Thoughts on the Study of Judicial Behavior' (2016) 57 *William and Mary Law Review* 2017.

EU law following that of judicial and political institutions.[23] According to this theory, enforcement by national courts will be weaker when national authorities oppose the application of EU law.

Faced with a judicial constitutional conflict, judges would look to their fellow domestic judicial authorities for guidance rather than the CJEU, because judges are in a weak institutional position. Under this model, national judges, operating in a restricted legal framework, will seek to avoid a judicial backlash from the national constitutional court and not follow the CJEU's rulings. Accordingly, national judges will be less likely to follow the CJEU's precedent when the constitutional court contradicts the position of the EU court (Hypothesis 3). Legal cultural models also reach a similar conclusion by offering a socialisation argument to justify the deference of national judges towards their national legal values and principles.[24] Such models set out that national constitutional courts may restrict the automatic reception and acceptance of EU law and doctrines in their rulings, signalling that the application of the CJEU's rulings could undermine the constitutional identity of their national legal order.[25]

Finally, judicial empowerment/neo-functionalist models argue that national judges may make strategic use of the CJEU's guidance and invoke the CJEU to legitimise their own power in the domestic context and divert criticism.[26] In these accounts, the national judges are driven by the need to protect their exercise of power and avoid the threats of overruling by their judicial superiors. Lower courts, therefore, will follow the CJEU in doctrinal conflicts and disregard their constitutional courts' precedents in favour of the CJEU's jurisprudence (Hypothesis 4).[27] Similarly, socio-legal trust-based accounts make a similar prediction highlighting that national judges' decisions depend on the confidence that such judges have for both institutions involved in the doctrinal conflict.[28] Accordingly, national judges may co-operate more with the CJEU when they believe that their supreme national judicial authority is untrustworthy. Lack of trust may be evidenced, for example, by their application of EU law,

---

[23] JA Mayoral, *The Politics of Judging EU Law: A New Approach to National Courts in the Legal Integration of Europe* (Madrid, Instituto Juan March de Estudios e Investigaciones, 2015).

[24] JE Rytter and M Wind, 'In Need of Juristocracy? The Silence of Denmark in the Development of European Legal Norms' (2011) 9 *International Journal of Constitutional Law* 470; Wind, 'The Nordics, the EU and the Reluctance Towards Supranational Judicial Review' (2010).

[25] Dyevre, 'Domestic Judicial Defiance and the Authority of International Legal Regimes' (2016); A Dyevre, 'European Integration and National Courts: Defending Sovereignty under Institutional Constraints?' (2013) 9 *European Constitutional Law Review* 139; Dyevre, 'Domestic Judicial Defiance in the European Union' (2016).

[26] Weiler, 'A Quiet Revolution' (1994); W Mattli and AM Slaughter, 'The Role of National Courts in the Process of European Integration: Accounting for Judicial Preferences and Constraints' in AM Slaughter, A Stone Sweet and JHH Weiler (eds) *The European Courts and National Courts. Doctrine and Jurisprudence. Legal Change in Its Social Context* (Oxford, Hart Publishing, 1998); Alter, *Establishing the Supremacy of European Law* (2001); Mayoral, *The Politics of Judging EU Law* (2015).

[27] Alter, *Establishing the Supremacy of European Law* (2001).

[28] JA Mayoral, 'In the CJEU Judges Trust: A New Approach in the Judicial Construction of Europe' (2017) 55 *Journal of Common Market Studies* 417.

lack of judicial independence, or lower courts' disagreement with the constitutional court's decisions.

IV. METHODOLOGY: USE OF VIGNETTES, CONVENIENCE SAMPLING AND THE PROBLEM OF DATA COLLECTION IN AUTHORITARIAN CONTEXTS

The use of vignettes is becoming more extended among scholars studying judicial behaviour.[29] In vignettes, individuals are asked questions about hypothetical real-life situations. A paradigmatic vignette study begins with a scenario that provides the framing for the actor's decision. Subsequently, the actor evaluates a series of vignettes in which crucial information is varied. Here, this information relates to the intervention of the PCC on an EU law matter. Because the scenarios are hypothetical, vignettes can be used to vary explanatory variables in an independent manner while they are likely to be much more correlated in practice. Accordingly, they can be particularly useful to discriminate between competing explanatory mechanisms.

Vignette studies have their own caveats.[30] First, as the respondents are asked to imagine themselves in a hypothetical scenario, the choices they make related to this scenario do not bear any real consequence for judicial decision makers. Incentives in driving these choices are likely to play a more limited role than in reality. Second, as the scenario is hypothetical, more potential sources of unreliability and bias can affect the interpretation of the actors' responses – judges may not act in accordance with their claimed intentions. Third, similar to laboratory experiments, the respondents can perceive vignette scenarios as rather artificial and this might compromise the validity of their decisions.

The survey data was collected by the author between 2011 and 2013 among judges from district and regional courts working in different Polish jurisdictions in collaboration with the European Centre of Natolin and the Polish Ministry of Justice. Those institutions disseminated the questionnaire and asked Polish judges to voluntarily answer it. With regard to the representativeness of the survey's design, carrying out a random probability sampling was extremely difficult due to the constraints in access to national judges and the distribution conditions imposed by the judiciary to co-operate.[31] Representativeness is important to ensure that all the relevant characteristics of the whole population of judges is in the sample, allowing for the generalisation of the findings.

---

[29] U Jaremba, *National Judges as EU Law Judges: The Polish Civil Law System* (Leiden, Brill, 2013); Nowak, Amtenbrink, Hertogh and Wissink, *National Judges as European Union Judges* (2011); Mayoral, *The Politics of Judging EU Law* (2015).

[30] D Barrera, V Buskens and W Raub, 'Embedded Trust: The Analytical Approach in Vignettes, Laboratory Experiments and Surveys' in F Lyon, G Mšllering and MNK Saunders (eds), *Handbook of Research Methods on Trust*, 2nd edn (Cheltenham, Edward Elgar Publishing, 2015).

[31] The questionnaire was distributed to the whole judiciary with no possibility of reminders or stratified sampling.

Nevertheless, a non-probability convenience sample was adopted, directed to as many available judges as possible rather than randomly selecting them from the whole judiciary. This type of design is suitable to demonstrate the extent that a particular trait or behaviour is present or occurs in the judiciary by sampling a group of judges. In this case, the objective was to test whether Polish judges may change their opinion and application of the CJEU's jurisprudence when the latter is challenged by their constitutional court, in other words in situations of constitutional judicial conflict between the CJEU and the PCC.

The data used was collected before 2015 when the attack on the rule of law and judicial independence in Poland began. Current literature on research design in challenging contexts has shown that respondents' fear of the government induces a significant bias on politically sensitive surveys in authoritarian situations compared to democratic ones.[32] Respondents adopt a self-censorship approach and, hence, are more likely to express support or trust in rulers, and more likely to distrust opposition leaders. Hence, any survey implemented in the current illiberal context in Poland where judges are under political pressure risks including a substantial bias in the responses. Many Polish judges would probably support the position of their pro-government constitutional court out of fear that the Polish authorities might use their responses to punish them. In this regard, we take advantage of the data collected before the democratic backsliding when the judiciary's independence was not yet compromised. This will help us gather more reliable conclusions about the behaviour of national judges in situations of judicial conflict.

V. WHAT WOULD HAPPEN IF THE POLISH CONSTITUTIONAL COURT LIMITED THE APPLICATION OF EU LAW? A COUNTERFACTUAL ANALYSIS

The analysis presents a scenario about the role of constitutional courts in conflicts between the European and the national legal orders. Such conflicts were avoided in a number of cases in Poland. In the *Brzeziński* case,[33] Polish judges from the Regional Administrative Court in Olsztyn sent out a question to the PCC questioning the constitutionality, in conjunction with Article 90 of the European Community Treaty, of the national provisions.[34] However, the PCC declared the case inadmissible, by asserting that Polish judges should direct their doubts about the compatibility of the Polish and EU law to the CJEU.[35]

---

[32] M Tannenberg, 'The Autocratic Trust Bias: Politically Sensitive Survey Items and Self-Censorhip', available at http://afrobarometer.org/sites/default/files/publications/Working%20papers/afropaperno176_autocratic_trust_bias.pdf.

[33] Regional Administrative Court in Olsztyn, Case I SA/Ol 374/05 on the submission of a legal question to the Constitutional Court, 16 November 2005.

[34] Excise Duty Act of 2004, Ustawa z dnia 23 stycznia 2004 r. o podatku akcyzowym.

[35] M Bobek, 'On the Application of European Law in (Not Only) the Courts of the New Member States: "Don't Do as I Say?"' (2008) 10 *Cambridge Yearbook of European Legal Studies* 1.

The PCC has, however, challenged the application of EU law in a number of cases. The PCC checked an EU regulation on its compatibility with Polish fundamental rights.[36] Even though it declared that the EU legal act was compatible with Polish fundamental rights, this decision was considered as a direct challenge to the principle of supremacy of EU law.[37] In other Member States, the highest national courts have expressly contradicted the CJEU in a number of cases; this includes the Czech Republic[38] and Denmark.[39]

In the Polish case, the scenario and context have changed because of the Polish Constitutional Court's lack of judicial independence. The lack of independence potentially makes the PCC more susceptible to limit the application of EU law and the CJEU's ruling and instead to protect the policies of the current populist government.[40] This begs the question of how Polish judges would react to a case of compatibility between EU and Polish law if the PCC had restricted the application of EU law. To answer this question, as was, I designed one vignette which was aimed especially at disentangling the signalling effects coming from two judicial authorities, the CJEU and the PCC. I presented a case to the surveyed Polish judges to test whether their position or decisions would have changed with the intervention of the Polish Constitutional Court. This aimed to uncover whether national judges in Poland are sensitive to the doctrinal constraints of the PCC. The survey examines the responses given by judges when asked to answer both of the questions below. Judges were asked to choose from three different paths of behaviour, allowing us to see whether and how their behaviour would alter if the PCC changed the rules of the game. The scenarios are:

Scenario without the intervention of the PCC: 'You are uncertain whether or not a national provision conflicts with an EU provision. In this case, the national provision is central to the resolution of the case. However, one of the litigants invokes a CJEU ruling stating that the national legislation is contrary to EU law and not applicable. Consequently …'

Scenario with the intervention of the PCC: 'You are uncertain whether or not a national provision conflicts with an EU provision. In this case, the national provision is central to the resolution of the case. However, one of the litigants invokes a CJEU ruling stating that the national legislation is contrary to EU law and not applicable. By contrast, the Constitutional Court has ruled that this EU provision should be applied restrictively because it is affecting fundamental national legal rules or values. Consequently …'

---

[36] Case SK 45/09, 16 November 2011.
[37] P Cebulak, 'European Constitutional Identity "Inside Out": Inherent Risks of the Pluralist Structure' (2013) 8 *Croatian Yearbook of European Law and Policy* 473.
[38] Komárek, 'Czech Constitutional Court Playing with Matches' (2012).
[39] MM Rask, OH Palmer and S Urška, 'Competing Supremacies and Clashing Institutional Rationalities: The Danish Supreme Court's Decision in the Ajos Case and the National Limits of Judicial Cooperation' (2017) 23 *European Law Journal* 140.
[40] Pech and Scheppele, 'Illiberalism Within' (2017).

For each question, judges were asked to choose from three alternatives on how they would react: A, B and C, representing their commitment to the application of the CJEU's rulings (see the wording in Table 11.1). The wording of option A was modified depending on whether the PCC had precluded the application of EU law or not.

Table 11.1 Aggregate responses of the Polish judges in the two scenarios

	Without PCC intervention	With PCC intervention
A) I would secure the national provision from the CJEU's interpretation/I would follow the Constitutional Court's interpretation	11.50%	58.26%
B) I would interpret national law in accordance with EU law	63.72%	20.87%
C) I would follow the CJEU's interpretation and apply EU law instead of the national law	24.78%	20.87%
Number of Polish judges	113	113

n=113 Polish judges.

Table 11.1 shows that the position of the judges certainly depended on the intervention of the PCC. Once the Constitutional Court signals or expresses a strong claim against the application of EU law, the percentage of judges saying they would follow the CJEU's interpretation and apply EU law instead of the national law decreases by around 4 per cent. More relevantly, in a situation where there has been no signalling from the PCC, the majority of judges declared that they would interpret national law in accordance with EU law, and thus make use of their judicial review powers of the national legislation without involving the CJEU. However, under a constitutionally constrained context, 43 per cent of these judges changed their position. Where the PCC intervened, the number of judges who supported the application of the PCC's ruling raised dramatically by 46 per cent.

Table 11.2 Transfer of judges' responses

	With PCC intervention		
Without PCC intervention	A: PCC	B: Interpret	C: CJEU
A: Apply national law	13 100%	0 0%	0 0%
B: Interpret	43 59.72%	23 31.94%	6 8.34%
C: CJEU	10 35.72%	1 3.57%	17 60.71%

n=113 Polish judges.

Table 11.2 sets out where these transfers took place. Each row shows how the responses of the judges in the scenario 'without PCC intervention' are allocated within the responses given for the second scenario 'with the PCC intervention'. This table informs whether judges would remain consistent with their behavioural path, or on the contrary, whether they would change their opinion depending on the position of the PCC with reference to EU law enforcement. The grey zones underline the areas where a transfer of opinions took place. Looking at the percentages reported, we see how a doctrinal clash between the PCC and the CJEU polarised the judges' responses, giving pre-eminence to the ruling of the PCC. Looking at the row corresponding to option B for the scenario without the intervention of the PCC, 60 per cent of the judges changed their position and sided with the Constitutional Court, while the transfer of those judges in favour to the CJEU is almost marginal (8 per cent). Also relevant is the congruence of all of the judges who chose option A before the intervention of the PCC, thereby maintaining their opinion (13 out of 113 judges). Finally, we can observe that some judges who previously supported the CJEU changed their position radically to the one supported by the PCC (35 per cent).

These findings illuminate the actions of judges in a context of heterarchical legal systems or, put differently, constitutional pluralism, 'where two or more high courts […] can claim authority to resolve legal disputes about the scope, content and applicability of a right, and no single high court can directly impose its authority on the other'.[41] In Poland, the pluralism in the constitutional system was settled after the decisions made by the PCC on the Polish Accession Treaty[42] and on the European Arrest Warrant.[43] Through these cases, the Polish court bestowed on itself the competence of reviewing and examining the application of EU law in the light of Polish fundamental legal principles. The counterfactual analysis shows the extent to which Polish judges are loyal and attached to the PCC. More extensively, the analysis demonstrates the extent to which the power of the CJEU and effectiveness of the EU's decentralised judicial system may be contested when the PCC is swayed by politics.

Nevertheless, it is worth pointing out that Polish judges, according to the data, may still use the CJEU to empower their own legal authority and subvert the rulings of the PCC.[44] This appears to have been the strategy of the Polish Supreme Court, which sent a preliminary reference to Luxembourg challenging the government's legislation forcing the Supreme Court's justices over 65 years old into early retirement.[45] The measures aimed to pack the Supreme Court with new judges selected by the ruling PiS party. A ruling from the CJEU could help

---

[41] A Stone Sweet and K Stranz, 'Rights Adjudication and Constitutional Pluralism in Germany and Europe' (2012) 19 *Journal of European Public Policy* 92, 97.
[42] Case K 18/4, 11 May 2005.
[43] Case P 1/05, 27 April 2005.
[44] Alter, *Establishing the Supremacy of European Law* (2001); Stone Sweet and Stranz (2012).
[45] Case III UZP 4/18, 2 August 2018.

national judges launch a counter-attack against a decision of the government endorsed by a politically subjugated constitutional court. The CJEU has laid down the groundwork for enforcing judicial independence as a general principle of EU law in *PPU Minister for Justice and Equality v LM* and *Associação Sindical dos Juízes Portugueses*.[46] This case law was further strengthened in the infringement case initiated by the European Commission where the CJEU ordered Poland in an interim injunction not to make any changes to the Supreme Court.[47] As a result, the Polish Government restored the Supreme Court judges to their positions until the final judgment.

This back and forth between the CJEU and the Portuguese and Polish courts is constructing the EU's rule of law framework, which may empower and encourage Polish judges to not only challenge their government, but also to disagree with the Polish Constitutional Court in EU law cases pertaining to sensitive political issues. Nevertheless, the capacity of national judges to dissent may be lost if the Polish Government is successful in submitting the entire judiciary to its will in the mid to long term. Any opportunity for judicial resistance against populist governments and co-opted higher courts may be conditional on the capacity of national judges to disagree with their judicial superiors and to review the executive's decisions. In Poland, this autonomy will be lost if PiS, despite the opposition of the EU and other Member States, persists and succeeds in its master plan to reduce the independence of the Polish judiciary.

VI. CONCLUSIONS

National courts of Member States have played an essential role in the process of legal integration by enforcing rights derived from EU law and the jurisprudence of the CJEU. However, the EU has recently been struggling as a rule of law community to make all its Member States uphold its laws and values. The Polish Government has increasingly attacked the rule of law and narrowed the independence of the judiciary and the Constitutional Court. This has raised the spectre of judicial conflicts between the CJEU and the PCC and concerns about national courts' enforcement of EU law and the CJEU's jurisprudence.

This chapter has analysed the degree to which the Polish Constitutional Court's behaviour may affect Polish courts' co-operation with the CJEU. Drawing on survey data collected between 2011 and 2013, it shows that Polish national judges may not follow the CJEU's jurisprudence when the Polish top court

---

[46] Judgment of 27 February 2018, *Associação Sindical Dos Juízes Portugueses*, C-64/16, EU:C:2018:117; for discussion see M Bonelli and M Claes, 'Judicial Serendipity: How Portuguese Judges Came to the Rescue of the Polish Judiciary: ECJ 27 February 2018, Case C-64/16, Associação Sindical Dos Juízes Portugueses' (2018) 14 *European Constitutional Law Review* 622; judgment of 25 July 2018, *LM*, C-216/18 PPU, EU:C:2018:586.

[47] Order of 17 December 2018, *Commission v Poland*, C-619/18 R, EU:C:2018:852.

disagrees with Luxembourg. The findings of this study highlight that governments that keep their constitutional courts on a short leash may systematically distort the application of EU law by national judges. Different theories predict different outcomes in this situation.

On the one hand, theories of empowerment and judicial trust predict that national judges, faced with a constitutional judicial conflict, will be less likely to endorse their highest court if they do not perceive their constitutional court as trustworthy, legitimate or independent. The capture of the Polish Constitutional Court reduces national judges' trust for the PCC. Judges increasingly feel that the PCC is no longer a trustworthy judicial authority.[48] According to these theories, the lower court judges, guided by professional ethics, will move away from the PCC's position and increasingly depend on either their own judgment or the CJEU's jurisprudence.

On the other hand, according to *realist/governmental* theories, the co-opting of the PCC will lead national judges to become more fearful of their judicial superiors, as judicial purges or lustration could lead lower court judges to fear for their jobs and/or careers, while at the same time potentially making the PCC more prone to strike down dissidents. According to these theories, recent developments may amplify the support for the PCC among Polish judges.

This chapter highlights several other findings. In the context of judicial pluralism or heterarchical legal systems, such as the EU's legal system, judicial conflicts may significantly restrict the development, reception and integration of the CJEU's rulings within the Member States' domestic systems. This resistance to the CJEU may be particularly important in centralised judicial review systems,[49] such as in Poland, where there exists a strong rivalry between constitutional courts and the CJEU according to inter-court competition theories.[50] We could expect different behaviour in countries where the dynamics of judicial competition are less present, like in the Netherlands with monist legal systems.

Moreover, this chapter's findings help us better understand national judges' use of preliminary references. In situations where the national constitutional court is openly opposed to the CJEU, judges will be more likely to submit cases on EU law to their constitutional court as opposed to making preliminary references. These findings challenge the inter-court competition theory's predictions that lower courts will use the preliminary reference's procedure to challenge their national superiors.

---

[48] Mayoral, *The Politics of Judging EU Law* (2015).
[49] The centralised model of constitutional adjudication is defined as a system where the constitutional court is the only judicial institution empowered to review all legislative acts and governmental decrees. In decentralised systems, ordinary courts are also bestowed with that power.
[50] Alter, *Establishing the Supremacy of European Law* (2001); Mattli and Slaughter, 'The Role of National Courts in the Process of European Integration' (1998); Mayoral, *The Politics of Judging EU Law* (2015).

Finally, one can speculate as to whether and when Polish courts may be an effective tool against democratic backsliding by enforcing the CJEU's rulings and EU legislation protecting democracy and the rule of law. In this regard, all the preconditions for a decentralised enforcement of EU law by political opponents and civil society before national courts against democratic backsliding are met:[51] 1) litigants who can invoke EU legal norms, 2) litigants with sufficient resources and organisational support, and 3) national and European courts which formulate legal interpretations supporting democracy and the rule of law. However, this judicial strategy's success may be limited. The disablement of the Polish judiciary may discourage any co-operation and implementation of the CJEU's rulings on compliance with democratic and rule of law principles. First, any attempt by national judges to challenge the populist government will be easily opposed by an obedient constitutional court with the means to discipline the rest of the judiciary. Second, the lack of independence at all levels of the Polish judiciary by discouraging Polish judges from behaving as EU judges and following the CJEU may reinforce conformity with the Constitutional Court in the situation of a judicial conflict.

---

[51] M Blauberger and RD Kelemen, 'Can Courts Rescue National Democracy? Judicial Safeguards against Democratic Backsliding in the EU' (2017) 24 *Journal of European Public Policy* 321.

Part V

Conclusions

12
National Resistance Against EU Law and Governance: Degrees and Manifestations

CLARA RAUCHEGGER* AND ANNA WALLERMAN

I. INTRODUCTION

'THE IDEA OF Europe is in peril. From all sides there are criticisms, insults and desertions from the cause.' These are the words used in a recent manifesto that was signed by 30 intellectuals from 21 countries and published by several newspapers.[1] The signatories warned against the consequences of populism, nationalism and Euroscepticism and they claimed that the current challenge to liberal democracy and its values was greater than any since the 1930s.

The overall aim of this book was to determine to what extent Eurosceptic attitudes have translated (or may translate) into actual legislative, administrative and judicial practices that challenge European Union (EU) law and governance in the Member States. Our wish was to divert attention from claims and pledges made by politicians to their specific consequences (or lack thereof) at the national level.

This chapter strives to bring together the main findings of the preceding 11 chapters in a coherent framework and to confront these findings with the academic literature on Euroscepticism and compliance. We do not attempt a conceptual definition of Euroscepticism. Instead, we present a spectrum of national resistance to the authority of EU law and governance that ranges from the drastic rejection of EU membership and disrespect of the EU's most

---

* Clara Rauchegger's work was supported by the Austrian Science Fund (FWF) [project J 4104-G16].
[1] 'Fight for Europe – or the Wreckers will Destroy It' (25 January 2019) *The Guardian*, available at www.theguardian.com/commentisfree/2019/jan/25/fight-europe-wreckers-patriots-nationalist.

fundamental values to unintentional practical obstacles that hinder the full effectiveness of EU law in the Member States. Some of the challenges discussed in this overview can be seen as expressions of Euroscepticism, but not all of them. The terms 'Euroreluctance' or 'Euroignorance' might more adequately capture some of these challenges.

The remainder of the chapter is divided into four sections. Section II discusses previous scholarship on the understanding, definition and classification of Euroscepticism, and relates it to the challenges discussed in this volume. Section III places these challenges on a spectrum from challenges brought on by hard-line, ideological Euroscepticism, to those that have their roots in more specific objections to the forms of European integration and finally to such challenges that are the effect of practical difficulties rather than political preferences. Section IV then turns the attention to remedies and in particular to the role of courts in countering manifestations of Euroscepticism. Lastly, section V offers some concluding remarks.

II. CLASSIFYING EUROSCEPTICISM

Although Euroscepticism has received considerable attention in the political science literature for the past two decades, no clear and common definition has emerged.[2] The dominant literature provides a number of dichotomies. In one of the most influential conceptualisations, Szczerbiak and Taggart distinguish between hard and soft Euroscepticism, where hard Euroscepticism signifies rejection of the European integration project as such, whereas soft Euroscepticism denotes a more qualified critique of EU policies.[3] Other commentators distinguish between diffuse and specific criticism of Europeanisation, where the former rejects the integration ideal, whereas the latter rejects the EU as the current embodiment of said ideal (without necessarily rejecting the ideal).[4] Yet others differentiate between political and instrumental Euroscepticism, with the former being of a more principled kind, whereas the latter is determined

---

[2] CE de Vries and EE Edwards, 'Taking Europe to its Extremes: Extremist Parties and Public Euroscepticism' (2009) 15 *Party Politics* 5; P Kaniok, 'Eurosceptics – Enemies or a Necessary Part of European Integration?' (2012) 12 *Romanian Journal of Political Science* 29; B Leruth, N Startin and S Usherwood, 'Defining Euroscepticism: From a Broad Concept to a Field of Study' in B Leruth, N Startin, S Usherwood (eds), *The Routledge Handbook of Euroscepticism* (Abingdon, Routledge, 2017).

[3] eg A Szczerbiak and P Taggart (eds), *Opposing Europe? The Comparative Party Politics of Euroscepticism, Volume 1: Case Studies and Country Surveys* (Oxford, Oxford University Press, 2008); A Szczerbiak and P Taggart (eds), *Opposing Europe? The Comparative Party Politics of Euroscepticism, Volume 2: Comparative and Theoretical Perspectives* (Oxford, Oxford University Press, 2008).

[4] P Kopecký and C Mudde, 'The Two Sides of Euroscepticism: Party Positions on European Integration in East Central Europe' (2002) 3 *European Union Politics* 297.

by whether oneself or one's own country is thought to gain from European co-operation.[5]

In legal scholarship, the term has been subject to less discussion, and consequently is even more indistinct. Euroscepticism is typically used as a broad term referring to all objections towards the EU (or European co-operation in general), its policies or its functioning.[6] Interestingly, however, a recent editorial in the *Common Market Law Review* took a literal perspective on the notion of *scepticism*, removing the most hard-line opposition from the concept altogether and differentiating between Euroscepticism on the one hand and outright hostility towards the EU on the other.[7]

The UK's decision to withdraw from the EU seems an obvious example of Euroscepticism and it could be classified as hard, diffuse and political Euroscepticism. The contributions to this volume, however, illustrate national policies and actions vis-à-vis EU law and governance that do not fit neatly with the dichotomies set out above. Most of these national policies and actions do not entail opposition to one's Member State remaining in the EU and could therefore be classified as soft Euroscepticism. However, this classification is unhelpful as it ignores the various facets of the challenges to EU law and governance set out in the different chapters and the significant differences between them. For this reason, we find that these challenges are better understood as positions on a continuum.[8] The benefit of this image, in contrast to dichotomies, is that it not only allows for clear-cut cases, but also for middle positions. Notably, it is suitable to distinguish different degrees and manifestations of Euroscepticism.

The spectrum of national measures that we propose in the following section is more than a subdivision of soft Euroscepticism. It includes all kinds of national resistances against the EU, not only those that can be termed Eurosceptic. In particular, the spectrum encompasses failures by the Member States to respect and implement EU law. Lack of compliance with EU law can be as dangerous to the authority of EU law in the Member States as outright Eurosceptic attitudes. However, it is not necessarily an expression of Euroscepticism, as some of the contributions to this volume clearly demonstrate. Sometimes, national resistance to the full effectiveness of EU law is not even intentional on the part of the

---

[5] M Lubbers and P Scheepers, 'Political versus Instrumental Euro-Scepticism: Mapping Scepticism in European Countries and Regions' (2005) 6 *European Union Politics* 223.

[6] See, eg, S Garben, 'Sky-High Controversy and High-Flying Claims? The Sturgeon Case Law in Light of Judicial Activism, Euroscepticism And Eurolegalism' (2013) 50 *Common Market Law Review* 15; S Douglas-Scott, 'Fundamental Rights, Not Euroscepticism: Why the UK Should Embrace the EU Charter of Fundamental Rights' in L Hodson, E Wicks and K Ziegler (eds), *The UK and European Human Rights: A Strained Relationship* (Oxford, Hart Publishing, 2015).

[7] 'Editorial Comments' (2019) 56 *Common Market Law Review* 2.

[8] Similarly see de Vries and Edwards, 'Taking Europe To Its Extremes' (2009) 11; L Hooghe and G Marks, 'Sources of Euroscepticism' (2007) 42 *Acta Politica* 119; A Krouwel and Y Kutiyski, 'Soft Sceptics and Hard Rejectionists: Identifying Two Types of Eurosceptic Voters' in B Leruth, N Startin, S Usherwood (eds), *The Roudledge Handbook of Euroscepticism* (Abingdon, Routledge, 2017) 190.

relevant national actor. Combing Eurosceptic resistances and other resistances to the EU in one scale allows us to reflect on the correlations between attitudes and actions at the national level.

Besides, the term Euroscepticism has strong negative connotations that should not be applied to any criticism of the EU or its developments.[9] Criticism is clearly legitimate in a democratic community based on the rule of law, as the EU strives to be. For instance, labelling Italian criticism of the asylum regime established by the Dublin III Regulation as solely Eurosceptic is hardly conducive to the improvement of either political debate or academic understanding, if the rationale of such criticism is mainly to foster a discussion on the distribution of responsibilities between the Member States.

Among the resistances against EU law and governance that are identified in the contributions to this volume, we can distinguish between, on the one hand, lawful resistances that stay within the limits provided by EU law and, on the other hand, unlawful resistances that undermine European integration by disregarding EU rules.[10] Fundamentally, this difference is illustrated by the difference between Brexit and the illiberal developments in Poland and Hungary. Brexit represents the ultimate rejection of European integration through withdrawal, but it is undertaken in accordance with Article 50 of the Treaty on European Union (TEU) and thus qualifies as a lawful challenge. On the contrary, the systemic rule of law backsliding in Poland and Hungary violates the EU's fundamental values that are enshrined in Article 2 TEU. Likewise, the Luxembourgish legislation examined by Warin in her chapter, as well as the Hungarian economic policy measures analysed by Papp and Varju, constitute unlawful resistances as they infringe EU free movement law. In contrast, the reintroduction of border controls in the wake of the migration crisis that Thalmann describes in his chapter is arguably lawful, relying on exceptions inbuilt in the Schengen regime.

III. SPECTRUM OF RESISTANCES AGAINST EU LAW AND GOVERNANCE

A. Fundamental Challenges to Core Values, Policies and Law of the EU

We have seen that Brexit is an example of hard Euroscepticism in the sense of an opposition to one's Member State remaining in the EU. However, there are various forms of national resistance against European integration that do not correspond to a wish to leave the EU. The combined effect of these challenges might be more dangerous for the EU than the UK's withdrawal as it undermines EU law and policy from within.

---

[9] Kaniok, 'Eurosceptics' (2012) 35.
[10] Similarly see MR Madsen, P Cebulak and M Wiebusch, 'Backlash against International Courts: Explaining the Forms and Patterns of Resistance to International Courts' (2018) 14 *International Journal of Law in Context* 197.

One such fundamental challenge for the EU is the rise of populist radical right-wing parties and their combined influence on established EU policies. These parties are not necessarily opposed to EU membership, but they are EU-hostile in the sense that they tend to call for the dismantling of EU policies rather than for policy extension. A second fundamental challenge consists in illiberal developments in some Member States, in particular Hungary and Poland. Rather than expressing an intention to leave the EU, governments and legislators in Poland and Hungary disregard the EU's core values and undermine the authority of EU law in their Member State by blatantly disregarding EU law that diverges from their perceived national interests.

Regarding the first challenge, the rise of populist radical right parties, Falkner and Plattner show in their chapter that these parties do not oppose any shift of competences to the EU level in principle. Where it might benefit their own Member State, they even demand enhanced co-operation within the EU's legal framework. Overall, Falkner and Plattner find significant incoherence in these parties' policy preferences. Their findings suggest that it is rather unlikely that populist radical right parties will join forces to reform the EU with a common goal in mind. The main danger seems to be that these parties will undermine EU policy making by opposing further integration in specific sectors. This opposition can have a significant impact on EU law and governance as the traditional pro-EU centre-right and centre-left parties continue to lose votes and seats, both at the national level and in the European Parliament.

The second challenge is twofold. First, systemic disrespect of the rule of law in Poland and Hungary threatens some of the values on which the EU is founded.[11] The European Commission has reacted to the rule of law backsliding in Poland by triggering an Article 7(1) TEU procedure against this Member State.[12] The European Parliament has done so in respect of Hungary.[13] It remains to be seen whether these attempts to safeguard the rule of law in Poland and Hungary will be successful.[14] The second problematic aspect of the illiberal developments in Poland and Hungary is that disrespect for the rule of law seems to coincide with

---

[11] For an explanation on how rule of law backsliding tends to happen and an assessment of the mechanisms the EU could rely on to address this problem see, eg, L Pech and KL Scheppele, 'Illiberalism Within: Rule of Law Backsliding in the EU' (2017) 19 *Cambridge Yearbook of European Legal Studies* 3. See also C Closa and D Kochenov, 'Reinforcement of the Rule of Law Oversight in the European Union: Key Options' in W Schroeder (ed), *Strengthening the Rule of Law in Europe: From a Common Concept to Mechanisms of Implementation* (Oxford, Hart Publishing, 2016).

[12] European Commission, 'Proposal for a Council Decision on the determination of a clear risk of a serious breach by the Republic of Poland of the rule of law' (2017) COM/2017/0835 final.

[13] European Parliament, Resolution of 12 September 2018 on a proposal calling on the Council to determine, pursuant to Article 7(1) of the Treaty on European Union, the existence of a clear risk of a serious breach by Hungary of the values on which the Union is founded (2018) 2017/2131(INL).

[14] Halmai argues that the traditional mechanisms that are aimed at safeguarding the rule of law in Member States are incapable of enforcing compliance and that there is a need for conditionality measures, such as cutting funds for Member States that fail to comply, see G Halmai, 'The Possibility and Desirability of Rule of Law Conditionality' (2018) *Hague Journal on the Rule of Law* 1.

non-compliance with EU law, at least to a certain extent. Two contributions to this volume suggest that blatant, public disregard of EU law is a corollary of the illiberal turn in Poland and Hungary. This aspect of the rule of law crisis has so far received less attention in the academic literature.

Tacik's chapter indicates that the Polish Government challenges the authority of EU law by refusing to comply with EU secondary law where it goes against (what the government considers to be) national interests. According to Tacik, the Białowieża forest case is more than an example of a standard failure to fulfil the obligations that arise from EU law. He suggests that the Polish Government not only failed to comply with EU secondary law on environmental protection by undertaking logging activities in the protected forest, but also engaged in a disinformation campaign on its logging activities and their legal assessment, and deliberately undermined the authority of the Court of Justice of the EU (CJEU). In the author's view, the Polish Government disrupted any rational communication with the EU institutions by advancing arguments that were manifestly inconsistent and unreasonable. Moreover, members of the Polish Government openly contested and ridiculed the authority of the CJEU, in particular by questioning the scientific evidence on which the CJEU based its assessment. Most importantly, the Polish authorities deliberately ignored the CJEU's order to stop logging except in cases of threat to public security. This was an unprecedented case of open and daring disregard of an interim measure of the CJEU.

Similarly, Papp and Varju's chapter details how Hungary, following the installation of the Orbán government in 2010, took a decidedly patriotic turn in its economic policy. They suggest that the Hungarian economic policy, which has frequently been struck down as incompatible with EU free movement law, is in fact a manifestation of 'deep-rooted ideological divisions'[15] between EU core values and Hungarian patriotism. In their view, the Hungarian Government not only challenges the EU's core democratic values, but also the market liberalism on which the EU's internal market is founded. It is hard to imagine a more thorough rejection of the Union's raison d'etre.

Most of the anti-EU policy preferences examined by Falkner and Plattner and the disregard for EU law identified by Tacik, Papp and Varju are expressions of instrumental Euroscepticism.[16] Many populist radical right parties are in favour of European integration where it may be of benefit to those who they consider as their own people. For example, Falkner and Plattner note that even the radically patriotic Hungarian far-right party Jobbik calls for an extension of the protection of minorities by the EU, albeit only in order to benefit its own ethnos. Similarly, the Polish KNP, a radically Eurosceptic Polish party, favours extending the free travel of people in the Schengen area as this extension

---

[15] Section IX, ch 10, this volume.
[16] On instrumental Euroscepticism, see Lubbers and Scheepers, 'Political versus Instrumental Euro-Scepticism' (2005).

would be likely to benefit Polish citizens. If populist radical right parties support EU membership, they appear to do so based on "instrumental Eurosupport", that is a hope or belief that membership is overall beneficial from a state-centric point of view. Conversely, populist far right parties tend to oppose EU policies that are seen as disadvantaging their own people. The two populist radical right parties that govern Hungary and Poland, Fidesz and PiS, seem to be amongst those that take such an instrumental approach. They support continued EU membership, but they fail to comply with EU environmental law or free movement law where it goes against their own interests.

Although the failures to comply with EU law described in the Polish and Hungarian case studies can be interpreted as instrumental Euroscepticism, it would be wrong to assume that Euroscepticism or Eurofriendliness explains compliance with EU law or lack thereof. Toshkov's contribution to this volume indicates that the overall degree of compliance with EU law in a Member State is largely unconnected to the Eurosceptic tendencies of its government or population. Likewise, Guastaferro and Gianniti indicate in their chapter that, while Italy traditionally had a Eurofriendly government and population, this has 'not necessarily turn[ed] into a speedy and correct implementation of EU law' in this Member State.[17] Conversely, the new Italian Government, which is composed of two Eurosceptic parties, has not (yet) engaged in any major reforms that question the authority of EU law in the national legal order. Thus, judging by these contributions, Euroscepticism does not appear to be the main cause for lack of compliance with EU law.

Compliance scholars have identified several different factors that influence compliance rates.[18] According to constructivism, one theoretical approach to understanding compliance with EU law, the normative cost of non-compliance must be high enough to encourage compliance. In Member States that are traditionally committed to the rule of law, blatantly disregarding EU law is unthinkable.[19] For this reason, loud and ardent political criticism of the EU does not necessarily lead to non-compliance in these Member States because their government ultimately concludes that it cannot clearly and publicly violate EU rules.[20] The difference between Eurosceptic rhetoric and actual policies in Italy could thus be explained from a constructivist perspective. While blatant non-compliance would be inappropriate, compliance can be incomplete insofar as the practical implementation and application of EU law is concerned – this seems

---

[17] Section I, ch 3, this volume.
[18] For an overview of political science perspectives on compliance with EU law, see L Conant, 'Compliance and What the EU Member States Make of It' in M Cremona (ed), *Compliance and the Enforcement of EU Law* (Oxford, Oxford University Press, 2012).
[19] ibid 6.
[20] ibid 22; D Beach, 'Why Governments Comply: An Integrative Compliance Model that Bridges the Gap between Instrumental and Normative Models of Compliance' (2005) 12 *Journal of European Public Policy* 113, 118–19.

to be the case in Italy. In Poland and Hungary, on the other hand, the lacking commitment to the rule of law in general adversely affects respect for EU law in these Member States; as Papp and Varju point out, the introduction of illiberal reform largely coincides with a fall in Hungarian compliance rates. Apparently, the Polish and Hungarian governments do not accept compliance with the law as an internalised obligation but they engage in a cost–benefit analysis.[21]

B. Sectoral Protectionism: Free Movement, Schengen and Third-Country Immigration

Several chapters of this volume highlight national challenges to the authority of EU law that arise in specific substantive areas of EU law and governance. The Member States in which these resistances occur are not necessarily ideologically opposed to European integration or values. Rather, they fail to comply with EU law in fields where it departs strongly from their national policies or political preferences. Free movement of persons, especially when it requires giving welfare benefits to migrant workers and their families, and the border-free Schengen system appear to be particularly controversial areas with low rates of compliance with EU law, even in Member States generally known as Europhile. The sectoral protectionism discussed in this section can be distinguished from the fundamental threats to EU authority in Hungary and Poland discussed in the last section in two ways. First, the resistances are confined to a particular policy area. Second, the Member States in which these resistances take place are generally committed to observing the rule of law.

Warin's chapter identifies obstacles to the free movement of persons in Luxembourg. As the author explains, Luxembourg is a Member State that proudly self-identifies as Europhile. Nevertheless, the cases discussed by Warin show that Luxembourg continuously engages in indirect discrimination on grounds of residence or nationality. Luxembourgish protectionism is specifically directed against frontier workers who make up a very high proportion of the labour force of this Member State. Frontier workers have been disproportionately discriminated by the Luxembourgish income tax law. In addition, they were deprived of family benefits and student financial support for their adult children whereas residents continued to receive these benefits. These forms of discrimination against frontier workers can be explained by financial considerations. However, Luxembourg also engages in protectionism where direct financial stakes are not involved. It has actively and consistently opposed the free movement of lawyers and introduced language barriers aimed at hindering foreign lawyers from establishing themselves in Luxembourg.

---

[21] Conant, 'Compliance' (2012) 7.

Luxembourg is not the only Member State that attempts to undermine the free movement of persons by diminishing social benefits of workers from other Member States. The first legislative initiative of the new Austrian Government, a coalition between the conservative ÖVP and the populist radical right FPÖ, was to curb family benefits and family tax reductions of migrant workers. New legislation that entered into force in January 2019 indexes family benefits and family tax reductions for migrant workers whose children are resident in another Member State.[22] Remarkably, the Austrian Government and Parliament were perfectly aware that indexing family benefits for migrant workers will, in all likelihood, violate EU law. The European Commission and the government's own civil service had warned that this kind of indexing was incompatible with EU secondary law as interpreted by the CJEU and this view was shared by a professor of EU law who provided expert advice to the Austrian Government and Parliament.[23] A recent academic article published in a renowned Austrian law journal concludes that the new law is definitely incompatible with EU secondary law in its current state.[24] Unsurprisingly, the European Commission has already launched an infringement procedure against Austria.[25]

Related to single market free movement is another area of EU law that has recently been undermined in a number of Member States: the border-free area established by the Schengen Borders Code. As Thalmann writes in his chapter, as a reaction to the so-called migration crisis of 2015–16, nine EU Member States and Schengen-associated states reintroduced temporary border controls along their borders with other Member States and six of these States continue to carry out border checks until the present day. Thalmann observes that the Member States justify these border controls by arguing that the influx of third-country nationals seeking international protection and the secondary movements of these migrants within the EU creates a serious threat to public policy or internal security in their national territory.

Challenges to the free movement of persons and the Schengen open border system might become even more acute with the rise of populist radical right parties in Member States and the European Parliament. Falkner and Plattner point out that most of the populist radical right parties support (at least sectoral) closing of their national markets. Besides, 77 per cent of the statements of populist radical right parties express opposition to free travel across national borders within the EU and the absence of internal borders. However, Falkner

---

[22] See S Mayr, 'Quod Licet Iovi, Non Licet Bovi? Die Indexierung der Familienbehilfe aus unionsrechtlicher Sicht' (2018) 73 *Zeitschrift für Öffentliches Recht* 317, 318.
[23] ibid 320–21.
[24] ibid 333.
[25] European Commission, Press Release, 'Indexation of Family Benefits: Commission Opens Infringement Procedure against Austria' (24 January 2019) IP/19/463; European Commission, 'Indexation of Family Benefits: Speaking Points of Commissioner Thyssen on the Launch of the Infringement Procedure against Austria' (24 January 2019) SPEECH/19/664.

and Plattner note that there is a stark difference between policy preferences of Eastern parties, which are advocating for open borders inside the EU, and Western and Northern parties, which want to restore national borders. One can speculate that Eastern European parties assume that their citizens will benefit from open borders, whereas parties from Western and Northern Member States want to protect their citizens from the influx of foreign nationals, be it third country nationals or EU migrants. Notably, all countries currently operating exceptions from the Schengen system would fall in the latter category.[26]

Furthermore, according to Falkner's and Plattner's findings, a majority of 70 per cent of the statements of populist radical right parties favour dismantling the EU's policy on external migration into the EU. The few calls for an extension of EU migration law and policy are not necessarily contradictory because they are mainly concerned with the strengthening of the EU's external border and the idea of a "fortress Europe", as Falkner and Plattner explain.

The common feature of the sectoral protectionism described in this section is that it is directed against the influx of foreigners. By introducing obstacles to the free movement of people, Member States such as Luxembourg and Austria try to promote their own citizens by treating them differently from other EU nationals. These obstacles can deter EU nationals from moving to this Member State. Exceptions to the Schengen open borders, for their part, are an expression of these Member States' intent to protect their citizens and national legal order from the consequences of immigration from outside the EU. The same applies to the calls of populist radical right parties to dismantle the EU's policy on external migration to the EU.

Although the protectionist measures are all targeted against non-nationals, the reasons behind the introduction of these measures by Member States do not necessarily coincide. The 'worlds of compliance' typology developed by Falkner and others can help to shed light on these reasons.[27]

In the 'world of law observance', which includes Denmark, Finland and Sweden, compliance typically overrides domestic concerns as there is an embedded compliance culture as well as legal and administrative capacity.[28] It might therefore seem surprising that Denmark and Sweden are among the Member States that continue to perform border controls at their borders with other EU Member States. However, Thalmann argues that these border controls may well be legitimate and proportionate and therefore compliant with EU law, although

---

[26] The Member States in question are: Austria, Denmark, France, Germany, Norway and Sweden.
[27] G Falkner and O Treib, 'Three Worlds of Compliance or Four? The EU-15 Compared to New Member States' (2008) 46 *Journal of Common Market Studies* 293. See also G Falkner, *Complying with Europe: EU Harmonisation and Soft Law in the Member States* (Cambridge, Cambridge University Press, 2005); G Falkner, M Hartlapp and O Treib, 'Worlds of Compliance: Why Leading Approaches to European Union Implementation are only "Sometimes-true Theories"' (2007) 46 *European Journal of Political Research* 395.
[28] Falkner and Treib, 'Three Worlds' (2008) 296.

a lack of empirical data prevents a definite conclusion. It can be speculated that Sweden and Denmark do not refrain from border controls because they could legitimately claim that they are not breaching EU law by doing so. Even though the border controls seem to be in line with EU law, they are likely to have considerable adverse effects on European integration. Thalmann and several EU institutions rightly emphasised that open internal borders are not a minor supplement to the internal market, but one of the most important and symbolic achievements of the EU.

In the 'world of domestic politics', which includes Austria, Belgium, Germany, the Netherlands, Spain and the UK, governments tend to engage in a cost–benefit analysis and non-compliance is a likely outcome if EU requirements conflict with domestic political interests.[29] In these Member States, political resistance is at the root of most compliance problems rather than capacity problems. The indexing of family benefits for workers from other Member States in Austria is a good example of this approach.

The third group of Member States, the 'world of transposition neglect', includes France, Greece, Luxembourg and Portugal. In these Member States, 'compliance with EU law is not a goal in itself' and 'the typical reaction to an EU-related implementation duty is inactivity'.[30] The most important motivation for compliance in these Member States is powerful enforcement action by supranational institutions. This description fits very well with Warin's case study. She demonstrates that the Luxembourgish Parliament repeatedly failed to sufficiently adapt domestic legislation to the requirements of EU free movement law. Domestic implementation of the relevant provisions of EU primary and secondary law was minimalistic in this area of EU law and it relied on a trial-and-error approach. National law was only brought in line with EU law when it was expressly declared to be incompatible with EU law by the CJEU and even this change of national law took a very long time. The typical reasons for non-compliance in the 'world of neglect' are preferences for national solutions and capacity problems.[31] Both reasons are apt to explain the neglect of EU law identified by Warin.

C. Obstacles Relating to Institutional, Regulatory and Constitutional Traditions

Two further types of resistance against EU law and governance emanate not so much from political policy disagreements, but from structural and constitutional discrepancies or practical problems and inabilities. These forms of

---

[29] ibid 297.
[30] ibid.
[31] ibid.

resistance manifest themselves in the chapters of this volume that focus on the implementation and interpretation of EU law by the judiciary. This section focuses on obstacles to the implementation of EU law that are due to conflicts between EU rules and pre-existing institutional and regulatory traditions in the Member States, whereas the next one looks at practical obstacles and capacity problems.

Mayoral's contribution demonstrates that the structure of the domestic judicial system and the deeply embedded traditions that correspond to this structure can hinder compliance with EU law. In his case study on Poland, he shows that national lower-instance courts are less prepared to refer to the CJEU and to follow its judgments when this would entail going against the national constitutional court. Importantly, he emphasises that this was the case even before the recent reforms of the Polish judiciary that are seen as incompatible with the rule of law.[32] Similarly, Glavina's interview study reported in this volume indicates that the engrained tradition of lower-instance courts to observe the case law of their apex court can adversely impact respect for EU law. She cites lower court judges from Slovenia who argue that complicated legal matters are best left to higher instance courts. By extension, this may also indicate that once the national supreme or constitutional court has resolved a matter, lower courts are unlikely to challenge its ruling.

Furthermore, national constitutional courts themselves might impede compliance with EU law if it directly conflicts with national constitutional law. From the EU's perspective, EU law enjoys primacy over conflicting national constitutional law and national constitutional courts have, in principle, accepted this rule of conflict.[33] However, recent case law of the German Federal Constitutional Court and of the Italian Constitutional Court indicates that these two courts are prepared to prevent the application of EU law in their jurisdiction if it infringes the identity, that is the very core, of their constitution.[34]

The strength of lower courts' institutionalised respect for higher instances can be illustrated by a case where it was stretched to its limit. In 2009 and 2010, the Swedish Supreme Courts declined to disapply national rules allowing for criminal sanctions to be imposed on tax evaders who had already been subjected to administrative penalty proceedings;[35] a system that was subsequently held incompatible with EU law in *Fransson*.[36] Both judgments were subject to

---

[32] See, eg, A Śledzińska-Simon, 'The Rise and Fall of Judicial Self-Government in Poland: On Judicial Reform Reversing Democratic Transition' (2018) 19 *German Law Journal* 1839.

[33] See, eg, judgment of 17 December 1970, *Internationale Handelsgesellschaft*, C-11/70, EU:C:1970:114; German Federal Constitutional Court, judgment of 22 October 1986, *Solange II*, 2 BvR 197/83, BVerfGE 73, 339.

[34] See, eg, German Federal Constitutional Court, Judgment of 15 December 2015, *Solange III*, 2 BvR 2735/14; Italian Constitutional Court, Order of 26 January 2017, *Taricco*, 24/2017.

[35] Swedish Supreme Administrative Court, judgment of 17 September 2009; Swedish Supreme Court, judgment of 31 March 2010.

[36] Judgment of 26 February 2013, *Åkerberg Fransson*, C-617/10, EU:C:2013:105.

widespread criticism from scholars who found the Swedish legislation manifestly incompatible with higher-ranking European rules.[37] Nevertheless, when a small number of lower-instance courts decided to disobey the supreme court rulings (which are not formally binding, anyway) to give effect to individual rights based on the European Convention on Human Rights and the Charter of Fundamental Rights, this was considered exceptional, with one commentator suggesting the lower court behaviour to be unparalleled since medieval times.[38] These reactions are testament to the institutional strength of the established judicial hierarchy – even in a Member State that does not apply a system of precedent proper and even when the higher courts are widely considered to be wrong.

The obstacles described in this section accord with the observation of comparative politics scholars, according to whom the degree of 'fit' or 'misfit' between EU rules and pre-existing institutional and regulatory traditions determines compliance with EU law or lack thereof. If EU law and national traditions fit well together, adaptational costs are low, which facilitates compliance. On the other hand, if EU law conflicts with deeply embedded domestic structures, adaptational costs are high, which makes compliance difficult.[39]

D. Practical Obstacles and Capacity Problems

The final type of resistance against EU law and governance consists in practical obstacles and capacity problems. Glavina's chapter points to a range of practical factors that determine whether national lower-instance courts are able to fulfil their EU law mandate. Drawing on interviews with Slovenian and Croatian judges, she argues that the decision of these judges to submit preliminary questions to the CJEU is determined, inter alia, by court resources, workload concerns, knowledge of EU law and the incentive structure of the specific court. Especially first-instance courts with heavy workloads and small expectations of ground-breaking legal analysis refrain from engaging with the preliminary reference system. These challenges to the full effectiveness of EU law in the Member States are not necessarily the product of political disagreements with EU policy. Instead, they emanate from the practical inability of national actors to fulfil the expectations of EU law.

We mentioned above that capacity problems are typical reasons for non-compliance in the 'world of neglect', which includes France, Greece, Luxembourg

---

[37] eg O Zetterquist, 'Högsta domstolens och Regeringsrättens bedömning av förenligheten av det svenska skattetillägget/skattebrottet med dubbelbestraffningförbudet i Europakonventionen' (2010) Europarättslig tidskrift 592; U Bernitz, 'Rättighetsskyddets genomslag i svensk rätt – konventionsrättsligt och unionsrättsligt' (2010–2011) Juridisk Tidskrift 821, 842.
[38] F Stenhammar, 'Internationell anarki i svenska domstolar? Ett folkrättsligt perspektiv på "HD-upproret" om skattetilläggen' (2011–2011) Juridisk Tidskrift 477.
[39] Conant, 'Compliance' (2012) 13.

and Portugal.[40] Warin's Luxembourgish case study seems to confirm this account. As she notes, the failure of Luxembourg to respect EU rules on free movement of persons might, to some extent, be related to the fact that transposing and implementing EU law is difficult for a Member State with an administration that is proportionate to its small size. Small Member States have smaller abilities to comply with EU law for the simple reason of having smaller administrations with fewer civil servants working to implement the abundant body of EU law that is, naturally, the same whether to be implemented in Germany or Malta.

Moreover, in the 'world of dead letters', which encompasses the Czech Republic, Hungary, Ireland, Italy, Slovakia and Slovenia, severe capacity limitations lead to widespread non-compliance with EU law when it comes to practical application and enforcement.[41] This cluster of Member States was identified based on the implementation of EU secondary legislation at the national level.[42] Glavina's interview study suggests that the readiness of national courts to refer to the CJEU is also (at least partly) influenced by practical and capacity problems. From a theoretical perspective, non-compliance due to practical problems and capacity limitations is in line with management theories of compliance. According to management theorists, non-compliance emerges due to capacity limitations and ambiguities of interpretation rather than deliberate defiance.[43]

IV. REMEDIES AND THE ROLE OF NATIONAL JUDGES AS GUARANTORS OF COMPLIANCE

A common challenge to the effectiveness of EU law in the Member States is the failure of national legislators to implement EU primary and secondary law in a correct and timely fashion. Warin's case study on Luxembourg as well as Papp and Varju's chapter on Hungary are good illustrations of this problem.

EU law has in-built mechanisms to address the problem of provisions of national law that are incompatible with EU law; most importantly the possibility of infringement procedures launched by the Commission. Furthermore, national courts must immediately disapply provisions of national law that conflict with EU law and they can (and in the case of last instance courts have to) refer to the CJEU when they have doubts on the interpretation of EU law. Overall, the contributions to this volume highlight the national judiciaries' role as guardians of EU law at the national level.

In the Luxembourgish example, the national judiciary was effective in ultimately leading the national legislator to gradually adapt national legislation

---

[40] See Falkner and Treib, 'Three Worlds' (2008) 297.
[41] ibid 308–09.
[42] ibid 300–07.
[43] Conant, 'Compliance' (2012) 7.

in line with EU law. The Luxembourgish courts were loyal to EU law. They diligently respected the CJEU's case law and disapplied national provisions that discriminated against frontier workers. Moreover, they repeatedly referred to the CJEU when they had doubts as to the compatibility of national legislation with EU free movement law.

This has not only happened in Luxembourg, which takes explicit pride in being Europhile. In Hungary, as well, it was the judiciary that stepped in to ensure compliance with EU law by forcing the executive to back down on its protectionist economic policy. According to Papp and Varju, the Hungarian courts' consideration of EU law in their own adjudication and their participation in the preliminary reference procedure were crucial for the continued application of EU law in Hungary. In this regard, it would be unfortunate if the CJEU, as it has hinted, were to deny that the ordinary courts in those Member States affected by rule of law backsliding are courts in the sense of Article 267 of the Treaty on the Functioning of the European Union (TFEU).[44]

Claassen's case study on Dutch competition courts is another illustration of the contribution of national courts to the application of EU law in the Member States. Claassen argues that national courts' loyalty to EU law should no longer be measured based on how many references they send to the CJEU.[45] In his view, positive explanations of low numbers of preliminary references tend to be overlooked. For example, Dutch competition courts are loyal to the EU in that they attempt to apply EU law in their adjudication, but they only rarely refer to the CJEU because they do not feel responsible for the general development of EU law. They consider themselves primarily as dispute resolution providers and not so much as constitutional actors. Given the increasingly heavy case load of the CJEU – albeit not as heavy as that of the European Court of Human Rights – a low number of references can even have some merits. The introduction of reasoned opinions as an alternative to full judgments of the CJEU indicates that the Court itself is starting to delegate more responsibilities to national courts. This could lead to a more independent attitude from the part of national courts.

In her contribution, Wallerman depicts the type of judge – referred to as judge Ariadne in analogy to Dworkin's judge Hercules – who refrains from referring to the CJEU without being opposed to European integration. She describes judge Ariadne as loyal to the law, free from personal agendas and fully committed to the supremacy of EU law as an integral and justiciable part of the national legal system. The Dutch competition courts examined by Claassen seemingly perfectly illustrate this type of judicial behaviour.

---

[44] Judgment of 27 February 2018, *Associação Sindical dos Juízes Portugueses*, C-64/16, EU:C:2018:117, para 43; judgment of 25 July 2018, *LM*, C-216/18 PPU, EU:C:2018:586, para 54.

[45] Similar points have been made in this volume by Glavina, Claassen and Wallerman. See also J Komárek, 'In the Court(s) We Trust? On the Need for Hierarchy and Differentiation in the Preliminary Ruling Procedure' (2007) 32 *European Law Review* 467.

For national courts to be loyal guarantors of EU law in the Member States, and thus for this behaviour to spread beyond the context of market regulation in the Netherlands, a number of requirements must be fulfilled. One of them is education. As illustrated by Glavina's contribution, national courts' knowledge of EU law is not on par with their knowledge of national law. This observation applies even to founding Member States like Germany.[46] Overcoming this challenge will be crucial to build national courts' capacity to ensure compliance with EU law at the national level. Imparting knowledge on EU law to national judges will require resources and time, both for the individual judges and in terms of investments into the judiciary as a whole.

Moreover, and perhaps most importantly, supreme and constitutional courts need to join the movement. Inter-court competition and lower court empowerment,[47] powerful as it may have been in the formative decades of the Union, is not capable of bringing the whole national judiciary to work towards the full implementation of EU law. Although many lower courts did, and still do, refer cases to the CJEU, many more do not, and the cases delivered and actions taken by (some) lower courts are not capable of setting national precedents. As is shown in this volume by Mayoral, the CJEU has not replaced the national highest instances as the most important precedent setter. However, where supreme and constitutional courts go, lower instances will follow. Thus, for national courts to be able to function as a force against challenges to EU law by Member States, national highest instances must lead the way. There is some evidence that this is indeed happening: highest instance courts have surpassed their colleagues on the lower instances and are now the CJEU's most frequent interlocutors.[48]

However, in Member States where rule of law backsliding is well advanced, there can be further limitations on national courts' ability to safeguard compliance with EU law. In particular, respect for (or fear of) national superiors may prevent national courts from fulfilling their EU law mandate. In this regard,

---

[46] JA Mayoral, U Jaremba and T Nowak, 'Creating EU Law Judges: The Role of Generational Differences, Legal Education and Judicial Career Paths in National Judges' Assessment Regarding EU Law Knowledge' (2014) 21 *Journal of European Public Policy* 1120; T Nowak, F Amtenbrink, M Hertogh and M Wissink, *National Judges as European Union Judges: Knowledge, Experiences and Attitudes of Lower Court Judges in Germany and the Netherlands* (The Hague, Eleven International Publishing, 2011); U Jaremba, 'At the Crossroads of National and European Union Law: Experiences of National Judges in a Multi-Level Legal Order' (2013) 6 *Erasmus Law Review* 191.

[47] See, eg, JHH Weiler, 'The Transformation of Europe' (1992) 100 *Yale Law Journal* 2403; K Alter, 'Explaining National Court Acceptance of European Court Jurisprudence: A Critical Evaluation of Theories of Legal Integration' in AM Slaughter, A Stone Sweet and JHH Weiler (eds), *The European Court and National Courts: Doctrine and Jurisprudence: Legal Change in Its Social Context* (Oxford, Hart Publishing, 1998).

[48] A Dyevre, A Atanasova and M Glavina, 'Who Asks Most? Institutional Incentives and Referral Activity in the European Union Legal Order' (2017) available at ssrn.com/abstract=3051659.

the disciplinary proceedings instituted against two Polish judges for having requested preliminary rulings from the CJEU are particularly worrisome.[49]

Generally, commentators have been pessimistic about the national or supranational judiciary's ability to have large-scale impact on more serious cases of Euroscepticism or rule of law backsliding.[50] Tacik's study on the Polish Government's reactions to the Białowieża Forest judgment highlights the risk that the authority of EU institutions is undermined by open defiance and/or incoherent, incorrect and incendiary speech acts. He also points to the risk of politicisation of judicial (and administrative) procedures.[51] These risks to European institutions' authority and legitimacy are particularly serious in light of the lack of centralised enforcement mechanisms in the Union.[52] Furthermore, judicial actions, be it through national courts or the CJEU, as well as administrative action, like the Article 126 TFEU procedure at the disposal of the Commission, by design can only deal with rather contained and clearly regulated matters. Fundamental values are often too vaguely regulated to be justiciable before national or supranational courts, rendering the most important norms the least protected.[53] One can question whether these mechanisms also lend themselves to counter more systemic challenges to the EU law and policy.[54]

Nevertheless, this volume, which sought to enquire into the challenges and problems faced by the EU in its relationship with Member States, has also pointed to answers to such threats. The contributions to this volume provide several examples of how national and EU-level remedies have proven effective and individual instances of rights violations and EU law infringements have thereby been righted.

For instance, in the case study described by Tacik, where domestic administrative authorities, supported by the Polish Government, were responsible for the logging activities in the Białowieża Forest, the EU was, ultimately, appropriately equipped to address this problem. The European Commission initiated infringement proceedings and the CJEU, for the first time and as a reaction to the previous non-compliance of the Polish authorities with an interim order,

---

[49] 'Polish Disciplinary Prosecutor Michał Lasota Launched a Case against Judge Igor Tuleya, Who Sent Pre-Judicial Queries to Luxembourg' (13 December 2018) *IUSTITIA*, available at www.iustitia.pl/en/2722-polish-disciplinary-prosecutor-michal-lasota-launched-a-case-against-judge-igor-tuleya-who-sent-pre-judical-queries-to-luxembourg.

[50] JW Müller, 'Should the EU Protect Democracy and the Rule of Law inside Member States?' (2015) 21 *European Law Journal* 141, 148; M Blauberger and RD Kelemen, 'Can Courts Rescue National Democracy? Judicial Safeguards against Democratic Backsliding in the EU' (2017) 24 *Journal of European Public Policy* 321; A Hofmann, 'Resistance against the Court of Justice of the European Union' (2018) 14 *International Journal of Law in Context* 258.

[51] This risk is also highlighted by M Blauberger and RD Kelemen, 'Can Courts Rescue National Democracy? Judicial Safeguards against Democratic Backsliding in the EU' (2017) 24 *Journal of European Public Policy* 321, 329 ff.

[52] See Hofmann, 'Resistance' (2018) 274.

[53] ibid 274; Blauberger and Kelemen, 'Can Courts Rescue National Democracy?' (2017) 325.

[54] Müller, 'Should the EU Protect Democracy' (2015) 147; 'Editorial Comments' (2019) 18.

interpreted Article 279 and Article 260 TFEU as allowing periodic penalty payments for non-compliance with interim measures. The disrespect of EU law ceased in the end, although this might also have been related, at least partly, to a change in the composition of the Polish Government, as Tacik suggests.

The Italian case study concerning the contested Italian budget for 2019, which was the first budget presented by the populist government emerging after the 2018 Italian parliamentary elections, also suggests that EU mechanisms can be effective. In that case, it appears that the prompt reactions of the Commission and other EU institutions, including a threat to instigate for the first time proceedings against excessive budget deficits under Article 126 TFEU, critically contributed to the proposed budget being amended and brought in conformity with the financial rules of the Union and the Eurozone. Again, however, the authors also stress that features of the national government's structure, in particular the role of the non-partisan Prime Minister, were instrumental in reaching this solution.

V. CONCLUDING REMARKS

As the contributors to this volume have pointed out, there is an underlying tension between, on the one hand, the Member States and their interests in providing what is best for their own territories and peoples and, on the other, the Union and its common goals and values. This is hardly new. Nor is, strictly speaking, popular or party-based scepticism towards the European project. More than 20 years ago, Joseph Weiler already noted that it had 'been evident for some time' that 'national Sleeping Beauty has woken up and discovered that she did not like the EU Prince at all'.[55] Alternatively, one needs only recall the several referenda in the Member States whereby voters rejected the deepening of European integration: the Danish referendum on the Maastricht Treaty in 1992; the Danish and Swedish referenda on the European Monetary Union of 2000 and 2003 respectively; the referenda on the draft Constitutional Treaty in France and the Netherlands in 2005; and the first Irish referendum on the Lisbon Treaty in 2008. As Michal Bobek points out in his prologue to this volume, the EU seems to be in almost constant crisis. *Plus ça change, plus c'est la même chose.*

But although the state of crisis may start to look permanent, the face of crisis is ever changing. This volume has attempted to shed light on (one of) its current incarnation(s); that of increasingly widespread and open scepticism for the European project gradually seeping into the mainstream of Member States'

---

[55] JHH Weiler, 'Epilogue: The European Courts of Justice: Beyond "Beyond Doctrine" or the Legitimacy Crisis of European Constitutionalism' in AM Slaughter, A Stone Sweet and JHH Weiler (eds), *The European Court and National Courts: Doctrine and Jurisprudence: Legal Change in Its Social Context* (Oxford, Hart Publishing, 1998).

political discourse and legislative reality.[56] Taken together, the contributions to this volume show that resistance to EU law and governance encompasses a whole spectrum of positions from the hard-line, outright rejection of the EU as a whole, through fundamental disagreements about European identity and basic values or certain EU policy areas, to the unwillingness or inability to implement and embrace Union law fully and loyally. In this sense, resistance, in some form or degree, is present in most or all of the Member States – including those that are (correctly) perceived as deeply committed to the Union. Furthermore, the contributions have shown that there is indeed a difference between Eurosceptic rhetoric and Eurosceptic actions. The actors who create the most noise and attract the most attention are not always the authors of the greatest challenges (although they sometimes are).

A question that remains unanswered by this volume is if, how, and for what reasons a specific Member State, a party, or a people moves across the Eurosceptic continuum. Can one, for instance, draw a direct causal link between the myth that the EU tried to ban the British pint and the UK's current withdrawal procedure?[57] Does incomplete or delayed implementation of Union law slowly chip away at the momentum and significance of European integration? Can temporary (although now in their fourth year) border controls open the floodgates of increased resistance to free movement and fuel xenophobia?

As for stopping and preventing such movements, we have seen examples of actors and mechanisms that may hinder such Eurosceptic sliding. In particular, courts, both at EU and Member State level, have tools available to them to counter challenges to EU law and authority. However, we have also seen that the effects of these remedies are more limited than the challenges national judges face, and several of the contributions raise questions as to whether national judges are indeed up for the task. As other commentators have concluded, judiciaries are unlikely to be the only answer to the challenge of Euroscepticism. This, however, goes for all other actors and institutions as well. This volume has endeavoured to illustrate the many faces of Euroscepticism; the remedies will likely have to be at least as numerous.

---

[56] See N Brack and N Startin, 'Introduction: Euroscepticism, From the Margins to the Mainstream' (2015) 36 *International Political Science Review* 239.

[57] See G Drewry, 'The Jurisprudence of British Euroscepticism: A Strange Banquet of Fish and Vegetables' (2007) 3 *Utrecht Law Review* 101, 103.

Index

Austria, compliance record, 126, 237, 238, 239

border control: *see* migration crisis (2015–17); Schengen Area

CJEU–constitutional/supreme court conflict (with particular reference to Poland): *see also* **Poland** (*Puszcza Białowieska* case)
  analysis of likely judicial behaviour in case of conflict
    methodology, 219–20
    impediments to reliable data collection, 220
  context: *see also* Poland, Constitutional Court (PCC), role
    CJEU–national courts as partners in enforcement of EU law, 213–15, 216
    examples of conflict (Poland, Czech Republic, Denmark), 221
    political constraints on independence of courts, 214
  factors possibly affecting judicial reaction to conflict
    concerns about trustworthiness of supreme national judicial authority, 218–19, 225
    confidence in CJEU as interpreter of EU law, 217
    constitutional court's reactions to EU infringements of constitutional identity of national legal order, 218, 240
    executive branch's negative attitude/ coercive political influence, 217–18
    inter-court competition, 225
    judicial empowerment, 218–19, 225
    reputational concerns, 203–4, 225
  future possibilities, 224–6
  impact of constitutional court (PCC) intervention on judicial decision-making, 220–4
    reference to CJEU as means of subverting PCC rulings, 223–4

  jurisprudence
    Associação Sindical Dos Juízes Portugueses, 224
    Brzeziński, 220
    Case I SA/Ol 374/05 16 November 2005 (submission of a legal question to PCC), 220
    Case III UZP 4/18, 2 August 2018 (Supreme court's referral of five questions to CJEU), 223–4
    Case K 18/4, 11 May 2005 (Polish Accession Treaty), 218, 223
    Case P 1/05, 27 April 2005 (European Arrest Warrant), 216, 223
    Case SK 45/09, 16 November 2011 (EC Regulation 44/2001 on the recognition and enforcement of judgments in civil and commercial matters), 221
    Commission v Poland (C-619/18 R), 224
common agricultural policy (CAP), 19
compliance: *see* **compliance, effect of Euroscepticism (empirical evidence); compliance, effect of Euroscepticism (theoretical considerations); compliance, factors affecting/ opportunities for non-compliance**
compliance, effect of Euroscepticism (empirical evidence)
  absence of discernible systematic negative effect of Euroscepticism/possible factors, 42–4, 235–6
    Commission's choice of battles, 44
    governments' playing down of Euroscepticism, 43
    mismatch between rhetoric and substance, 48–9, 54–6, 58–9, 235–6
    political disassociation from implementation process, 43
  CJEU infringement case patterns
    decline in cases/trust in Commission/ support for EU (Figure 2.1), 41–2
    delivered judgments (Table 2.2), 41–2

Member State 'wins' (Table 2.3), 42
methodology, 38–40
registered cases (Table 2.1), 40
factors of possible relevance
express disagreement with directive, 38
government attitude to EU, 37–8
literature review of, 36–8
pre-accession transposition record, 38
public attitude to EU, 36–7, 38
future research, 41
sectoral protectionism, 236–9: *see also* sectoral protectionism
compliance, effect of Euroscepticism (theoretical considerations)
factors reducing the political impact of compliance
political disassociation from implementation process, 35–6
strategic aspects of enforcement, 34–5
unwillingness to comply (Eurosceptics) benefits, 30
Eurosceptic public's lack of interest in notifying compliance failures, 31
hard-to-spot obstruction of implementation, 31
hostility to increasing reach of EU laws, 31
lack of interest in timely compliance, 31
unwillingness to comply (general)
change of government, 30
conflict between departments responsible for negotiation and application, 30
free-rider approach to common policies, 30–1
substantive disagreement with legal act, 30
compliance, factors affecting/ opportunities for non-compliance, 28, 31–5
bureaucracy, 47
capacity/willingness, 29–30, 47
CJEU judgment, uncertainties of implementation, 33
compliance culture, 239–40
delays between adoption of act and date for implementation, 32
difficulties presented by national actors, 34
disincentives to infringement proceedings, 34
margin of appreciation considerations, 31–2
negotiated settlement/no penalties as Commission's preference, 32–3
political resistance, 239

sanctions, delay and obstacles to, 32
'transposition neglect', 239, 241–2
weak enforcement mechanisms, 32, 239
Croatia: *see* **preliminary references (TFEU 267) (Croatia and Slovenia)**

death penalty, 18
Dublin regime: *see* **migration crisis (2015–17), allocation of responsibility for handling protection applications (Dublin Regulation III)**

economic patriotism: *see also* **Hungary (economic patriotism)**
conflict between EU obligations and national interests, 91–3, 234
definition/characteristics, 91, 92–3
financial crisis, role, 87–91
national electorate as driving force, 91
environmental protection, populist parties' (PRRP's) attitude towards, 19–20
Euroscepticism
definitions/classification as, 31, 230–2
Brexit, 2, 231, 232, 233
as catch-all term, 231
as a continuum, 231
diffuse vs specific criticism of Europeanisation, 230
hard vs soft Euroscepticism, 230, 232
lawful vs unlawful resistances, 232
legitimate criticism distinguished, 231
political vs instrumental Euroscepticism, 230–1, 234–5
unintentional non-compliance distinguished, 231–2
fundamental challenges to core values, policies and EU law, 233–6
PRRPs, 233: *see also* populist parties (PRRPs)
growth in, 27
populists' selective 'our own people' Euroscepticism, 234–5, 238
rule of law, threat to, 27

free movement of persons (Austria) (indexing migrant workers' family benefits), 237, 239
free movement of persons (general)
correlative obligations of national authorities, 137
free movement of workers (EC 48), 136

Index   251

free movement of workers (Regulation (EEC)
    No 1612/68 of 15 October 1968), 136
freedom of establishment (EEC 52), 136
freedom of movement and residence for
    EU citizens (TEU 8(a)), 136
jurisprudence
    Baumbast, 136n7
    Commission v Belgium (C-408/0), 137
    Grzelczyk, 136n7
    Martínez Sala, 137
    Pusa (AG Jacobs' Opinion), 137
    Van Gend en Loos, 136
non-discrimination obligation (EC 48(2)),
    139–41
non-discrimination obligation (TFEU 18),
    136–7
    indirect discrimination, 137
**free movement of persons (Luxembourg)
    ('Euroreluctance')**
background
    frontier workers as chief target, 236
    Luxembourg's European credentials,
        135, 236
    population structure, 137
compliance with EU obligations
    dependence on clear CJEU ruling, 239
    legislative delay in implementing
        EU legislation, 138, 142–3, 149,
        151–2
    national courts' role/willingness to
        make preliminary reference, 139–40,
        141–3, 145–7, 151–2, 242–3
direct discrimination (*ASTI*), 138–9
indirect discrimination (frontier workers),
    discriminatory income taxation of
    non-resident workers, 139–42
    EC 48(2) obligations, failure to meet,
        139–41
    jurisprudence
        Administrative Appeal Court
            decisions, 140, 141–2
        Biehl, 139–40
        Commission v Luxembourg
            (C-151/94), 140
        Lakebrink, 141–2
        Schumacker, 140
    revisions to LIR (Income Tax Law), 141–2
indirect discrimination (frontier workers),
    social benefits (changes to law on
    higher education financial aid),
    143–7, 236
    changes to the law, 143–4

Commission views on, 144
hastiness of introduction, 144
jurisprudence
    Administrative Appeal Court's refusal
        to make preliminary reference
        (16 February 2017), 146–7
    Administrative Tribunal decisions,
        145–6
    Bragança Linares Verruga, 146
    Depesme and Kerrou, 146
    Giersch, 145
    legislative response to *Giersch*, 145–6
indirect discrimination (lawyers: language
    requirements (law implementing
    Directive 98/5/EC)), 147–50, 236
    Conseil de l'Ordre's role, 149–50
    jurisprudence
        Reyners, 148
        Wilson, 148–9
    practising lawyers in Luxembourg, 147–8,
        150
    reasons for, 151–2
freedom of establishment: *see* **free movement
    of persons (general); free movement
    of persons (Luxembourg)
    ('Euroreluctance'), indirect
    discrimination (lawyers: language
    requirements (law implementing
    Directive 98/5/EC))**
frontier workers: *see* **free movement
    of persons (Luxembourg)
    ('Euroreluctance')**

Hungary (economic patriotism): *see also*
    economic patriotism
agricultural and forestry land transactions,
    Act CXXII 2013 as example of
    exclusion of non-nationals from
        agricultural property market as
        purpose, 103
    property rights (CFR 17), as possible
        breach of, 104
    restrictions on acquisition and use
        of land, 103
        Commission's opinion, 103n68
    restrictions on usufruct rights
        CJEU proceedings (*SEGRO and
            Günther Horváth*), 104
        national court proceedings, 103–4
    similarity of legislation in other CEE
        countries, 103
    summary of provisions, 103–4

compliance enforcement (CJEU proceedings)
    alternatives to, 94, 99–100
    infringement proceedings, 95
    preliminary references (TFEU 267), 95, 243
compliance record, 87–8, 93–5
context
    CEE economies post-crisis, 89–90
    change of government, 87–8
    conflict between EU neoliberalism and Member States' patriotism, 88–9, 105
    EU response to problem, 105–6
    global financial crisis, 87–91
    Hungarian policy patriotism pre-crisis, 90–1
monopolisation of service markets as example of
    CJEU infringement proceedings, 97
    gambling and betting monopolies (preliminary references), 97–9
        Berlington, 97–8
        Commission's decision to leave handling of complaints to national courts, 97
        Sporting Odds, 98
        Unibet, 98–9
    national mobile payment monopoly, 96–7
        CJEU infringement proceedings, 98
    national school book distribution
        EU law, limitations of, 99
        Könyv-Tár Kft, 99–100
        national courts, admissibility/jurisdiction failures, 99
        Vékony, 99n51
    restructuring tax-free remuneration voucher market, 95–6
        BIT-based arbitration, 96
        Commission/CJEU rulings, 95–6
tax law changes to market conditions as example of
    general considerations
        discrimination/distortion of competition as key features, 100
        effectiveness of method, 100
        obstacles to detection of infringement of EU law, 100
    indirectly discriminatory retail tax, 100–1
        abolition of tax/national Court's follow-up ruling, 101
        preliminary ruling (*Hervis*), 101
        selective sectoral taxation (Commission Decisions/sectors considered), 101–2

internal security: *see* public policy/internal security, classification as
Italy–EU relationship before 2018 election/Euro-friendliness, 47
    compliance record, 47
    Constitutional openness to limitations of sovereignty (Constitution 11), 48–9
    judicial support for, 49
    primacy of EU law, 49
    implementation of EU law, instruments governing, 49
    parliamentary involvement in decision-making process, 49
    ready endorsement of European integration process, 48
Italy–EU relationship following 2018 election/Euroscepticism
    changing landscape
        bipolarism of election campaign, 51
        Fiscal Compact (2012)/constitutional 'balanced budget' amendment, effect, 50
    Eurosceptic parties' positions (Five Stars Movement/Di Maio)
        Beppe Grillo, 51
        calls for referendum on the euro, 51, 52
        omission of foreign and EU policy from manifesto, 51
        softening of pre-election anti-EU stance, 51–2
    Eurosceptic parties' positions (League/Salvini) ('EU-heavy' manifesto)
        'Back to pre-Maastricht', 52
        guaranteeing sovereignty, 52
        post-Brexit adjustments, 53
        recovering sovereignties, 53
    mismatch between rhetoric and substance, 2, 48–9, 54–6, 58–9, 235–6
    negotiation of 2019–21 budget package, 61–3
        'anomalous acceleration' of parliamentary processes, 63–4
        EU-encouraged executive dominance, 64–5
    post-election Conti government, approach to the EU
        Contract of Government, modification in favour of traditional Italian position, 55
        involvement of Parliament in EU-decision-making process, 55–6
        Prime Minister's non-partisan role, 63–5, 246

post-election Conti government, establishment
  composition, 51, 53–4
  Contract of Government, 54
  nuanced position on EU, 54
  President Mattarella's role, 54
post-election Conti government, PM's speeches to Parliament on EU matters
  5 June 2018 (confidence motion), 56–7
  27 June 2018 (pre-European Council meeting), 57–9
  16 October 2018 (European Council/Euro Summit meetings), 59–60
  11 December 2018 (European Council/Euro Summit meetings), 60–1
  non-divisive approach, 57–61

Luxembourg: *see* free movement of persons (Luxembourg) ('Euroreluctance')

migration crisis (2015–17): *see also* Schengen Area
  allocation of responsibility for handling protection applications (Dublin Regulation III), 117–18
  amendments to (draft Dublin IV), 133–4
  effect on Member States' right to invoke a serious threat to public policy/internal security (TFEU 72/TEU 4(2)), 127–8
  Eurodac obligation to take and share fingerprints, 118
  obligation of Member State of first entry to take back applicant rejected by another Member State, 228
  solidarity and fair sharing of responsibility principle (TFEU 80), 118
  events of 2015–17
    arrival statistics, 118–19
    countries of origin/first arrival, 118–19
    secondary migration, reasons for/failure to prevent
      failure to comply with fingerprint obligation, 119
      Germany's decision to waive to transfer Syrian nationals back to Member State of irregular first entry, 119, 127
      ineffectiveness of return decisions, 120

obligation to give applicant access to lengthy asylum procedure, 119, 130
transfer of migrants back to Greece as risk of inhuman or degrading treatment (CFR 4/Dublin III), 119–20
Member States' reactions
  reintroduction and prolongation of controls, 120–2
    by country, 121
    numbers (2015–19), 120–1
    reasons given, 121–2
    TFEU 72 (maintenance of law and order)/TEU 4(2) (internal security) as potential basis for, 122
  relocation decisions
    EU–Turkey Statement (March 2016), 120
    Italy and Greece (Council Decisions of 14 and 22 September 2015), 120, 127

national judges' role: *see also* preliminary references (TFEU 267)
  concerns about effectiveness, 245–6
  Hungary, 94–5, 243
  Luxembourg, 139–40, 141–3, 145–7, 151–2, 242–3
  Netherlands, 176–7, 243: *see also* preliminary references (TFEU 267) (Netherlands competition law (TFEU 101) cases (2013–17))
  Poland, 245–6: *see also* CJEU–constitutional/supreme court conflict (with particular reference to Poland); Poland, Constitutional Court (PCC), PiS measures curtailing powers; Poland (*Puszcza Białowieska* case)
  reform proposals, 244–5
national security: *see* public policy/internal security, classification as
necessity for internal border controls
  availability of alternative measures
    police measures (SBC 23(a)), 131–2
    technical or financial support measure (SBC 30(1)), 132
  SBC provisions
    'as a last resort' (SBC 26), 131
    'shall not exceed what is strictly necessary' (SBC 25(1)), 131

Netherlands: *see* preliminary references (TFEU 267) (Netherlands competition law (TFEU 101) cases (2013–17))
non-discrimination: *see* free movement of persons (Luxembourg) ('Euroreluctance')

patriotism: *see* economic patriotism; Hungary (economic patriotism)
Poland
   Constitutional Court (PCC), PiS measures curtailing powers, 67, 216
      co-option as enforcer of EU law, 216
      partial revocation (19 October 2018), 68
      potential impact of PiS measures, 216: *see also* CJEU–constitutional/supreme court conflict (with particular reference to Poland)
      Rule of Law Framework dialogue (TEU 7(1)), 68, 83, 84, 224
   Constitutional Court (PCC), role
      populist challenge to, 216
      as promoter of constitutional democracy/Europeanisation, 215
Poland (*Puszcza Białowieska* case): *see also* CJEU–constitutional/supreme court conflict (with particular reference to Poland)
   background
      environmental significance of Białowieża Forest, 70–1
      Government decision to allow increase in logging activity (2016 Annex), 70–2
      initiation of infringement proceedings (alleged breach of TFEU 258), Commission's allegations, 71
   interim measures order (27 July 2017), 71–4
      government's defiance of, 73–4
      grounds, 72–3
      precautionary principle, 72–3
   interim measures order (20 November 2017), 74–6
      continued defiance/disinformation campaign, 76–8
      periodic penalty payments for non-compliance (TFEU 260/TFEU 271), 74, 75–6
   judgment on merits (1117 April 2018), 79–80
      AG Bot's Opinion, 79
   populist strategies for undermining relations with CJEU, 67–9, 80–5, 234
      denial of judicial/CJEU authority, 81–2, 234
      disinformation, 80–1, 234
      ill-based dismissal of CJEU's scientific findings, 76–8, 234
      inconsistent and manifestly unreasonable argument, 80–1, 234
      nationalist demonisation of liberal/international critics, 67–8, 83–5
      politicisation of the judiciary, 82–3
populist parties (PRRPs) (background)
   definition/characteristics, 9
   Fidesz, status, 10
   participation in government (November 2018), 8 Table 1.1
   parties identified as, 9
   representation in the EP (2018), 10 Table 1.2
   risks presented by
      challenge to freedom of movement principle, 237–8
      coalition formation, 7–8
      cohesive policy-making, 7–8, 233
      opposition to further integration, 233
   selective 'our own people' Euroscepticism, 234–5, 238
populist parties (PRRPs) (measuring coherence)
   background
      definitions
         absolute coherence, 12
         coherence, 12
         core state powers, 13
         depth of change, 12
         direction of change, 12
         goal coherence, 12
      evidence, 11
      methodology, 11–12
   Cluster 1: core state powers (common foreign, defence and security policies)
      border controls, 15–16
      CFSP, 14
      CSDP, 14–15

Index

EU Army, 15
EU counter-terrorism activities, 15
free movement of persons, 15–16
free movement of workers, 15–16
geopolitical orientation, 14
Joint Procurement, 15
Cluster 1: core state powers (economic and monetary policies)
   Economic Union, 248
   Monetary Union, 16–17
Cluster 1: core state powers (overview)
   depth of change, 13 Table 1.3
   direction of change, 13 Table 1.4
   summary, 16–17, 24–6
Cluster 2: 'new politics' (anti-discrimination policies)
   death penalty, 18
   ethnic minorities, 18
   freedom of religion, 18
   gender equality, 18
   right of non-sexual couples to found family, 18
Cluster 2: 'new politics' (environmental protection)
   common agricultural policy (CAP), 19
   Emissions Trading System, 20
   Energy Security Strategy, 20
   Food Information to Consumers, 20
   low-carbon economy, 19
   Renewable Energy Directive, 20
   renewal energy, 19
   safe food policy, 20
Cluster 2: 'new politics' (migration policies)
   Common Policy on Asylum, 20–1
   Common Policy on Immigration, 20
   Common Policy on Monitoring and Management of EU External Borders, 21
   Dublin Regulation, 21
   Family Reunification Directive, 21
Cluster 2: 'new politics' (overview)
   depth of change, 17 Table 1.5
   direction of change, 17 Table 1.6
   examples of incoherence, 18, 20
   summary, 21, 24–6
cluster 3: socio-economic policies (overview)
   depth of change, 22 Table 1.7
   direction of change, 22 Table 1.8
   summary, 24–6

cluster 3: socio-economic policies (single market)
   EU-wide energy market, 22–3
   four freedoms (TFEU 26), 22–3
   social policy, 23–4
preliminary references (TFEU 267): *see also* **CJEU–constitutional/supreme court conflict (with particular reference to Poland)**
   Eurosceptic governments' and national judges' approach to, 171–2, 189, 210
   variation between Member States, 172–3
   motivation for referral/factors possibly affecting (national courts), 156
   CJEU's responses to previous references, 94–5, 184, 195–6, 243
   competence of national courts to apply EU law, 176, 189
   confidence in CJEU as interpreter of EU law, 217
   constitutional court's reactions to EU infringements of constituational identity of national legal order, 218, 240
   constitutional culture, 160
   democratic system, 195
   executive branch's negative attitude/coercive political influence, 176, 217–18, 245
   fear of a negative effect of ruling on national policy, 147
   ideological differences between referring judge and CJEU, 196
   judicial empowerment, 160, 170, 194–5, 201
   judicial hierarchy (domestic courts), 240–1, 244
   judicial review availability, 195
   legal culture, 195
   length of EU membership, 195
   levels of intra-EU trade, 195
   litigation rate/practice, 160, 195, 208–9
   'maturity' of EU law, 183, 186
   parties' wishes, 182
   population size, 160, 195
   public support for European integration, 160, 176, 195
   rapid development of CJEU jurisprudence, 186

relative relevance of EU law, 160
time/resource constraints, 244
transnational economic exchange, 195
motivation for referral/factors possibly
affecting (national judges)
attitude towards CJEU, 161
concerns about trustworthiness of
supreme national judicial authority,
218–19, 225
education in and knowledge of EU law,
161, 169, 187–8, 189, 197, 201, 206,
207–8, 210, 244
example of Supreme Court/higher courts,
206–7, 244
judicial empowerment, 201, 218–19,
225
language skills, 202
perception of the relevance of EU
legislation, 161
perception of role in promoting
uniformity of EU law, 186, 189
personal characteristics, 161–8, 172–3
procedural knowledge, 202
reaction to tone of previous CJEU
responses, 184, 195–6
reputational concerns, 203–4, 225
time/resource constraints, 169, 196–7,
202, 204–6, 207–8, 210, 242, 244
national courts' level of participation
Croatia and Slovenia: *see* preliminary
references (TFEU 267) (Croatia and
Slovenia)
Denmark, 176, 195
France, 159
Germany, 159
Hungary, 94–5
Italy, 195
Luxembourg, 139–40, 141–3, 145–7,
151–2, 242–3
Netherlands: *see* preliminary references
(TFEU 267) (Netherlands
competition law (TFEU 101) cases
(2013–17))
patchiness/judicial resistance, 159
Spain, 159
participation as measure of sincere
cooperation/loyalty (TEU 4(3)), 147,
151–2, 175–6
challenging non-referrals, reasons for/
significance, 168–70
challenging referrals, importance of
design, 170–1

success or not?
CJEU enthusiasm for, 156–7, 175
contribution to integration process, 175
national courts' lynch-pin role, 157–8,
213–14
referrals (1961–2017) (Figure 10.1), 193
uniform application of EU law,
dependence on, 175, 189, 192,
193–4
**preliminary references (TFEU 267) (Croatia
and Slovenia)**, 198–211
motivation for non-referral/factors possibly
affecting (general)
analytical methodology, 198–9
Euroscepticism, 210
litigation rate/practice, 208–9
summary (Table 10.1), 200
motivation for referral/factors possibly
affecting (national judges)
education in and knowledge of EU law,
201–2, 206, 207–8, 210
example of Supreme Court, 206–7
judicial empowerment, 201
language skills, 202
procedural knowledge, 202
reputational concerns, 203–4
time/resource constraints, 202, 204–6,
207–8, 210
**preliminary references (TFEU 267)
(Netherlands competition law
(TFEU 101) cases (2013–17))**,
175–89
EU competition law, scope for involvement
of national courts, 176–7
ex officio/ex proprio motu application of
TFEU 101, 186–7
Netherlands implementation of TFEU
101, 177–8
possibilities for a preliminary reference,
177–8
executive branch's negative attitude towards
preliminary reference (asylum
cases), 176
low rate of referrals
CJEU's responses, 178–9
comparison with Netherlands references
on matters other than TFEU 101,
179
comparison with other Member States,
179
questions referred (*T-Mobile,
UPC Nederland, FNV*), 178–9

motivation for non-referral/factors possibly affecting
  analytical methodology, 180–1
  competence of national courts to apply EU law, 176, 189
  divergence between national courts' treatment of issue, 184–6
  Euroscepticism, 189
  FNV (referral) vs *Zilveruien* and *Eerstejaars plantuien* (non-referral), 181–2
  knowledge of/specialisation in EU law, 187–8, 189
  'maturity' of EU law, 183, 186, 189
  parties' wishes, 182
  perception of role in promoting uniformity of EU law, 186, 189
  rapid development of CJEU jurisprudence, 186
  reaction to tone of previous CJEU responses, 184
proportionality of internal border control, 128–33
  Commission's Opinion on the necessity and proportionality of the controls reintroduced by Germany and Austria (SBC (2006) 24(4)), 121, 126
  criteria (Regulation 1051/2013), 129
  proportionality *stricto senso*, 129, 132–3
  SBC provisions, 128–9
    'likely impact ... on free movement' (SBC 30(1)(c)), 132
    'necessity and proportionality' (SBC 28(3)), 116
    'shall assess the proportionality of the measure in relation to that threat' (SBC 26/SBC 30(1)), 117
    'what is strictly necessary' (SBC 25), 115
  suitability/'likely to remedy' test (SBC 26/SBC 30(1)), 129–31
    migration management/threat of terrorism or other serious crime, 130
    right of access to the asylum procedure, 119, 130
    right to refuse entry (SBC 6) vs *non-refoulement* obligation (ECHR 2 and 3/SBC 3(b)), 130
    serious threat from administrative overload/frustrate efforts to manage migration, 130

TFEU 72/TEU 4(2) measures, applicability to, 129, 132–3
German Constitution/*Lisbon Judgment*, 132
public policy/internal security, classification as: *see also* **'serious threat' (SBC 25–30), classification of migration crisis as**
internal security
  absence of definition/self-contained interpretation, 124–5
  as independent justification, 124
  jurisprudence
    Albore, 124–5
    Campus Oil, 125
    Richardt, 124–5
    suggested coverage derived from, 125
  as part of external security, 124–5
public policy
  absence of definition, 122
  alternative terminology ('public order'/'law and order'), 122
  jurisprudence
    Achughbabian, 124
    Adil, 124
    Boscher, 123
    Bouchereau, 123, 125
    Centre Leclerc, 123
    Commission v Italy (C-128/89), 123
    Commission v Italy (C-426/92), 123
    de Peijper, 123
    Deutsches Milchkontor, 123
    JN, 124
    Omega, 123
    Orfanopoulos, 124
    Ringelhan, 123
    Schmidberger, 123
    Spanish Strawberries, 122n95
    Thompson, 123
    van Duyn, 122–3
    Vo, 124
    Zh and O, 124
  strict interpretation
    examples, 122–3
    SBC preamble, recital 27, 124

Schengen Area: *see also* **migration crisis (2015–17)**
definitions
  'border checks' (SBC 2(11)), 112n17
  'border control' (SBC 22(10)), 112n17

258 *Index*

'border surveillance' (SBC 2(12)), 112n17
Westphalian model, 110
general matters
  borders, function, 109–10
  PRRPs' opposition to/risk of growing challenges to freedom of movement principle, 237–8
  scope for amendment, 133–4
  Westphalia (nation state model) vs EU integration/supranationalisation of border control, 3, 110–11, 134
legal status of open internal borders principle
  as autonomous legal value, 113
  endorsement of political value by Commission and EU Council, 114
  as EU competence (TFEU 77), 113
  as extra-Community regime (1985 Schengen Agreement/1990 Schengen Implementing Convention), 113
  SBC (2016) as EU instrument (TFEU 77), 113
  SBC as nucleus of AFSJ integration efforts, 114
  'The Union shall offer its citizens an area … without internal frontiers' (TEU 3(2)), 113
'membership' of
  exemption of Member States from, 112n18
  new Member States' obligation to accept *acquis*, 112n18
  non-EU members, 112
obligations
  abolition of all border controls (SBC 22), 112–13
  removal of obstacles to fluid traffic control (SBC 24(1)), 112n20
permitted controls (SBC 23(a)), 112–13
temporary reintroduction of border controls (SBC 25–30)
  cases requiring immediate action (SBC 28)
    French checks on border with Italy (April 2011), 116
    requirements, 116
    Sweden and Norway (July 2011) (bomb explosion in Oslo and shooting on the island of Utøya), 116

  cases where serious external border control deficiencies constitute a serious threat to public policy or internal security of the Schengen Area (SBC 29(1)), 116–17
    amendments to, 116, 117
    Commission evaluation report requirements (SBC 21), 117
    Member State's non-compliance with a Council decision (Frontex Regulation 19(1)), 117
    prolongation, 117
  examples of use prior to migration crisis, 115, 116
  Member States' responsibilities for law and order and internal security (TFEU 72/TEU 4(2)) as support for/as alternative basis, 113, 123
  overview, 114–17
  prior Commission proposal/Council recommendation, need for, 117
  proportionality requirement (SBC 30(1)), 117
  requirements: *see also* public policy/internal security, classification as
    'a serious threat to public policy or internal security in a Member State', 114, 237
    authorisation by EU institutions, absence, 115, 116
    as exception for limited period (SBC 25(1)), 115, 117
    notification to Commission and other Member States (SBC 27(1)), 115, 116
    proportionality (SBC 26), 114
    submission of information to EP and Council (SBC 27(2)), 115
  resurrection of Westphalian/nation state model, 3, 110–11
sectoral protectionism, 236–9: *see also* **free movement of persons; Schengen Area**
Euroscepticism, relevance, 236
'serious threat' (SBC 25–30), classification of migration crisis as: *see also* **public policy/internal security, classification as; Schengen Area**
administrative overload as, 126, 133
automatic classification of migration as, exclusion
  EU's commitment to fundamental values (TEU 2/TFEU 67(1)), 125
  instinctive presumption against, 125

perception of Member States reinstating
border checks, 125–6
SBC preamble, recital 26, 125
Bouchereau, 123, 125
ex ante assessment, 125
frustration of migration management as
asymmetry of the Dublin system, 127–8, 133–4
deficient external border controls/
secondary migration, 126–7

effects of unmanaged migration
of third-country nationals, 127, 133
threats of terrorism or serious crime as, 128, 133

Slovenia: *see* **preliminary references
(TFEU 267) (Croatia and Slovenia)**

Westphalia, Peace of (1948): *see* **Schengen
Area**